W9-DAT-480

780.72
Che

100958

Cheyette.
Teaching music creatively
in the elementary
school.

Date Due

DISCARDED

The Library
Nazareth College of Rochester, N.Y.

 PRINTED IN U.S.A,

TEACHING
MUSIC
CREATIVELY
IN THE
ELEMENTARY
SCHOOL

TEACHING MUSIC CREATIVELY IN THE ELEMENTARY SCHOOL

Irving Cheyette
Director of Music Education
Professor of Education
State University of New York at Buffalo

Herbert Cheyette
Columbia Broadcasting System, Inc.

**McGraw-Hill
Book Company**

New York
St. Louis
San Francisco
London
Sydney
Toronto
Mexico
Panama

DISCARDED
NAZARETH COLLEGE LIBRARY

TEACHING MUSIC CREATIVELY IN THE ELEMENTARY SCHOOL

Copyright © 1969 by Irving and Herbert Cheyette. All rights reserved.
Printed in the United States of America. No part of this
publication may be reproduced, stored in a retrieval system,
or transmitted, in any form or by any means, electronic,
mechanical, photocopying, recording, or otherwise, without
the prior written permission of the authors.

Library of Congress Catalog Card Number 68-54851

10745

1 2 3 4 5 6 7 8 9 0   HDBP   7 5 4 3 2 1 0 6 9 8

100958

7280.72
Cle

TO RUTH

Blame not my lute for he must sound
Of this and that as liketh me.
For lack of wit the lute is bound
To give such tunes as pleaseth me.

Sir Thomas Wyatt

PREFACE

This book concerns the teaching of an art, and therefore also the art of teaching. The art taught is music, the concern is for children attending classes in the elementary schools.

The authors' purpose has been to describe methods by which the elements of music may be made intelligible, which implicitly requires that music first be made enjoyable. That which makes learning music enjoyable enhances learning in general: an enthusiastic teacher who comprehends the interests and attitudes of children; a teacher whose objectives are restrained by common sense, but whose satisfactions are not constrained by the classroom.

The music-education student and practicing music teacher are the authors' particular audience. The classroom teacher, teaching music in a school system with limited financial and musical resources, will find this book a comprehensive guide to music fundamentals, and methods for their successful exposition.

Since this book is designed to be a useful source, musical skills integrated in classroom units are treated separately by chapter. The motivating impulse for that integration, however, will be found in Chapter One, *Developing Musical Literacy*, and in Chapter Nine, *Developing the Innate Creativity of Children*. For reasons of parsimony rather than redundancy, these chapters have not been printed twice. The conscientious student will remedy this defect by reading them first and last.

Chapter Two, *An Outline for an Elementary Music Curriculum*, constitutes a key to the selection of musical activities at various grade levels. The teacher may then refer to appropriate chapters for extended treatment of the activities selected.

For those whose interests include principles as well as practice, Chapter Twelve consists of a brief history of theories of music education in the United States.

A comprehensive bibliography and list of available teaching materials are appended.

For reading the manuscript and suggesting improvements, thanks are extended to Professors William Tallmadge, Catherine English, and Silas Boyd of State University College at Buffalo; Professor Richard Colwell of the University of Illinois; Dr. Everett Gates, Director of Music Education at the Eastman School of Music; Assistant Professors Dowell Multer and Jacklin Bolton, State University of New York at Buffalo, and special thanks to Miss Marilyn Honings.

For permissions to quote, credits are extended to Professor Mary R. Tolbert,

Professor Mary E. Whitner, Professor William Tallmadge, Dr. William C. Hartshorn, Dr. Kate Hevner Mueller, Mr. Augustus D. Zanzig, Miss Janet E. Tobitt, Mr. Mack Perry, Professor Earl W. Count, Mrs. Elizabeth Rugg, Mrs. Helen Worden Cranmer, and to the following publishers: Follett Publishing Company; M. Baron Company; Silver Burdett Company; Harvard University Press; W. W. Norton & Company, Inc.; Prentice-Hall, Inc.; Appleton-Century-Crofts, Inc.; National Education Association, Music Educators National Conference, National Society for the Study of Education, Random House, Inc.; Alfred A. Knopf, Inc.; Association for Higher Education; The Westminster Press; G. P. Putnam's Sons; McGraw-Hill Book Company; Ginn and Company; American Book Company; Summy-Birchard Company; Blaisdell Publishing Company; The Key Reporter; Edward B. Marks Music Corporation; Cooperative Recreation Service; Allyn and Bacon, Inc.

For photographs and illustrations, thanks are due to Professor Phyllis Dorman, Dr. Mitchell Oestreich, Buffalo, New York; and to the following companies: Peripole, Inc.; M. Hohner & Company; American Music Conference; Bowmar Records, Inc.; Melody Flute Company; Scherl & Roth; Vega Instrument Company.

Irving Cheyette
Herbert Cheyette

CONTENTS

Preface   vii

Musical Illustrations   xxiii

**CHAPTER ONE   DEVELOPING MUSICAL LITERACY:
FROM EAR TO VOICE TO EYE**   1

The Meaning of Language   2

How Imagery Enriches Concepts   3

Conveying Musical Meanings   3

**CHAPTER TWO   AN OUTLINE OF AN ELEMENTARY SCHOOL MUSIC
CURRICULUM**   7

Kindergarten-Primary: Ages Five through Eight   7

Attitudes to Be Developed   8

Appropriate Musical Activities and Objectives   9

   Vocal Skills   9

   Motor-rhythmic Skills   9

   Ear Training for Pitch and Mood   9

   Listening Skills   9

   Instrumental Skills   10

   Creative Activities to Be Encouraged   10

Time for Music   10

Relating Music to Other Activities   11

                                                                 ix

The Music Corner 12

    Music for Quiet Listening 13

    Recorded Music 14

Intermediate Grades: Ages Eight through Ten 14

Musical Development 15

Attitudes to Be Developed 15

Appropriate Musical Activities and Objectives 15

    Vocal Skills 15

    Motor-rhythmic Skills 15

    Harmonic Skills 16

    Reading and Writing Notation 16

    Critical Skills 16

Relating Music to Other Activities 17

Upper Elementary Grades: Ages Ten through Twelve 17

Musical Development 17

Appropriate Musical Activities and Objectives 18

    Vocal Skills 18

    Motor-rhythmic Skills 18

    Harmonic Skills 19

    Notational Skills 19

    Critical Skills 19

    Creative Skills 20

    Instrumental Skills 20

Relating Music to Other Activities 21

Music Symbols 21

Useful Terminology to Be Included in a Music Notebook 22

    Tempo Terms 22

    Dynamic Terms 22

    Clef Signs 22

    Staff Symbols 22

    Form Symbols 23

    Key Signatures and Symbols 23

Scale Ladder Graphs on Permanent Charts 25

    Meter Signatures 25

Selecting a Basic Series 25

    Content 26

Songs	26
Accompaniment Material	27
Music Reading	27
Teaching Aids	27
Recordings	28
Philosophy of Approach	28
Applying Pedagogical Principles to Learning Music Skills	28
Principles of Lesson Planning	29
Summary (Evaluation of Teaching and Learning)	30

CHAPTER THREE DEVELOPING CONCEPTS OF MELODY: PRIMARY GRADES | 32 |

Teaching a New Song	34
Initial Preparation	34
The Phrase Method or Rote Approach	34
The Question Approach	34
Sensing Tonal Beauty	35
Developing Pitch Consciousness	35
Possible Pitch Difficulties	36
Voice Play	37
Demonstrating Tonal Relations by Sign Language	37
Key to Musical Sign Language	37
From Ear to Voice to Eye	39
Introducing the Meaning of Scale	42
Teaching the Major Scale	42
The Half-step Interval	44
Games of Musical Speech	44
Learning the Scale Tones	45
Measuring Pitch Distance with the Hands	46
Visual Aids for Measuring Pitch Intervals	46
The Melody Graph	46
Graphing Musical Names	46
Figure Illustrations for Songs	47
Staff Notation	48

Deriving Treble Clef Notation from the Hand Staff   49

The John Curwen Hand Signals   50

Summary (Outline of Procedures for Teaching a Song)   51

CHAPTER FOUR   DEVELOPING CONCEPTS OF RHYTHM   53

Rhythm of Everyday Activities   53

Free Expression   54

Instrumental Rhythmic Expression   55

Sensing Phrase Rhythm   55

Interpreting Music Symbols   56

Sensing $\frac{2}{4}$ Meter   56

Syllabic Rhythm   57

Symbolizing Duration Values   59

Listening for Rhythm   59

Using Flash Cards for Rhythm Patterns   59

Sensing Notes of Long Duration   60

Sensing Pulse Silently   62

Drum Talk   63

Dramatizing Three Rhythms with the Story of the Three Bears 63

Sensing Faster Rhythms in $\frac{2}{4}$ 64

Developing a Rhythm Score   64

Syncopation in $\frac{2}{4}$ 66

Tempo and Mood   68

Sensing $\frac{3}{4}$ Meter and Rhythms   68

Sensing Tempo Changes in $\frac{3}{4}$ 73

Flash Cards   73

Sensing $\frac{3}{8}$ Meter   74

Physical Movement to $\frac{3}{8}$ 74

Sensing Tempo Changes   77

Flash Cards in $\frac{3}{8}$ and $\frac{1}{4}$.   77

Sensing $\frac{6}{8}$ Meter   78

$\frac{6}{8}$ Beat   78

Physical Responses   78

Drum Talk   78

Fast ⅜ in Song — 79

Sensing Mood and Tempo Changes in ⅜ — 81

Sensing Compound Meters — 81

Interpreting Other Compound Meters — 82

Illustrating Varieties of Notation for Beat in Upper Grades — 83

Summary — 86

CHAPTER FIVE   DEVELOPING CONCEPTS OF CHORD SKIPS — 87

How Melodies Are Composed — 88

Teaching a 1 Chord Song — 90

Introducing the Idea of the Tonic Chord — 90

Flash Cards for Ear-training Purposes — 91

Examples of 5 x 7 Flash Cards for Ear-training Games — 91

Music Dictation Games — 92

Using the One-octave Orchestra Bells or Xylophones — 93

Black Keys, Then White — 93

Improving Reading Ability in the Upper Grades — 94

The Dominant Seventh Chord — 94

Recognizing the Sound of the V7 Chord — 96

The Subdominant or IV Chord — 96

Secondary Chords — 99

Eye and Ear Training in Chord Harmony — 103

Improving Song Tone in the Upper Grades — 106

Introducing Chromatic Accidentals — 106

Summary — 109

CHAPTER SIX   DEVELOPING CONCEPTS OF SCALE IN UPPER GRADES — 110

Pentatonic Scales — 112

Encourage Experimentation — 114

Transposition on the Piano Keyboard — 114

Vocal Pitch Placement — 115

Relating the Vocalizes and Scale Ladder to the Piano Keyboard — 116

Constructing Major Scales in Various Keys — 118

Constructing Minor Scales 120

    Using the Scale Finder for Minor Scales at the Piano 120

    Aeolian Minor 120

    Melodic Minor Scale 122

    Harmonic Minor 123

    Dorian Minor 124

Mixed Modes 125

Modes and Exotic Scales 126

    Phrygian Mode 126

    Modified Phrygian Modes 127

    Other Modes 129

    Locrian Mode on the Seventh Scale Step 129

    Near Eastern Exotic Modes 130

Bass Clef Notation 132

Teaching Scale Fingerings for the Piano 133

Summary 135

CHAPTER SEVEN   DEVELOPING CONCEPTS OF HARMONY IN THE UPPER GRADES 136

Partials 137

Tendential Resolution of Scale Tones 138

Mood Qualities of Chords 139

Harmonic Development 140

Introducing Harmonic Concepts to Children 140

    Canons and Rounds 141

    Partner Songs 142

    Combining Rounds with Other Songs 143

    Adding a Drone Organ Point 143

    Adding a Chordal Descant 143

    Adding a Harmony Choir 147

Adding Barbershop Thirds by Finger Harmony, Rounds, and Improvisation 148

    Adding a Drone in Open Fifths to Scottish, Indian, and Oriental Songs 151

Hand Harmonizing Triads 154

    Key to Hand Harmonizing 154

    Building Chords 154

    Hand Harmonizing Procedure 155

Humming Choir and Chanting Choir　156

Hand Harmonizing Sequence of I, IV, V, I Chords　156

Songs with I, iii, IV, V7, vi Chords　157

Developing Harmonic Awareness Vocally　158

Adding Instrumental Color to Voices　159

Memorizing Chord Sequences for Major and Minor Scales in Upper Grades　160

Transposition by Voices　160

Harmonizing the Minor Scale　161

Hand Harmonizing for Minor Songs　161

Relating Minor Chord Hand Harmonizing to a Song　162

Summary　165

CHAPTER EIGHT   DEVELOPING A CLASSROOM ORCHESTRA　166

Objectives for a Classroom Orchestra of Homemade and Manufactured String, Wind, and Percussion Instruments Requiring Simple Techniques　167

Suggested Procedures for Teaching Tonette, Flutophone, and Other Simple Pipes　167

Simple Wind Instruments　169

Pop Bottle Band　169

Common or Transverse Flute　170

The Shepherd's Pipe　171

Pandean Pipes　172

Melody Wind Instruments　172

Melody Flute in C or in D　174

Homemade Instruments　175

Wind Instruments　175

Percussion Instruments　176

Manufactured Rhythm Instruments　177

Manufactured Melodic Percussion Instruments　178

Individual Tone Bells: Resonator or Swiss　178

Building Chord Bells　180

Tuned Swiss Bells　181

"Build a Tune" Tone Bars　182

Xylophones　184

Melody Chimes　184

The String Family: The Principle of Vibration and Resonance 185

Initial Procedures for Teaching Autoharp, Fretted String Instruments, and Piano in Class 185

    The Autoharp 185

    The Psaltery 187

The Fretted String Instruments 187

    Procedure for Teaching the Fretted String Instruments 187

    Peripole Duobass 188

    The Two-string Ukulele or Pianolin 189

More Complex String Instruments 189

    The Four-string Ukulele 189

    The Tenor Banjo 191

    The Six-string Guitar 192

    The Mandolin 194

The Bowed Nonfretted String Family 196

Latin American Percussion 199

Complex Pipes 202

    The Recorders 202

    The Mouth Organ or Harmonica 205

Keyboard Instruments 205

    The Melodica 205

    The Piano Accordion 206

    Piano Accordian Bass Keyboard Chart 207

    Basic Piano Keyboard Harmony 209

    Basic Chording at the Piano 212

Summary 215

CHAPTER NINE   DEVELOPING THE INNATE CREATIVITY OF CHILDREN 216

Inspiring Creative Activity 220

    Motivation 220

    Selection 220

Notation 222

Finding the Song's Expressive Elements 223

Selecting Tonality and Mode 224

    Transferring the Melody to the Piano Keyboard 225

Music Notation 225
   Terms of Tempo 227
   Terms of Mood 227
   Sensing the Beats 229
   Sensing the Phrase Line 230
   Adding Rhythmic Sound Effects 230
   Adding Harmonic Background 230
   Adding Simple Melodic Instruments 231
   Correcting Errors in Singing and Playing 232
Evaluation 233
   Tape Recording 233
   Notebooks 233
   Recorded Music 233
   List of Procedures in a Creative Music Lesson 234
Developing Creative Activities Using Contemporary Musical Techniques 234
   Discovering Sound Sources 234
Creative Activities Employing Sound Painting 236
   Primary Grades 236
   Improvising Irregular Rhythms in a Chance Arrangement 237
   Polyrhythms 238
In Upper Grades: Developing an Awareness of Contemporary Techniques of Music Composition 239
Making a School Sound Studio 242
Sound Kits for the Sound Studio 242
   Percussion 242
   Wind: Breath-supported 249
   Strings 253
Constructing Musical Instruments 254
Summary 259

CHAPTER TEN DEVELOPING LISTENING SKILLS 260

Tone 261
Melody: Pitch and Intonation 262
Rhythm 262
Tempo 263

Meter 264

Dynamic Intensity 264

Expressive Inflection 264

Mode, Scale, and Tonality 265

Modality 266

Tonality 266

Harmony 270

Timbre 271

Style 272

Structures of Musical Form 273

Planning Listening Lessons 274

Sample Listening Lesson 276

Listening to Contemporary Music 278

New Sound Sources 278

Expanded Tonal and Rhythmic Spectrum 278

New Performing Techniques 281

Strings 282

Brasses 282

Woodwinds 282

Prepared Piano 283

Percussion 283

Electronic Amplification 283

Electronic Alteration of Tempo 283

Spoken Voices 283

Checklist for Listening Activities in Upper Grades 283

Outline of Development of Musical Forms and Types of Orchestration 285

Summary 287

CHAPTER ELEVEN THE MUSIC TEACHER AS SUPERVISOR AND
RESOURCE AND UNIT CONSULTANT 288

Some Procedures for Supervision of Classroom Teachers 289

Questionnaire for Classroom Teachers 289

Outline for Classroom Teachers 290

A Sample Lesson Plan for Second Grade 290

The Music Teacher as Unit Consultant 294

The Correlated Unit of Instruction   **296**

Curriculum Units Prepared by Music Specialists   **306**

A Unit Plan for Upper Grades on Negro Afro-American Music   **310**

Workshops for the Musical Preparation of the Classroom Teacher   **317**

   Vocal Abilities   **318**

   Keyboard Skills   **318**

   Instrumental Skills   **319**

   Rhythmic Skills   **319**

   Song Leading Skills   **319**

   Theoretical Music Skills   **320**

   Teaching Skills   **320**

   Cultural Skills   **321**

Methods of Teaching Classroom Teachers   **321**

Programmed Instruction in Music Education   **322**

   Program Construction   **322**

   Using the Electronic Music Board for Immediate Playback   **326**

   Using Prepared Tapes for Feedback   **326**

Measurement and Evaluation in Music Education   **327**

Some Criteria for Constructing Tests   **327**

Some Devices for Measuring Musical Aptitude Employed in Standardized
Tests   **328**

Tests for Measuring Musical Imagery and Sensitivity   **329**

Music Achievement Tests   **330**

Types of Objective Tests   **332**

Music Symbols Tests   **332**

Some Standardized Music Aptitude and Achievement Tests   **333**

Musical Aptitude Tests   **334**

Music Achievement Tests   **335**

Keeping Student Records   **336**

Keeping Inventory Records   **337**

   Music Series   **337**

   Recordings   **337**

   Choral Music   **338**

   Orchestra and Band Music   **338**

   Orchestra and Band Instruments   **338**

Summary   **340**

CHAPTER TWELVE   CHANGING CONCEPTS OF MUSIC EDUCATION   341

    Factors Influencing Discrimination and Judgment   348

        Attitudes toward Music   349

        Standards and Ideals   349

    Sociological Aspects   350

    Musicological Aspects   351

        Skills   351

        Imagery   352

    Changing Concepts of Musical Learning   353

    The Space Age and Research Orientation   355

    Foreign Influences   355

        The Orff System   355

        The Kodály Method   357

        Suzuki Talent Education   358

        Current Objectives   358

    Summary   361

APPENDIX I   THE MATERIALS OF TEACHING   362

Audio-visual   362

Audio-visual Equipment and Materials   363

Sources of Display Materials   364

General Curriculum Building   364

Catalog Sources for Recordings, Tapes, and Filmstrips   365

Sources for Free Catalogues Describing Rhythm, Melody, and Accompanying Instruments   365

Films for Music Education   366

Sources for Correlating Music with Social Studies, Physical Education   366

Supplementary Songbooks   367

Recordings for Rhythmic Activities (Primary Grades)   368

Reference Materials for Action Songs, Free Rhythmic Play, Game Songs   369

Materials for Folk and Square Dances   369

Materials for Rhythm Instruments   370

Materials for Melody Flutes   370

Materials for Recorder Instruction   370

Materials for Bells, Flutophones, Tonettes, Melody Flutes   371

Materials for Autoharp Instruction   371

Materials for Melodica Instruction 371

Additional Bibliography on Creative Music Teaching 371

APPENDIX II A BIBLIOGRAPHY OF MUSIC MATERIALS FOR AN ELEMENTARY SCHOOL LIBRARY 373

Biography 373

Symphony 374

Opera 375

Instruments 375

Stories that Inspired Musical Settings in Ballet, Opera, Suite 376

APPENDIX III SOURCE MATERIALS FOR LISTENING ACTIVITIES 377

Bibliography 377

   Children's Reading 377

Teacher's Readings 378

Complete Programs for Elementary School Listening Activities 378

Complete Programs of Recorded Music to Illustrate Historical Periods in Music 379

Films and Film Strips 380

Sources for Educational Records for Children 381

APPENDIX IV BIBLIOGRAPHY OF MATERIALS FOR THE MUSICAL EDUCATION OF THE MUSIC TEACHER 382

Aesthetics and Integration of the Arts 382

Basic Musicanship 383

   Theory of Music 383

   Counterpoint 384

   Keyboard Harmony 385

   Sight Singing 385

   Orchestration-band Arrangements 386

   Conducting Choral Ensembles 386

   Conducting Instrumental Ensembles 386

Guidance to Musical Careers 387

History of Music 387

Philosophy of Music Education 390

Instrumental Methods 390

   Percussion 390

String Instruments   391

Recreational Instruments   391

Wind Instruments—Brass and Woodwind   391

Piano as a Minor Instrument   392

Vocal Methods   392

Methods of Teaching Music   392

Elementary   392

Junior High   393

Senior High   394

Musical Acoustics (Science of Sound)   394

Music Supervision and Administration   395

Psychology of Music   395

APPENDIX V   BASIC MUSIC SERIES OF THE LAST 100 YEARS   397

Nineteenth-century Music Series for Public Schools   397

Early Twentieth-century Music Series   397

Music Series from 1925 to 1950   398

Modern Music Series Currently in Use   398

APPENDIX VI   BIBLIOGRAPHY OF MATERIALS FOR THE MUSICAL EDUCATION OF THE CLASSROOM TEACHER   400

Vocal Methods   400

Vocal Ear Training   400

Keyboard Skills   401

Instrumental Skills   401

Fundamentals of Music   401

Teaching Methods   402

Music Literature   402

About Music for Layman   402

Glossary of Musical Terms   403

APPENDIX VII   KEY TO MUSICAL ILLUSTRATIONS IN THIS BOOK   406

Index   409

MUSICAL ILLUSTRATIONS

	Chapter	Page
The Barnyard Song	3	41
The Steeple Bells	3	43
Baa, Baa, Black Sheep	4	60
Old Brass Wagon	4	64
Tinga Layo	4	67
The Skaters' Waltz	4	69
See-saw Margery Daw	4	75
To Market, to Market	4	79
Ten Little Indians	4	82
Twinkle, Twinkle, Little Star	4	84
Oranges and Lemons	4	84
Hickory, Dickory, Dock	4	85
Beautiful Dreamer	4	85
Silent Night	4	86
Greeting Song	5	90
Clementine	5	95
The Little Mohee	5	97
Sweet Betsy from Pike	5	100
Old Hundredth	5	100
A Song to Remember	5	102
Swing the Shining Sickle	5	107
Hide-and-Seek	6	113
Trot, Pony Trot	6	114
Wayfaring Stranger	6	115
The Wraggle-taggle Gypsies	6	121
Foom! Foom! Foom!	6	123

Old King Cole	6	124
Old Joe Clarke	6	125
Humpty Dumpty	7	141
Sing a Song of Sixpence	7	141
Three Blind Mice	7	143
Frère Jacques	7	143
The Lone Star Trail	7	144
Oh, Susanna	7	145
Camptown Races	7	145
Old Folks at Home	7	145
Humoresque	7	145
Patsy	7	146
Goodbye, My Lover, Goodbye	7	150
The Campbells Are Coming	7	151
Happy Song	7	152
On Yoshino Mountain	7	153
This Old Man	7	156
Sweet Betsy from Pike	7	157
Erie Canal	7	162
Our Halloween Song	9	228
Frère Jacques	9	240
Twinkle, Twinkle, Little Star (Variations)	10	277
If You're Happy	11	295
Oranges and Lemons	11	296
Lullaby	11	297

TEACHING
MUSIC
CREATIVELY
IN THE
ELEMENTARY
SCHOOL

CHAPTER ONE

DEVELOPING MUSICAL LITERACY: FROM EAR TO VOICE TO EYE

Written communication consists of symbols, which, to have meaning, presuppose an awareness of sensory images and intellectual concepts. The child, to enjoy and use music, must become musically literate. However, learning music notation, if it is not to stifle musical interest, must be integrally related to experience and motivated by the desire to share that experience with others.

According to Tolbert:

Any discussion of literacy recognizes that it involves the process of learning a complex language, in this case, a non-verbal language without literal meaning except when combined with poetry for song lyrics. Therefore, attention must be focused upon the structural elements and the musical meaning, even though song lyrics are also a part of the problem of musical literacy. . . . Literacy has more than a single dimension in music education. In a literal sense, this term means the ability to interpret the printed page, to read and write symbols which represent the elements out of which music is made. It means to recognize the structures, or form, which hold these basic ingredients together in a systematic way. In a broader sense, music literacy means the comprehension of what these symbols and forms represent in an art created by and for human needs and wants. It means the understanding of significant music literature. Competence in reading and writing should enlarge a person's musical vista. It should extend his independence in creating, performing and listening to music literature.[1]

Music and dance can be transmitted by oral or visual tradition, or by recording. Some types of recording can be interpreted by machines (phonograph records, sound tracks), some by instruments (piano rolls), but most music, being recorded only in printed music notation, requires interpretation by human performers. The desire of the child to create and *share* his creation enables the teacher to point out the need for its preservation. Mechanically recording a performance is an expensive process whose potential audience is limited to those within range of the amplifier. Printed music notation, however, cheaply reproduced, may be performed by anyone, anywhere its terminology is understood.

THE MEANING OF LANGUAGE

To understand writing, prior direct experience must have given meaning to its symbols. When a mother dresses her baby, she describes each item of apparel. She may say, "Let's put on your dress, your booties, your sweater, your hat." In due time after many repetitions a baby will learn to associate certain sounds with certain objects. When asked, "Where is your hat?" he will reach for his head, and at "Where are your booties?" he will reach for his feet. When taken for a stroll in his carriage, mother will point out a dog, a cat, a horse, a policeman, a fire engine, and innumerable other objects. About the house the baby will learn to identify table objects used for his feeding: a spoon, a fork, a knife, a glass, a cup. At the zoo, he will learn to identify animals by the same association of sound and shape. The baby also learns to associate sounds with sensations: hot and cold, sweet and sour, soft and hard, the acrid smell of burning tobacco, the aroma of fresh flowers, the odor of cooked food. Besides learning various colors, he will recognize the touch of hand to hand; the feel of rough and smooth surfaces in textiles, wood, and a thousand other objects. With each of these activities he will eventually associate certain muscular reactions of the lips and vocal chords, and the sounds so produced.

As he grows into his second year, the child's mother will substitute pictures for the objects. He can now recognize a dog, a cat, a monkey, a fork, a spoon, an egg, and innumerable other objects from symbols. Even though the pictures reduce the object in size, his concept of the actual object's characteristics will enable him to recognize it. At the age of four or five he will have a vocabulary that is largely the result of direct experience. As few children of this age can read, his symbolic knowl-

---

[1] Tolbert, Mary, "Musical Literacy in the Elementary School, What and How," in *Changing Emphases in Elementary School Music*, Music Educators National Conference, March, 1964, Philadelphia, Pa.

edge will be confined to the ability to recognize a few numbers, some of the words found on shop windows, and of course pictures, especially trade marks seen in television commercials.

As a result of five years of training, the child brings to his first day in school a background of experience for which he will eventually learn word symbols to convey concepts of objects, ideas, and feelings. Without a background of experience, however, the word symbols would lack meaning. Thus a five-year-old, after hearing the verse of the Twenty-third Psalm in Sunday School, "Surely goodness and mercy shall follow me all the days of my life," can ask his mother, "Why must good Mrs. Murphy follow me all the days of my life?" "Mrs. Murphy" is comprehensible, "goodness and mercy" is not.[2]

HOW IMAGERY ENRICHES CONCEPTS

To help children become aware of their personal reservoir of imagery, ask them to imagine a deeply colored orange on their desk, about 3 inches in diameter.

Let them pretend to pick up the orange in their left hand, shaping their fingers around it. Ask them to peel it from top to bottom with an imaginary paring knife. Can they imagine the cool texture of the orange skin; the whiteness inside the peel, the veined gold of the pulp?

The orange is very juicy. Can they smell the juice dripping over their fingers and feel it stick? Tell them to make believe they are removing a section of the orange and placing it in their mouths. Can they image the taste? Can they hear the munching of their teeth?

They can imagine seeing the orange, feeling the orange, peeling the orange, smelling the orange, tasting the orange, because they have each actually done such things.[3]

CONVEYING MUSICAL MEANINGS

In order to read, the child must have already encountered the visual, auditory, tactile, olfactory, and gustatory sensations to which many words refer. In addition, from the isolated perception of sense data, he must have developed certain basic concepts representing combinations of perceptions, although some concepts, such as temporal sequence and cause, may be innate. By the time the child enters school, he

[2] Without additional information, can you determine whether the syllables "ha," "va," "na," "gi," "la," refer to an Israeli hora, "Havah Nagillah," or a Cuban love song, "Havana Gila"?
[3] This exercise illustrates the power of "affective memory," which is the foundation of so-called method acting. See Konstantin Stanislavski, *An Actor Prepares,* Theater Art Books, New York, 1948; Lee Strasberg, *Acting and the Training of the Actor,* in John Gassner (ed.), *Producing the Play,* Holt, Rinehart and Winston, Inc., New York, 1941, pp. 143ff.

will also have acquired some knowledge of linguistic structure in the process of learning to speak.[4]

In order to teach music symbols, the music teacher must duplicate the same process of linguistic formation which preceded the child's learning to read. The language of music must be introduced gradually and flow directly from circumstances requiring its use. Just as the mother relates the sound of words to objects and ideas, then substitutes symbols and relates the same word to the symbol, so the teacher should gradually introduce music symbolism into various music activities: singing, eurythmics, building musical instruments, instrumental performance, creative periods of song, dance, and drama, and above all, that most difficult of activities, listening. Only as the child accumulates percepts of music can he develop the concepts needed to understand its symbols.

The first step in the development of a concept is direct perception of the thing to which the concept refers. Thus the first step in developing a musical concept is direct perception of music, for that is the thing to which the concept will refer. . . . The only sensory perception of music is aural, for the distinguishing characteristic of music is tone and tone is perceived through the ear. But it is not enough that the sound of music reach the physical ear. It must reach the mind and become a part of the conscious thought of the learner. This is an indispensable foundation for the development of musical concepts. Unquestionably the child who can think tone has developed tonal concepts. . . . The next step in the development of a concept is the analysis of what has been perceived . . . some form of notation may be used even in the primary grades to provide a visual symbol for what has been experienced aurally. . . . Their ability to perceive (musical) relationships aurally provides the foundation upon which (musical) concepts can be developed through musical activities. . . . The development of musical concepts requires that children think musically.[5]

The means of acquiring language proceeds from the ear to the voice to the eye. Mother speaks word sounds to the child. The child identifies word sounds with the object, learns to imitate the word sounds, and eventually associates the word sounds with a written symbol for the object or idea. The process of learning musical language too proceeds from ear to voice to eye. The child must hear musical sounds in his environment, must learn to identify them through the ear, perhaps to imitate them vocally or instrumentally, and then to identify them symbolically. Music symbolism involves a music staff, various shapes of notes, rests, clef signs, time signatures, key signatures, foreign words for tempo and dynamic terms, and dynamic markings.

[4] Compare the theories of cognition in: David Hume, *An Enquiry Concerning Human Understanding,* A. Selby Bigge (ed.), Clarendon Press, Oxford (1902); Immanuel Kant, *Critique of Pure Reason,* trans. Norman Kemp Smith, St. Martin's Press, Inc., New York; Jean Piaget, *The Origins of Intelligence in Children,* International Universities Press, Inc., New York, 1952, (see especially Chapter I, "The Biological Problem of Intelligence"). A summary of modern psychological theory concerning the intellectual development of children will be found in *Child Psychology,* National Society for the Study of Education, University of Chicago, Chicago, 1963.

[5] Hartshorn, William C., "The Development of Musical Concepts in the Elementary School," in *Changing Emphases in Elementary School Music,* Music Educators National Conference, March, 1964, Philadelphia.

Distinction

Nevertheless, *symbols are not music*. They do not become music until they are translated into a "vocabulary" of musical sounds.

The introduction of notation divorced from a background of direct experience is meaningless and leads to frustration and discouragement. To teach notation in the abstract is like asking the child to translate a paragraph from a foreign language, or to listen to a specialist discuss higher mathematics. Children must realize that notation is the composer's alphabet for conveying musical ideas, and that learning to read it is a prerequisite for communicating musical ideas.

The succeeding chapters present procedures and materials designed to develop the various concepts and sensory images that give meaning to musical communication. The multiplicity and variety of these concepts are illustrated in the following example:

OLD FOLKS AT HOME

Andante   **Stephen Foster**

Way down up - on the Swan - ee Ri - ver, Far, far a - way,

mp ———————— *mf*   *decrescendo*

The text is recognizable as a phrase, to be sung without break or pause, perhaps on a single sustained breath. Its fragmentary character is duplicated by the music, which halts irresolutely above the tonic F. The sequence of notes on the staff designates the rise and fall of the melodic line, which, according to the key signature, is in the scale of F Major.

The treble staff denotes that the A on which the melody commences has a frequency of 440 vibrations per second. The time or meter signature indicates that there are four quarter notes or their equivalent within each measure to be sung Andante, the tempo of a slow stroll. Note shape designates comparative duration of pitch within the meter at a given tempo, while the flow of the text is also rhythmically indicative. Dynamic intensity may be derived from the relationships of the symbols *mp* and *mf*, moderately soft and moderately loud respectively. The widening arrow demands increasing loudness, and the word *decrescendo* the reverse.

To perform the melody as the composer intended, the performer must have sufficient musical knowledge to interpret all the aforementioned symbols. In addition, he must be able to translate that interpretation into the muscular and mechanical techniques required by his instrument. A singer must not only be able to match indicated pitch, but he must also be able to enunciate the text with appropriate articulation of tongue, lips, and jaw. The violinist must know the strings to play and their fingering, which part of the bow to use, and the pressure to exert. The flutist must sense the breath to expend, the keys to close, the speed of tongue articulation. The cornetist must know the requisite tension of cheek and lip muscles, the valves to depress, the breath to expend.

If a pianist desires to play both melody and accompaniment, he must know the chord sequence within the key tonality so as to make quick perceptive judgments as to harmonic propriety. To develop this skill, he must have studied keyboard harmony (the practical application to the keyboard of the grammar of music), the construction of chords, their resolution in terms of traditional usage, techniques of modulation to remote keys, and techniques of modern harmonization. (A limited harmonic facility, described in Chapters 7 and 8, will suffice for almost all classroom needs.)

A music symbol, of course, has limitations inherent in the idea of symbol.[6] Any sign, to be identifiable as a symbol, must be standardized so as to be recognized. What the mark stands for, however, whether a swelling or diminishing of sound, a quickening or slowing of pace, should never be exactly the same in any two musical occurrences even though the sign in each instance is identical. Music consists not only of separate sounds, but of sounds organized in definite relations as to vibration and temporal sequence.[7] By reason of this sequential relation, any variation of sound or sequence at any instant of performance will change all subsequent musical relationships in such performance. Yet precisely because music is an art as well as a science, such nuances in performance are both inevitable and desirable. Mastery of nuance is the skill that makes an artist of a technician, a refinement of intuition only acquired by study of the performance of other artists.

[6]Is musical notation more closely related to letters or numbers? See John Chadwick, *The Decipherment of Linear B,* Random House, Inc., New York, pp. 41ff. How many types of symbols are there? See Dante, *The Divine Comedy,* trans. Dorothy L. Sayers, Penguin Books, London, 1949, Introduction. Can there be allegorical music? Compare the program notes to *Death and Transfiguration* by Richard Strauss to Dante's letter quoted by Miss Sayers. See also Martin Foss, *Symbol and Metaphor in Human Experience,* Princeton University Press, Princeton, New Jersey, 1949, pp. 13ff.; 148. If a work of art is composed of various levels of meaning, can differing interpretations be equally valid? See Angel Flores, *The Kafka Problem,* Octagon Books, New York, 1963. Compare any recorded performance by Toscanini with a recording of the same work by Bruno Walter. Are the tempos the same? Do other elements differ? Is one interpretation right and the other wrong?

[7]Hartshorn, *op. cit.*

CHAPTER TWO

AN OUTLINE
OF AN ELEMENTARY
SCHOOL MUSIC
CURRICULUM

It is wise to plan a trip before setting out. An educational trip is no exception to this rule. The teacher, as guide, must plan the route, determine and find the educational transport, and recognize the road's various landmarks. He must also teach young travelers in music appropriate behavior to ensure a successful journey. They must learn how to conduct themselves when singing; how to sit quietly and listen; and how to follow directions with good grace. The teacher must encourage his travelers in music to participate in rhythmic activities, game songs, and dramatizations; to share in the handling of music equipment and to experiment with it on their own; to create songs, chants, artwork, poetry, and dance movements; and to build and use simple rhythm and melody instruments. A knowledge of the appropriate conduct when engaging in these activities is essential to their success.

KINDERGARTEN-PRIMARY: AGES FIVE THROUGH EIGHT[1]

Children from ages five through eight exhibit rapid physical growth, tremendous curiosity, and a short attention span. They experience emotional difficulty in ad-

[1]See Chapters 1 and 3.

justing to the demands of the group. The desire to learn through each sense produces constant experimentation. The child wants to see, touch, taste, smell, and hear everything; he is frequently frustrated by the reprimands: "don't touch," "take that out of your mouth," "this is for grown-ups," "don't put that to your nose."

He is sensitive to loud and soft sounds, to vocal qualities expressed in moods of fear, anger, friendliness, and affection. Still lacking in fine muscular coordination, he enjoys activities such as tumbling, swinging, running, skipping, and hopping that primarily require the larger muscles.

The child's voice quality is light, thin, and pitched quite high within the range represented by the treble staff. His eye muscles have not matured to read fine print.

Teachers in the primary grades soon recognize that the young child learns best when permitted to gratify his sensory curiosity. The music teacher must, therefore, utilize as many musical activities as possible requiring direct sensory perception.

ATTITUDES TO BE DEVELOPED[2]

Children enter school not as a blank staff, but imprinted with a variety of musical attitudes that are based upon music they have heard in their homes, usually popular dance music and commercial jingles. The following reactions to music described by a group of second graders is typical:

I like it just to listen to with Batman and the movies.
There's a lot of games we have to have music with.
How could you say "Happy Birthday To You" without singing it?
I can't wait until the band comes in a parade.
I don't like it in church when the lady sings and makes her voice wobble.
Why do you shiver your wrist when you play the violin?
Everybody sings on the bus. Sure, I know the songs, but I didn't learn 'em in school.
My daddy is in a barbershop quartet, but I never will be.
I'm a nonsinger, teacher says. It's a good thing we have somebody in my family who can sing.
Oh, music's good on radio, but why do we have to learn to read it in school?
We have lots of records at our house.[3]

Obviously the teacher must attempt to discover such attitudes so as to construct a lesson plan and devise individual instruction accordingly. The motivation of positive attitudes toward music must be a primary objective.

Children should enjoy music sufficiently to be willing to devote time to achieving greater skill in performance. Cooperating with others in making music in and out of school should be a source of increasing pleasure.

[2] See Chapters 1 and 3.
[3] Pillar, Mary, "Helping the Classroom Teacher with Music," term paper, Seminar in Music Education, University of Buffalo, Buffalo, N.Y., 1955.

APPROPRIATE MUSICAL ACTIVITIES AND OBJECTIVES[4]
Vocal Skills[5]

1. To sing simple songs with gradually improving pitch intonation
2. To sing responses to question and answer songs with reasonable improvement
3. To refine gradually the ability to recognize changes in vocal dynamics
4. To alter voice quality to suit the mood of a song
5. To identify and sing the melody of a familiar song when only the text is given, or rhythmic pattern tapped
6. To acquire a repertoire of enjoyable songs
7. To sing a major scale with numbers and syllables

Motor-Rhythmic Skills

1. To imitate rhythmic patterns by voice, rhythm sticks, and clapping
2. To sense accent in duple and triple meter
3. To follow directions for changes in rhythmic movement, as pulse, tempo, and mood may dictate
4. To recognize changes in tempo, and to express them in bodily movement

Ear Training for Pitch and Mood[6]

1. To respond with improving feeling and by appropriate bodily expression to music representing movement and mood
2. To use simple equipment such as scarves, strips of crepe paper, balls, balloons, and rhythm instruments to express mood and rhythm
3. To recognize changes in pitch range and to describe such changes by appropriate hand motions
4. To identify from neutral syllables or numbers, melodies or tone patterns in the major scales and the tonic chords in such scales

Listening Skills[7]

1. To identify many of the piano pieces and the recorded music performed in class
2. To sit and listen with attention and good concert behavior to short musical programs

---

[4] Fleming, Jessie, "A List of Desirable Musical Experiences for Elementary School Children in the Maryland Public Schools," *Journal of Research in Music Education,* I:1, Spring, 1953, pp. 59–67.
[5] See Chapters 3 to 5.
[6] See Chapters 3 to 5.
[7] See Chapter 10.

Instrumental Skills[8]

1. To use simple rhythm instruments, melody bells, water glasses

Creative Activities to Be Encouraged[9]

1. Composing and singing sentence songs and chants about usual or unusual experiences: a new tooth, a new baby, a trip, an airplane ride, spring flowers, the return of birds

2. Adding new verses to familiar songs

3. Setting a favorite poem to an original melody

4. Adding instrumental rhythmic accompaniments to familiar songs by melody bells, xylophone, water glasses, bottle chimes, and homemade rhythm instruments

5. Improvising rhythmic movements to dramatize suitable songs, piano pieces, and recorded music

6. Making rhythm instruments: bongo drums from a large oatmeal and smaller salt box; triangles from large nails; cymbals from pie pans; claves from sawed-off broomsticks; maracas by encasing and then breaking a light bulb in papier-mâché; shakers from small coffee cans containing pebbles or rice; an Indian tom-tom by stretching a drumhead or heavy piece of inner tube over a butter tub; rattles by loosely nailing bottle tops, cork filler removed, to the ends of dowl sticks

7. Illustrating favorite songs with crayon drawings

8. Bringing to class pictures from magazines and newspapers, recordings, and souvenirs to illustrate music activities

9. Relating music activities to other subjects

10. Synthesizing music skills to prepare assembly programs for special occasions

TIME FOR MUSIC

Both teacher and class should consider singing to be a form of recreation that lifts the spirit, sets a mood, heightens experience. Singing improves after rest periods because children are relaxed. It also improves when used as an adjunct to other activities. Action songs can be sung at recess; sawing and hammering songs while at the workbench; planting or raking songs while gardening; and fun songs, the children sitting in a circle around the teacher, at any time. Even though the teacher is intent on improving voice quality, helping the weaker singers, matching tones, or imitating familiar sounds, singing must remain a happy interlude. Since the voice is an integral part of each child's personality, the teacher must encourage singing rather than demand technique; promote enjoyment, not perfection.

Because of the child's short attention span, musical activity must be constantly

[8]See Chapters 4 and 8.
[9]See Chapters 3, 4, 8, and 9.

varied by *focusing attention* on different musical elements at each repetition. For instance, ask the class to:

1. Identify the subject of a song
2. Listen for and find repeated tonal or rhythmic elements
3. Determine, after familiarity, where rhythm instruments should be introduced for enhanced sound effects
4. Determine where phrases end
5. Indicate by hand movements the rise and fall of melodic lines
6. Chart melodic scale line and chord skips against a scale ladder drawn on the board
7. Find melodic patterns on a set of bells, a xylophone, or water glasses
8. Chart duration values under a text written on the chalkboard
9. Dramatize a song if it lends itself to rhythmic movement
10. Add tonic or dominant bell tones as an accompaniment

The creative activities enumerated earlier should also occupy part of the music lesson.

Do not expect accuracy of tone or rhythmic precision on the first singing. Initially the child perceives the outline of a song rather vaguely but, after difficult passages have been isolated and practiced, will eventually understand its form.

If the piano is used for accompaniment, play softly so the children can hear their own voices. Otherwise they will rely on the piano to the point of quitting when it stops. If recordings are used, turn down the volume for the same reason. Do not constantly play the melody after a tune has been learned. The bass or root of each accompanying chord will suffice to keep the class on pitch with good intonation. A delightfully soft accompaniment adding color and charm can be provided by chording on an autoharp while the chord root is played on tone bells.

In lower grades, the music period should be as informal as possible, with the children seated around the teacher in a semicircle that allows plenty of space beyond the chairs for free rhythmic play and games. *Plan the music lesson!* Save improvisation for the piano, not the classroom. The scale of class reaction to an insecure teacher is rarely tempered.

A sequence of musical signals can be developed to eliminate most verbal direction. A quietly played chord can mean "Ready for music"; a single bell tone, "Ready for rhythms"; a sequence of *do-mi-sol,* "Return to your seats."

RELATING MUSIC TO OTHER ACTIVITIES

You will find that most songbook series for the primary grades and their supplements are organized about subject matter such as:

1. Myself: who I am, my name, my hair color, eye color, height
2. Home: daily activities, playtime, mealtime, bedtime, toys
3. Family: Daddy, mother, sister, brother, baby
4. Pets: animals, birds, fish, dolls

5. Seasons: summer, spring, fall, winter, and corresponding effects on nature, people, and environment

6. Devotion: prayer, praise, and thankfulness

7. Community: policemen, firemen, grocer, mailmen, etc.

8. Travel: by water, land, air, space

9. Holidays: by month or season, legal, religious, others

10. Occupations: shoemaker, carpenter, sailor, miner, railroader, pilot, etc.

11. Zoo: wild and domestic animals

12. Circus: wild animals, trainers, trapeze artists, clowns, bareback riders

13. Strange lands and peoples: Indians, Eskimos, Africans, Asians, etc.

14. Folksongs: Latin American and European

Such books also contain:

1. Action songs
  a. Finger play and dramatization
  b. Rhythmic interpretation: march, walk, run, skip, hop, jump, gallop, tiptoe, bounce ball, jump rope, tap balloon, swirl scarves, etc.
  c. Game, clapping, and dance songs

2. Sound effect and imitation songs about clocks, telephones, trains, boats, planes, autos, rockets, wild and domestic animals.

3. Songs illustrating musical concepts:
  a. High and low, loud and soft
  b. Quiet, boisterous, mysterious, rhythmic moods
  c. Musical instrument imitations
  d. Varying modes: pentatonic, major, minor, Oriental
  e. Motive and rhythm sequence in melodic patterns, phrases
  f. Styles and forms: march, waltz, Indian, cowboy

THE MUSIC CORNER

Encourage classroom teachers to set up a music corner in their rooms where children, individually or in small groups, will feel free to experiment with musical sounds and develop spontaneous musical activities. The teacher may assign to committees of children the responsibility for keeping the corner in good housekeeping order; tuning the water glasses as needed; setting up the classroom for rhythm activities; distributing books and instruments.

Materials for such a music corner may include homemade rhythm instruments, water glasses, and a pitcher; bottle chimes; resonator tone bells or Swiss melody bells; autoharp; a record player and recordings; melody flutes, tonettes, or flutophones; music books for singing and playing instruments; books about music and musicians.

If possible include the following rhythm instruments, which are sufficient to equip a medium-sized class: a large drum, a few small drums, two or three triangles, tambourines, wood blocks, rattles, sand blocks, jingle bells, castanets on sticks, one pair of cymbals, and twelve pairs of rhythm sticks. These can be implemented with home-made claves, maracas, guiros, scrapers, rattles, and various shakers.

The teacher will need a pitch pipe and staff liner.

If a separate music corner in each classroom is impracticable a visiting music teacher can use a handcart, like that found in school cafeterias, to transport equipment, books, and instruments.

MUSIC FOR QUIET LISTENING[10]

Music for listening should not be confined to a particular period. Rather, the teacher will discover many instances when such listening will be welcome: during rest periods; while the class is assembling in the morning; while it is finishing its daily activities. Above all, the children must learn to listen quietly when one of their own number, or a child from an upper grade, is performing. Youngsters enjoy hearing older children perform, not least because of the possibility of some day imitating them. However, do not make inordinate demands on their attention span.

Primary Grades

All musical activity, vocal or instrumental, solo or ensemble, requires *focused* listening. Such listening demands and produces a variety of additional responses: intellectual, physiological, and motor. The child must learn to immerse himself in the music without drowning, to enjoy its balmy reaches, but to navigate, not drift. Musical landmarks can be recognized by

1. Listening to
   a. Rhythms for marching, running, skipping, and other fundamental movements
   b. Dynamic changes
   c. Melodic lines and pitch relationships
   d. Timbre of musical instruments and voices
   e. Mood: light and airy, heavy and somber, dramatic and gay
   f. Tempo: slow, fast, moderate
   g. Comparative beauty of tone (contrast tape recordings of class performance with recorded performances of professionals)
2. Comprehending
   a. The story of program music (*Peter and the Wolf*)
   b. The mood of descriptive music (Nocturne from *A Midsummer Night's Dream*)
   c. The purpose of martial, funeral, dance music
3. Recognizing characteristics of
   a. American Indian music
   b. Cowboy music
   c. Marches, waltzes, gallops, and skip rhythms

[10]See Chapter 10 and Appendix III.

Intermediate and Upper Grades

Amplify listening by background material on the works heard. Introduce:

1. Characteristic national and ethnic music: American, Negro, Latin American, Calypso, European, Asian, Oriental, African

2. Forms of opera, symphony, folk songs, concerto, oratorio

3. Forms of dance such as minuet, gavotte, cha-cha-cha, samba, fox-trot, polka, square dances, rock-and-roll, etc.

4. Characteristics of various periods in music history through related studies: Baroque, Classic, Romantic, Impressionist, Modern, Contemporary. Have the children attempt recognition of: orchestral, band, and recreational instruments by sight and sound; compound meters at varying tempos—$\frac{6}{8}$, $\frac{9}{8}$, perhaps $\frac{5}{4}$; modality: major, minor, and perhaps Dorian, modified Phrygian; voice registers: soprano, contralto, tenor, baritone, and bass; and variations in caliber of performance of the same work by different artists.

Recorded Music

Today, the number and variety of recordings for children makes their use imperative but their selection difficult. A list of major manufacturers and distributors will be found in Appendix III. In selecting recordings, these criteria may be helpful:

1. Does the quality of singing provide a worthwhile vocal standard?

2. Does the instrumental accompaniment stimulate musical imagination and lead to musical insight?

3. Is the diction easily understood? Are the instruments played in a characteristic and idiomatic manner?

4. Is the music memorable?

5. Are the pieces short enough to hold the child's attention?

6. Is the subject of the text of interest, its vocabulary understandable?

7. Do the recordings provide a variety of voice types and instrumental colors?

8. Are the musical forms and moods readily identifiable at later hearings? Will the child want to hear them again?

9. May the recordings be related to other activities: rhythms, singing, dancing, drawing, dramatizing, story telling?

INTERMEDIATE GRADES: AGES EIGHT THROUGH TEN

Around his eighth year, the child begins to control smaller muscles, developing an interest as a result in physical and manipulative skills. He has finer eye-hand coordination, his eyes having matured to adjust to both near and far vision; he is interested in competitive games using marbles, immies, and jacks, in wrestling and climbing, and in team sports, over which he becomes very argumentative. Increasing participation in group activities is accompanied by a desire to belong to the peer group of his sex. Pockets are filled with odd items of which mother can never be rid. Interests have broadened to include community activities: camping, cub scouting, little league baseball, boys' and girls' clubs. He enthusiastically studies materials concerning other peoples and countries.

MUSICAL DEVELOPMENT

The voice range of boys in the ten-year-old group shifts slightly lower, so that songs can be pitched at about middle C. Girls' voices sound more mature in quality and stronger in the upper register. Because of increased muscular control, organized rhythmic folk dances requiring finer coordination and a longer memory span can be mastered, as can beginning instrumental skills and reading rudimentary music notation.

ATTITUDES TO BE DEVELOPED[11]

1. The desire to achieve greater skill in performance
2. Recognition that music is an important activity of life
3. A desire to cooperate with others in making music in and out of school

APPROPRIATE MUSICAL ACTIVITIES AND OBJECTIVES

Vocal Skills[12]

1. Match tones to enable those singing incorrectly to improve pitch mastery
2. Sing longer songs that require increased vocabulary. Emphasize diction, accuracy of intonation, expression, rhythm
3. Introduce rounds, canons, descants. Develop original chants. Hand harmonize I, IV, and V chords. Develop recognition of these chords by ear
4. Provide the opportunity for individual singing through dialogue, antiphonal, answer, and partner songs. Combine rounds such as "Three Blind Mice" and "Are You Sleeping?", as well as other songs
5. Demand careful listening to vowel sounds, diction, and pronunciation
6. Develop a selected choir consisting of those children especially interested in music to sing unison and two-part songs

Motor-Rhythmic Skills[13]

1. Action songs
2. Party and game songs

---

[11] See Chapter 12.
[12] See Chapters 3, 5, 6, and 7.
[13] See Chapters 3, 4, 8, and 9; Appendix I.

3. Square and folk dances
4. Sensing meter in $\frac{4}{4}$, $\frac{3}{8}$, $\frac{6}{8}$ in varying tempos
5. Sensing tempo changes
6. Recognition and identification of learned rhythms by use of bodily movement
7. Latin American rhythms and syncopation introduced through folk music: singing, dancing, adding rhythm instrument accompaniment
8. "Sound painting": organizing instrumental and vocal sounds and noises into metrical and nonmetrical forms (see Chapter 9)

Harmonic Skills[14]

1. Rounds and canons
2. Descants and chants
3. Partner songs
4. Dialogue songs
5. Simple two-part diatonic harmony in thirds and sixths
6. Hand harmonize I, IV, and V chords (see Chapter 7)
7. Develop recognition of I, IV, and V chords by ear. Add them to familiar melodies vocally by a harmony choir and instrumentally by autoharp, Swiss melody bells, resonator tone bells, water glasses, bottle chimes, bottle band, or flutes

Reading and Writing Notation[15]

1. Teach music notation, utilizing rote and original songs. Practice transfer of the scale ladder to the music staff
2. Develop a percussion score from text and melodic rhythms. Translate syllabic duration of common names and words into note values (see Chapter 4)
3. Teach terminology for tempo, dynamics, expression, rhythms, easier key and meter signatures. Collect a glossary of musical materials for a music notebook
4. In place of learning only published songs, create songs and develop their notation (see Chapter 9)

Critical Skills[16]

1. Evaluate performance by use of tape recordings. Compare class performance with a professional recording of the same work to develop critical judgment of tone quality and accuracy of performance
2. Discuss outside music listening
3. Develop recognition of musical instruments: violin, viola, cello, bass, clarinet, oboe, bassoon, trumpet, French horn, trombone, tuba, percussion battery. Develop recognition of qualities of singing voices at various ranges. Compare tone quality and

[14]See Chapters 5, 7, and 8.
[15]See Chapters 1, 3, 4, and 9.
[16]See Chapters 10 and 11.

style of favorite singers. Compare orchestral sounds of strings, woodwinds, brass, percussion

4. Develop a class repertoire of recorded music consisting of shorter works by master composers in varied musical forms: dance, suite, opera, ballet, oratorio, chamber music, symphony, novelties

RELATING MUSIC TO OTHER ACTIVITIES[17]

1. American songs: Indian, cowboy, Negro, work, explorers (*voyageurs*), chanteys, heroes and folk characters (John Bunyan, Johnny Appleseed), patriotic
2. Folk and patriotic songs of other nations (including songs in foreign languages)
3. Devotional and holiday songs
4. Fun songs for camping, bus riding, games, and parties
5. Stephen Foster and other minstrelseys
6. Seasonal songs describing nature in varying moods
7. Story songs that can be dramatized
8. Transportation, chanteys, railroad, riverboat songs
9. Choral speech and chants
10. Musical plays and ballets for dance dramatization
11. Songs that need to be completed: melodies without texts, texts without melodies, parodies
12. Songs to which classroom orchestration may be added
13. Songs about the space age
14. Songs imitating orchestral instruments
Source materials for all music activities will be found in Appendix I.

UPPER ELEMENTARY GRADES: AGES TEN THROUGH TWELVE

Children of this age experience rapid growth, developing voracious appetites. There is wide variation in physical maturation and it occurs unevenly on the child's body, girls seeming to mature more rapidly than boys.

The gang spirit develops strongly in boys, although both sexes become clannish. Increasing sex differentiation leads to teasing and antagonism, boys being especially afraid of "sissy" fraternizing. There is a tendency toward hypercriticism, rebelliousness, and independence. These feelings are reinforced by the child's ability to earn money for the first time by performing chores.

MUSICAL DEVELOPMENT

Tone quality improves in the girls' upper register. Increasing heaviness in the boys' voices requires lower ranges. Both sexes enjoy dancing of all types, and want to play band, orchestra, and recreational instruments. Harmonic interest develops

[17]See Chapters 11 and 12; Appendix I.

strongly with the wish to carry independent parts. The child enjoys making simple musical instruments, particularly Latin American ones: claves, maracas, conga, bongo, and rhumba drums, and guiros.

Because of his expanding interests, the child is delighted to relate music to other subjects, and to incorporate personal research into class units of instruction he has helped to plan (see Chapter 11).

APPROPRIATE MUSICAL ACTIVITIES AND OBJECTIVES

Vocal Skills[18]

1. Refine tone quality. Demand greater accuracy of pitch intonation, rhythmic sense, dynamic feeling, expression, diction, and pronunciation

2. Develop ability to carry an independent second or third part against the melody

3. Develop ability to sense and carry a musical phrase with proper breath control

4. Develop recognition and ability to sing by *sol-fa* syllables scales in the minor modes and chromatic alteration of accidentals

5. Develop ability to sense changes in harmonic feeling between the I, IV, and V chords

6. Widen the range of song interests and increase ability to sing and remember songs of longer duration

7. Develop elementary choral groups to sing two- and three-part songs

Motor-Rhythmic Skills[19]

1. Teach party games

2. Teach square and social dances, including those related to units of instruction: minuet and gavotte for Colonial Unit, reels and jigs for unit on Western Exploration, etc.

3. Complex rhythms in $\frac{2}{4}$, $\frac{2}{2}$, $\frac{3}{4}$, $\frac{4}{4}$, $\frac{3}{8}$, $\frac{6}{8}$, $\frac{6}{4}$, $\frac{9}{8}$

4. Use eurhythmics to develop memory recognition and identification of familiar rhythms. Develop feeling of $\frac{3}{4}$ time for contrasting waltz and minuet tempos. For $\frac{2}{4}$ time contrast tempos of street, processional, funeral, and cavalry marches

5. Increase awareness of effect of tempo on mood by contrasting the Scherzo and Nocturne of Mendelssohn's *Midsummer Night's Dream,* operatic excerpts, other appropriate works

6. Develop ability to sense and perform syncopated rhythms of Latin American and Calypso music on rhythm instruments

[18] See Chapters 5, 6, and 7; Appendix I.
[19] See Chapters 4, 8, and 11; Appendix I.

Harmonic Skills[20]

1. Develop independence in carrying parts in two- and three-part songs, rounds, canons, descants, and chants

2. Develop ability to hear, and to sing with good intonation, harmonic alteration, chromatic sequence in second and third parts

3. Use keyboard charts to build I, IV, and V chords in major and minor modes

4. Develop the ability to play a pizzicato bass part on the open strings of a viola, cello, or bass from chord symbols. Perhaps the class can also learn the fingering of the other bass notes

5. Develop ability to play accompaniments from chord symbols on the autoharp and harmolin

6. Translate hand harmonizing to numbers, syllables, and notation

7. Develop class ability to use I, IV, and V chords to provide accompaniment to familiar songs, and to sense possible harmonic background for those composed by themselves

8. Harmonize chords with Swiss bells, tone bells, bottle band, recreational and orchestral instruments

Notational Skills[21]

1. Read music notation in treble clef including accidentals

2. Sing minor scales from *la* to *la*, including natural, melodic, and harmonic forms with chromatic alterations

3. Sing I, IV, and V chords in minor mode

4. Sing modal scales, particularly Dorian and Phrygian, and modal songs. Practice the identification of modes by ear

5. Increase knowledge of music notation for major and minor scales through three sharps and three flats. Introduce terminology for tempo, dynamics, meter, and expression. Teach the principles underlying recognition of key signatures

6. Develop scores for percussion and melodic accompaniment to be played by a classroom orchestra that includes recreational, orchestral, and band instruments

7. Expand music notebook to include a music dictionary, biographical sketches, original songs, art illustrations, current events in music, and theoretical information

8. Compose accompaniments for rhythm and recreational instruments, piano, autoharp, and voices (see Chapter 9)

Critical Skills[22]

1. Use tape recordings to refine the child's critical sense of his own performance and that of others. Develop critical judgment of his tone quality, accuracy of pitch,

---

[20]See Chapters 5, 7, and 8.
[21]See Chapters 1, 3, 5, 6, 7, 8, 9, and 11.
[22]See Chapters 9, 10, and 11.

rhythm, dynamics, and feeling for mood and interpretation. Record performances to permit self-criticism

2. Discuss outside listening

3. Develop aural discrimination of instrumental sounds, including unusual percussion: celeste, chimes. Develop the ability to identify coloratura, dramatic and lyric sopranos; mezzo, contralto, tenor, baritone, and bass voices

4. Develop the ability to research materials pertinent to music: biography, opera, ballet, and related literature

5. Increase knowledge of varied forms, including works in Baroque, Classic, Romantic, Impressionist, and Contemporary styles. Encourage the sharing of favorite recordings with classmates

Creative Skills[23]

1. Compose songs and dances

2. Add new texts, chants, descants, and harmonized parts to familiar songs

3. Add as accompaniment to songs and dances: voice, piano, autoharp, bells, rhythm, recreational, orchestral, and band instruments

4. Add dance movements to recorded literature and combine songs, dances, and instruments in rhythmic activities

5. Find poetry, art, and architecture to illustrate comparable moods and forms in music. Post appropriate pictures in notebooks, on bulletin boards

6. Find recorded music to match moods of works in other arts

7. Enjoy the sharing of music and recognition of differences in musical preference

8. Play orchestral and band instruments

9. Dramatize song, operetta, and ballet stories

10. Prepare assembly programs utilizing music as part of related units of instruction

Instrumental Skills[24]

1. Class lessons in piano, orchestral, and band instruments

2. Introduce melody flutes and other similar flute-type instruments

3. Teach basic piano in regular music class. Teach scale and chord construction with Keyboard Scale and Chord Finder

4. Teach accompaniment by pizzicato playing of chord roots or bass line on the open strings of the viola, cello, and bass

5. Teach accompaniment by autoharp

6. Offer voluntary class lessons in the plectrum instruments, such as the ukulele, guitar, and banjo. Also offer lessons on the piano accordion

7. Combine simple melody and orchestral instruments into a classroom orchestra

8. Encourage the creation of small ensembles of any combination of instruments

[23]See Chapters 8 and 9.
[24]See Chapters 8 and 9.

for home music making. Provide each participant with a list of neighboring young instrumentalists, as well as a collection of ensemble music

9. On Saturday mornings rehearse an elementary band and orchestra made up of players from the school or several schools (the need for extra salary for instrumental teachers participating in such a program seems obvious)

10. Encourage solo work utilizing the song materials from basic elementary school music series as well as graded literature for each instrument. Provide opportunities for solo appearances in regular classroom music class, assemblies, school music clubs

11. Use instruments in regular music class to accompany singing and dancing

12. To assist the reading of rhythmic notation, teach easier drum rudiments using drum sticks on a drum pad

RELATING MUSIC TO OTHER ACTIVITIES

Songs, dances, lists of recordings, works of art, and literature characteristic of the following periods will all be found in any basic elementary school music series and its supplementary materials.

1. American Indian
2. Early settlers: Dutch, English, French, Spanish
3. Importation of slave labor: Negro Afro-American music
4. Songs of early exploration: *voyageurs*, chanteys, riverboat songs
5. Westward exploration and expansion
6. Colonial times
7. Revolutionary times
8. Westward Ho! and the Industrial Revolution
9. War Between the States and Reconstruction: minstrel shows
10. Gay Nineties
11. First World War
12. The Flapper Twenties and Recession Thirties
13. The Space Age

MUSIC SYMBOLS[25]

The learning of concepts of music must precede learning the symbols for such concepts. To be meaningful, both concepts and symbols must be organically related to the musical activities in which they are employed. Music theory divorced from music making remains only theory. In the method described in the succeeding chapters, notation and terminology are introduced only as they are needed to enhance and enrich the child's direct sensory musical experience.

[25] See Chapters 1, 3, 4, 7, and 10.

To facilitate the learning of notation, ask the class to make 4 x 7 flash cards for incorporation into individual notebooks, and 8 x 11 wall charts for bulletin board display. A collection of flash cards, perhaps called "My Music Dictionary," can be used by the child for future reference.

USEFUL TERMINOLOGY DERIVED FROM SONG SERIES TO BE INCLUDED IN A MUSIC NOTEBOOK

Tempo Terms

1. Adagio: very slow
2. Andante: walking time
3. Moderato: in a moderate tempo, like a slow waltz
4. Allegretto: gaily
5. Allegro: quite fast
6. Vivo: very fast
7. Presto: as fast as possible

Dynamic Terms

1. *ff:* abbreviation for *fortissimo*—very loud
2. *f:* abbreviation for *forte*—loud
3. *mf:* abbreviation for *mezzoforte*—moderately loud
4. *mp:* abbreviation for *mezzopiano*—moderately soft
5. *p:* abbreviation for *piano*—soft
6. *pp:* abbreviation for *pianissimo*—very soft

Clef Signs Denote Range of Pitch

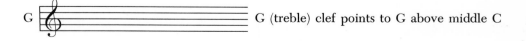

G   G (treble) clef points to G above middle C

F   F (bass) clef points to F below middle C

Staff Symbols

Repeat sign, meaning repeat from previous such double bar or, if none, from beginning

Double bar, meaning end of phrase, section, or song

Light double bar, marks end of either section or introduction

Fermata, meaning hold longer than note value or until released by conductor

Form Symbols

D.C.: Abbreviation for *Da Capo,* meaning repeat from the beginning to the place marked *Fine* (pronounced fee-nay), the finish or end

D.S. al Fine: Abbreviation for *Dal Segno al Fine,* meaning return to the sign 𝄋 and sing or play again until reaching the word Fine or Coda

First ending written above the staff means stop and go back to the beginning the first time through; skip this ending on the repetition and go to the second ending

Denotes the second ending on the repetition referred to above

Coda sign, appearing frequently on a Da Capo or Dal Segno repetition, means skip from the place where this sign appears to the other Coda sign, and then play to Fine

Key Signatures and Symbols

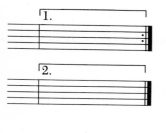

Key of D

How to locate tonic *do* or first step on a scale with sharps or flats:

1. In sharp keys the last sharp to the right is the seventh step of the scale ascending. Going up one scale step gives the keynote or tonic

Key of B♭

**C Major or
A Minor**

2. In flat keys the last flat to the right is the fourth step of the scale. Counting down four steps will then give the keynote of the scale. Also, if more than one flat is in the key signature, the next to the last flat to the right is the key signature

3. Minor keys take the same key signature as their relative major keys. The relative major key of any given minor key is found by deeming the minor tonic the sixth step of the major scale and counting up two steps (a minor third) to the eighth step of the scale. Thus A Minor takes its key signature from C Major, two steps up from A. The relative minor key of any major is the key of the sixth step of the major scale

4. A *cancel* or *natural sign* alters a flatted or sharped tone back to its normal pitch in the scale

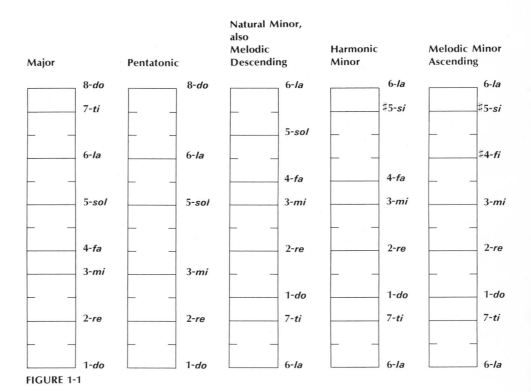

FIGURE 1-1

SCALE LADDER GRAPHS ON PERMANENT CHARTS

The comparative table of scales given in Figure 1-1 will help children visualize the measurement of musical intervals. Each scale should be placed on separate charts aligned along the chalkboard edge so that children may compare scale construction to charts of the piano keyboard. Pitch names of notes in a given key may be placed on the chalkboard alongside a chart to facilitate the eventual relating of the scale ladder to the music staff. Additional scale graphs will be found in Chapters 3, 5, 6, and 7.

METER SIGNATURES

Many basic series now follow Carl Orff's recommendation that the meter signature be written with a note instead of a numeral as the lower figure, as follows:

2/4 is 2/4	3/4 is 3/4	4/4 is 4/4	6/4 is 6/4	
3/♪ is 3/8	4/♪ is 4/8	6/♪ is 6/8	9/♪ is 9/8	12/♪ is 12/8

In rapid tempo

1/♩. is 3/8	2/♩. is 6/8	3/♩. is 9/8	4/♩. is 12/8
2/♩ is 2/2 or ¢	3/♩ is 3/2	4/♩ is 4/2	

SELECTING A BASIC SERIES

The advent of new educational philosophies requires that the school's basic series of elementary music books be periodically changed. The selection will usually be made by a committee of administrators, classroom teachers, and music specialists, and to aid such committees, the music education faculty of the State University of New York, College at Buffalo has developed the following checklist of Evaluative Criteria for the Selection and Purchase of Music Textbooks.[26]

Name of Series:

Publisher and Address:

[26]"Evaluative Criteria for the Selection and Purchase of Music Textbooks," State University of New York, College at Buffalo, N.Y., 1961.

Authors:

Copyright Dates:

Cost of Teacher's Books:

Cost of Student's Books by Grade: K 1 2 3 4 5 6 7 8

Cost of Recordings by Grade:

In answering each question score Superior, Excellent, Average, Mediocre, Poor: *Total.*
                                                        5   4   3   2   1

Content

1. Does the material arouse the child's curiosity and interest?
2. Does it offer a logical and psychological sequence graded for the development of musical growth?
3. Is the material in each book organized into units of interest and activity to stimulate child participation?
4. Is the material sufficient to provide (a) melodic; (b) rhythmic; (c) instrumental; (d) dramatic; (e) creative; and (f) harmonic experiences?
5. Is there material suitable for musical and literary appreciation (attentive listening)?
6. Do the illustrations capture, enhance, and interpret the spirit and character of the songs?
7. Are there biographical sketches of composers and performers?

Songs

1. Are the songs of fine musical quality, yet within the range and intervals of the children's voices and abilities?
2. Are the texts of quality, yet within the understanding and experience of children of the grade level for which the book is intended?
3. Are there a large number of familiar rote songs for the primary grades?
4. Are there enough songs of more than average length?
5. Is the rhythm of the music well fitted to the rhythm of the words?
6. Is the reading vocabulary appropriate for each grade level?
7. Does the selection of songs in the books for junior high school indicate an understanding of adolescent psychology?
8. Are there songs for the seventh and eighth grades in which boys with changing voices have the opportunity to sing the melody?
9. Do the altos (second sopranos) sing the melody in some of the songs while the sopranos sing harmony or a descant?
10. Is there a sufficient variety of holiday songs?
11. Is the amount of composed music and folk songs approximately the same?
12. Is there a variety of song material so that music may be related to social

studies, including: (a) American citizenship education; (b) Foreign languages; (c) Science (weather, birds and animals, space travel)?

13. Do books for the primary and early intermediate grades anticipate part singing by offering a sufficient number of rounds, canons, partner songs, conversation (dialogue) songs, descants, and optional two-part songs?

Accompaniment Material

1. Do a large number of songs have:

    a. Autoharp markings (either roman numerals or chord symbols)?
    b. Parts for melody bells, tone bells and/or chimes?
    c. Parts for song flutes, recorders, melody flutes?
    d. Rhythm band percussion instruments?
    e. Easy piano accompaniments?
    f. Challenging, interesting piano accompaniments?
    g. Obbligatos and/or descants?
    h. Classroom orchestrations for rhythmic instruments, recreational instruments, and orchestral and band instruments?

Music Reading

1. Does the approach to music reading follow the child's normal progress in reading, according to current psychological and physiological theory?

2. Are oversized notes and good-size print used in the books for the lower primary grades?

3. Is there a graduated rhythm sequence of basic rhythmic patterns, games, dances, and imaginative responses?

4. Are songs chosen and ordered to help students see and hear familiar rhythmic patterns?

5. Are these patterns repeated and reviewed sufficiently for children to learn to recognize them at sight?

6. Are numbers and syllables used sufficiently to help pupils find the keynote?

Teaching Aids

1. Is there a suggested procedure for teaching each song in relation to its recording?

2. Are the guides completely and understandably organized?

3. Do they meet the needs of the nonspecialist classroom teacher as well as those of the music specialist?

4. Are there piano accompaniments for all the songs in the children's books?

5. Will the book bindings permit the book to remain open on the piano music rack?

6. Are the books printed on easily erasable high-quality paper?

7. Are the illustrations in color?

8. Are teachers' editions available throughout the entire series?

Recordings

1. Are songs recorded so as to permit any classroom teacher unable to read music to learn unfamiliar songs by listening?

2. Have the performers on the recordings captured the "feel" of the classroom?

3. Do the performers sing with such imagination and expression that the record may be used as a model of interpretation, diction, tempo, and intonation?

4. Are the recordings edited in such a way that any selection may be found quickly and easily?

5. Are the recordings of unbreakable vinylite, rugged enough for use by children?

6. Are the recordings packaged for durability, protection, and long-term storage?

7. Are there a sufficient number of songs and other selections for the primary grades to provide a variety of appropriate music for fundamental rhythms: marching, skipping, running, jumping, swaying, etc.?

8. Are there instrumental as well as vocal performances for a graduated course in music appreciation covering diverse forms, nationalities, and periods of history?

9. Does the introduction of each recorded song help the student and teacher to find its starting note?

10. Do the record labels indicate both the page number and title of songs in the student books?

11. Are there references in the teacher guides to other recorded materials?

Philosophy of Approach[27]

1. How well does this series meet the needs of the curriculum?

2. Can you as a teacher enthusiastically teach this series?

3. What specific suggestions are needed to modify format, content, organization, underlying psychological theory, editing, to suit this series to your school?

Select the series with the highest score.

APPLYING PEDAGOGICAL PRINCIPLES TO LEARNING MUSIC SKILLS

To learn to perform is to learn a skill. Learning a skill requires repetition, which should be organized in the most effective psychological sequence:

1. The learner must have a definite purpose before he begins the formation of a habit. A habit is a learned response to certain stimuli that upon continued repetition becomes automatic, thereby freeing the performer from the necessity of consciously organizing the details of the desired response.

[27] Determine from teachers manuals and guides for each basic music series. For listing see Appendix V.

2. Before beginning each exercise or lesson, the student must plan its sequence. Bad habits arise frequently from lack of procedural knowledge. In musical, as in all learning, analysis of subject matter and the logical order of its presentation is essential.

3. A habit must be started correctly, and continued correctly whenever the student performs.

4. All practice must be conducted attentively, varying details of drill to motivate mastery.

5. Correct performance is the best evidence of growth in skill.

6. The length and frequency of practice should be decreased as skill increases. Music previously mastered should be performed less often and for shorter periods than music known less well.

7. Use acquired skills in the course of acquiring new ones. A skill once mastered does not remain so unless used.

PRINCIPLES OF LESSON PLANNING

The first objective of a properly organized series of lessons is to induce the child to desire to accomplish a sequence of clearly outlined tasks. A task accomplished creates a feeling of confidence. An understanding of problems solved is expressed in a willingness for new undertakings. It has become axiomatic in educational philosophy that a lesson well planned is more than half taught.

The following criteria should be borne in mind when setting up music lesson plans:

1. The plan must be interesting, and must make a real appeal to the interests and traits of developing children. The teacher should become familiar with theories of learning.

2. The plan must contain a challenge and create a desire to accomplish a given task.

3. The plan must reveal a purpose and contain all directions needed for its accomplishment. The purpose must seem worthwhile not only to the teacher, but to the children. The class must always be fully aware of what is required to complete the task.

4. The plan must define the skills to be acquired and the information to be presented.

5. Requirements should be gauged to the recognized abilities and needs of the pupils. No plan should be inflexible. Making impossible demands of children hinders learning.

6. The plan should be of proper length. The attention span of children will vary according to their interest.

7. There should be provision for students to use their own initiative in suggesting methods of problem-solving.

8. The plan must give incentive and opportunity for children to use skills and information acquired in non-school music activities.

9. Each step should follow easily and logically from those previously mastered.

10. Learning difficulties must be anticipated, new terminology and new ways of performing explained. Specialized terminology must be taught as a natural product of circumstance, much as speech is taught to the young child. Concepts are derived from experience, and words denote concepts. Words with known meaning can be abbreviated as symbols.

11. Provision should be made for practice in the use of the requisite tools and techniques.

12. All necessary materials should be assembled beforehand.

13. The plan must evoke the teacher's sincere and enthusiastic interest. Nothing will discourage a child more than a teacher who is indifferent or unprepared.

A program of music education must help each child develop to full capacity a love and understanding of the *use* of music. If the influence of music is used wisely, it will serve to enrich his life by focusing emotional feeling and by strengthening bonds of brotherhood and common culture. A program of music education must give the child the opportunity to listen to fine performances, to perform himself, and must be designed to reinforce and supplement school and non-school activities.

The report of the American Association of School Administrators in 1959 stated:

We believe in a well-balanced school curriculum in which music, drama, poetry, sculpture, architecture, and the like are included side by side with other important subjects such as mathematics, history and science. It is important that pupils, as a part of general education, learn to appreciate, to understand, to create, and to criticize with discrimination those products of the mind, the voice, the hand, and the body which give dignity to the person and exalt the spirit of man.[28]

SUMMARY (Evaluation of Teaching and Learning)

The following checklist should aid the teacher to discover how successfully music has been taught through the sixth grade. By then the child should have achieved the following skills:

1. Sensing meter: to recognize $\frac{3}{8}$, $\frac{6}{8}$, $\frac{9}{8}$, in addition to simpler meters; to feel pulse accents.

2. Sensing tempo: to move with rhythmic feeling to game and party songs; to dance, to sing, and to perform on percussion and melody instruments to changing tempos.

3. Sensing mood: to translate musical moods clearly into words and/or bodily movement.

4. Sensing mode: to recognize major, minor, and pentatonic melodies, as well as major and minor chords and their qualities.

5. Sensing style: to recognize rhythms of some Latin American dance styles, and some Calypso and jazz idioms; to recognize general characteristics of ethnic folk music

[28]Official report, American Association of School Administrators, Atlantic City Conference, 1959, Atlantic City, N.J., p. 248.

such as Spanish, Hungarian, Gypsy, Russian, American (Indian, Western, Negro); to distinguish general characteristics of some musical periods such as Baroque, Classic, Romantic, Impressionistic, Contemporary.

6. Sensing form: to recognize period dances of European and American origin as the result of units correlated to social studies; to recognize ballets such as the *Nutcracker Suite, Sleeping Beauty, Rodeo, Billy the Kid;* suites such as the *Baroque Dance Suite* and *Peer Gynt;* oratorios such as *The Messiah;* a Mozart or Haydn symphony; a piano or violin concerto.

7. To evince enjoyment of music in attitudes in class and to participate in curricular and extracurricular music activities.

8. To recognize by ear music learned in class.

9. To identify by sight and sound all string, woodwind, brass, plectrum, and percussion instruments.

10. To recognize from tape recordings of his own performance deficiencies in tonal beauty, diction, pronunciation, and dynamic contrasts and to improve his performance as a result.

11. To compare accurately recordings of his own performance with recordings of professional performances of the same music.

12. To be able to carry a descant, chant, or second or third part against a melody line.

13. To possess a repertoire of songs; to enjoy sight reading in two- and three-part harmony.

14. To identify the keys of the piano keyboard.

15. To identify tonic, dominant, and subdominant chords and other tonal groups in the major mode by syllables, number, and pitch name.

16. To sense changes from tonic to dominant or subdominant in harmonic accompaniment.

17. To recognize key signatures through three sharps and three flats in the major mode, and to be able to place the appropriate keynote on the staff.

18. To write basic symbols for rhythmic and dynamic values; to know pitch by name, number, and syllable, and be able to relate these to the music staff by notation.

19. To illustrate duration values by tapping the rhythm of familiar songs on drum, desk, or hand, including sixteenth notes and triplet figures in all meters.

20. To pluck appropriate pizzicato bass on the open strings of the viola, cello, and bass to accompany songs in the keys of C, G, and D.

21. To strum an autoharp with assured reading of chord symbols.

CHAPTER THREE

DEVELOPING CONCEPTS OF MELODY: PRIMARY GRADES

In the primary grades, a principal objective of music education is to develop aesthetic sensitivity to music by creating musical literacy, the ability to comprehend music symbols. Such symbols will convey meaning to the child only if he has experienced the materials represented. This chapter deals with methods of introducing those musical elements from which the imagery and concepts needed to understand musical communication are built.

A young child exposed to varied musical sounds will gradually realize that musical pitch exists everywhere: in a struck drinking glass, in a soda pop bottle converted into a flute, in his mother's crockery, in his voice, and in musical instruments. Such exposure will also bring recognition that few sounds are the same.

The voice of a child differs from the voice of an adult. The sounding of the brass is not that of string or percussive instruments; the sound of wood instruments is not that of instruments of metal or membrane. Musical sounds are pitched high or low, are loud or soft, rhythmically fast or slow.

The child can also be made aware of the varied sources of rhythmic movement: the natural rhythms of his own body and those of animals, the swaying of trees, the arc of the swing, the inflection of words and animal sounds, mechanical rhythms in the noise of machines and vehicles. Once conscious of pitch and rhythm, he will be able to understand that the sounds called music are those organized solely for the purpose of creating recognizable patterns.

A sense of form brings sense of mood: gaiety, sadness, martial spirit, quiet serenity. Such recognition ultimately permits discrimination among modal forms, the realization that the major mode is frequently gay, the minor mode sometimes sad.

Zanzig suggests that there is an innate musical potential in most young children.

Evidently all young children are by nature possessed of certain impulses and sensibilities which, if not all readily recognizable as being musical, are in essence enough like the elements of musical expression or response to be suspected of being kin thereto—as baby talk is to literature. In degree of these native powers, children differ very greatly; but in kinds of them, they are likely to be alike. What are the kinds, as indicated even in infancy?

1. To hear and to distinguish sounds, of bird, bell, auto horn, airplane, voice, drum, violin, etc., often with an apparently acute and full response. To hear also and to feel and enjoy the RHYTHM of music, poetry, rhymes and jingles.

2. To move rhythmically, jouncing with or without music at age of eight or nine months; later swaying, crawling, toddling or walking, pushing and pulling, hippity-hopping, skipping; all often jubilantly and in a rhythm of each child's own (which may or may not yet, however, be ready to keep in time with music).

3. To express oneself vocally, and to play with the voice, commencing with the babbling, gurgling and crooning of infancy; later speaking in words or in baby talk, sometimes if not often, with a vivid and highly inflected expressiveness not far from being melody; chanting or making up jingles, usually while engaged in an absorbing activity; or singing tunefully without bidding or in ready imitation.

4. To strike, shake or scrape things for the sounds they make, his first toy a rattle; later striking or really playing the piano keys or a set of tuned bells or the like in a fashion of his own; delighting to blow on a whistle, a simple flute or toy trumpet.

5. To make up things—imaginative play in "acting," story-telling, song-making or chanting, or in being a giant, fairy, bird or airplane, galloping horse, swaying tree or whatever else he wills.

6. To respond to his world, inner and outer, with apparently vivid feelings of grief, joy, desire, aggression, wonder, humor, restlessness or serenity, or of beauty or at least a rapt sensory response, any of which may be found expressed in real music to which even young children can respond. But most important is the underlying urge to LIVE fully, which seems to be especially expansive in young children.

Let us assume, then, that it is mainly through all of these natural approaches to music, used with a wise progressiveness, that we shall proceed with the children; through singing and voice play, rhythmic movement; listening; playing with simple instruments, song making; acting out songs; instrumental pieces and stories with music; and finding ideal expression, free yet orderly, of children's feelings.

Still another strand of activity must be mentioned as interestingly interwoven in the whole fabric of musical experiences. It is one that probably is entirely new to most if not all of the children when it is introduced. It is the beginning of SEEING music in a line of notes, getting ready to READ MUSIC.[1]

[1]Zanzig, Augustus D., *Education Through Music,* mimeographed form, Public Schools of Brookline, Mass., 1955, pp. 1–3.

TEACHING A NEW SONG

The child's aesthetic instinct, bolstered by his developing social needs, provides the natural basis for a program of school music. Since the child lives not only in the formality of the classroom, but in his family and among his playmates, he will find those school skills most enjoyable which also have extracurricular use. Not the least of such skills is the ability to perform music.

Initial Preparation

The child's first experience of classroom music must be made sufficiently pleasurable to make him *want* to participate. This requires approaching him through his emotions, exploiting mood and feeling of music and text. Most simple songs have as text a narrative of some sort, which permits presentation of related stories and pictures. Before singing, the teacher should always read the text to explain meaning and mood, being careful to define and articulate new and difficult words. If the child knows the context of a song, he will not commit such malapropisms as "Where the deer and the cantelope play."

Even as familiar a song as "Jack and Jill" should be read aloud in the first grade. Words such as "fetch" and "crown" in the first verse, and "caper" in the second should be written on the board and explained, as should the reference to the old remedy of vinegar and brown paper to staunch the flow of blood from a scrape. Thus prepared, the child can sing with appreciation and understanding.

The Phrase Method or Rote Approach

The most commonly used and traditional approach to song teaching consists of singing the entire song to the class, then singing each phrase separately, the class replying antiphonally. The sequence is usually: first phrase, second phrase, first and second phrase, third phrase, fourth phrase, third and fourth phrase, entire song; the class imitating the teacher in each instance. This method is commonly referred to as teaching *by rote*.

The Question Approach

Rather than relying on memorization, the teacher focuses attention on some particular aspect of the song by asking questions relating to the text or the expressive elements of the music. In teaching "Jack and Jill" to a first grade, for example, the teacher asks before the first singing: "Listen and tell me the names of the children described in the song." Before the second: "What did Jack do in this song?" Before the third: "What did Jill do?"

On further repetition the song can be divided between class and teacher on the basis of the story, the class singing that part of the first line which tells where Jack and Jill went:

Teacher sings: "Jack and Jill."
Children sing: "Went up the hill to fetch a pail of water."

Or the children can sing what happened after Jack got the pail of water:

Teacher sings: "Jack and Jill went up the hill to fetch a pail of water."
Children sing: "Jack fell down and broke his crown and Jill came tumbling after."

Thus the children must focus their listening on the story being told, concentrating not only on the line of the melody, but on suiting it to the context of the song's pitch, rhythm, and mood. They must also, of course, remember their part.

Experience shows that the *question approach* stimulates greater interest than rote learning, creating a musical and intellectual challenge that requires an active response. Moreover, the child does not have to grasp the entire song, but merely the particular idea or musical motive the teacher is emphasizing. By adept questioning, the sequence of initial preparation can be varied to incorporate rote procedures as needed. For instance, if a first grader is asked to listen for words he does not understand in "Jack and Jill," he will discover the unusual words: "caper," "crown," and "fetch." If his singing of parts of the tune is incorrect, such passages can be isolated later for rote drill, the teacher singing the passage correctly for the class to imitate.

Sufficient elements are involved in creating vocal and rhythmic sound to permit a shift in emphasis on each repetition. After pitch intonation, focus on rhythm, then dynamics, expression, diction, phrasing, form, style, mood, mode, tempo, scoring for instrumental or chant accompaniment, and dramatization. Thus a song may be repeated many times with heightening interest because new musical ideas constantly emerge.

Sensing Tonal Beauty

Since the child learns most efficiently from direct sensory experience, the stronger the sensation, the greater the likelihood of learning. The most conspicuous sensuous quality of music is *tone*, and it is therefore tone on which the first classroom music should be focused.

The teacher will no doubt rely primarily on phonograph recordings, but it is imperative that these be of performances of the highest quality. Beauty may be truth, but it is seldom popular. If the child is to develop any but the common standards of musical taste, the classroom must be the source. Should a fine recording of a familiar song be available, let the children hear it often. Later, if possible, make a tape recording of the class's performance for comparison. Such comparisons should be encouraged in all grades.[2]

Developing Pitch Consciousness

For little children, pitch is easily confused with tonal volume: high and low being equated with large and small. The pitch of the low or bass strings of the piano

[2]See James L. Mursell, *The Psychology of Music*, W. W. Norton & Company, Inc., New York, 1937, pp. 26–27.

seems larger rather than lower than the higher pitched strings, which the child will describe as having a smaller sound. This is a natural reaction, since most higher pitched instruments are smaller than those whose pitch is lower: that is, a child is smaller than an adult, a violin smaller than a cello, a piccolo smaller than a flute, a trumpet smaller than a tuba.

Possible Pitch Difficulties

Don't expect all children to be able to match pitch accurately. Pitch placement is frequently achieved only through maturation and practice. Its development may

FIGURE 3-1 Imitating Familiar Sounds and Musical Instruments

be hindered by an inability to hear pitch accurately. If, after a year or two of practice, a child still has difficulty in matching pitch levels, an audiometer check by the school nurse is advisable.

Voice Play[3]

Children with adequate hearing may nevertheless have difficulty reproducing pitch because of an inability to recognize the direction of melodic movement. For practice ask them to imitate familiar sounds such as a police siren (starting low and becoming more shrill), a squeaking mouse, a howling winter wind, a clanging fire bell, the song of the cuckoo, the ding-dong of a railroad engine bell, and the tones of various instruments (see Figure 3-1).

DEMONSTRATING TONAL RELATIONS BY SIGN LANGUAGE

Musical sign language, equating pitch with hand movements in relation to the body, will help children convert larger-smaller to higher-lower pitch imagery. Since the easiest interval to grasp aurally is the octave, let the lowest tone of an octave be represented by the hands hanging at the side and its octave by placing hands on top of the head. The intervening scale tones will be represented by pointing to areas between. With these signs a musical signature or "singing commercial" of tones within the octave may be created and signalled for each child in the class. Thus "Mary" can be an octave skip, the first syllable "Ma-" falling on the bottom tone, and "-ry" on its octave. In sign language this will be represented by hands hanging at the side, then moving to the top of the head. As shown in Figure 3-2, all the tones of a major scale may be represented by sign language.

Key to Musical Sign Language

Hands alongside the body are scale step 1 (*do*); hands on hips are step 2 (*re*); hands on waist are step 3 (*mi*); hands parallel to chest are step 4 (*fa*); hands on shoulders are step 5 (*sol*); hands at chin are step 6 (*la*); hands opposite the eyes are step 7 (*ti*); hands on top of the head are step 8 (high *do*). Certain tones below low *do* (1) may be signaled as indicated in Figure 3-2. Tones above high *do* (8) may be added by moving hands above the head sideways for high *re* (2) and about 6 inches above the head for high *mi* (3). In teaching sign language always reinforce the relationship of *sol-fa* syllables to numbers by requiring both to be sung on each pitch.

As each child's musical signature is created, both teacher and class should sing and demonstrate the hand signals.

Similar to the musical signature for the name Mary, a tone group can represent any name, regardless of the number of syllables.[4]

[3] See Kindergarten or Book 1 of any series of basic music books for the elementary schools.
[4] This technique, of course, has been used by many composers. The most famous example is Schumann's setting of "Chiarina," the pet name of his wife, Clara, as one of the pieces of *Carnival*.

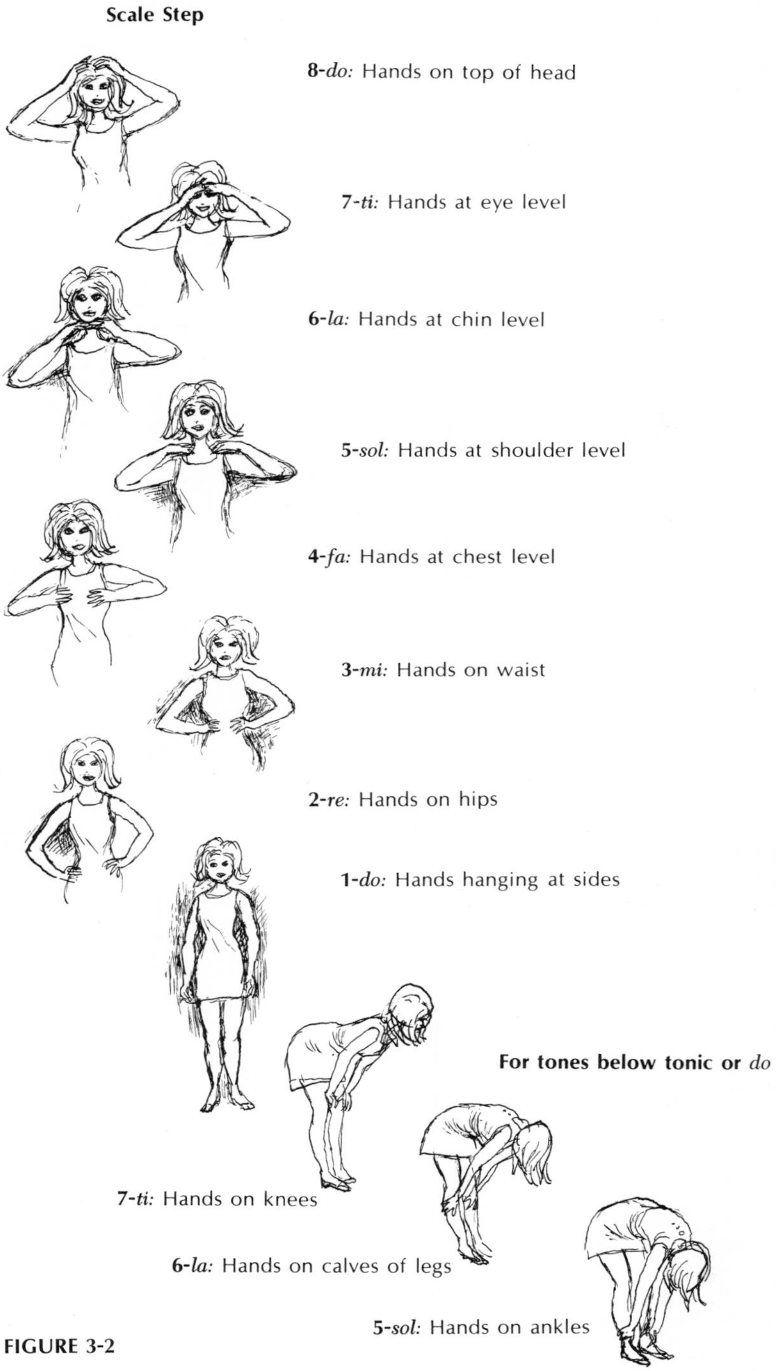

Scale Step

8-*do*: Hands on top of head

7-*ti*: Hands at eye level

6-*la*: Hands at chin level

5-*sol*: Hands at shoulder level

4-*fa*: Hands at chest level

3-*mi*: Hands on waist

2-*re*: Hands on hips

1-*do*: Hands hanging at sides

For tones below tonic or *do*

7-*ti*: Hands on knees

6-*la*: Hands on calves of legs

5-*sol*: Hands on ankles

FIGURE 3-2

Two-syllable names	Three-syllable names	Four-syllable names
John-ny: *do-mi,* 1–3	Maryann: *do-mi-sol,* 1–3–5	Elizabeth: *do-mi-sol-do,* etc.
David: *do-sol,* 1–5	Gwendolyn: *do-re-mi,* 1–2–3	Jeremiah: *do-re-mi-fa*
Sophie: *mi-sol,* 3–5	Jonathan: *mi-sol-do,* 3–5–8	Ezekiel: *sol-la-ti-do*

Once the class is familiar with the sign language for each child's signature, ask the children to guess signatures signed by either the teacher or a child, the class singing the name guessed. For variation, let the child who first sings the right name give the next signature sign.

Later, merely sing, with a neutral syllable such as "loo," the tone pattern representing the child's name. When the class identifies the signature, the named child must give the appropriate signs. Divide the class into two teams. Each member in turn must signal the signature of someone on the opposing team who, on recognizing the signal, must sing his name. The teams should alternate, first a child on one side signalling, then a child on the other. The game may also be played by substituting for signs neutral syllables or numbers sung to the signature tone patterns. Before playing, always be sure to sound the tonic of *do* so there is no doubt as to the tonality of the scale octave.

FROM EAR TO VOICE TO EYE

The entire scale can be taught by challenging the child and exploiting his natural delight in games, translating songs into sign language and sign language into numbers and syllables. However, since all musical learning must proceed from training the ear, to training the voice, to training the eye or body, the first music symbols presented to the child should represent the tone groups most natural to his voice.

Children's game and street songs can be translated into sign language.[5] In these songs, as in the child's natural mimicry, the falling minor third (5–3) *sol-mi* and (8–6) *do-la,* and the major ascending second (5–6) *sol-la* and (1–2) *do-re,* occur most often. There are innumerable combinations of these intervals, as the following example shows:

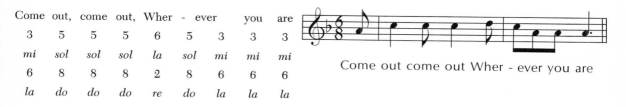

Come	out,	come	out,	Wher	-	ever		you	are
3	5	5	5	6	5	3		3	3
mi	*sol*	*sol*	*sol*	*la*	*sol*	*mi*		*mi*	*mi*
6	8	8	8	2	8	6		6	6
la	*do*	*do*	*do*	*re*	*do*	*la*		*la*	*la*

Come out come out Wher - ever you are

[5]See generally, Iona Opie and Peter Opie, *The Lore and Language of School Children,* Oxford University Press, Fair Lawn, N.J., 1960.

Or as in

Ma	-	ry	has	a	fel	-	low
5		5	3	6	5		3
sol		*sol*	*mi*	*la*	*sol*		*mi*
8		8	6	2	8		6
do		*do*	*la*	*re*	*do*		*la*

A	-	tis	-	ket	A	-	tas	-	ket
3		5		3	3		5		3
mi		*sol*		*mi*	*mi*		*sol*		*mi*
6		8		6	6		8		6
la		*do*		*la*	*la*		*do*		*la*

I	found	a	yel	-	low	bas	-	ket
3	5	5	3		6	5		3
mi	*sol*	*sol*	*mi*		*la*	*sol*		*mi*
6	8	8	6		2	8		6
la	*do*	*do*	*la*		*re*	*do*		*la*

When teaching the symbols for these musical phrases and for the passing second step *mi-re-do,* which is also found in a variety of songs, follow the methods outlined previously, translating pitch into sign language, numbers, and *sol-fa* syllables.

"The Barnyard Song," given below (Figure 3-3), built on the five tones of the pentatonic scale and the child's natural pitch intervals, is the type of song appropriate for a child's introduction to written symbols.

Assume the class has originally learned the song by the question and answer method previously described, acted it out, and added rhythm accompaniment. Assume further that the children have mastered musical sign language and have some experience translating musical phrases into signs. Reverse the process. See if the class can recognize the melody of "The Barnyard Song" merely from sign language. Once the children learn the sequence of hand positions for the melody, gradually substitute numbers, then *sol-fa* syllables. Other songs should gradually be related to numbers and syllables by the same method.

On the left side of the chalkboard draw a scale ladder for a pentatonic or five-tone scale. In drawing scale ladders, always show all twelve half steps to help the children relate one scale to another and the ladder itself to the piano keyboard and music staff.

The pentatonic scale is found most frequently in the less sophisticated melodies of children and in primitive cultures. It is the easiest of all scales to sing since it contains the melodic intervals that fall most naturally to the human voice. After a

THE BARNYARD SONG*

Gaily   Kentucky Mountain Folk Song

1. I had a cat and the cat pleased me, I fed my cat by yon-der tree;
2. I had a hen and the hen pleased me, I fed my hen by yon-der tree;

Cat goes fid-dle- i -fee. Hen goes chim-my-chuck, chim-my-chuck,

cat goes fid-dle-i-fee.

3. Duck goes quack, quack   6. Pig goes oinck, oinck
4. Goose goes sssss, sssss   7. Cow goes moo, moo
5. Sheep goes baa, baa   8. Horse goes neigh, neigh

FIGURE 3-3

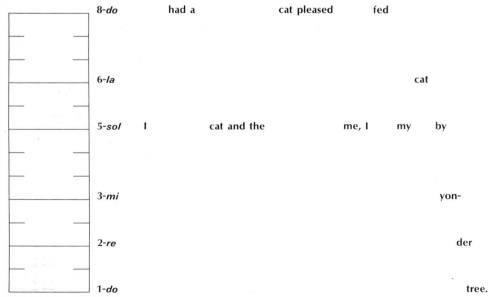

FIGURE 3-4 Pentatonic Scale Ladder

*From "Singing Every Day" of Our Singing World Series, ⓒ Copyright by Ginn and Company, Boston, 1950, 1957, 1959. Used with permission.

few songs in this scale have been learned by ear (pentatonic songs can be found in any series of basic music books for elementary schools), the class will enjoy plotting the melodic intervals on the scale ladder, then singing the melodies with numbers and syllables.

The children should copy the pentatonic scale ladder into their music notebooks, adding the scale step 5 (*sol*) below *do*-1, since pentatonic melodies frequently begin on that step (for example, "Auld Lang Syne," "Whoopy Ti Yi Yo").

The full major scale requires the addition to the pentatonic scale of the passing fourth step or *fa* and the passing seventh step or *ti*. Some songs employ only five or six steps of the scale while others, with descending melodic lines, include the seventh step or leading tone.

After teaching songs in the major scale using rote and question methods, translate the songs into musical sign language and then, having measured the intervals of the melody on the chalkboard scale ladder, substitute numbers and syllables for the text. All basic music series contain songs of limited as well as octave range in the major scale.

Introduction of the major scale requires special drill on the additional intervals of *do-ti*, *sol-fa*, and *mi-fa*, using scale numbers first, then a neutral syllable such as "loo." Play a game identifying tones, sung with a neutral syllable, a child writing the appropriate *sol-fa* syllables and numbers on the chalkboard, or finding them on the scale ladder.

INTRODUCING THE MEANING OF SCALE

A simple way to explain the meaning of a musical scale is to compare it to the units that measure weight and distance, intervals being a unit of measurement of music, as pounds are of weight, and feet are of distance. Just as numbers designate pounds and feet, the numbers from 1 to 8 designate the steps of the octave. Octave steps are also designated by *sol-fa* syllables, and by the first seven letters of the alphabet. To aid in explaining the scale, draw either a ladder or a staircase figure on the chalkboard, each rung or step having the sequence of numbers of the major scale and their corresponding syllables. The scale image thus created will give the class a new concept of musical high and low, capable of being related not only to the body by sign language, but also to the stairs in school: the octave being the floors and the scale the stairs between.

Teaching the Major Scale

The song "The Steeple Bells" (Figure 3-5) is a fine device for teaching the major scale, since it contains the scale ladder, the scale numbers, and the pitch names in their proper place on the music staff. The interesting combination of voices and bells challenges children to join in with appropriate pitch and rhythm at the proper time, thereby providing excellent motivation for learning.

THE STEEPLE BELLS*

English Folk Song
Words by Irving Cheyette

1. The stee-ple bells chime ever-y day.
2. I know the tune that they will play.
(or)
3. They sound the same song that we play
4. Do La Fa Re Ti Sol Mi Do.
   8 6 4 2 7 5 3 1
   C A F D B G E C

Do Ti La Sol Fa Mi Re Do, Our mu-sic bells can sound the same we
(or) 8 7 6 5 4 3 2 1,

play, C B A G F E D C, Now we all sing and play.

FIGURE 3-5

FIGURE 3-6 **Major Scale Ladder and Stair Chart**

*See Appendix VII for other versions of this song.

If Swiss bells or tone resonator bells are available, set them in scale sequence, each child having one bell to play as required. Upon each repetition of the scale on the bells, have the children sing along with numbers, then with syllables, then with pitch names. A "change" of the bells may be rung by playing an ascending instead of a descending scale in the first three measures, or by playing instead of singing measures 3 and 4, or 7 and 8. Ask the class to create other "changes."

The Half-step Interval

Most children will immediately observe that, in the major scale ladder represented in Figure 3-6, the distance between the steps is not uniform, steps 3 and 4 and 7 and 8 being separated by intervals only half the distance of the others. The major mode scale sequence will remain merely an abstraction, however, unless the child is taught to discriminate pitch by ear and to feel it in his voice muscles. Here the syllabic scale has one advantage over the use of numbers. The vowel sound "ee" of *mi* and *ti* (steps 3 and 7) designates the lower step of the half-step intervals in the major scale, thus aiding their recognition.

Games of Musical Speech

Sing questions to the class, pointing to the various tones of the question on the scale ladder. A child must answer in song, similarly pointing out his tones. Thus, always being sure first to sound *do* to enable the class to measure intervals accurately, the teacher may ask the musical question:

Where	do	you	live?
1	3	4	5
do	*mi*	*fa*	*sol*

The class should repeat the question, singing words, then numbers, then syllables. One child can then sing an answer, pointing to the scale ladder and trying to identify his tone pattern, which may well be:

I live on Sixth Street
5	3	2	3	1
sol	*mi*	*re*	*mi*	*do*

Or

Where	is	John?		Is	he	in	the	li-bra-ry?
3	2	1		1	2	3	5	6 6 5
	or			*do*	*re*	*mi*	*sol*	*la la sol*
5	4	3						

Children soon discover that numbers and syllables become an interesting form of musical shorthand. Divide the class into teams and keep score of satisfactory answers to question songs.

A similar game consists of constructing a series of unfinished melodic motives whose tone patterns are to be completed by a child's singing the omitted last note. Before playing, be sure that everyone *hears* the key center from which the game starts. Since this game is more difficult, sing not only the tonic *do* with the class, but also the tonic chord triad *do-mi-sol-mi-do*. After the key has been established, play the game by singing intervals to individual children who must respond by supplying the final note of the group of three or four:

3 - 2 - ? or 5 - 6 - ? or 1 - 6 - ? or 5 - 4 - 2 - 7 - ? or 4 - 3 - 2 - ?

mi - re - ?   *sol - la - ?*   *do - la - ?*   *sol - fa - re - ti - ?*   *fa - mi - re - ?*

This game will help the child sense *tendential resolution:* the tendency of *active* tones in the scale to move to a logical resolution on a *rest tone* or nearest neighbor. Thus the simple descending scale relationship of *sol-fa* creates the feeling that the tones should continue downward to *mi.* Similarly, the sequence *do-ti* suggests going back to *do* or down to *la* (see Chapter 7).

Learning the Scale Tones

The class will now have progressed from musical sign language to a chalkboard scale ladder or stair on which the numbers and syllables are designated. Designating pitch by syllables is called the *movable do* or *sol-fa system.* Although each country numbers notes in its own language, almost all have adopted the medieval Latin syllable sequence, thereby implicitly proving the axiom that music is the true international language. (The pitch syllabary is even more widely used than the Italian musical terminology for tempo, dynamics, and expression.)

Children enjoy learning the scale by numbers in foreign languages. Moreover, the difficulties of learning several words for the same pitch will emphasize to them the value of a universal musical syllabary that enables anyone anywhere to find the same intervals given the same keynote.

English	French	German	Japanese	Musical Latin
one	un (uhn)	eins (eins)	ichi (itchy)	*do*
two	deux (duh)	zwei (tzvai)	ni (nee)	*re*
three	trois (trwa)	drei (dry)	san (sahn)	*mi*
four	quatre (kahtr)	vier (fear)	shi (shee)	*fa*
five	cinq (sank)	fünf (finf)	go	*sol*
six	six (sees)	sechs (zex)	roku (rokue)	*la*
seven	sept (set)	sieben (zeeben)	shichi (sheechee)	*ti or si*
eight	huit (weet)	acht (ahkht)	hachi (hahchee)	*do*

Measuring Pitch Distance with the Hands

Melodies, like scales, may also be illustrated by sign language. This requires only that the distance from waist to head encompass the scale range of the song rather than the mere octave. To "sign" a song, move the hands up or down as the melody moves to higher or lower pitch. Ask the class to measure the song's range by moving the hands from the waist to the top of the head, then adjust the measure of its lesser intervals. Sensing pitch relationships muscularly will aid the child to place pitch in his voice.

VISUAL AIDS FOR MEASURING PITCH INTERVALS

The Melody Graph

The melody graph simulates the bouncing ball once used by the movies for group singing, the placement and length of horizontal lines uncomplicated by a music staff indicating melodic flow, pitch duration, and pitch interval. If the scale numbers and syllables are placed vertically in rising sequence at the left of a chalkboard, a simple melody such as "Hot Cross Buns" below may be graphed, each note being represented by a line whose height designates its pitch and whose length its duration:

3-*mi*	H<u>ot</u>		H<u>ot</u>				H<u>ot</u>	
2-*re*		Cr<u>oss</u>		Cr<u>oss</u>		two a pen-n<u>y</u>		Cr<u>oss</u>
1-*do*			<u>Buns</u>		<u>Buns</u>, One a pen-n<u>y</u>			<u>Buns</u>

Note that the graph not only provides a representation of the melodic line, but also of its numbers, syllables, and text. It is constructed from left to right, the pitch numbers and syllables being indicated on the left as the ordinate axis, and the duration of each note by the length of its line along the abscissa.

Ask the children to attempt to graph at the chalkboard, or in their music notebooks, a simple familiar melody as it is sung to the neutral syllable of "loo." As always, before singing the melody be sure to sound its keynote. The children will be intrigued to collect melody graphs in their notebooks so as to have a record of their improving skill.

Graphing Musical Names

Just as the sign language of musical signatures can be employed in guessing games, so can a melody graph, each child being required to graph his musical signature on the scale ladder.

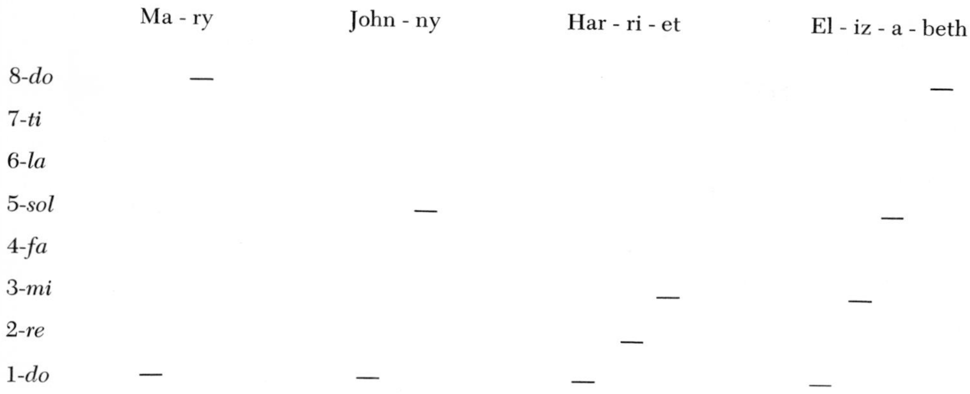

	Ma - ry	John - ny	Har - ri - et	El - iz - a - beth
8-*do*	—			—
7-*ti*				
6-*la*				
5-*sol*		—		—
4-*fa*				
3-*mi*			—	—
2-*re*			—	
1-*do*	—	—	—	—

Figure Illustrations for Songs

Whenever possible, employ the other arts to enrich music. For instance, instead of lines, utilize the child's natural interest in drawing to make illustrated melody graphs in chalk- or flannel board. If flannel board, have the class make cut-outs of appropriate figures for placement at the proper pitch level. Thus, "Twinkle, Twinkle Little Star" may be represented by placing variously colored small stars for quarter notes, and large or double stars for half notes, appropriately on the graph, as in Figure 3-7:

TWINKLE, TWINKLE LITTLE STAR

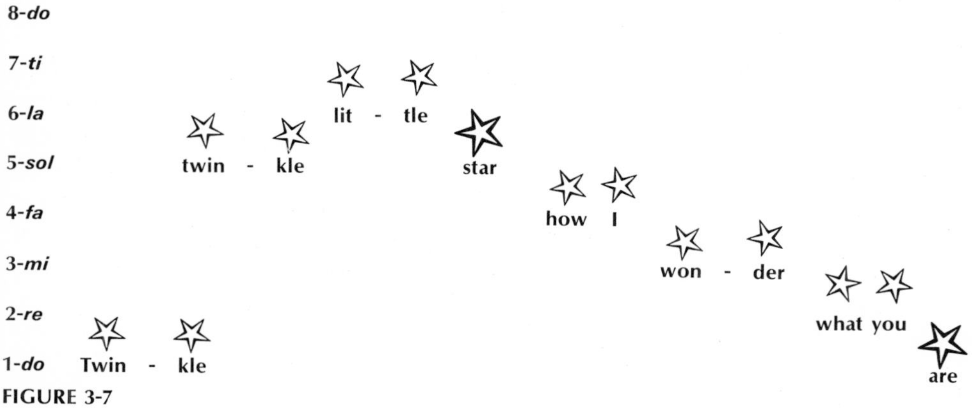

FIGURE 3-7

Call attention to the fact that the tones for the words "star" and "far" are held twice as long as the others, and are, therefore, represented by either a star figure twice the size of the other stars, or a double star.

A song like "Oranges and Lemons Say the Bells of St. Clemens" (Figure 3-8) is ideal for illustration.

ORANGES AND LEMONS

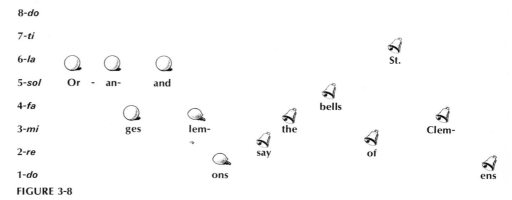

FIGURE 3-8

Drawing and coloring oranges, lemons, and bells, the children will need little encouragement to graph many of their favorite songs in their notebooks.

STAFF NOTATION

After much singing using sign language, scale ladders, stairs, and melody graphs, the class should be ready to transfer the scale ladder to the *music staff,* which is the notation system of musicians the world over. The only difference between the staff and the scale ladder with which the children are already familiar is that instead of using only the rungs of the ladder, staff notation employs both the rungs and the spaces between them.

The music staff may be simply explained as an extension of the fingers. Place the back of the left hand against the chalkboard with fingers parallel to the floor. Draw a straight line from each finger. The result will be five equidistant lines, separated by four spaces, as in Figure 3-9.

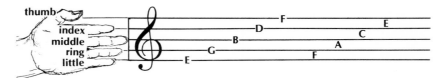

FIGURE 3-9   **Drawing the Hand Staff**

A traditional mnemonic device for remembering the pitch names represented by the five lines of the treble staff is the sentence, "Every good boy does fine," the sequence of first letters being the sequence of staff line pitches. The sequence of pitch in the four spaces constitutes the word "face."

Since an octave consists of eight notes, and *do* is repeated, only the first seven letters of the alphabet denote tones. The piano keyboard repeats the octave sequence A to G seven times and adds four extra tones. Short lines (*leger* or light lines) represent the continuance of the music staff above or below the staff range.

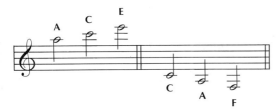

FIGURE 3-10 Adding Leger Lines and Treble Clef Sign

At the extreme left of the staff is placed a *clef* symbol (literally "key"), which locates the octave in which most of the music on the staff is composed. The sign of the treble or G clef, a free version of the letter G, is written so as to cross the second line, the tone G, four times. The word "treble" refers to high voice. There are other clef signs: the C clef marking the placement of middle C, the area of altos and tenors, and the F or bass clef, identifying F below middle C, the range of the lowest voices.

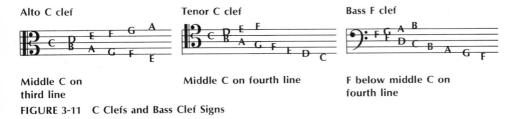

Alto C clef   Tenor C clef   Bass F clef

Middle C on
third line   Middle C on fourth line   F below middle C on
fourth line

FIGURE 3-11 C Clefs and Bass Clef Signs

Deriving Treble Clef Notation from the Hand Staff

Ask the children to imagine a music staff by holding their left palm in front of them parallel to their body with fingers spread. The five fingers represent the lines, and the spaces between the fingers the spaces of the staff. Indicate the lower leger line of middle C by wiggling the index finger of the right hand under the left hand. Practice identifying pitch position on the staff, using the right hand to point to the appropriate finger or space. The class will immediately recognize that the *hand staff* is merely a modified form of sign language. After becoming familiar with pitch position on the hand staff, the class can hand sign the melody of any familiar song. The teacher should start, of course, with songs of limited range such as "Hot Cross Buns" or "Merrily We Roll Along," using middle C as *do* (1) of the scale before increasing the difficulty of the hand-staff repertoire. Always relate a melody learned with a song text to pitch names, numbers, and *sol-fa* syllables.

Ask the children to draw the hand staff into their music notebooks, marking pitch in the lines and spaces, as in Figure 3-12.

Tonal memory can be developed by sounding *do*, then describing on the hand staff a tonal pattern such as *mi-re-do*, from a familiar song. Ask the children to think the tones carefully, then to sing the pattern while marking it on their fingers. Gradually expand the tonal groups in length, until the children can identify full phrases. Have individuals describe tonal patterns on their fingers within a given key tonality for

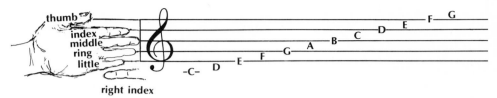

FIGURE 3-12   Hand Staff Pitch Identification

the class to identify by singing the pitch names. Try this first with *do* on C, then move *do* to the space below the staff on D, then up to the first line on E. When a pattern has been illustrated on the fingers, have the children sing it with a neutral syllable such as "loo," then with pitch names, syllables, and numbers.

The John Curwen Hand Signals

Musical sign language has existed in various forms since Guido of Arezzo in the eleventh century devised a system of stationary hand positions to represent a fixed six-tone scale. In 1870 the English musician, John Curwen, developed a sign system that could be related to the steps of any diatonic major scale (Figure 3-13),

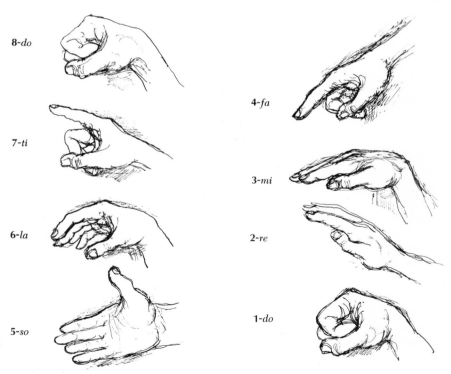

8-*do*

7-*ti*

6-*la*

5-*so*

4-*fa*

3-*mi*

2-*re*

1-*do*

FIGURE 3-13   Original Curwen Signals

a radical departure from the then current "fixed *do*" conservatory system that related the syllables solely to the C Major scale.

The Curwen system has recently been revived in American schools with some modifications by Arpad Darazs, a disciple of the Hungarian composer and teacher, Zoltan Kodály.[6] Some teachers may be interested in using it in the upper elementary grades after the children have learned to identify scale steps and chord intervals by ear. The variations in hand position of the Curwen system are too subtle to be easily distinguished by younger children, and are not directly related to their feeling about pitch position in the scale.

SUMMARY (Outline of Procedures for Teaching a Song)

I. Synthesis: presentation of a song for enjoyment.
  A. Focus listening through questions about the song text.
  B. Sing as beautifully as possible or play a recording of the song.
  C. Question about musical elements.
II. Analysis: learning through focused listening.
  A. Sing parts of the song calling attention to and correcting inaccuracies in:
    1. Melodic line (pitch and intonation).
    2. Rhythm (duration, accent, pause).
    3. Dynamics (loud and soft).
    4. Expressive inflection (nuance and shading).
    5. Diction (enunciation and pronunciation).
    6. Phrasing (proper breath control).
    7. Beauty of tone (quality of voice).
    8. Form (sequentials, motives, phrases, sections in upper grades).
    9. Style (dance, lullaby, march, impressionistic).
    10. Mood (sad, gay, light, martial, ponderous).
    11. Mode (major, minor, pentatonic, modal in upper grades).
    12. Tempo (rate of speed suitable to the song).
  B. Add accompaniment of rhythm and melodic instruments.
  C. Dramatize action and rhythm.
  D. Create chants from text.
  E. Create descants from harmonic background (upper grades only).
  F. Identify harmonic quality and chords (upper grades only).
  G. Associate learned songs with symbols.
  H. Demonstrate tonal relations using body and hand sign language, scale interval numbers, *sol-fa* syllables, scale ladder and/or stair, pitch names on the scale ladder, and melody graphs.

[6]Darazs, Arpad, and Stephen Jay, *Sight and Sound,* Boosey and Hawkes, New York, 1965, Teacher's Book and Student Manual.

100958

      I. Correlate neutral syllables, numbers, *sol-fa* syllables, and pitch names.

      J. Have tone intervals copied into music notebooks using numbers, syllables, and objects illustrating familiar songs.

      K. Draw the music staff using the analogy of the fingers of the left hand.

      L. Explain the meaning of the clef sign.

III. Synthesis: heightened enjoyment in singing and listening. Develop

      A. Information about musical elements,

      B. Skills in singing, playing, listening,

      C. Improved performance through critical evaluation of class activity.

CHAPTER FOUR

DEVELOPING CONCEPTS OF RHYTHM

Rhythm is a muscular feeling produced by sounds organized into patterns of *accent, duration,* and *pause:* accent and pause being opposites, and duration being the period either of such states exist. *Rhythm* is time organized into emotional idiosyncratic relationships, as distinct from clocktime, which is time organized into rational uniform relations. Clocktime can be understood; rhythm must be felt.[1] Human beings instinctively divide reiterated sound into metrical groups of two or three, or compound groups of four, six, nine, or twelve. Thus, the clack of train wheels is invariably broken into a sequence of twos or threes, depending on when seeming accents and pauses occur.

Rhythm of Everyday Activities

Human beings naturally act rhythmically in any reiterated activity. They breathe, walk, skip, hop, jump, run, dance, row, paddle, swing, slide, hammer, saw, and stir with accent, duration, and pause. Athletes strive to coordinate the rhythms of various muscles so as to reduce effort and increase speed. The rhythm of all such activities can be represented by music notation.

Common words preserve unconscious feelings and attitudes. Contrast the short

[1] Cooper, Grosvenor and Leonard B. Meyer, *The Rhythmic Structure of Music,* University of Chicago Press, Chicago, 1960, part I.

NAZARETH COLLEGE LIBRARY

vowel sounds in the verbs: "run," "hop," "skip," "jump," "fast," with the long vowels in "walk," "stroll," "crawl," "slide," "slow."

The difference in the vowels corresponds to the difference in tempo of the activities referred to. Moreover, all the latter words have long soft consonants—mostly "l" and "s"—while the consonants of the former are mostly short and hard. The contrast between the groups can be represented in music notation by symbolizing the verbs denoting fast movement by eighth notes, and those denoting slow movement by quarter notes. Create appropriate notation for various multisyllabic verbs denoting physical activity.[2]

Since rhythm consists of the alternation of accented and unaccented beats, a prerequisite for developing rhythmic feeling is the ability to distinguish the two. Musical tempos—the surge of the march, the whirl of the waltz, the skip of the polka, the stateliness of the minuet, and the swing of the gallop—are felt overtly and covertly: overtly through muscular activity, covertly through mental response.[3] As between the two modes of feeling, tempo is sensed more strongly when accompanied by overt physical response, as any dancer can testify. Therefore, children should be continually encouraged to interpret rhythms in dance and song, as well as by playing percussive instruments.

Free Expression

Teachers in the primary grades should be concerned to develop the child's ability to express himself rhythmically. Try plotting and acting feelings and ideas evoked by music. Ask the class to:

1. Dramatize by interpretive dance and movement ballet plots such as the *Nutcracker Suite*, stories and fairy tales, poems, nursery rhymes

2. Interpret through movement the moods of lullabies, marches, gallops. Show the children how to imitate familiar moving objects: a falling leaf, a moving train, a tolling church bell

3. Swing to the pulse of music in duple and triple meter and their compounds (see recording lists and bibliography in Appendixes I and III

4. Add sound effects with rhythm instruments to rhythmic movement

[2] Cf. Mario Pei, *The Story of Language,* J. B. Lippincott Company, Philadelphia, 1949, pp. 161ff,; H. L. Mencken, *The American Language,* Alfred A. Knopf, Inc., New York, 1943, pp. 164ff. (and the supplements thereto). Soft sounds actually occur with greater frequency than hard in common English. See Godfrey Dewey, *Relative Frequency English Speech Sounds,* Harvard University Press, Cambridge, Mass., 1923, Table 17.

[3] In his *A Treatise on Human Nature,* David Hume remarks: "The victory is not gained by the men at arms who manage the pike and sword; but by the trumpeters, drummers and musicians of the Army." What does he mean? Hume's immediately preceding sentence is: "Amidst all this bustle, 'tis not reason which carries the prize, but eloquence; and no man need ever despair of gaining proselytes for the most extravagant hypothesis, who has art enough to represent it in any favourable colours." How does music, and especially rhythm, affect human beings? Cf. Thomas Mann, *The Magic Mountain,* Alfred A. Knopf, Inc., New York, 1927, Chapters III and VII, especially the section entitled "Politically Suspect"; see also Martin Foss, *Symbol and Metaphor in Human Experience,* Princeton University Press, Princeton, N.J., 1949, pp. 150ff.; and Friedrich Nietzsche, *The Birth of Tragedy.*

5. Develop rhythmic interpretations of occupations related to curriculum units such as farming, building, railroading, loading. Social study units are most apt for this purpose. Create original chants to accompany interpretations

6. Add new texts in rhyme to familiar songs. Nursery rhymes and rhymed game songs appeal to the instinctive rhythmic need of children. Dramatizing rhymes and songs can be of great aid in developing rhythmic feeling

The physical education teacher, a delighted collaborator in developing game and square dance skills, is an excellent source of information for materials and recordings. In teaching musical games and square dances always remember that although training children to follow directions is important, equally so is encouraging them to be creatively expressive.

Instrumental Rhythmic Expression

Melodic, harmonic, and rhythmic percussion instruments accent singing and dancing by changing dynamics, pitch, and timbre. Let the class experiment, using percussion to produce desired effects (see Chapter 8).

Sensing Phrase Rhythm

As the children learn each phrase or sentence of a song, ask them to try to represent the onward flow of the phrase by rotating the right arm from left to right as in Figure 4-1.

At the end of each phrase reverse direction:

FIGURE 4-1   Phrasing Diagram

Explain that phrases end when a brief stop or point of rest occurs, although the melody may continue.

In dramatizing rhythms through bodily movement, ask the children to alternate direction with each phrase, the end of the phrase being marked by the recurrence of rhythmic or melodic accent.

Interpreting Music Symbols

Rhythmic notation must be related to activities with which the child is familiar. The purpose of teaching rhythmic notation is to rigorize the child's increasing rhythmic ability, but (as already stressed) conceptual skills cannot be developed until the meaning of the concepts is rooted in the child's experience. Only after the child has interpreted rhythm by song, dance, speech, and percussive instrument is he capable of learning its symbolic representation. Unless kinesthetic training precedes symbolic learning the child will be unable to translate notation into the muscular movements required for rhythmic performance, or meter signatures into the swing of rhythm in twos and threes, or tempo markings into relative rhythmic speed.

The proper method of teaching music must always be *deductively* ascertained by the teacher so as to provide an *inductive* experience for the child. This sequence of learning, from familiar activity, to general concept, to symbolic representation of that concept, is applied in the remainder of this chapter to each rhythmic element.

SENSING $\frac{2}{4}$ METER

Since rhythmic feeling occurs in the muscles, development of rhythmic sense must start with everyday physical activity. Ask a child to demonstrate how fast he walks to, and then from, school. There will probably be a difference. Ask the class to tap two fingers against the palm to the rhythm of his varying pace as a child beats a drum to the cadence. The cadence can be represented on the chalkboard by drawing a foot and leg for each step, drawing the foot with the side of a small piece of chalk, then bringing the end of the chalk straight up to make the leg ♩. A series of such walking notes will appear:

See if the class can follow the sequence, tapping their left foot on each odd note and clapping on each even.

Once the children can follow the notes, ask them to beat time in a down-up conducting movement and to chant the word "beat" on each step. As the children conduct, count two beat measures, accenting the first step as follows:

Teacher: ONE, two, ONE, two

Class: Down   Up ↑
ONE ↓   two ↖

Reverse the procedure, the class counting the notes of the measure as they conduct, while the teacher repeats: "Beat, beat."

Since human beings have only two legs, place the number 2 before the series of walking notes. Counting in twos from the beginning, place a bar line after every second note. The bar line will now show every time the child has moved both legs. Explain that to prevent the child from getting mixed up, every step with his left foot is given a strong beat, and every step with his right foot a weak one.

In conducting the two steps, the first beat was down, the second up. This movement can be represented by turning the stems of all the first notes down.

2 | L   R | L   R | L   R

1   2 | 1   2 | 1   2

When a child walks, he uses two legs and makes two movements. To show the child is walking using two legs, the 2 at the beginning of the notes will be changed to the symbol $\frac{2}{\flat} = \frac{2}{4}$.

Syllabic Rhythm

Words not only convey rhythmic attitudes, but the rhythmic feeling of the muscles of the tongue and lips in producing word sounds is easily transmitted to other muscles. Such rhythmic transmission can be demonstrated by showing the child that his name provides a rhythmic as well as written signature.

Names of one syllable are always in a walking tempo: two-syllable names always run:

Jack Jones   Ann Smith   Frank Brown   Mary Johnson   Leonard Bernstein

Write the names on the chalkboard and above them the music notation representing their syllabic rhythm.

Ask a child with a one-syllable name like John and a child with a two-syllable name like Mary to come to the front of the class. Write their names with rhythmic notation on the chalkboard:

♩   ♩   ♩   ♩

John John John John, a walking name.

♫   ♫   ♫   ♫

Ma-ry Ma-ry Ma-ry Ma-ry, a running name.

In the same time it takes John to walk a step, ask Mary to run two steps. Ask half the class to tap John's rhythm lightly with their toes, while the rest lightly clap Mary's rhythm. Obviously, there are twice as many running notes in "Ma-ry Ma-ry" as there are walking notes in "John John." When John has taken four steps, Mary has taken eight. Therefore, if 4 represents one of John's notes, 8 will represent one of Mary's.

See if the class can identify all children who have walking-note first names (quarter-note names ♩), and all who have running-note first names (eighth-note names ♫).

Surnames consist of either "walk," "running," "running-walk," "walk-running," or "running-running" rhythmic combinations. Write the names on the board and above each its appropriate music notation. Indicate the accented beat by turning its stem down:

John Bradley   Frances Jones   Mary Franklin

Ask the children to tap the two beats of the walking notes lightly with their left toe while simultaneously chanting the various names rhythmically in the same tempo. Then ask them to clap the rhythm of the names lightly while tapping the two-beat rhythm. Notate this two-line rhythm pattern on the board.

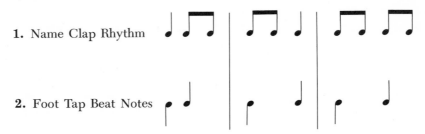

1. Name Clap Rhythm

2. Foot Tap Beat Notes

Divide the class in half, each side pronouncing the names of the notes in the upper and lower lines respectively, simultaneously in tempo, holding the sound of each note for its appropriate rhythmic duration.

1. Quarter, eighth, eighth, etc.
2. Quarter, quar-ter, etc.

Symbolizing Duration Values

Duration values can be indicated by underlining a text, the length of the line representing the rhythmic emphasis to be given each word. Children enjoy the rhythmic diagramming of nursery rhymes.

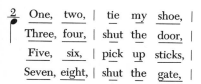

2   One, two, tie my shoe.   Rain, rain, go a-way.

Place the meter symbol 2 in front of the pattern and ask the children to conduct time with their right forearm as they recite it. Following their directions, underline its duration values. See if they can determine where to place the bar lines to divide the text into two-beat measures:

2   One, two, | tie my shoe, | 2   Rain, rain, | go a-way |
    Three, four, | shut the door, | Come a-gain an | other day.
    Five, six, | pick up sticks, |
    Seven, eight, | shut the gate, |

Listening for Rhythm

Let the class try to identify the tapped rhythm of familiar nursery rhymes and the rhythms of names of children in the class.

On the chalkboard place duration value lines representing the rhythm of a familiar nursery rhyme and see if the children can identify it. Once identified, ask a child to write its notation.

Thus: "Rain, rain, go away" is notated as:

Of course, the entire class can play by attempting to notate the rhythms in their music notebooks.

Using Flash Cards for Rhythm Patterns

Place a series of 5 x 7 flash cards containing the notation of various familiar rhythms along the chalkboard. After establishing the tempo by counting a measure of two beats, conduct the class in the unison tapping or clapping of the various rhythms, as in Figure 4-2.

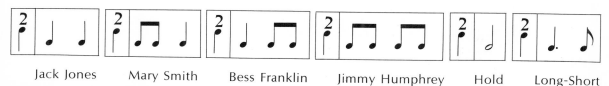

Jack Jones   Mary Smith   Bess Franklin   Jimmy Humphrey   Hold   Long-Short

FIGURE 4-2 Flash Cards for Name Rhythms

Recite a name or word group, the rhythm of which is represented by the notation of one of these patterns, asking a child to find the appropriate flash card.

If a flannel board is available, make up quarter and eighth notes for the children to attach to the board to represent the rhythm of various word groups given by the teacher.

Sensing Notes of Long Duration

Here is the familiar nursery rhyme "Baa, Baa, Black Sheep" (Figure 4-3) set to a familiar tune.

BAA, BAA, BLACK SHEEP

FIGURE 4-3   Baa, Baa, Black Sheep

1. After the class has learned the music, write the text on the chalkboard. As the class sings, place an appropriate duration line corresponding to the length of the word sounds under each word. Always try to have the length of the duration line approximately the same for each similarly held syllable.

[4]See Musical Illustrations, Appendix VII, for sources of songs.

2
Baa, baa, black sheep, have you any wool?

Yes, sir, yes, sir, three bags full.

One for my mas-ter and one for my dame, And

One for the little boy who lives down the lane.

2. Write the duration pattern on another part of the board.

3. Ask the children to count the two beats of each measure, tapping the strong first beat with their left toe while they conduct in two. Tapping the first beat will enable them to differentiate between the strong first accent and the two-beat pulse.

4. Call attention to the varied duration lengths and add approximate note values above them.

5. Ask a child to place a bar line before the first beat of every measure on the board, which when completed will look like this:

6. Call attention to the long note over the word "wool," and explain that it is a "holding" or half note which is held for a measure's two full counts.

7. Analyze the duration value converted into the dotted quarter note on the word "dame" in the third line. The dot shows that the first note of the measure is held long enough to include not only beat 1, but half of beat 2, a dot always adding one-half the duration value of the note to which the dot is annexed. Thus "dame" in the third line is held for the same duration as the combined value of the two notes of "master" two measures before it.

One for my | mas - ter and | one for my | dame, And

8. Recite the rhythmic pattern of the rhyme, substituting the word "walk" for quarter notes, "running" for two eighth notes, "hold" for a half note, and "walking" for a dotted quarter note. Then substitute recitation of the rhythmic designation of the notes: that is, quarter, eighth, eighth, etc.

9. Divide the class into three groups:
  a. Group One taps the strong first beat of each measure with the left toe.
  b. Group Two conducts two-beat measures with downward-upward motions.
  c. Group Three claps the rhythm of the words lightly, using two fingers of the right hand on the palm of the left hand.

10. Introduce the term *rest* to represent a musical "rest." Notate the rhythms tapped by Group One on the board. Indicate that the "rest" on the second beat is symbolized by a quarter rest.

11. Notate the rhythm of strong beat, pulse beat, and melody:

Baa, baa, | black sheep, | have you any | wool?

12. Give one child in each group a rhythm instrument so that the group's rhythmic pattern may be played instrumentally. To the child in Group One give an instrument that makes a loud sound, such as a drum; to the child in Group Two an instrument with a softer sound, such as a pair of rhythm sticks; and to the child in Group Three a triangle. Be sure that each group has an opportunity to play each of the three rhythms, changing players within each group as well.

Sensing Pulse Silently

Let the children attempt to alternately tap a $\frac{2}{4}$ measure in a walking tempo and think a measure in $\frac{2}{4}$, the test being whether they can resume the beat at the proper time in proper tempo. Gradually increase the number of silent measures. Illustrate the rhythmic notation of $\frac{2}{4}$ on the chalkboard, indicating silent measures by both half-rest and quarter-rest symbols. Point out that notes indicate sound, and rests indicate silence. The board diagram should look like this with notes and rests on a single line.

If the children have difficulty thinking tempo at first, let them beat time with their right hand through the tapped and silent measures; then only in the silent measures; then eliminate beating time entirely.

Drum Talk

1. Divide the class into two teams.
2. Establish a walking tempo with the drum, while counting two-beat measures.
3. Ask the children to listen carefully to the following four-measure phrase on the drum:

4. See if the class can repeat the phrase, clapping the rhythm while tapping the left toe on the strong beat.
5. Ask a child on Team One to describe the components of the phrase, using the words "walk," "run," and "hold," that is,

"Walk, walk, running, running, walk, walk, hold."

6. Ask the same child to demonstrate his interpretation of the drum rhythm by performing the appropriate steps at the proper tempo. If he interprets accurately, his team scores a point.
7. After his interpretation, the child must tap a different rhythm of four measures, using similar phrases, which a member of Team Two must describe and perform as in steps 5 and 6.
8. Try to include music rests in the game, rests being demonstrated by stopping for the appropriate beats.
9. Symbolize the drum patterns with duration lines and then by notation. Symbolize rhythm patterns from familiar songs in $\frac{2}{4}$.

Dramatizing Three Rhythms with the Story of the Three Bears

It has been previously noted that musical rhythms generally consist of three major components: stress on an accented or strong beat; unaccented beats grouped between strong beats (called the *pulse beat*); and finally, irregular sounds within the framework of the pulse beat corresponding to the rhythm of the melody or words.[5]

The difference between these three forms of rhythm can be illustrated by the story of the three bears. Papa Bear being a large bear moves very slowly, taking a step only when he hears the strong beat. Mama Bear being smaller moves to the pulse beat of the measure. Baby Bear gambols around them on each syllable, marking the *melody rhythm* pattern.

---

[5] Hindemith compares meter to a clock and rhythm to the natural events of man's activities. Clocktime is the result of analysis; rhythm the result of character, circumstance, and purpose. See Paul Hindemith, *Elementary Training for Musicians*, Associated Music Publ., Inc., New York, p. 93. See also Albert L. Stoutamire, "Teaching Rhythmic Notation," *Music Educators Journal*, I:2 (Nov.–Dec., 1964), pp. 91–95.

Thus in a $\frac{2}{4}$ tempo, Papa Bear lumbers forward only on the stress beat of 1. Mama Bear takes dainty steps on both beats 1 and 2, while Baby Bear runs on all of the syllables. Have three children act out the rhythms so that the class can see and hear them simultaneously. Utilizing different-sounding rhythm instruments, have children play the strong beat, pulse beat, and word rhythms respectively as others act them. Practice sensing each of the rhythms, first strong beat, then pulse beat, then word rhythm. Let the class notate at the board and in their music notebooks the constituent rhythms of many familiar $\frac{2}{4}$ songs.

Sensing Faster Rhythms in $\frac{2}{4}$

After singing various songs, such as "Old Brass Wagon" in Figure 4-4, that employ march or fast dance rhythms in $\frac{2}{4}$, follow the procedures outlined previously for establishing strong beat, pulse beat, and melody rhythm.

OLD BRASS WAGON*

Play Party Song

1. Cir-cle to the left, Old Brass Wag-on, Cir-cle to the left, Old Brass Wag-on,
2. Cir-cle to the right, Old Brass Wag-on, Cir-cle to the right, Old Brass Wag-on,

1. Cir-cle to the left, Old Brass Wag - on, You're the one, my dar - ling.
2. Cir-cle to the right, Old Brass Wag - on, You're the one, my dar - ling.

FIGURE 4-4 Old Brass Wagon

Developing a Rhythm Score

After the children have learned to sing "Old Brass Wagon" and enjoyed doing the dance suggested in the songbook (accompanied perhaps by rhythm instruments), develop a rhythm score.

1. Establish tempo and meter with the tap, hand clap, and the "down-up" conducting pattern.

2. Write the duration values under the text. Use a dot to symbolize the fast

*From "Music Now and Long Ago" in Music For Living Series, © Copyright 1956, Silver Burdett Company, Morristown, N.J. Rhythm modified slightly. Used by permission.

sixteenth notes, a short dash for the eighth notes, and a longer dash for the quarter
notes:

Circle to the left, Old Brass Wagon,
Circle to the left, Old Brass Wagon,
Circle to the left, Old Brass Wagon,
You're the one, my dar - ling.

3. Isolate the dot-dash duration symbols. Above them add the rhythmic notation:

Circle to the left, Old Brass Wagon,

You're the one, my dar - ling.

4. Ask the children to pick out word patterns that fit specific rhythms and write
them below the notation, such as:

5. Have a child place bar lines before every down beat in the word and rhythm
pattern charts on the board as indicated

Bar lines for pulse:

6. Explain that a sixteenth note is symbolized by a *double beam* or double flag.
7. Distinguish the duration of the sixteenth and the dotted eighth notes. Show
that the aggregate duration of ( ), a dotted eighth and sixteenth note, is equivalent
to that given the word "You're" in the phrase "You're the one, my dar-ling."
8. Remind the children that a dot annexed to a dotted quarter note adds another
half value to the note in front of the dot. The same rule applies to eighth and sixteenth
notes.
9. Divide the class into three groups, each group to play a different rhythmic
component:

Strong beat — Toe tap
Pulse beat — Hand clap
Melody rhythm — Word pattern

10. In the third grade or higher, the children should be able simultaneously to tap the strong beat with their left toe, clap the pulse beat, and chant the word rhythm.

11. Set up a rhythm score to accompany singing and dancing, using rhythm patterns (which are generally termed *rhythmic motives*) from a song. Let the children choose the instruments to play each motive, taking into consideration the ability of the instrument to be struck or shaken rapidly or slowly, and its dynamic quality (degree of loudness).

Word Pattern	Meter	Rhythmic Notation	Instrument
1. Dar-ling	$\frac{2}{2}=\frac{2}{4}$		drum
2. Old Brass Wagon			triangle
3. You're the one, my			tambourine
4. Circle to the left,			rhythm sticks

Be sure that the placement of the notation of the rhythm matches the duration values of the words, so that the children get an accurate visual impression of the relationship of rhythmic values: namely, two eighths under a quarter, four sixteenths under a quarter, etc.

Syncopation in $\frac{2}{4}$

Select a song like "Tinga Layo" (Figure 4-5) and follow the procedures outlined previously for developing sense of beat, pulse, and word rhythm by toe tapping, clapping, and conducting. Always remember, however, that a class should first learn a song just for the fun of singing.

1. Have the children make a rhythm score for Latin American instruments using the rhythmic motives of strong beat, pulse beat, and the word rhythms.

2. Analyze each rhythm—the entire class clapping the words while tapping the strong beat with the toe.

3. Diagram the rhythm score, which may look like this:

Rhythm Score for "Tinga Layo"

Instrument	Rhythm Source	Meter	Notation
Conga drum	Strong beat	$\frac{2}{P} = \frac{2}{4}$	
Claves	Pulse beat		
Tambourine	Come, Tin-ga		
Castanets	Come, my don-key		
Maracas	Come, lit-tle don-key		

TINGA LAYO*

With a beat   **West Indian Song**

Tin - ga   Lay - yo!   Come, lit - tle don - key,   come; Tin - ga   La - yo!

Come, lit - tle don - key,   come. My don - key   walk, my don - key   talk, my don - key

eat   with   a   knife   and   fork.   Tin - ga   Lay - yo!   Come, lit - tle   don - key,

come. Tin - ga   Lay - yo!   Come, lit - tle don - key   come;   my   don - key,

Come, lit - tle   don - key,   come.

FIGURE 4-5   Tinga Layo

*Copyright 1943, M. Baron Company, Oyster Bay, N.Y. Used by permission.

Have the children find other words with the same rhythmic pattern.

4. After each rhythm has been analyzed, and all rhythmic motives notated, distribute a different instrument to each of five children who will become section leaders of five groups. As the section leaders play, each group will clap their leader's respective part while tapping the strong beat with their left foot.

5. Build a ten-measure introduction to the song, starting with the rhythm of one instrument and group and adding another every two measures. When all groups have been playing for two measures singing can begin.

6. The Merengue is danced to a rhythmic motive of four eighth notes to a measure. The class can learn it by following these simple instructions (L and R stand for left and right foot):

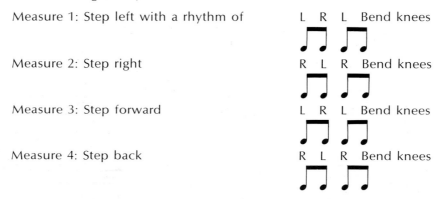

Measure 1: Step left with a rhythm of   L   R   L   Bend knees

Measure 2: Step right   R   L   R   Bend knees

Measure 3: Step forward   L   R   L   Bend knees

Measure 4: Step back   R   L   R   Bend knees

7. The children should take turns playing the rhythm instruments. Switch the rhythms among the groups.

Tempo and Mood

In order to help children understand how tempo affects mood, take any of the songs usually sung at a rapid tempo, such as "Oh, Susanna" or "Polly Wolly Doodle," and sing them at a very slow tempo. Conversely, take a lullaby or other song in a slow tempo and sing it quickly. A few such illustrations will suffice to demonstrate the influence of tempo on mood and the resulting importance of proper tempo to song interpretation.

Action and play party songs, square dances, piano pieces, and recordings suitable for rhythmic activities are listed in Appendix I according to age group. Also listed are pieces for quiet listening with which to illustrate the effect of tempo on mood.

SENSING $\frac{3}{4}$ METER AND RHYTHMS

Teach the class various songs in $\frac{3}{4}$ meter. Everyday movements that occur in $\frac{3}{4}$ time are ice and roller skating, see-sawing and swinging. For the purpose of developing rhythmic feeling in this meter, use a song such as "The Skaters' Waltz," Figure 4-6.

THE SKATERS' WALTZ*

With a swing

Emil Waldteufel

FIGURE 4-6 The Skaters' Waltz

1. While remaining in their seats, have the children move their feet forward and backward in imaginary skating movements in slow waltz time to the word "skat - ing." Ask them to imagine that their left and right hands are at opposite ends of a seesaw, one moving up and the other down to the tempo of "see-saw." Have them move their bodies from left to right, or forward and backward, to the word "swing-ing."

2. Divide the class. Half the class will count 1, 2, 3, while describing a right triangle in the air with their right hand. Drawing each side of the triangle takes one beat: down on 1, right on 2, up on 3. Meanwhile the remainder of the class should say the word "skat-ing," taking the same three beats. Alternate the parts.

3. Write the text on the chalkboard:

*See Appendix VII for other versions of this song. The text is added.

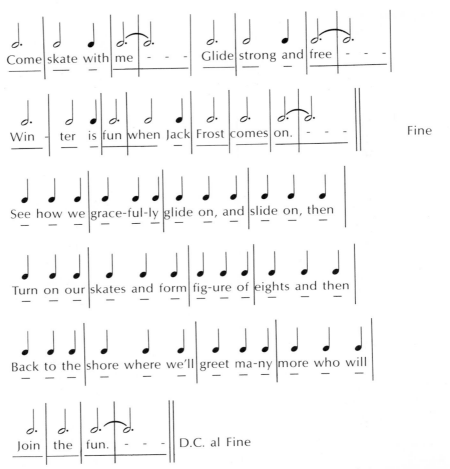

As the children sing, indicate the duration pattern under the words: the quarter line short, the half twice its length, and the dotted half three times as long.

4. Write the duration pattern on the board as the children sing the song again. This will enable them to concentrate on the rhythmic pattern of the words.

5. Divide the class. While half the children sing the words and the rest sing the beat count of each measure, number the beats of each measure below the duration pattern.

6. Add the meter signature: $\frac{3}{} = \frac{3}{4}$, explaining that songs whose swing has a pulse beat of threes are composed in this meter. To facilitate recognizing each group of three beats, separate them by a bar or measure line. Add the measure lines to the chart, duration pattern, and text. [Explain the meaning of Italian terms: *Fine* (fee-nay) meaning "the end" and *Da Capo* (D.C.) meaning "repeat from the beginning." Also explain that the light double-bar line indicates the end of a section of a song, while the light bar line followed by a heavy bar line indicates the end of the whole song.]

7. See if the class can devise two ways to write the notation for a measure containing three beats. The children already know that quarter notes designate sounds held for the duration of one count, and half notes designate sounds held for the duration of two counts. Therefore, placing a quarter and a half note together in a measure totals three counts. The class also knows that a dot placed after a note increases that note's duration value by half; therefore a dotted half note also equals three counts.

8. As the class sings the words, ask a few children to sing the beat count as in paragraph 5 above. Add notation values above the duration pattern and text. Let the two groups conduct as they sing, using the triangular conducting pattern previously described.

9. Explain that sounds must sometimes be held longer than the beats of one measure. Such duration is indicated by tying the notes of two measures together with a curved line called a *tie.*

10. Ask most of the class to sing the song with the text, while a few children sing the phrase "Strong, weak, weak" in each measure.

11. Draw a rhythm chart showing the strong beat with stem down and the weak beats with stems up:

Ask half the class to tap the strong beat with their left toe while the rest clap the weak second and third beats using two fingers against the palm.

12. Write a rhythm line indicating a strong beat followed by a two-beat rest in each measure:

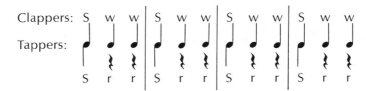

Ask the class to tap and sing only those words and the notes of the song that fall on the first beat of each measure, thinking but not singing the words and notes for the remaining two beats.

13. Half the class should now tap on the first beat of each measure and sing the word "rest" for the remainder while the other half claps all three beats. Write this rhythm on the board:

Clappers: S   w   w │ S   w   w │ S   w   w │ S   w   w

Tappers:

S   r   r │ S   r   r │ S   r   r │ S   r   r

14. Next, have the class alternately sing and remain silent a measure. This will require the children to imagine pulse and pitch during the silent measures so as to accurately sing pitch at the right time. Make a rhythm chart showing the alternating measures of rest. The symbol for a full measure rest is a rectangle suspended from a line, ▬.

15. Set up three groups in the class:

    A. Group A to tap their toes on the first strong beat of each measure
    B. Group B to clap the pulse on all three beats
    C. Group C to clap the melodic rhythm

Assign several children instruments with qualities reminiscent of sounds heard while ice skating or sleigh riding: sandpaper blocks to represent the swish of skates on ice; a triangle or tone bells to represent sleigh bells; a slap stick to represent the crack of the whip. Assign one instrumentalist to each of the above groups as leader. Interchange the playing of the rhythm patterns among the groups. Construct a rhythm chart combining all three rhythm patterns. The resulting combination of sounds can be termed *polyrhythmic* since many rhythms are played at once.

A. Strong beat: whip snap with slap stick

B. Pulse beat: sleigh bells or triangle

C. Melody rhythm: rhythm stick on cymbal

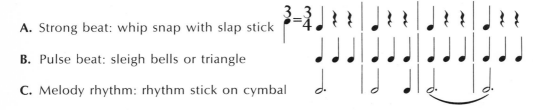

The introduction of an occasional measure of rest will test the children's ability to sense pulse and tempo.

16. Dramatize the rhythm by bringing three children to the front of the class representing:

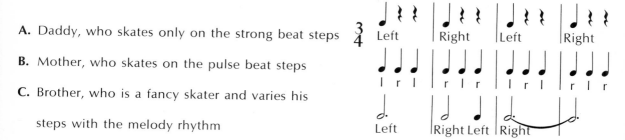

A. Daddy, who skates only on the strong beat steps

B. Mother, who skates on the pulse beat steps

C. Brother, who is a fancy skater and varies his

steps with the melody rhythm

17. Add resonator or Swiss bells and melody flutes to the score.

Utilize the procedures outlined above to help the children sense the rhythm of other songs in ¾.

Sensing Tempo Changes in ¾

Select songs in faster and slower ¾ tempos, such as the Mexican song "Chiapane-cas" and the Brahms "Lullaby." After the children have learned the songs, ask the class to dramatize the lullaby by pretending to rock a cradle or a baby in their arms to the meter. Explain that Andante describes the tempo of a lullaby and Allegro the tempo of a fast dance.

Flash Cards

Place two sets of flash cards along the chalkboard. The first should contain the notation of rhythms and the second the tempo terms previously learned. Ask the class to tap or clap the rhythms in unison at various tempos. Always establish the tempo by counting and conducting a measure before the class starts. Flash cards for tempo terms, form, and ¾ rhythms might be similar to those shown in Figure 4-7.

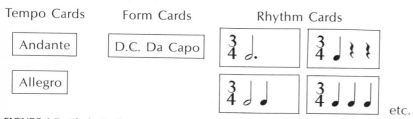

FIGURE 4-7 Flash Cards—Tempo, Form, Rhythm

Ask the children to assist in making permanent flash cards. Keep these filed under headings such as Rhythm, Scales, Chords, Scale Ladders, etc. They can be a valuable visual aid.

SENSING $\frac{3}{8}$ METER

Up to now the class will have sung songs in $\frac{2}{4}$ and $\frac{3}{4}$ time. In both of these meters a quarter note represents a beat. In $\frac{3}{8}$ time, however, a beat is represented by an eighth note. $\frac{3}{8}$ time corresponds to fast actions patterned in rhythms of threes. For instance: "galloping," whose movement and three equal syllables suggest "gal-lop-ing,"

may be represented by three eighth notes( ). "Jump-ing" is analyzable as "jump-ing."

"See-saw," its syllables sustained, becomes "see - saw," each syllable a separate meas-

ure. The children will sense the accent required on the first beat of the measure if they tap their left toe as they pronounce the first syllable of each word.

$\frac{3}{8}$ can be played so fast as to have but one beat to a measure. In this tempo a note to be held for the full beat of a measure will be symbolized by a dotted quarter (♩.). On the other hand, a triplet pattern or group of three notes of equal duration to be played at the speed of one beat can be indicated by three tied eighth notes. Such a group is the syllabic pattern of "Saturday"( ). These rhythms should be notated in relation to each other:

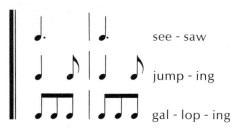

Physical Movement to $\frac{3}{8}$

1. The children can sense the feeling of "galloping" while remaining in their seats by chanting each syllable separately, and clapping their hands on the syllable "gal-," striking their right thigh with their right hand on "-lop-," and striking their left hand on their left thigh on "-ing."

2. Ask the children to chant "jump-ing," striking their palms to their thighs on "jump-" and clapping on "-ing."

3. Create a seesaw feeling by pretending each hand is on the opposite end of a seesaw that teeters on each syllable.

4. Write the notation pattern for $\frac{3}{8}$ on the chalkboard, placing under it duration lines and under the duration lines the beat count in three. Explain that an eighth rest (ɤ) lasts just long enough to take a quick breath.

5. Ask one child to dramatize "galloping" rhythmically, another to dramatize "jumping." Let two others pretend to be on opposite ends of a seesaw. As the actors move, the class should chant the appropriate words, relating the syllabic rhythm to the rhythm of the actors.

6. $\frac{3}{8}$ is conducted in exactly the same triangular pattern as $\frac{3}{4}$ 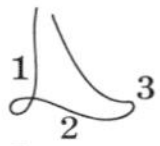 ¹⟍₂ ₃, except the tempo is usually faster in $\frac{3}{8}$. Let the class conduct while chanting the rhythm pattern of the words, then while reciting the beat count.

7. Ask a child to tap "galloping," "jumping," and "seesaw" rhythms on a drum, the class attempting to identify the action represented. Organize teams and keep score.

8. Write the eighth note symbols used to represent $\frac{3}{8}$ time.

9. After "See-Saw, Margery Daw" (Figure 4-8) has been learned by the question and answer approach, write the text on the board:

SEE-SAW MARGERY DAW

Mother Goose Rhyme
Traditional Melody

See - Saw Mar - ge - ry Daw, Jack shall have a new mas - ter,

He shall have but a pen-ny a day, Be - cause he won't work an - y fas - ter.

FIGURE 4-8 See-Saw Margery Daw

10. As the children sing, add the duration pattern, Figure 4-9, under the text:

See   -   Saw Mar   -   ger   -   y Daw, Jack shall have a new mas   -   ter,

He shall have but a pen - ny a day, Be   -   cause he won't work an   -   y fas   -   ter.

FIGURE 4-9 Duration Chart

11. Write the duration pattern on the board, placing beneath it the numbers of the beats. Ask the children to sing the melody, substituting the numbers of the beats for the text. Have them tap their toe on beat 1 while conducting the three-beat measures with their right hand. The tapping will establish accent, the conducting the pulse or meter, and the voices the melodic rhythm and phrasing:

12. Place the meter symbol of $\frac{3}{4}$ or $\frac{3}{8}$ in front of the rhythm chart. Explain that the bar lines simplify counting, making it easier to see the groups of threes.

13. Add notation above the duration lines as the children tap the meter, clap the melodic rhythm, and sing to the melody the names of the various rhythms: dotted quarter, dotted quarter, eighth eighth eighth, dotted quarter. Again explain the meaning of the dot and eighth rest symbols.

14. Divide the class into three groups:

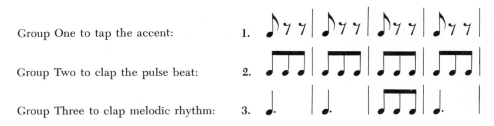

Group One to tap the accent:

Group Two to clap the pulse beat:

Group Three to clap melodic rhythm:

15. Add three different-sounding instruments, one to play the rhythm of each group. Rotate the rhythms among the groups and the instruments among the members.

16. Explain the similarity of feeling between the meters of $\frac{3}{4}$ and $\frac{3}{8}$. The children must realize that the same rhythm may be notated in either of these meters to be identically performed.

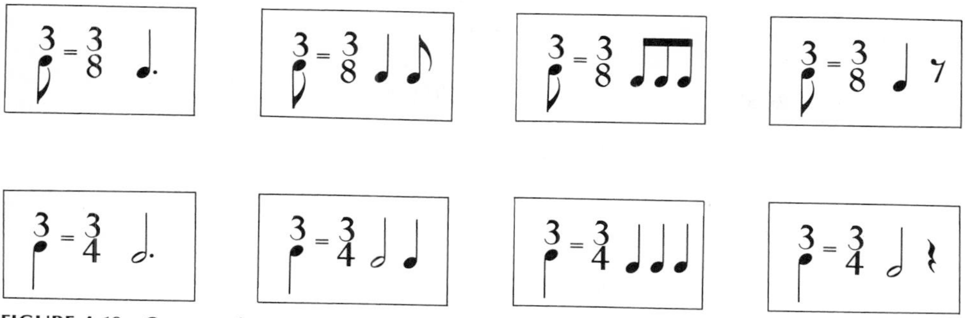

FIGURE 4-10 Comparative Meter Chart

17. In the upper grades, beginning perhaps with the fourth, try to make the children realize that the duration of a beat may be represented by a quarter note, ♩ = 4; by an eighth note, ♪ = 8; by a half note, 𝅗𝅥 = 2; or by a dotted quarter note, ♩.. In the meter signature the lower numeral designates the unit of measurement of rhythmic notation for each measure; that is, quarter, eighth, half note; the upper numeral designates the number of these rhythmic units (or their rhythmic equivalent) in a measure. Do not be confused into thinking that the lower numeral necessarily represents the unit of beat. *Beat* refers to the sensation of pulse felt in music. Some composers do employ a "beat" signature that indicates the rhythmic notation symbol of that rhythmic unit which receives one beat as determined by tempo. Thus a fast $\frac{3}{8}$ may have as a beat signature $\frac{1}{♩.}$. (See Chapter 10 on Meters.) Beat is determined by the tempo of the music.

Sensing Tempo Changes

It is important for children to learn that the tempo of the music, not the meter signature, determines the number of beats to be sensed in a measure. Thus a fast song in $\frac{3}{8}$ should be sensed with a whole measure, not an eighth note, to a beat. The more accurate beat signature is $\frac{1}{♩.}$ rather than $\frac{3}{8}$. The distinction can be illustrated by singing "See-Saw" as normally indicated in a fast tempo, then slowly with each eighth note as a *beat* note. Conversely, sing a slow $\frac{3}{4}$ or $\frac{3}{8}$ song at a fast tempo.

Flash Cards in $\frac{3}{8}$ and $\frac{1}{♩.}$

Make a series of flash cards comparing known rhythms notated in $\frac{3}{8}$ to comparable rhythms notated in $\frac{3}{4}$ (see Figure 4-10).

After the children can tap and clap rhythms notated in $\frac{3}{8}$, ask them to tap the same rhythms notated in $\frac{3}{4}$. Explain, as suggested in paragraph 16 above, the interchangeability of $\frac{3}{8}$ and $\frac{3}{4}$ notations, demonstrating that different symbols can represent the same rhythmic feeling. Additional songs in $\frac{3}{8}$ meter will be found in any series of basic music books.

SENSING $\frac{6}{8}$ METER

The appropriate sequence for teaching meter should by now be familiar. Start with large physical responses to rhythm, then sing various songs in the meter, tapping and clapping accent, pulse beat, and the rhythm of melodic phrase.

Many nursery rhymes and game songs in $\frac{6}{8}$ contain dramatic action—for example, "Humpty-Dumpty," "Hickory, Dickory, Dock," "Little Bo-Peep," "Farmer in the Dell," "Jack and Jill," "To Market, To Market," and "Oh Dear, What Can the Matter Be?"

$\frac{6}{8}$ Beat

The slow $\frac{6}{8}$ measures of "Silent Night" contain a full six beats, but those of the quick "Hickory, Dickory, Dock" contain but two (see Figure 4-14, p. 85). Remember, however, that although the meter of a fast $\frac{6}{8}$ may swing in two, the rhythmic groups within each measure are accented in threes. A measure in a quick $\frac{6}{8}$ therefore may be the equivalent of two measures in $\frac{3}{8}$. Since a dotted quarter note constituted a one-beat measure in fast $\frac{3}{8}$, two dotted quarter notes will represent the two beats of a measure in fast $\frac{6}{8}$. This can be indicated in the meter signature by placing a dotted quarter note under the numeral 2 to signify that there are only two beats to a measure: $\frac{6}{8} = \frac{2}{\bullet\cdot}$.

Physical Responses

The large muscular movements of familiar activities appropriate for fast $\frac{3}{8}$ rhythms such as galloping, skipping, hop-along, also give the sense of fast $\frac{6}{8}$. Symbolize the rhythmic pattern with duration lines and notation as previously discussed, this time placing the bar lines following groups of six eighth notes or their equivalent, rather than after groups of three eighth notes.

Drum Talk

1. Place duration lines under words representing $\frac{6}{8}$ rhythms: "galloping," "skipping," "hop-along."

2. Write the same duration patterns separately with their equivalent music notation above:

Gal - lop - ing   Skip - ping   Hop - a - long

3. Ask the children to clap the indicated rhythms and tap them on a drum. See if they can suggest words whose syllable sequence matches the duration sequence of $\frac{6}{8}$ rhythm patterns:

Galloping rhythm   Skipping rhythm   Hop-along rhythm

4. Explain the meaning of $\frac{6}{8} = \frac{2}{\bullet}$, the meter signature of a fast $\frac{6}{8}$ tempo. Although there may be six eighth notes or their equivalent in a measure, the swing of the pulse beats actually will be in twos. $\frac{2}{\bullet}$ therefore indicates the meter. Stress that the clue as to whether there are two or six beats in a measure lies in the tempo and spirit of the song.

5. Explain that the sequence of a dotted eighth, sixteenth, and eighth note is equivalent to the syllabic rhythm of "hop-a-long" (♪.♬♪).

Fast $\frac{6}{8}$ in Song

In the song "To Market, To Market" (Figure 4-11), galloping and hop-along rhythms can be heard.

TO MARKET, TO MARKET*

Gaily: Introduction soft to loud

Nursery Rhyme
Traditional Melody

Play the Introduction and Coda on wood blocks.

FIGURE 4-11   To Market, To Market*

*See Appendix VII for other versions of this song.

1. Teach the song using the question and answer approach.

2. Ask the class to tap their left toe on the first beat and right toe on the
second as they say "jig-gi-ty jig" in $\frac{2}{P}$ meter. This will establish a pulse beat against
the rhythm of the melody.

3. Ask the class to clap the rhythm of "jig-gi-ty jig" using two fingers against
the palm of their opposite hand, while tapping the pulse beat with their toes as in
paragraph 2 above.

4. Write the repeat, crescendo, and decrescendo signs around the words "jig-gi-ty
jig" as indicated below. Explain the meaning of such markings.

Soft to Loud   Loud to Soft

‖: Jig-gi-ty-jig 7 | Jig-gi-ty-jig 7 :‖

Draw the duration pattern under the words.

Explain the eighth *rest symbol* (7), a place to pause for breath.

Explain the *fermata* (⌢) hold, indicating that a tone is to be sustained until the signal
for release is given by the conductor.

5. While the children sing, write the duration pattern of the song text on the
chalkboard. Use a dot to represent the short sixteenth note. Below the duration pattern
number each of the six counts of each measure inserting the bar lines. Where there
is an eighth rest use the appropriate rest symbol.

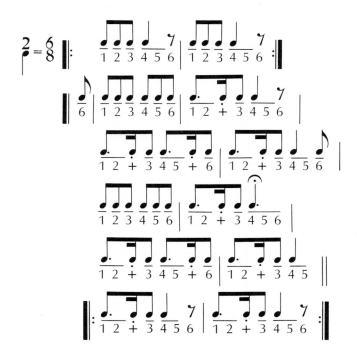

6. Explain that the dot adds half the duration value of the note it follows to that note.

7. Divide the class. While half sing the words, tapping the meter with their toes and clapping the word "rhythm," the remainder are to sing the count of the eighth notes indicated in each measure below the duration-lines. Alternate the parts.

8. Add notation above the duration patterns in the rhythm chart and above the text.

9. Prepare flash cards of newly learned rhythms in $\frac{6}{8}$. Ask the children to suggest appropriate rhythm patterns. Clap the rhythms to help them. Be sure that the rhythms are derived from familiar songs or dances in both slow and fast tempos.

FIGURE 4-12 Flash Cards in $\frac{6}{8}$

Sensing Mood and Tempo Changes in $\frac{6}{8}$

Choose a song such as "Silent Night." Analyze it in the same manner as "To Market, To Market," extracting duration values, numbering metrics under the duration pattern, and adding notation above. Point out that in slow $\frac{6}{8}$ there is actually a feeling of six beats, so that each eighth note represents a beat. When using flash cards with $\frac{6}{8}$ rhythms, always be sure to establish tempo before asking a rhythm to be tapped or clapped. This means the class must be told whether the eighth note, if the tempo is slow, or the dotted quarter note, if it is fast, represents a beat.

SENSING COMPOUND METERS

$\frac{4}{4}$ Meter

$\frac{4}{♩}$ ($\frac{4}{4}$) is a combination of two groups of $\frac{2}{♩}$ ($\frac{2}{4}$). However, the first beat of each measure is usually given a stronger accent than the third beat. In teaching $\frac{4}{4}$ rhythms, follow the same procedures as previously outlined:

1. Have the class interpret $\frac{4}{4}$ rhythms by bodily movement

2. Create syllabic sequences to represent duration patterns

3. Isolate the duration pattern and add the notation patterns above it

4. Distinguish the strong beat, pulse beat, and melodic phrase rhythms. After each is clapped separately, clap them simultaneously

5. Create rhythm charts for rhythm band accompaniment

6. Use flash cards

"Ten Little Indians" (Figure 4-13) illustrates $\frac{4}{4}$ as a compound of two groups of $\frac{2}{4}$:

TEN LITTLE INDIANS*

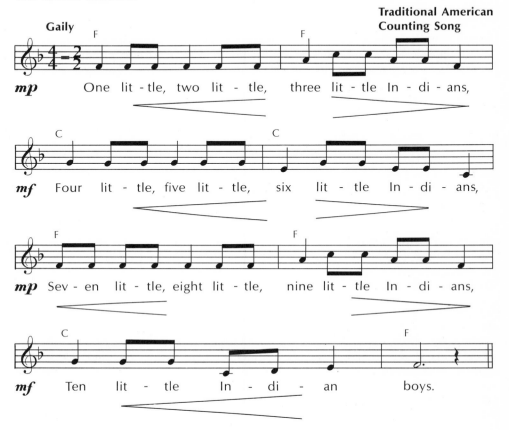

Also sing this song counting backwards.

FIGURE 4-13   Ten Little Indians

Interpreting Other Compound Meters

Standard music notation contains many symbols to represent rhythms. The more complicated meters should be left for the upper grades, when children have had more experience singing, listening, moving rhythmically to music, and playing percussion and simple melody instruments.

The following chart, illustrating beat notation in various meters, presents some of the more complex patterns to be found in vocal and instrumental music literature.

*From "The First Grade Book" of Our Singing World, Ginn & Company, Boston, © 1949, 1957, 1959. Used by permission. Transposed from key of G.

The Measurement of Meter in Music (the upper numeral states the number of units in each measure; the lower numeral states the kind of unit to which the upper number refers)

Lower Numerals	Note Name	Note Symbol	Rest Symbol	Upper Numeral of Meter Signature					
				1	2	3	4	5	6
1	Whole			1					
2	Half			2					
4	Quarter			4					
8	Eighth			8					
16	Sixteenth			16					

etc.

ILLUSTRATING VARIETIES OF NOTATION FOR BEAT IN UPPER GRADES

To help children understand the use of different meters demonstrate that a song may be variously notated, yet sung at the same tempo. (The tempo indication and metronome marking, by equating the beat note with a given metronome speed, will compensate for the increasing or decreasing notation value of a beat.) Children should have had some addition, subtraction, and division (Grades 4 to 6), for this to make sense.

Figure 4-14 gives examples of songs notated in various meter signatures but identical tempos because the beat note has identical time value.

TWINKLE, TWINKLE, LITTLE STAR

ORANGES AND LEMONS

FIGURE 4-14   Twinkle, Twinkle, Little Star; Oranges And Lemons; Hickory, Dickory, Dock; Beautiful Dreamer; Silent Night

HICKORY, DICKORY, DOCK

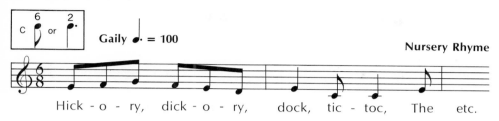

Gaily ♩. = 100

Nursery Rhyme

Hick - o - ry, dick - o - ry, dock, tic - toc, The etc.

Gaily ♩. = 100

Gaily 𝅝. = 100

BEAUTIFUL DREAMER

Gently ♩. = 60

Stephen Foster

Beau - ti - ful Dream - er, Wake un - to me,

Gently ♩. = 60

SILENT NIGHT

Si - lent night, Ho - ly night, All is calm, All is bright, etc.

Franz Gruber

SUMMARY

1. Measures contain either two units of measurement, called *duple meter,* or three units of measurement, called *triple meter,* or a multiple of these.

2. The number of beats in a measure depends upon the speed or tempo of the music.

3. There are many possible rhythmic subdivisions of each unit of measurement.

4. There are many instances in which a triple rhythm is superimposed on duple rhythm or alternated with duple rhythm. These are called *compound rhythms.*

5. A dot placed after any note unit adds half the duration value to the measurement unit.

CHAPTER FIVE

DEVELOPING
CONCEPTS
OF CHORD SKIPS

Melodies are constructed either on the basis of scale or on the basis of chord intervals, *chords* being tones at given scale intervals sounding simultaneously. The ratio of the vibrations per second of the medium producing each component tone of the chord to the vibrations per second of the medium producing the other component tones determines the chord's particular aesthetic quality.

Some chords are called *primary* or *major triads* and others *secondary* or *minor triads*. The major triads are those built on the first, fourth, and fifth tones of the scale: the minor triads those built on the second, third, and sixth.[1] The primary triads may be regarded as a family—the *tonic* or *I chord* being the father chord, the *V chord* the mother chord (since it is frequently referred to as the *dominant*) and the *IV chord*, their child. Like a good family, the primary chords are great believers in togetherness; they hang around together. The IV chord in fact habitually clutches at either its mother or father—a tendency musicians refer to as *tendential resolution*. The bulk of most folk music is built on the harmonies of these three chords plus the ii chord, a child

[1]See Chapters 6 and 7.

of the mother chord by another marriage.[2] In the table following, note that the ii chord differs from the IV chord by only one note—the second step which replaces the tonic.

The learning sequence from ear to voice to eye is as apposite to teaching chord notation as it is to teaching melody and rhythm. Chord intervals must be heard and sung before being read. Therefore, the most effective procedure is to:

1. Teach a song that incorporates the chord intervals to be learned.

2. Focus attention on the chords used in the song's accompaniment.

3. Teach visual and vocal recognition of the chords by means of visual aids and musical games.

HOW MELODIES ARE COMPOSED

All melodies consist of a series of tones separated by either scale or chord intervals. A consonant chord can be built on any tone by adding tones at intervals of thirds.

Chord Name	Chord Number	Chord Root	Scale Steps Used	Quality Sound
tonic	I	scale step 1	1 + 3 − 5	major
supertonic	ii	2	2 − 4 + 6	minor
mediant	iii	3	3 − 5 + 7	minor
subdominant	IV	4	4 + 6 − 8	major
dominant	V7	5	5 + 7 − 2 − 4	major
submediant	vi	6	6 − 8 + 3	minor
leading tone	vii°	7	7 − 2 − 4	diminished
+ major third				
− minor third				

Chords may be *inverted*, that is, reorganized so that the chord bottom is a tone other than the root tone. For example, a I chord can be sung (reading from low to high) as 1–3–5, 3–5–8, or 5–8–3. Inversion changes the sequence of intervals but does not change the major or minor quality.

The following illustration shows notation for chords in the key of C.

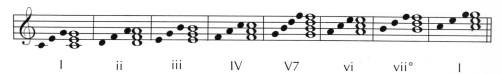

I　　　　ii　　　　iii　　　　IV　　　　V7　　　　vi　　　　vii°　　　　I

[2]If possible, have your local educational television station obtain the charming television series by Max Morath entitled *The Ragtime Era*, produced by the National Educational Television Association and Radio Center and KRMA-TV, Denver. See especially Program 3—"Barbershop Harmony." The family metaphor used here is borrowed from that program.

Two-tone chords are known as *duads* and three-tone chords as *triads*. However, a chord of four tones separated by intervals of thirds is called a *seventh chord*, because it spans seven scale steps. In the illustration above, all the chords are triads except the V7, which is a seventh chord.

A composer harmonizes a melody utilizing chords adapted to his aesthetic intentions and melodic requirements. If the melodic line employs any combination of scale steps 1–3–5, a I chord is his obvious choice. Melodic combinations of scale steps 2–4–5–7 on the other hand suggest a V7 chord.

Scale intervals are identified by arabic numbers: 1, 2, 3, 4, 5, 6, 7, 8. Chords are identified by roman numerals: primary major chords by roman capital numerals, secondary minor chords by lowercase roman numerals, and diminished chords by lowercase roman numerals followed by a small raised circle.

Chords may be constructed in the following sequence:

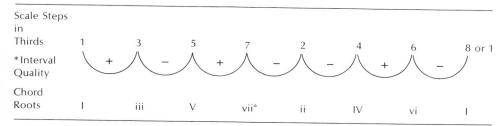

Scale Steps in Thirds	1	3	5	7	2	4	6	8 or 1
*Interval Quality	+	−	+	−	−	+	−	
Chord Roots	I	iii	V	vii°	ii	IV	vi	I

*A plus sign identifies an interval of a major third consisting of two whole steps; a minus sign identifies an interval of a minor third consisting of a whole and a half step; ° indicates the root of a chord consisting of two minor thirds.

To build a triad (three-tone chord) start with any root and add two consecutive numbers to its right.

To build a seventh chord (four-tone chord) start with any root and add three consecutive numbers to its right.

To build a ninth chord, start with any root and add four consecutive numbers to its right.

Major chord triads, designated by uppercase roman numerals, consist of a major and a minor third.

Minor chord triads, designated by lowercase roman numerals, consist of a minor and a major third.

A diminished seventh chord, shown as vii°, is a chord consisting of two minor thirds.

The structure of major and minor chords is described in Chapter 7.[3] As a result of the relationship of their component major and minor thirds, and concomitant quality, the I, IV, and V7 chords are called *major*, and the ii, iii, and vi chords *minor*. The vii° chord, called *diminished*, is neither major nor minor since it consists of two minor thirds, rather than a major and a minor third. Actually the vii° chord is a rarity, seeming

[3]See p. 139; see also pp. 103–104, below.

to demand the dominant, a major third below its root, whose addition creates the V7 chord (see table of chords above). Children quickly learn to detect major and minor chord quality.

TEACHING A I CHORD SONG

The following "Greeting Song" employs only tones of the I or tonic chord (tones 1–3–5–8, *do-mi-sol-do*). Substitute other verses for the second line. For instance: "My name is Mary, and what is your name?" Relate the melody to the chalkboard scale ladder. Then, as the class sings by number and then syllable, transfer the notation to the staff. Transposing the song from D to E (*do* on the first line) and F (*do* in the first space) on flash cards will help develop a sense of I chord intervals independent of a particular key.

GREETING SONG

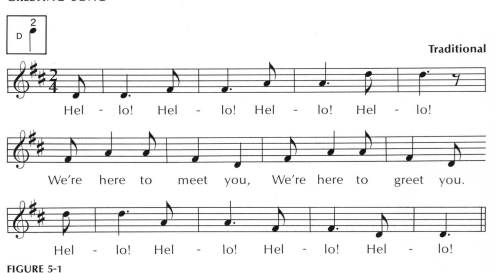

Traditional

Hel - lo! Hel - lo! Hel - lo! Hel - lo!

We're here to meet you, We're here to greet you.

Hel - lo! Hel - lo! Hel - lo! Hel - lo!

FIGURE 5-1

Introducing the Idea of the Tonic Chord

Indicate the placement of *do* on the music staff by a convenient symbol such as an X (as in X marks the spot) or the word DO (the letter d if the English system is used).

Key of D

The tonic triad of *do-mi-sol* can then be identified on the music staff.

Songs built on the tonic chord are to be found in any basic music book for elementary schools. After the children have learned such songs by ear, employ the various procedures previously suggested. Translate the melody into sign language, into numbers on the chalkboard, into steps on the scale ladder, into steps on the hand staff, and finally into pitch names on the music staff.[4]

FLASH CARDS FOR EAR-TRAINING PURPOSES

Charts and games are of inestimable help in introducing the concept of key. Illustrate a series of tone groups on 5 x 7 flash cards using either numbers, syllables, or staff notation. Since competition heightens interest, divide the class into teams, recording successful responses to the flash cards by each team member. When a card is shown, a child must sing the tones indicated, supplying those forms of tone designation omitted from the card, whether numbers, notation, or syllables.

To reverse this game, place the cards with the staff notation along the chalkboard edge. When the teacher sings a tone group using numbers, syllables, pitch names, or a neutral syllable, a team member must identify the flash card on which that tone pattern occurs and supply the missing elements.

No game should be carried on for more than a few minutes. Before playing, always designate the key—that of a song to be sung after the game—by singing its tonic chord (1–3–5–3–1).

Examples of 5 x 7 Flash Cards for Ear-training Games

By numbers, read both up and down

| 5 3 1 | 5 1 3 | 3 1 5 | 1 5 3 | 3 5 1 | 3 2 1 | 2 3 1 | 5 4 3 | 8 5 3 | etc. |

By syllables, on reverse side of card

| sol mi do | sol do mi | mi do sol | do sol mi | mi sol do | mi re do | re mi do | sol fa mi | do sol mi |

FIGURE 5-2

Make flash cards containing the notation in various tone sequences for the I chord triad of each of the tones of the C Major scale. *Do* will move to a different line or space as the chord is built, and each chord group, of course, will be in a different key. Similar cards should eventually be made to represent all major (primary) and minor (secondary) chord intervals. *Do* should be marked on each card.

[4]See Chapters 2 and 3.

Notation flash cards with *do* in a space

Notation flash cards with *do* on a line

FIGURE 5-3

Music Dictation Games

Divide the class into teams. Bring six children to the chalkboard to represent Team A. The members of Team B must sing a tone group by syllables for which Team A must write the numbers. Conversely, Team B can sing numbers for which Team A must write the corresponding syllables.

Draw a music staff across the board with a staff liner, allowing each child at the board about two feet of music staff to be divided into six equal measures. Identify *do*, varying its position on the staff from game to game. As a tone group is sung by an individual member of one team, the members of the other team must notate it on the board, using a measure for each group. Scores should be kept to permit each child to evaluate his ability to "see what he hears and hear what he sees."

Another variation of the tone group game is to distribute easily mimeographed blank music-staff paper, asking the class to notate by number, syllable, and pitch name melodic motives sung to a neutral syllable such as "loo." The class should always repeat the pattern to the same neutral syllable before trying to identify it. Be sure each child follows the sequence of writing numbers first, then syllables, then pitch names, before attempting to relate notation to the staff. The fourth grade is not too early to start such training.

Below are two charts helpful in promoting recognition of the relationship of syllables to staff notation. The first typifies keys in which *do* is on a space, the second keys in which it is on a line. (Review "The Steeple Bells" from Chapter 3 for this sequence.)

Call attention to the fact that in major scales the vowel sound "ee" of a *sol-fa* syllable always identifies the lower step of a half-tone interval; that is, *mi-fa* and *ti-do*. When *do* or 1 of the scale is in a space, *mi-sol-ti* are also in spaces, while *re-fa-la* and high *do* are on lines. Conversely, when *do* is on a line, *mi-sol-ti* are also on the lines, and *re-fa-la* and high *do* are in the spaces. Ask the class to demonstrate these relationships on the hand staff.[5]

It will be helpful if the scales of F and E♭ are sung in unison, first by number, then syllable, then pitch name, and the charts copied by the children into their music notebooks.

Using the One-octave Orchestra Bells or Xylophone

Hang a xylophone or set of bells at the side of the chalkboard. Draw a music staff as an extension of the xylophone bars so that each staff line or space is opposite its counterpart on the instrument. A flannel-board staff on which the class can notate various motives with flannel note heads can be hung similarly.

FIGURE 5-4 **Hung Bells**

After sounding *do*, sing a melodic motive with a neutral syllable. Ask a child to sing the motive by number, syllable, and pitch name, while accompanying himself on the xylophone.

BLACK KEYS, THEN WHITE

Probably the best visual aid in learning staff notation is the piano keyboard. For this reason each child should have a keyboard chart in his music notebook (Most modern music books for elementary schools contain such charts inside the back covers. If not, they can be easily made.)

The pentatonic scale is clearly pictured on the piano's black keys. Starting with

[5]Teaching the scale is discussed at length in Chapter 6.

the first black key of the group of three, the black keys sound the ascending syllabic steps of *do-re-mi-sol-la-do*. Children should be encouraged to pick out and identify the notes of pentatonic melodies by scale number, syllable, and pitch name, because this will facilitate the learning of sharps and flats.

After the children have become acquainted with the black keys, introduce the white by means of the scale in the key of C, C being the first white key in front of two black keys.

The class will remember, from learning the scale ladder, that half steps occur in the major scale between steps 3 and 4 and 7 and 8 (*mi-fa* and *ti-do*). Counting from C on the white keys of the keyboard, there is no black key between the white keys at these intervals. Thus half steps in the key of C are intervals that do not have a black key between them.

IMPROVING READING ABILITY IN THE UPPER GRADES

The Dominant Seventh or V7 Chord Intervals

Since all melodies are based on either scale or chord tone patterns, skill in reading music primarily consists of the ability to recognize such patterns, their relation to each other, and probable sequence. Next to the scale and tonic (I) chord pattern in frequency is that of the dominant seventh (V7) chord (5–7–2–4). Because the V chord is harmonically a prelude to the tonic (I) chord, although the V chord sometimes occurs as the triad 5–7–2, the fourth step is most often included to make a V7 chord. The addition of the fourth, whose tendency is to resolve into the third step of the tonic chord, reinforces the tendency of the seventh step to resolve into the eighth. This tendency is known as *tendential resolution*.

Tendential resolution is strongly felt in the delightful folk song, "Clementine" (Figure 5-5), which employs only tonic and dominant chords (I and V7).

After the song has been learned, ask the class to locate all I, V, and V7 chord and scale patterns in its melody. Point out the pattern of melodic phrases. Phrases 1 and 3 are identical, as are phrases 2 and 4. "Clementine" is a strophic song for which there are many verses. Its structure of two contrasting phrases may be symbolized as A-B form.

After the children have learned a variety of songs employing the patterns of V and V7 chords, make a series of flash cards containing the tone patterns as numbers, *sol-fa* syllables, and music notation. There should be one series with *do* in a space, another with *do* on a line. When playing identification games with the V7 flash cards be sure that the class always starts and finishes with a card showing the tonic or I chord tones. Thus, before presenting a flash card with the V7 chord, the teacher should always sing the tones *do-mi-sol* (1–3–5), so that the children can measure the interval to the chord's starting tone.

CLEMENTINE*

Sadly

American Ballad
Traditional

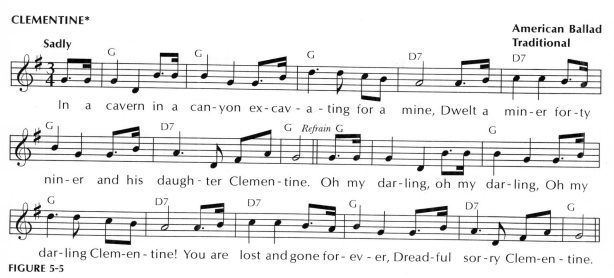

In a cavern in a can-yon ex-cav-a-ting for a mine, Dwelt a min-er for-ty

nin-er and his daugh-ter Clemen-tine. Oh my dar-ling, oh my dar-ling, Oh my

dar-ling Clem-en-tine! You are lost and gone for-ev-er, Dread-ful sor-ry Clem-en-tine.

FIGURE 5-5

Horizontal Forms

I	V	V7	V7	V7
1-3-5	5-2-7 to 1	5-4-2-7 to 1	2-4-5-7 to 8	2-5-4-7 to 8

Vertical Forms

Teacher sings down, children respond with any of these variations*

I Chord	V7	V7	V7	V7	V7	V7
1	5	4	2	2	4	5
3	4	5	4	5	2	4
5	2	2	5	4	5	7,
	7, to 1	7, to 1	7' to 8	7, to 1	7' to 8	2 to 1

On reverse side

I Chord	V7	V7	V7	V7	V7	V7
do	sol	fa	re	re	fa	sol
mi	fa	sol	fa	sol	re	fa
sol	re	re	sol	fa	sol	ti,
	ti,-do	ti,-do	ti'-do	ti,-do	ti'-do	re-do

*A single quotation mark placed above seven (7') means high seven in the scale going to 8. A quote mark placed after seven (7,) means low seven in the octave below *do* going to 1.

FIGURE 5-6   V7 Chord Flash Cards

*From Music In Our Country, © 1956, 1962, Silver Burdett Company. Rhythm slightly modified. Used by permission.

The resolving tone of a V7 chord should always be included on its flash card. This helps to develop a sense of tendential resolution. Examples of flash cards are shown in Figure 5-6.

Additional flash cards should be made showing these patterns in notation; one set with *do* marked on a space, another with *do* marked on a line, as in Figure 5-7:

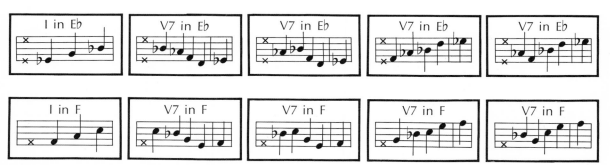

FIGURE 5-7   V7 Chord Notation Flash Cards

When employing cards be sure to mark the appropriate key signature on a music staff on the chalkboard.

Once the children have learned the syllables, teaching the simplified *English system*—which designates syllables by their first letter—will not only facilitate the reading of flash cards but also of British editions of music.

Recognizing the Sound of the V7 Chord

Sing a familiar song that employs both the I and V7 chords, such as "Clementine," to the accompaniment of a recurrent I chord. Ask the class if the accompaniment sounds strange and incorrect in some places. Sing the song again, accompanying as before, this time asking the children to raise their hands when they hear a discord that seems to require a change. They will not take long to recognize the occasions requiring a V7 chord.

Analyze the notation to determine where the melody employs V7 chord tones rather than those of the I chord. Finding chord patterns can be made into a game, two sections of the class competing to properly identify tone patterns in a group of songs. Keep score to measure progress during the year.

The Subdominant or IV Chord

The next most frequently encountered tone intervals are those of the chord built on the fourth step of the scale, called *subdominant* because it is that major chord below the dominant (V7) chord.

Again following the principle of ear to voice to eye, play I, IV, and V7 chords on the piano or autoharp until the children are able to recognize the new chord by its quality. Then play a familiar song containing intervals of the three primary chords in its melody, such as "The Little Mohee" (Figure 5-8), or "Home On The Range," accompanying, however, solely by a I chord.

THE LITTLE MOHEE*

FIGURE 5-8

Ask the children to sing the song, listening carefully to the accompaniment, and to hold up four fingers when they think a IV chord is demanded, and five fingers when they think a V7 chord. With a little practice, their designations should become quite accurate. Play several songs in this way.

The numbers and syllables of the tones of the IV chord should be written on opposite sides of flash cards. Other cards should contain music notation for the chord: one set with *do* on D, another with *do* on middle C, the space and the leger line below the staff respectively.

*From Birchard Music Series, Book 6, Copyright © 1962, Summy-Birchard Company, Evanston, Illinois. All rights reserved. Used by permission.

IV chord	IV	IV	IV	IV	IV
4	6	8-1	6	4	8-1
6	8-1	6	4	8-1	4
8-1	4	4	8-1	6	6

IV chord	IV	IV	IV	IV	IV
f	l	d	l	f	d
l	d	l	f	d	f
d	f	f	d	l	l

FIGURE 5-9   IV Chord Number and Syllable Flash Cards

Note: Since 8 and 1 are both keynotes (*do*), either note may be sung, but tell the children which is called for. After the class has learned to recognize pitch by ear, substitute the single letters of the English system for the *sol-fa* syllables. The chord may be sung either up or down the card.

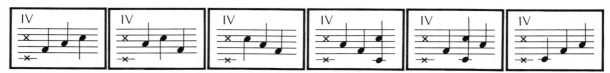

FIGURE 5-10   Examples of IV Chord Flash Cards in Notation with *Do* on Middle C

Make up additional cards with *do* on D.

When playing tonal games with flash cards, set up several possible resolutions for the IV chord intervals, either by moving to the I chord directly, or to the V7, which in turn resolves to the I chord.

Figures 5-11 and 5-12, show examples of such resolutions using I, IV, and V7 chords for flash cards. The flash cards can be taped to the chalkboard.

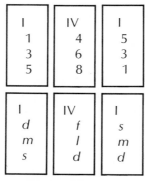

I	IV	I
1	4	5
3	6	3
5	8	1

I	IV	I
d	f	s
m	l	m
s	d	d

Notation in key of D

FIGURE 5-11   Flash Card Game Combining I-IV-I Chords

I	IV	V7	I
1	6	2	8
3	4	4	5
5	1	5	1
		7	

I	IV	V7	I
d	*l*	*r*	*d*
m	*f*	*f*	*s*
s	*d*	*s*	*d*
		t	

Notation with *do* on D

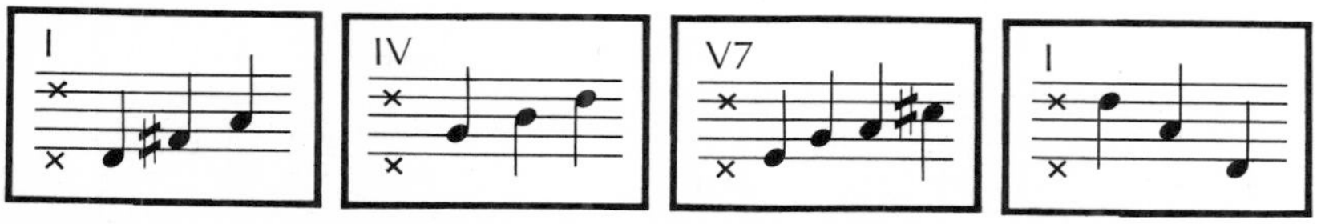

FIGURE 5-12 Flash Card Game Combining I-IV-V7-I Chords

When using flash cards, always remember to sing the I chord pattern, *do-mi-sol-mi-do,* so that the class can judge the starting tone of the intervals listed on the next card.

Secondary Chords

The class now will have learned songs built on I, IV, and V7 chord intervals, the primary or major triads. Many songs are built on chord intervals beginning on the second, third, and sixth steps of the scale, the secondary chords or minor triads. As discussed in Chapter 10, these triads consist of a minor third below a major third, the reverse of the first, fourth, and fifth step triads.

The chord built on the second step, logically designated a ii chord or *supertonic* because it is just above the tonic (I) chord, contains the intervals 2–4–6, *re-fa-la.* The chord built on the third step (the iii chord), called the *mediant,* contains the intervals 3–5–7, syllables *mi-sol-ti.* The chord built on the sixth step (vi chord), called *submediant,* contains intervals 6–8–3, syllables *la-do-mi.* "Sweet Betsy from Pike" (Figure 5-13 below) employs intervals of these chords.

Sometimes in a melody a chord tone is carried into the following one. Such a technique is known as a *suspension* because a tone is literally suspended over from one chord to another. Sometimes a chord tone anticipates the resolving chord, in which case it is known as an *anticipation* or *appogiatura* (meaning a "leaning" tone; it "leans on" the resolving tone). In Figure 5-13 suspensions and anticipations are marked by asterisks.

"Old Hundredth" (Figure 5-14) illustrates the use of secondary chords to harmonize a scale line melody. The arabic number under the roman numeral refers to the first or second inversion of the chord for the bass line.

SWEET BETSY FROM PIKE*

American Song

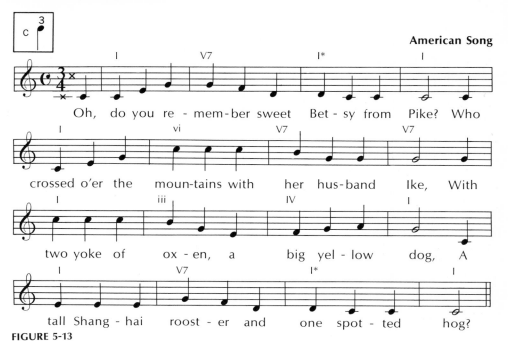

Oh, do you re-mem-ber sweet Bet-sy from Pike? Who crossed o'er the moun-tains with her hus-band Ike, With two yoke of ox-en, a big yel-low dog, A tall Shang-hai roost-er and one spot-ted hog?

FIGURE 5-13

OLD HUNDREDTH

Doxology by
Bishop Thomas Ken, 1695

Tune commonly known
as "Old Hundredth"
Attributed to Louis
Bourgeois c. 1535

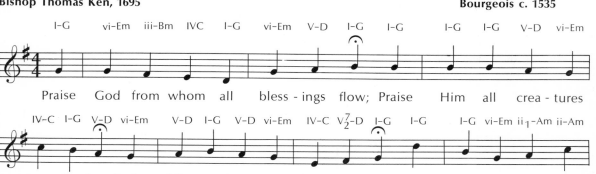

Praise God from whom all bless-ings flow; Praise Him all crea-tures here be-low; Praise Him a-bove ye heav'n-ly host; Praise Fa-ther, Son and

Ho-ly Ghost. A-men.

FIGURE 5-14

*From This Is Music, Book IV, by W. R. Sur, Mary R. Tolbert, W. R. Fisher, and Gladys Pitcher, copyright © 1961, 1967, Allyn & Bacon, Inc., Boston. Used by permission.

After the class has learned several songs employing intervals in the secondary triads, the intervals should be isolated for flash card drills and ear-training games of a few minutes' duration similar to those previously described.

Secondary chord flash cards should be made in either vertical or horizontal form using numbers and syllables, as in Figure 5-15.

ii Chord	ii	ii	ii	ii
2	4	6	2	4
4	6	4	6	2
6	2	2	4	6

Reverse sides

ii Chord	ii	ii	ii	ii
r	f	l	r	f
f	l	f	l	r
l	r	r	f	l

iii Chord	iii	iii	iii	iii
3	5	7	3	5
5	7	3	7	3
7	3	5	5	7

Reverse sides

iii Chord	iii	iii	iii	iii
m	s	t	m	s
s	t	m	t	m
t	m	s	s	t

vi Chord	vi	vi	vi	vi
6	8	3	6	3
8	3	6	3	8
3	6	8	8	6

Reverse sides

vi Chord	vi	vi	vi	vi
l	d	m	l	m
d	m	l	m	d
m	l	d	d	l

FIGURE 5-15 **Secondary Chord Flash Cards**

A SONG TO REMEMBER
(Descending)

Irving Cheyette

1. This is just a simple song that never leads me wrong, because it
2. This is I chord, this is iii chord, this is IV chord, now on I chord,

1. Helps me recognize the chords I need to make a song.
2. Here is ii chord, back on I chord V7 leads me home.

A SONG TO REMEMBER
(Ascending)

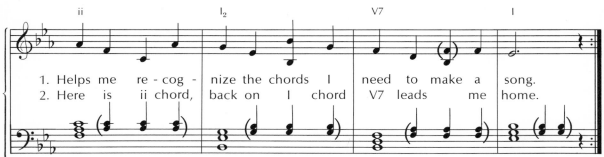

1. This is still another song that helps me as I sing along the
2. This is I chord, now on V7, back to I chord, here is IV chord,

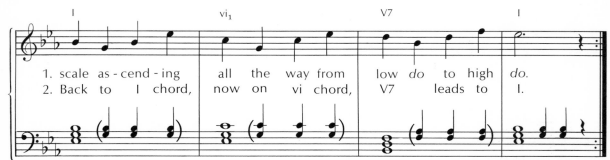

1. scale ascending all the way from low *do* to high *do*.
2. Back to I chord, now on vi chord, V7 leads to I.

FIGURE 5-16

Once these secondary chord intervals have been learned, their melodic use should be analyzed in familiar songs. Intervals of the secondary triads in a melody are usually followed by (resolve into) intervals of the primary triads. Typically, intervals of a iii chord will resolve to a IV chord, those of a ii chord will resolve to a IV or V7 chord, and those of a vi chord will resolve to a IV or V7 chord. Figure 5-16, "A Song To Remember," provides examples of such harmonic anticipation—the tendential resolution of chord intervals. It should be memorized, transposed to different keys, and sung by both numbers and syllables.

Once the class has progressed this far, ear-training games employing flash cards should include most of the chord intervals found in children's songs.

The following chord sequences (Figure 5-17) are from "Sweet Betsy from Pike." They should be sung both down and up, translated into syllables, and eventually notated by pitch name on the staff in the song's key of C.

I Chord	vi Chord	V7 Chord	I Chord
1	8	7	3
3	6	5	5
5	3	4	8

Also

I Chord	iii Chord	IV Chord	I Chord
8	7	6	5
5	5	4	3
3	3	1	1

FIGURE 5-17   Chord Sequences

EYE AND EAR TRAINING IN CHORD HARMONY

With the singing of secondary chord intervals, the children should begin to hear the difference between major and minor chord qualities. Since the eye can be used to reinforce the ear, symbolizing the interval distances of the minor chords on the scale ladder and finding such chords on the piano keyboard with the aid of the Keyboard Scale and Chord Finder will help the children conceptualize the distinction.[6]

As previously explained, in major chords (I, IV, V) the interval from the root step on which the chord is built to the next chord step consists of two whole steps or a major third, and the upper interval from the middle to upper note of the triad consists of a step and a half or a minor third. This is the structure of all major triads.

[6]The Keyboard Scale and Chord Finder is a type of slide rule. When placed on the piano keyboard it indicates by arrows the construction of major and minor scales, and, through correlation with primary and secondary colors, the primary and secondary chords in any key. It is produced by the Carl Van Roy Co., 51–17 Rockaway Beach Blvd., Far Rockaway, N.Y., 11691. There is an accompanying four-octave cardboard keyboard imprinted with the notation and vocal ranges of all human voices.

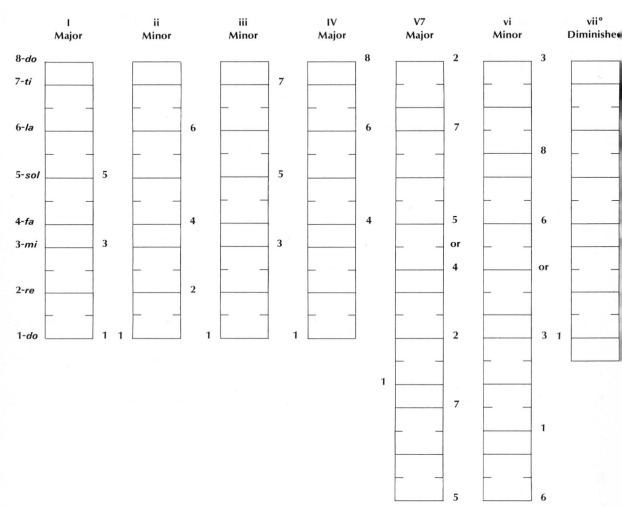

FIGURE 5-18 Interval Chord Construction

Conversely, the ii, iii, and vi chords are built with the minor third, a whole and half step, between the root of the chord and its middle step, and a major third, two whole steps, between the middle and upper note. Children should be given an opportunity to investigate this for themselves at the piano keyboard. (Other distinctions between major and minor are described in Chapter 7). The diminished triad in the vii° chord, consisting of two minor third intervals, produces a strong feeling of irresolution.

The class should now be ready to create appropriate chord accompaniments for the ascending and descending scale intervals of many familiar songs. A sense of harmony, even if never developed beyond the ability to "chord," provides incalculable pleasure. Using the flash cards of chord intervals previously prepared, set up the following sequences of chords for harmonizing ascending and descending scales, such as are found in "Joy to the World" or "Bells in the Steeple."

Chords Used for Ascending Scale Passages

Scale step:	1	2	3	4	5	6	7	8
Chord used:	I	V7	I	IV	I	vi	V7	I

Chords Used for Descending Scale Passages

Scale step:	8	7	6	5	4	3	2	1
Chord used:	I	iii	IV	I	ii	I	V7	I

Vocalizes in the key of the song to be sung following the exercise should be sung by numbers, *sol-fa* syllables, and neutral syllables.

To play a game, tack or tape flash cards with tone patterns in a row above the chalkboard. Under the flash cards draw a music staff at a level at which the children will be able to write, marking off measures for each chord. After finding the keynote

Flash cards

I Chord	V7 Chord	I Chord	IV Chord	I Chord	vi Chord	V7 Chord	I Chord
1	2	3	4	5	6	7	8
3	4	1	1	3	3	5	5
5	5	5	6	8	8	4	1
	7					2	

By syllables, reverse side

d	*r*	*m*	*f*	*s*	*l*	*t*	*d*
m	*f*	*d*	*d*	*m*	*m*	*s*	*s*
s	*s*	*s*	*l*	*d*	*d*	*f*	*d*
	t					*r*	

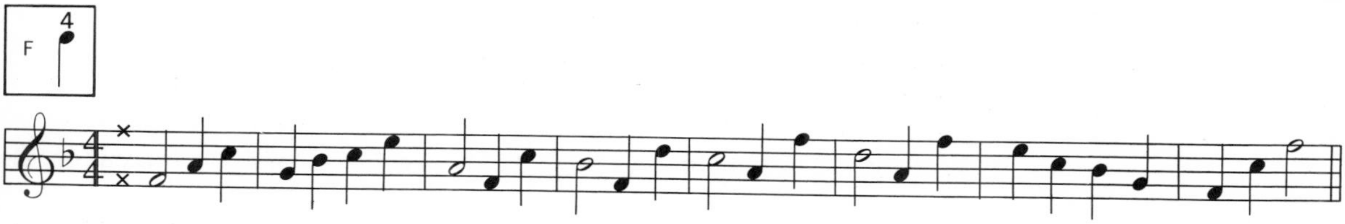

Also descending forms

FIGURE 5-19. Examples of Notation of Vocalizes

and marking it on the staff, call individual children to the board to notate each tone in the pattern as the class sings its pitch name.

Spend a few minutes of each period having the class take music dictation. After first singing the tonic chord (1–3–5–3–1, *do-mi-sol-mi-do*) to establish the key, and identifying it on the music staff, sing chord intervals on a neutral syllable. The children must identify the tones by writing in their notebooks the number, syllable, and pitch name. Remember that musical skill, even with practice, develops only gradually over the years. Some children may achieve accurate pitch and rhythm sense quickly; others will accomplish few of the skills described thus far.

Improving Song Tone in the Upper Grades

Chord and scale tone groups may be organized into exercises to be sung on sustained neutral vowel sounds, such as "lah, leh, lee, lo, loo." Sustain each pitch until voices blend, asking the children to listen carefully to the quality of the sound. If chord triads are sung up and down in this manner for a few minutes each class period, a marked improvement in tone quality should result.

The children should also be encouraged to hum vocal exercises on an "nnh" sound, the tongue behind the lower teeth. Call their attention to the resonance in the upper nasal channels and forehead resulting from humming correctly.

After the class learns to sing with the neutral "lah, leh, lee, lo, loo," add variety to the exercise by changing the initial consonants to labials such as "bah, pah, mah," lingual consonants "dah, tah, lah, rah, sah, yah, nah, vah," gutteral consonants "gah, kah, quah, xah," and breathed consonants "fah, hah, chah, jah."

Clarity of sound release is also important. To this end, sing exercises at varying tempos using a syllable that ends in a hard consonant such as "let" with the accent on the "t." Try to make all voices complete the "t" of each tone at the same time.

Introducing Chromatic Accidentals

Chromatic tones are any tones that do not belong to a given scale tonality (key). For this reason the signs altering or reverting to scale in a given measure are known as *accidentals*. Thus, the added sharps (♯) and canceling naturals (♮) in "Swing the Shining Sickle" (Figure 5-20) are accidentals. The cancel (♮) returns the note to the given key tonality of C.

1. Teach the song by using the question and answer approach, without reference to notation.

2. Draw a ladder of the major scale on the chalkboard.

3. Find the tone groups in the song having accidentals and write them on the board (see step 7 below).

4. Explain that placing a sharp in front of a note raises the pitch of that note a half step. Fit the sharped accidentals appropriately into the scale ladder between the whole steps, adding a sharp to the number and changing the vowel sounds of

SWING THE SHINING SICKLE*

Alice Riley
In strong rhythm

Janet Gaynor

1. Swing the shin - ing sick - le, cut the ri - pened grain

Flash it in the sun - light, swing it once a - gain,

Tie the gold - en grain heads in - to shin - ing sheaves,

Beau - ti - ful their col - ors as the au - tumn leaves.

FIGURE 5-20

No.	Syllable	Pitch		New No.	New Syllable	New Pitch
8	do	C				
7	ti	B				
6	la	A		♭7 or ♯6	te or li	B♭ or A♯
5	sol	G		♭6 or ♯5	le or si	A♭ or G♯
4	fa	F		♭5 or ♯4	seh or fi	G♭ or F♯
3	mi	E				
2	re	D		♭3 or ♯2	me or ri	E♭ or D♯
1	do	C		♭2 or ♯1	ra or di	D♭ or C♯

FIGURE 5-21   Scale Ladder for Measuring Chromatics in Key of C

*From Music Now and Long Ago, copyright © 1956–1962, Silver Burdett Company. Transposed from key of D to key of C. Used by permission.

the syllables to an "ee," as in *ti* or *mi*. Thus *fa* sharped becomes *fi*, and *sol* sharped becomes *si*.

5. Explain that placing a flat before a note lowers that note a half step, and changes the syllable to an "eh" sound. Thus when *ti* is flatted, it becomes *te*. However, *re*, already an "eh" sound, becomes *ra*.

6. To bring an accidental back to its original sound in a key, a cancel mark or natural sign is placed in front of the note the first time it occurs thereafter.

7. Practice singing the chromatically altered tone groups notated on the board (see step 3) with syllables, numbers, and pitch names.

Key of C

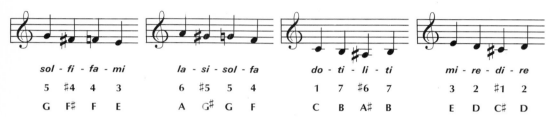

sol - fi - fa - mi	la - si - sol - fa	do - ti - li - ti	mi - re - di - re
5 ♯4 4 3	6 ♯5 5 4	1 7 ♯6 7	3 2 ♯1 2
G F♯ F E	A G♯ G F	C B A♯ B	E D C♯ D

May also be written:

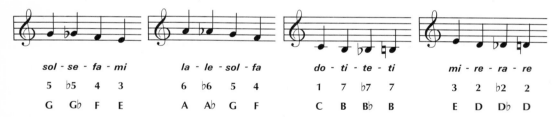

sol - se - fa - mi	la - le - sol - fa	do - ti - te - ti	mi - re - ra - re
5 ♭5 4 3	6 ♭6 5 4	1 7 ♭7 7	3 2 ♭2 2
G G♭ F E	A A♭ G F	C B B♭ B	E D D♭ D

FIGURE 5-22 Chromatic Notation Drills

8. Help the children to find the altered tones of the song (Figure 5-22) on the keyboard chart using the Keyboard Scale and Chord Finder with *do* on C.

9. Add instrumental accompaniments with tone bells, melody flutes, and auto-harp, teaching the fingering for the altered notes. Dramatize with swing rhythms in time to the pulse beat.

After the children have sung a variety of songs containing chromatic alterations, they should be ready to learn the numbers and syllables of the ascending and descending chromatic scale. In the upper grades, large permanent wall charts, visible to the entire class, should be made of the chromatic scale ladder. As new songs employing accidentals are learned, the tone groups should be isolated and related to the scale ladder for special drills. (Charts can be attached to the chalkboard by masking tape, pitch names being written as needed.)

Ascending Form
Add pitch names as needed

8 - _do_	
7 - _ti_	
_	♯**6 - _li_**
6 - _la_	
_	♯**5 - _si_**
5 - _sol_	
_	♯**4 - _fi_**
4 - fa	
3 - _mi_	
_	♯**2 - _ri_**
2 - re	
_	♯**1 - _di_**
1 - _do_	

Descending Form
Add pitch names as needed

8 - _do_		
7 - _ti_		
_	_	♭**7 - _te_**
6 - _la_		
_	_	♭**6 - _le_**
5 - _sol_		
_	_	♭**5 - _se_**
4 - _fa_		
3 - _mi_		
_	_	♭**3 - _me_**
2 - _re_		
_	_	♭**2 - _ra_**
1 - _do_		

FIGURE 5-23   Chromatic Scale Ladders

SUMMARY

The child cannot grasp relationships between triads sounding as a chordal unit until his ear has become attuned to their sound in arpeggiated form. Such arpeggiation must be introduced by songs the child enjoys. Only after joyful singing should a song's specific tone patterns be isolated for analysis. Joyful singing is also the test of analysis, and performance should improve as a result of keener appreciation of structure. Music consists of artistic wholes. Though subject to conceptual division, no work of art is merely the sum of its parts.

CHAPTER SIX

DEVELOPING CONCEPTS OF SCALE IN UPPER GRADES

An *octave* is the musical interval between two tones vibrating in a ratio of 1:2, the higher tone vibrating at exactly double the frequency of the lower. Sounding an octave produces an apparent reinforced unison, the range of overtones merely being extended. The scale organizes the sequence of tones whose frequencies lie between those of the octave to suit particular cultural needs. European cultures divide the octave into a twelve-tone *chromatic* scale. By contrast the Balinese and Indians of Asia fractionalize their scales into seventeen and twenty-two steps respectively.

The simplest division of the octave, corresponding to the natural divisions of the human voice, is the pentatonic scale of primitive and less musically sophisticated peoples, the scale of much folk music, and many songs of childhood.[1] Children can pick out a pentatonic scale easily simply by playing the black keys of the piano. Ask some to do so while the class accompanies on keyboard charts.

The Keyboard Scale and Chord Finder illustrated in Figure 6-1 indicates the tones of one pentatonic scale resulting from playing the black keys of the piano. The

[1] Cf. Curt Sachs, *The Rise of Music in the Ancient World, East and West,* W. W. Norton & Company, Inc., New York, 1943, p. 43; also our Chapter 10, p. 267.

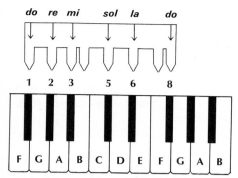

FIGURE 6-1   Keyboard Scale and Chord Finder over Piano Keyboard

key is G♭ Major, but note that the corresponding steps of any major scale constitute the same pentatonic scale, the interval sequence being identical.

Since the following folk songs are built on the pentatonic scale, they can be played on the black keys of the piano:

Scottish Songs: "Auld Lang Syne," "Loch Lomond."
Negro Spirituals: "Swing Low, Sweet Chariot," "Deep River."
Cowboy Songs: "Whoopy Ti Yi Yo," "Bury Me Not on the Lone Prairie."
American Indian Songs: "Sun Worshippers," "In the Land of the Sky Blue Water."

Similar songs of other nationalities can be found in any basic music series for elementary grades.

Interval numbers written above a song text as shorthand notation can later be related to the corresponding keys of the piano.

5   1   1   1   3   2   1   2
Should auld acquaintance be forgot

3   1   1   3   5   6
And never brought to mind,

6   5   3   3   1   2   1   2
Should auld acquaintance be forgot

3   1   6   6   5   1
And days of auld lang syne.

Vocally measuring the distance of each tone from *do*, ask the children to notate the text of various familiar pentatonic songs as indicated. Make a large poster-size chart showing the scale finder pointing to the black keys on the piano keyboard as in Figure 6-1 and another showing a pentatonic scale ladder (Figure 6-2). On both charts extend the scale range down to the fifth step below *do* (that is, C♯ below F♯) and to the third step above high *do* (A♯ above F♯).

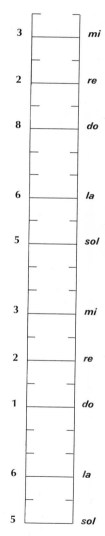

**FIGURE 6-2
Pentatonic
Scale Ladder**

PENTATONIC SCALES

Mode, meaning quality of scale, is not determined by starting pitch, but rather by sequence of scale intervals. The scale of "Auld Lang Syne" is produced by playing an octave on the black keys beginning with the first of the group of three. As Figure 6-2 indicates, the steps are separated by intervals of whole tone, whole tone, whole-and-a-half tone, whole tone, whole-and-a-half tone.

Demonstrate the sound of a major second (1–2 or 2–3) and a minor third (3–5 or 6–8). Ask the class to count the number of half steps on the scale ladder and keyboard between these intervals.

Merely moving the scale finder half a step on the piano and playing the keys now designated by the arrows numbered 1, 2, 3, 5, 6, and 8 will demonstrate that the same mode, termed the *Ionian,* can be played on any of the various combinations of white and black notes, kind of scale being determined by the pattern of intervals, not by pitch. Moving pitch of scale or melody is called *transposition,* tones changing but interval sequence remaining constant.

If a pentatonic scale is constructed on the black keys of the piano starting with the second in the group of three, the intervals between the scale steps become whole tone, whole-and-a-half tone, whole tone, whole-and-a-half tone, whole tone (see Figure 6-3). This pentatonic scale has an entirely different quality from the scale of "Auld Lang Syne." It is, in fact, one favored by much Japanese, Korean, and Chinese folk music, for example, "Hide-and-Seek" (Figure 6-4).[2]

[2]May, Elizabeth, "The Influence of the Meiji Period on Japanese Children's Music," *Journal of Research in Music Education,* XIII: 2 (Summer, 1965), pp. 110–120.

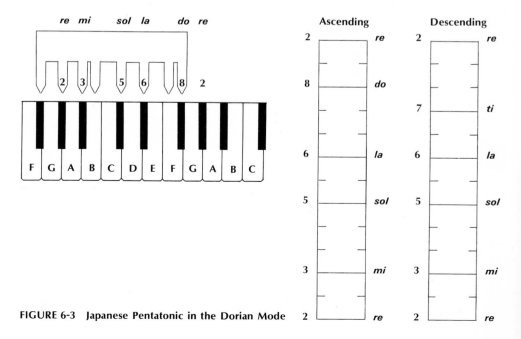

FIGURE 6-3 Japanese Pentatonic in the Dorian Mode

HIDE-AND-SEEK*

Japanese Folk Tune
Words Adapted by
Irving Cheyette

Gaily

Come on out and join the fun, we'll play Hide - and - Seek.

Let's throw Jan Ken Pon to find who the "devil" is,

Jan Ken Pon, It looks ev - en, One more throw, Now I guess I'm It.
Are you ready? No we're not, Here I come! Try to find us now.

FIGURE 6-4

Both Oriental and Western cultures use that pentatonic scale produced by playing an octave on the black keys of the piano commencing with the second of the group of two. The scale intervals are whole-and-a-half tone, whole tone, whole tone, whole-and-a-half tone, whole tone. Contrast the Chinese song "Trot, Pony Trot" (Figure 6-6) with the American white spiritual "Wayfaring Stranger"[3] (Figure 6-7).

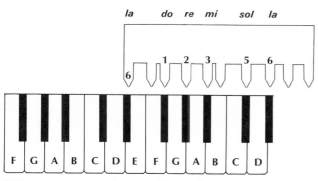

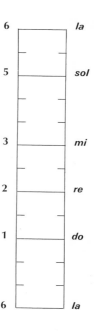

FIGURE 6-5 Pentatonic in Aeolian Mode

[3] See footnote 1, above.

*In Japanese Hide-and-Seek, the person who is "It" is called the "devil." Jan Ken Pon is a children's game to choose a winner, with two extended fingers representing a scissor, a fist representing a rock, and a cupped hand a paper. Rock breaks scissor, scissor cuts paper, paper covers rock. Each child throws his choice and must win two out of three.

TROT, PONY TROT*

1. Trot, trot, po - ny trot! Trot to Grand - ma's gate - way.
2. Trot, trot, po - ny trot, Home from Grand - ma's gate - way.

1. She comes out and calls the dog, And then we'll ride on jog - a - jog,
2. Mo - ther calls it's time to eat, And we'll have dum - plings stuffed with meat,

1. Trot, trot, trot, trot, trot, trot.
2. Trot, trot, trot, trot, trot, trot.

FIGURE 6-6

Encourage Experimentation

Invite the children to experiment, creating different scales on the black keys of the piano. See if they can pick out, translating from notation to scale number to keyboard, the pentatonic melodies of various nationalities.

The scale ladders of the pentatonic scales of Western and Oriental cultures, together with the numbers and syllables relating their intervals to the major scale, are diagrammed in Chapter 10. Draw the appropriate scale ladder on the chalkboard whenever a song employing a pentatonic scale is taught.

The pentatonic scales enumerated are not all the five-tone scales possible. Any five tones within the octave may be combined to suit the musical needs of a composer. Ask the children to try constructing scales within the framework of the various modes described later in this chapter.

Transposition on the Piano Keyboard

So far, scales have been confined to the black keys of the piano. Play the pentatonic scales beginning on the white key to the right of a black key; then beginning on the white key to the left, measuring the intervals with the scale finder in terms of major seconds and minor thirds. The tonic (*do*), as the other tones, will be a half

*From *Music through the Year,* © 1955, Follett Publishing Company, Chicago. Used by permission.

WAYFARING STRANGER*

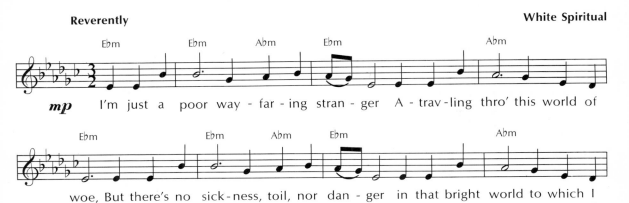

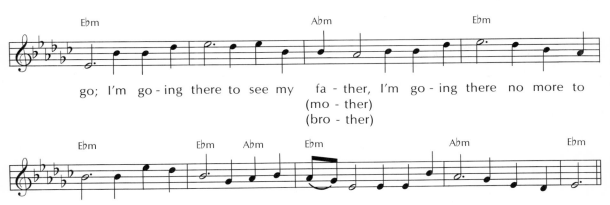

FIGURE 6-7

step higher and a half step lower respectively than the scale played on the black keys.

The scale finder permits any scale to be transposed into another key by simply placing tonic (*do*) on the key desired and playing the tones indicated. Figure 6-8 illustrates transposition from black keys to white.

Vocal Pitch Placement

As all but the most modern songs are constructed on major or minor scales and their chords, the child must learn to place interval distances vocally as well as on the piano. Starting with any given key, he should learn to measure the intervals

*From Music for Young Americans, Book 6, American Book Company, New York, ©1960. Transposed from D Minor to E♭ Minor to permit playing on the black keys of the piano. Used by permission.

to higher and lower octaves of the major scale. Once pitch intervals are "placed" in the voice, numbers, syllables, and pitch names of each tone should be related to the music staff.[4] A series of such vocalizes in the major scale follows:

Pentatonic Scale on the Black Keys

Pentatonic Transposed Down a Half Step

Pentatonic Transposed Up a Half Step

FIGURE 6-8

Example 1:	1–2,	1–3,	1–4,	1–5,	1–6,	1–7,	1–8–1.
	d–r,	d–m,	d–f,	d–s,	d–l,	d–t,	d–d'–d.
Pitches:	c–d,	c–e,	c–f,	c–g,	c–a,	c–b,	c–c'–c.
Example 2:	8–7,	8–6,	8–5,	8–4,	8–3,	8–2,	8–1–8.
	d–t,	d–l,	d–s,	d–f,	d–m,	d–r,	d–d,–d.
Pitches:	c–b,	c–a,	c–g,	c–f,	c–e,	c–d,	c–c–c.
Example 3:	1–3,	2–4,	3–5,	4–6,	5–7,	6–8,	7–2'–1.
	d–m,	r–f,	m–s,	f–l,	s–t,	l–d,	t–r'–d.
Pitches:	c–e,	d–f,	e–g,	f–a,	g–b,	a–c,	b–d'–c.
Example 4:	8–6,	7–5,	6–4,	5–3,	4–2,	3–1,	2–7,–1.
	d–l,	t–s,	l–f,	s–m,	f–r,	m–d,	r–t,–d.
Pitches:	c–a,	b–g,	a–f,	g–e,	f–d,	e–c,	d–b,–c.

Make up additional vocalizes using intervals of fourths, fifths, sixths, and those of the chromatic scale.

RELATING THE VOCALIZES AND SCALE LADDER TO THE PIANO KEYBOARD

In Figure 6-9 the scale finder points to the C Major scale, which is played entirely on the piano's white keys. Since the major scale intervals are: whole tone, whole

[4]For upper grades see Irving Cheyette, *Tune Ups for Choral Groups*, Schmitt, Hall & McCreary, Minneapolis, Minn., 1951, 8pp.

tone, half tone, whole tone, whole tone, whole tone, half tone, beginning the major scale on any note other than C requires some use of the black keys. With the help of the scale finder let the children discover the black keys needed to play various familiar songs such as "Joy to the World" or "The Steeple Bells" in major keys.

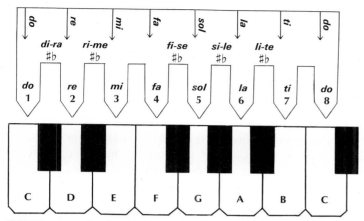

FIGURE 6-9 Scale Finder on the Keyboard, C Major Scale

When the arrow marked *do* = 1 of the scale finder is pointed to any note, the remaining arrows will automatically designate the other notes (sharps or flats) of the major scale of the key on which *do* rests. Thus in Figure 6-10, the scale finder placed with *do* on D points to the remaining steps of the D Major scale.

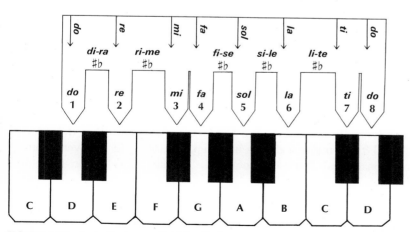

FIGURE 6-10 Scale Finder on D Major Scale

Attach a chart of the piano keyboard horizontally across the chalkboard with masking tape. Underneath draw a music staff, with a mark indicating the space or line of *do* for a given song. Then, by use of the scale finder, ask the class to determine the sharps or flats of the key signature. The D Major scale illustrated in Figure 6-10 requires F♯ and C♯, such sharps being notated on the music staff to the left of the meter signature as follows:

Key Signature Indicates D Major

CONSTRUCTING MAJOR SCALES IN VARIOUS KEYS

The misleading nature of the terms *sharp* and *flat* is seldom realized by musicians. In teaching the major and minor scale sequence the child must be made to realize that the "natural" quality of the key of C is not inherent but merely convenient. The tones of the black keys do not differ in kind from those of white: the scales are integrated, not segregated. What defines a major scale is the sequence of seven intervals that separates its eight tones: the third and seventh intervals being half steps and the remainder whole. Arbitrarily, the tones falling within this scale when played commencing with C have been termed *natural* (white keys on the piano), and the remainder *sharps* or *flats* (black keys). Actually, the key of C provides not a "natural quality," but merely a convenient notational base.

Once the class realizes that, in a major scale, the seventh ascending step must fall a mere half step below the octave, it can determine at once from inspection of the piano keyboard that, with the exception of C and F Major, the seventh step must fall on a black key since the intervals E–F (3–4) and B–C (7–8) are the only half steps in the key of C.

Analysis will show that the sequence of intervals from C to F in the C Major scale is an exact duplicate of the sequence from G to C; that is, in the major scale the arrangement of intervals from the first to the fourth step is duplicated by the arrangement from the fifth to the eighth. Therefore, the upper four tones of any major scale must also constitute the lower four tones of another major scale commencing on its fifth. Thus the upper four tones (tetrachord) of the C Major scale are identical to the lower four tones (tetrachord) of the G Major scale. Aware that the interval between steps 7 and 8 in a major scale is a half step, the class will discover in building a major scale on G that F must become F♯. The key of G Major, therefore, requires one sharp.

Comparable to the relationship between the C Major and G Major scales, the class should be able to determine that the sequence of tones from the dominant in the G Major scale to the octave (D to G) must be duplicated by the interval sequence in the D Major scale from A to D. Thus, remembering that the seventh interval must be a half step, the class will find that the D Major scale requires both F and C sharps.

By this method the class should be able to derive the key signatures of all major keys through F♯. The class will also realize in the process that the key cycle moves in fifths, the fifth being the most powerful overtone of any pitch other than its octave.

The additional sharp in the succeeding key in the cycle is added to make the seventh interval a half step.

Notice one curious fact: deriving all keys in the key cycle through F♯ includes all major keys commencing on tones in the C Major scale except F.

Construction of the major scale requires that the sequence of intervals in the lower and upper tetrachord be identical. The major keys requiring sharps could be deduced precisely because the upper tetrachord in one key had to be the lower tetrachord in another. The converse must also be true: the lower tetrachord in one key must be the upper tetrachord of another. But the lower tetrachord ascending in the key of C ends with F. Therefore, descending from F the class will discover that the major scale sequence demands B♭. Moreover, the B♭ is in turn the fourth note of the lower tetrachord in the key of F. This tetrachord is also, therefore, the upper tetrachord of the key of B♭, which descending demands the addition of E♭ to maintain the major sequence. Similarly, the cycle of all keys requiring flats can be derived.

Let one child derive as many keys as possible by ascending by fifths from C, and another by descending by fifths from C. The fact that key denotation by sharp or flat is purely a matter of convention will rapidly become apparent.

Thus each key requires sharps or flats only in terms of its relation to the sequence of tones in C Major, but the relationship is solely for the purpose of notational convenience. With a little ingenuity, it is possible to demonstrate that any other key could be taken as "natural," sharps and flats designating deviations from this base key with equal facility.

By the visual and auditory methods previously described, teach new songs in the major keys, referring to the piano keyboard chart with the scale finder to enable the class to add the major key signatures to a blank music staff. Vocalizes, as have been suggested, pitched in the key of a given song and utilizing both scale runs and chord skips, will also help develop the child's sense of mode and pitch.

Figure 6-11 is a reference chart illustrating the number of sharps or flats needed in each major key.

Scale Step	Syllable		Sharp Keys								Flat Keys						
			0	1♯	2♯	3♯	4♯	5♯	6♯	7♯	1♭	2♭	3♭	4♭	5♭	6♭	7♭
8	do	Key of	C	G	D	A	E	B	F♯	C♯	F	B♭	E♭	A♭	D♭	G♭	C♭
7	ti		B	F♯	C♯	G♯	D♯	A♯	E♯	B♯	E	A	D	G	C	F	B♭
6	la		A	E	B	F♯	C♯	G♯	D♯	A♯	D	G	C	F	B♭	E♭	A♭
5	sol		G	D	A	E	B	F♯	C♯	G♯	C	F	B♭	E♭	A♭	D♭	G♭
4	fa		F	C	G	D	A	E	B	F♯	B♭	E♭	A♭	D♭	G♭	C♭	F♭
3	mi		E	B	F♯	C♯	G♯	D♯	A♯	E♯	A	D	G	C	F	B♭	E♭
2	re		D	A	E	B	F♯	C♯	G♯	D♯	G	C	F	B♭	E♭	A♭	D♭
1	do	Key of	C	G	D	A	E	B	F♯	C♯	F	B♭	E♭	A♭	D♭	G♭	C♭

FIGURE 6-11 Diagram of Major Diatonic Scales

This chart might be mimeographed and distributed to upper grades for inclusion in their music notebooks. Remember that its information will be absorbed only as children learn to sing various major keys. Using the piano keyboard and keyboard charts to demonstrate key signatures should accelerate this process.

CONSTRUCTING MINOR SCALES

Much traditional Occidental and Oriental music is based on scales in the minor modes, particularly the Aeolian and Dorian. Scale ladders for the minor modes appear in Chapter 10.[5]

Using the Scale Finder for Minor Scales at the Piano

Using the Keyboard Scale and Chord Finder, begin with scale step 6 or *la* on the piano keyboard. By placing the finder on the piano keyboard, a child can see exactly how any major or minor scale is constructed.

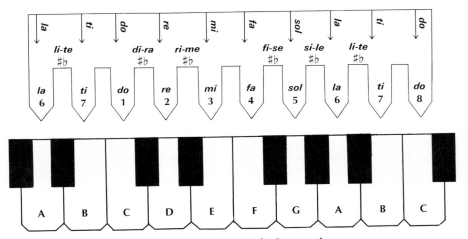

FIGURE 6-12   Keyboard Scale Finder for Minor Scale Construction

Aeolian Minor

The *Aeolian mode*, the most common of all minors, has three variations termed *natural, harmonic,* and *melodic.* Commencing on *la* = 6 of any major scale and playing the octave in the key of the tonic (*do*) will alter the major sequence of intervals to produce Aeolian natural minor. Thus the key signature of natural minor is always the same as the major scale to which it is related. For example, when a C Major scale is transformed into an Aeolian minor scale in A by playing the octave commencing on *la* = 6, instead of *do* = 1, the key signature remains without sharps or flats. This

[5]See footnote 1, above.

is technically known as building a natural minor scale in the Aeolian mode on the sixth step of the relative major.

To explain this relationship:

Natural Minor Scale

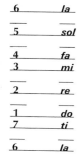

1. Use the scale finder to play an octave scale on the white keys of the piano commencing on A-6.

2. Sing the scale ascending and descending by number and syllable. See if the class can sing the intervals unaided.

3. Compare the interval sequence to that of the major scale. The second and fifth intervals are half steps, instead of the third and seventh.

4. Demonstrate that this interval sequence will result if the octave is played in a major scale commencing on its sixth step.

5. Because the scale played on the white keys commencing on A has the same notes as the C Major scale, A Minor is called the relative minor of C Major, and takes the same key signature as its relative major, C Major.

6. In the fourth and higher grades use the scale finder to find the sixth step of other major scales. Ask the class to play and sing their related minor scales with numbers, syllables, and pitch names.

See if the children can sing this lovely song (Figure 6-13) in the Aeolian natural

THE WRAGGLE-TAGGLE GYPSIES*

Old English Ballad

FIGURE 6-13

*From *Music in Our Country*, © 1956, 1962, Silver Burdett Company, Morristown, N.J. Used by permission.

minor mode in the mood of the text, following the suggested procedures of the question and answer approach.

Melodic Minor Scale

Many songs, and much instrumental music, have been composed in the melodic minor scale, which has separate ascending and descending forms requiring the use of accidentals.[6] Note that melodic minor differs from natural minor only on the ascending form in which *fa* and *sol* are sharped to become *fi* and *si*.

Ascending Form		Descending Form	
6	*la*	6	*la*
♯5	*si*	5	*sol*
♯4	*fi*	4	*fa*
3	*mi*	3	*mi*
2	*re*	2	*re*
1	*do*	1	*do*
7	*ti*	7	*ti*
6	*la*	6	*la*

FIGURE 6-14 Melodic minor ladders

For sharps the vowel of the *sol-fa* syllables becomes "i" (pronounced "ee"). For flats the syllable vowel becomes "e" (pronounced "eh"), except *re* which when flatted becomes *ra*.

Number minor scale steps to stress their relation to the major. The number 1 (*do*) is used as the key center for the major scale, the number 6 (*la*) as the key center for the minor scales, and the number 2 (*re*) as the key center for the Dorian minor scale.

In the fourth and higher grades, construct minor scales on the piano keyboard beginning with the sixth step of the various major scales using the scale finder. Ask the class to write pitch names, including sharps or flats, as needed.

Older children should also be able to detect the difference in modality between songs in major and songs in minor modes. Alter a familiar song in a major key by lowering the third step of its scale a half step to produce the melodic minor. Singing the song in both modalities should help the class "feel" the differing modal quality.

The text of the following song in melodic minor, "Foom! Foom! Foom!" (Figure 6-15), suggests many additional embellishments such as bells, descant, and chants. Note that its middle section is in the relative key of C Major, but the final line moves back to A minor. Such mixing of modes is frequent in folk melodies of European origin.

[6]See p. 106, above.

FOOM! FOOM! FOOM!*

FIGURE 6-15

Encourage the children to verbalize the feelings evoked by music in minor modes; associating verbal characteristics will sharpen their modal discrimination.

Harmonic Minor

Central European folk music frequently employs the harmonic minor scale which, unlike melodic minor, is uniform ascending and descending. In this scale, the seventh ascending step is sharped, creating the large interval *fa–si* (4–♯5), termed an *augmented second*, because it has been stretched to a step and a half.[7]

---

[7] The distinction between a "minor third" and an "augmented second" is merely that of notational accident. The interval is identical. If the constituent tones skip a letter, as A–C, it is a minor third. If they do not, as E♭–F♯, it is an augmented second.

*Add an instrumental Introduction by having tambourine and recorder play the first four measures. Add an instrumental Coda by having tambourine and guitar play the last five measures. These instruments with autoharp or guitar may also accompany throughout.

From Music for Young Americans, Book 6, © 1960, American Book Company, New York. Used by permission.

Harmonic Minor

6	*la*
♯5	*si*
*	
4	*fa*
3	*mi*
2	*re*
1	*do*
7	*ti*
6	*la*

Ask the class to:

1. Note the large interval between steps 4 and ♯5, *fa* and *si*. This interval, a whole plus a half step called either an augmented second or a minor third, though the terms are not used interchangeably, is one to which both ear and voice must become accustomed. The child may find difficulty at first in placing its limits
2. Use the scale finder to construct harmonic minor scales on the piano keyboard beginning with the sixth step (*la*) of the various major keys. Ask the class to write the pitch names, including the sharps or flats as needed

Here is a charming old English folk song, "Old King Cole," in the harmonic minor mode (Figure 6-16). Other melodies in the minor modes will be found in any music series for elementary schools.

OLD KING COLE

English Folk Song

Old King Cole was a mer-ry old — soul, And a mer-ry old soul was he — He

called for his pipe, And he called for his bowl, And he called for his fidd-lers   three.

FIGURE 6-16

Dorian Minor

Many lovely songs are composed in the Dorian minor mode, the scale that results from playing an octave commencing on the second step of the major scale as illustrated:

Dorian Scale

2	*re*
1	*do*
7	*ti*
6	*la*
5	*sol*
4	*fa*
3	*mi*
2	*re*

Ask the class to:

1. Play the scale on the piano beginning on D, using only white keys
2. Sing the ascending and descending scale by number and syllable
3. Try to memorize the sound of the Dorian minor
4. Use the scale finder to find the second step of other major scales. From the second step construct Dorian scales in the same key as the major, singing them by pitch name and *sol-fa* syllable

The song shown in Figure 6-17, "Old Joe Clarke," is in the Dorian mode:

OLD JOE CLARKE*

FIGURE 6-17

MIXED MODES

Many songs provide contrast and color by varying modes, as in "Erie Canal" (see Chapter 7). Illustrate shifting modalities by appropriate recordings. The ability to recognize such changes will enhance appreciation.

Major and minor key relationships can be illustrated for grades 5 and 6 by mimeographing the chart below (Figure 6-18), asking the class to add the pitch names of the related minor keys. The upper line indicates the key signature of the major key, and therefore that of the related minor key as well. Remember that in melodic minor, accidentals are required on the ascending but not the descending scale, while in harmonic minor, the accidental remains for both. Natural minor employs no accidentals.

Do not forget that theoretical information is merely an adjunct to the music curriculum, not its object. *The object is joyful music making.* Information is learned, music must be made.

*From *Music for Young Americans*, Book 5, © 1959, American Book Company, New York. Transposed down from E Minor to D Minor. Used by permission.

Major Key Signature

	0	1♯	2♯	3♯	4♯	5♯	6♯	7♯	1♭	2♭	3♭	4♭	5♭	6♭	7♭
	C	G	D	A	E	B	F♯	C♯	F	B♭	E♭	A♭	D♭	G♭	C♭

Minor Scale Ladder

Natural	Melodic	Harmonic															
6 la		A															
	♯5 *Si*	♯5 *Si*															
5 sol		G♯															
	♯4 *Fi*																
4 fa		F															
3 mi		E															
2 re		D															
1 do		C															
7 ti		B															
6 la		A															

Related Minor Keys	A	E	B	F♯	C♯	G♯	D♯	A♯	D	G	C	F	B♭	E♭	A♭

FIGURE 6-18 Major Key Signatures

MODES AND EXOTIC SCALES

Scales may be constructed commencing on any pitch. Each creates a unique feeling, possessing a quality not always distinguishable as major or minor. The modes, with names appropriated from ancient Greek, have an archaic, primitive sound easily demonstrated on the white keys of the piano. Gregorian chant and much Oriental, Near Eastern, and Central European folk music is of modal construction.

Phrygian Mode

This mode, resulting from an octave played commencing on the third step (*mi*) of a major scale, provides the basis for the lovely Japanese folk song "Sakura," meaning cherry blossoms, Figure 6-19.

Phrygian Scale

3	*mi*
2	*re*
1	*do*
7	*ti*
6	*la*
5	*sol*
4	*fa*
3	*mi*

1. Sing the scale beginning on third step in the key of C by number, syllable, and pitch name
2. As the class sings, let each child simulate playing the scale on the piano keyboard chart using the scale finder to designate the notes
3. Ask the class to try to remember the sound of the scale
4. Notate the scale in music notebooks

SAKURA*
(Cherry Blossoms)

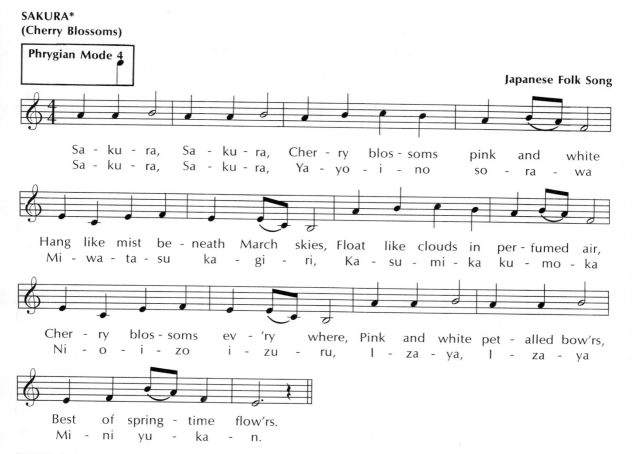

Phrygian Mode 4

Japanese Folk Song

Sa - ku - ra, Sa - ku - ra, Cher - ry blos - soms pink and white
Sa - ku - ra, Sa - ku - ra, Ya - yo - i - no so - ra - wa

Hang like mist be - neath March skies, Float like clouds in per - fumed air,
Mi - wa - ta - su ka - gi - ri, Ka - su - mi - ka ku - mo - ka

Cher - ry blos - soms ev - 'ry where, Pink and white pet - alled bow'rs,
Ni - o - i - zo i - zu - ru, I - za - ya, I - za - ya

Best of spring - time flow'rs.
Mi - ni yu - ka - n.

FIGURE 6-19

Part of the loveliness of the song lies in the fullness of the Japanese vowel sounds. The "gi" is a hard "g" sound, and the "i" sound is "ee." The melody of "Sakura" was incorporated by Puccini in the opera *Madame Butterfly* and can also be heard in the sound track of the motion picture *Sayonara*.

Modified Phrygian Modes

The Phrygian mode is found in much Central European folk music in a modified form, sometimes called the *Gypsy scale*, favored by such composers as Franz Liszt, Johannes Brahms, Georges Enesco, and Béla Bartók. The *Rumanian Rhapsody* of Enesco presents one of the more colorful examples of this scale in an orchestral setting. Israeli music such as the popular Hora, "Havah Nagilah" (Figure 6-20), is also, modally, modified Phrygian.

*From *Children's Songs From Japan*, © 1960, E. B. Marks Music Corp., New York. Used by permission.

Modified Phrygian Scale

3	mi
2	re
1	do
7	ti
6	la
♯5	si
4	fa
3	mi

1. Sing the scale beginning on third step, in the key of C by number, syllable, and pitch name
2. See if the class can play the scale beginning on E
3. Use the scale finder to transpose the scale to other keys
4. Ask the class to try to remember its sound
5. Draw the scale ladder into music notebooks
6. Note the heightened emotional quality derived from the augmented second

HAVAH NAGILAH (Hora)*

Gaily, with increasing tempo

Adapted Words Israeli Folk Dance Song

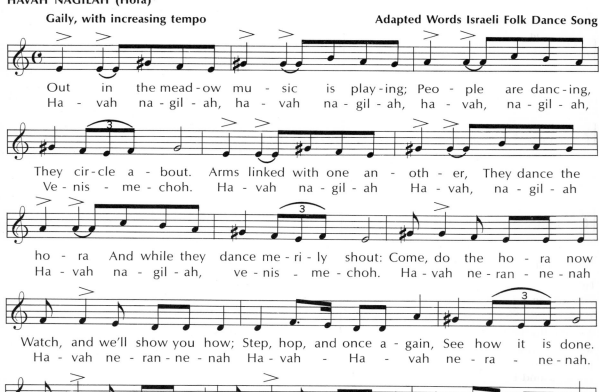

Out in the mead-ow mu - sic is play-ing; Peo - ple are danc-ing,
Ha - vah na-gil-ah, ha - vah na-gil-ah, ha - vah, na-gil-ah,

They cir-cle a - bout. Arms linked with one an - oth - er, They dance the
Ve - nis - me - choh. Ha - vah na - gil-ah Ha - vah, na-gil - ah

ho - ra And while they dance me - ri - ly shout: Come, do the ho - ra now
Ha - vah na - gil - ah, ve - nis - me - choh. Ha - vah ne - ran - ne - nah

Watch, and we'll show you how; Step, hop, and once a - gain, See how it is done.
Ha - vah ne - ran - ne - nah Ha - vah - Ha - vah ne - ra - ne - nah.

Hear how we keep the beat, Step - ping with live - ly feet; Come, join our cir - cle now;
Ha - vah ne - ran - ne - nah, Ha - vah ne - ran - ne-nah, Ha - vah - Ha - vah

*Literal translation from the Hebrew text is "Come, let us be gay and joyful! Come, let us rejoice: Awake, brothers, with a joyful heart."

From Music for Young Americans, Book 6, © 1959, American Book Company, New York. Used by permission. Transposed to A minor, Hebrew text added.

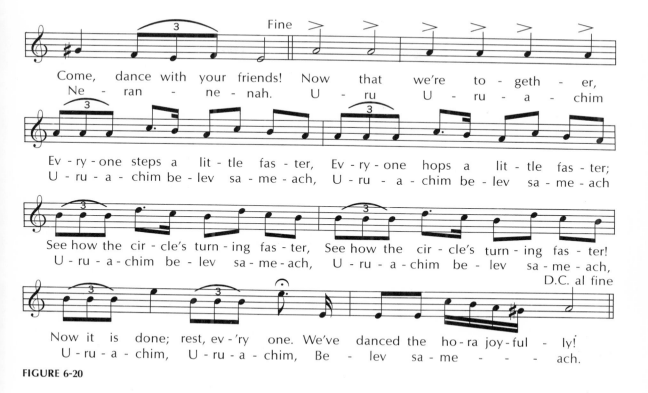

Come, dance with your friends! Now that we're to - geth - er,
Ne - ran - ne - nah. U - ru U - ru - a - chim

Ev - ry - one steps a lit - tle fas - ter, Ev - ry - one hops a lit - tle fas - ter;
U - ru - a - chim be - lev sa - me - ach, U - ru - a - chim be - lev sa - me - ach

See how the cir - cle's turn - ing fas - ter, See how the cir - cle's turn - ing fas - ter!
U - ru - a - chim be - lev sa - me - ach, U - ru - a - chim be - lev sa - me - ach,

Now it is done; rest, ev - 'ry one. We've danced the ho - ra joy - ful - ly!
U - ru - a - chim, U - ru - a - chim, Be - lev sa - me - ach.

FIGURE 6-20

Other Modes

The Lydian mode, based on the fourth step of the major scale, and the Mixo-Lydian mode, based on the fifth step, are outlined in Chapter 10. Following the usual method, ask the class to listen to these scales, identify their intervals on the scale ladder, sing them, play them on the keyboard, and write their notation. Lydian and Mixo-Lydian patterns are frequently interwoven into solo, orchestral, and choral literature.

Locrian Mode on the Seventh Scale Step

This scale, unusual in the West, is common in the Orient, particularly in Japan. An example is "Counting Song," Figure 6-21.

The class may well ask if there is a limit to the number of modes a composer may use in a single composition. To answer, play a recording of the first movement of the C Major Sonata No. 15 in which Mozart builds modal scales on each step of the major scale, and from which the popular song "In An Eighteenth-Century Garden" is derived. See how many modes the class is able to identify by aural and visual analysis.

COUNTING SONG*

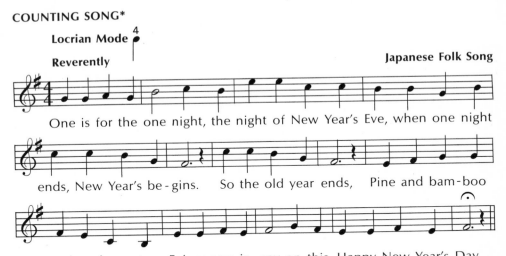

FIGURE 6-21

Near Eastern Exotic Modes (modified Aeolian mode)

"Tumba" (Figure 6-22) is a delightful Arabian song based on the sixth step of the scale but employing the augmented second step characteristic of the Mediterranean region of North Africa, Asia Minor, and the Black Sea. Ask the class to sing the ascending and descending forms of these scales, but only after they have first learned the song and accompanied the singing with tambourine and drum.

Ascending		Descending	
6	*la*	6	*la*
♯5	*si*		
		5	*sol*
4	*fa*	4	*fa*
3	*mi*	3	*mi*
♯2	*ri*		
		2	*re*
		♯1	*di*
1	*do*		
7	*ti*		
		♭7	*te*
6	*la*	6	*la*

Ask the class to:

1. Sing the scale in the key of C Minor by number, syllable, and pitch name

2. Find the scale on the keyboard charts and piano, measuring the intervals

3. Listen to recordings that employ exotic scales, such as *Scheherazade* by Rimski-Korsakov; *Polovtsian Dances* by Borodin; and "Danse Arabe" from the *Nutcracker Suite*

4. Note particularly the unusual construction of the ascending scale

5. Write the scale forms into their music notebooks

6. See if the class can transpose the scale in other keys

7. Try playing the scale with melody bells. Ask the children studying orchestral instruments to play the scale. Simple melody flutes, tonettes, or flutophones emphasize the Oriental flavor

*From *Children's Songs from Japan,* ⓒ 1960, E. B. Marks Music Corp., New York. Used by permission.

TUMBA*

Tambourine Tap

Drum
FIGURE 6-22

*Songs without words or with nonsense words are found among all peoples.
**Pronounced "toom-ba."

From Birchard Music Series, Book 6, © 1962, Summy-Birchard Company, Evanston, Ill. Slightly modified melodically. Used by permission.

BASS CLEF NOTATION

In upper grades, the children will learn to use the open strings of the larger string instruments such as the cello and bass viol for accompaniments.[8] Playing these instruments requires a knowledge of the bass clef.

Placing the back of the left hand against the chalkboard, draw five lines from the extended fingers. Place on this staff the symbol for the F clef, showing that the fourth line marks the pitch of F sounding below middle C. Using the piano keyboard charts, help the children locate the F symbolized by the clef sign, and identify the clef lines and spaces:

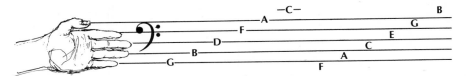

FIGURE 6-23   Deriving Bass Clef Notation from the Hand

Note that pitch designations differ from those of the treble clef. Above the bass clef draw another staff so that the children may see the relationship of the treble to the bass clef. By putting both staves together, as in piano or choral music for four voices, the difference in the designations of the lines and spaces will become apparent. Demonstrate the necessity of inserting a leger line between the two clefs to bridge from one to the other, as in the Grand Staff chart in Figure 6-24:

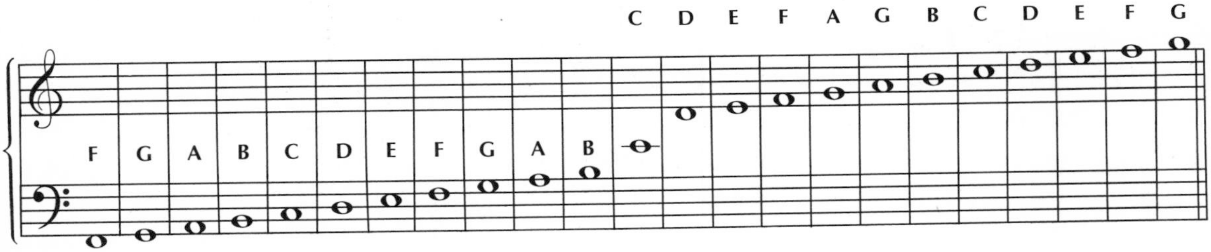

FIGURE 6-24   Grand Staff Found on Keyboard Chart

A keyboard chart provides opportunity for finding the bass clef notes. Let children take turns coming to the piano to play the root of song chords designated by letter name. Initially, use songs requiring the I and V chords, then add others after the class has gained familiarity with reading the bass clef.

[8]See Chapter 8.

TEACHING SCALE FINGERINGS FOR THE PIANO

1. Place the Keyboard Scale and Chord Finder with *1 - Do* on the key of the scale to be played. Arrows will point to the remaining tones of the major scale.

2. On mimeographed charts of the piano keyboard, such as in Figure 6-25, ask the children to write the names of the scale tones on the applicable piano keys. When sharps or flats are required, place the letter name and sign above the note.

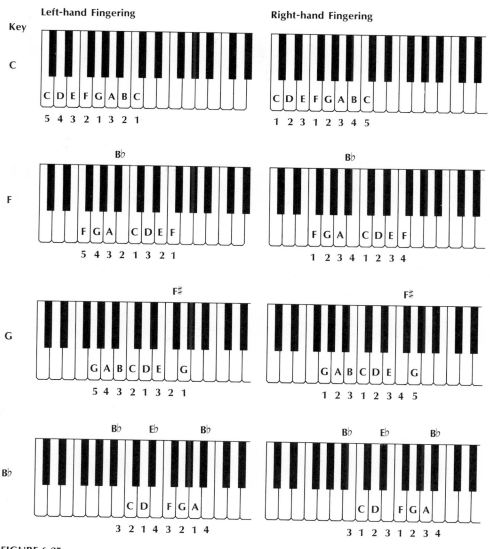

FIGURE 6-25

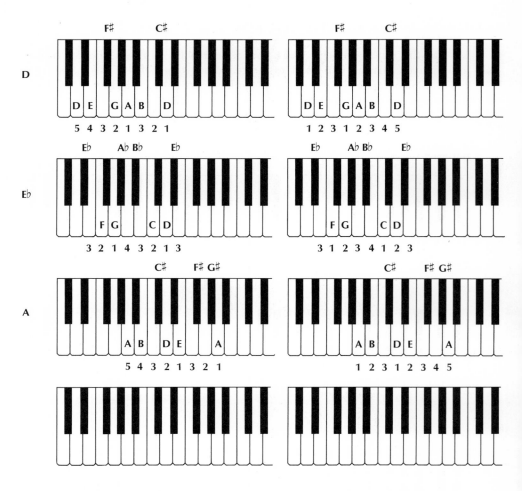

3. Identify the finger number of each hand as below. Ask the children to mark the appropriate fingering under each scale.

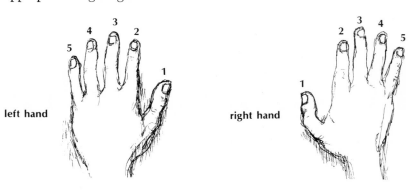

left hand   right hand

4. Explain that to play the ascending scale in right-hand fingering, the thumb (1) crosses under the palm of the hand; but in playing the descending scale, the third or fourth finger lifts over the thumb. Left-hand fingering reverses the order of movement.

5. To play a minor scale, utilize the same fingering as for the major scale.

SUMMARY

Melody is the primary musical means by which the variety of human emotion may be expressed. Since all melody is based on scale, scale is the most easily accessible element of composition and the most characteristic. Aesthetically, scale evokes mood. Conceptually, scale betrays degree of sophistication and ethnic background. It bears much the same relation to music that pronunciation bears to speech.

Learning to recognize type of scale will not only lend intellectual interest to listening but will stimulate further research about the structure of music.

CHAPTER SEVEN

DEVELOPING CONCEPTS OF HARMONY IN THE UPPER GRADES

The music of Western civilization is primarily a harmonic art whose sensuous appeal lies in the varying relationships of vocal and instrumental parts: the architectonic structure of combinations of musical tones. Combined tones that fuse in a sensuously pleasing fashion are generally termed *consonant*, while those that clash are called *dissonant*. Dissonant sounds create an aesthetic tension that demands release. This polarity of feeling is the emotional field of music in which harmonic sequences seem to flow from dissonance to consonance. Unresolved dissonance can be as discomforting as holding one's breath.[1]

[1]The emotional protest of much contemporary music consists in its refusal to resolve the tensions of its dissonance. It creates fury but provides no catharsis. Schoenberg, his pupil John Cage, and their respective disciples have sought to eliminate concepts of consonance and dissonance by reducing harmony to mere relationships of time. This simplistic approach equates the aesthetic of Beethoven with that of a watch. The logical corollary to Cage's celebrated statement "All is music" is "Nothing is music." Cage's doctrine of "purposeless play," that music should not "attempt to bring order out of chaos, nor to suggest improvements in creation, but simply [be] a way of waking up to the very life we're living, which is so excellent once one gets one's desires out of its way and lets it act of its own accord," is Buddhism applied to composition. The purpose of the Buddha

PARTIALS

Every tone is really a chord consisting of a *fundamental* or lowest tone, and an invariable series of higher overtones known as *partials*. Much as ripples are produced by a stone cast into a pond, sound is produced by the movement of a body in enveloping air. Assume for the sake of argument that a stone thrown into a pond displaces water not only by its entire bulk, producing a large ripple, but by smaller portions of itself, producing separate smaller ripples. Something similar occurs when a string vibrates or a pipe resonates. The string or pipe vibrates or resonates along its entire length producing the fundamental tone, and also at one-half, two-thirds, three-fourths, and other smaller proportions of its length producing higher partials of the fundamental tone. The smaller the length of the vibrations, the greater the frequency and, therefore, the higher the pitch. The loudness or intensity of the partials determines to some extent the quality of the overall sound, although the highest partials are inaudible to the human ear.[2] Since the relation of fundamental and partial tones is constant, the combination of fundamental and partials is called the *chord of nature*. The sequence of partials within the chord of nature is known as the *harmonic series*.

Traditional harmony developed by the gradual introduction of higher partials into musical composition and their grudging public acceptance in closer and louder relationships. Fortunately, so far as harmony is concerned, familiarity does not breed contempt, but makes content; the public ear, once acclimated to new sounds, finds little as pleasurable as the expected. Critics are frequently upset not so much by what is dissonant as by what is new, and the edginess of strange harmonic sequences is dulled by repeated hearings. Thus the progressions of Stravinsky's *Le Sacre du Printemps*, which provoked a riot at its premier, are now the lugubrious commonplace of the program annotator.[3]

Fundamental on C with successive partials (overtones)

FIGURE 7-1   **Chord of Nature in C**

---

was to enable man to emancipate himself from the burden of existence. The purpose of aleatory music, presumably, is to emancipate composers from the burden of composition. In the light of this analogy, the Oriental quality of the auditory pointillism of such serial composers as Webern and Foss is metaphysically just, if not humanly satisfying. "The twelve toners behave as if music should be seen and not heard," Ned Rorem, *The Paris Diary of Ned Rorem*, George Braziller, Inc., New York, 1966, p. 171.

[2] Redfield, John, *Music, A Science and An Art*, Alfred A. Knopf, Inc., New York, 1928, pp. 22–79.

[3] Stravinsky, Igor, and Robert Craft, *Expositions and Developments*, Doubleday & Company, Garden City, N.Y., 1962, pp. 163ff. See also Joseph Machlis, *Introduction to Contemporary Music*, W. W. Norton & Company, Inc., New York, 1961, pp. 653–654, for an explanation of the employment of higher partials.

The ratio of the vibration of a given partial to the vibration of the fundamental tone is the same as the number of the partial: that is, the sixth partial in Figure 7-1 (G) vibrates at six times the speed of C below the bass clef staff—the fundamental tone.

TENDENTIAL RESOLUTION OF SCALE TONES

What has been called the most consonant sound in harmony is the major chord: the fundamental tone and the first five overtones (partials) of the chord of nature. Steps 1, 3, 5, and 8 of a major scale, derived from the audible lower partials, seem restful or passive in relation to the fundamental tone, much as if the fundamental itself were being repeated. These scale steps provide a base in traditional harmony to which the melody always repairs. On the other hand, scale steps 2, 4, 6, and 7 of a major scale are not only higher partials of the fundamental but are also lower partials of its dominant third partial. Although consisting of tones not as acoustically intimate to the original fundamental as the third and fifth, the dominant's chord of nature more closely approximates the chord of nature of the tonic than does any other. This approximation creates a sense of progression, of harmonic purpose: the tendency in traditional harmony of the second, fourth, sixth, and seventh steps of the major scale and their chords to resolve to steps 1, 3, 5, and 8, and their chords. When key tonality is established in a piece of music, the logic of the mind's ear demands and anticipates resolution of the melodic and harmonic lines in terms of the active higher, and passive lower, partials of the fundamental tones.

Figure 7-2 illustrates the pull of the dominant and subdominant to the tonic in the major scale:

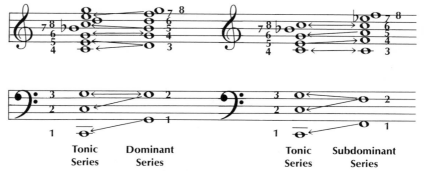

FIGURE 7-2 Tonic, Dominant, and Subdominant Chords of Nature in Key of C to Resolutions

Notice that the dominant-tonic relationship tends toward the tonic, whereas that of subdominant to tonic vacillates according to context. This is because any tonic in a major scale is the dominant in the key of its subdominant.[4] Thus partials 4, 5, 6, and 7 of fundamental C also constitute the dominant chord in the key of F, the subdominant of C.

[4] See the discussion of the creation of major scales, Chapter 6, pp. 118ff, above.

Tendential resolution is readily demonstrable by singing the first two tones of a scale. A sense of incompleteness, immediately felt, demands addition of the third step or the reiteration of the first. Similarly, the sequential frustration of a tonic followed by a dominant or a subdominant chord (Figure 7-3) can be alleviated by a return to the tonic or further modulation.

Unresolved Tonic and Dominant   **Unresolved Tonic and Subdominant**

FIGURE 7-3

MOOD QUALITIES OF CHORDS

Besides the active and passive harmonic relationships of scale tones and chords, any sequence of major, minor, or diminished intervals possesses emotional connotations. Major modes frequently seem gay, triumphant, or martial, while minor are plaintive and somber. Diminished chords in themselves seem indecisive.

Whether a triad (three-tone chord) is major, minor, or diminished is determined by the relationships of the middle tone of the chord to the root. A major chord consists of a major third surmounted by a minor third; a minor chord is the reverse; while in a diminished chord both thirds are minor (see Chapter 5).

Do not be confused into thinking that a major scale may only be harmonized by major chords—or a minor only by minor. Rather, building in thirds on the steps of any major scale: chords I, IV, and V, termed *primary*, are major (that is, the tonic, subdominant, and dominant); chords ii, iii, vi, termed *secondary*, are minor; and the vii° chord is diminished. Thus the C Major triads are as follows:

Primary-Major   Secondary-Minor   Diminished

I   IV   V   ii   iii   vi   vii°

Remember that the order of intervals of a minor scale is that resulting from starting with step 6 of a major scale. Therefore, in a natural minor scale, the sequence of major-minor triads is the same as the major scale sequence commencing with the vi chord. This results in the tonic and subdominant (i and iv) chords in a minor scale sequence becoming minor; the III, VI, and VII° chords becoming major; and the ii chord diminished.[5]

For example, this is the sequence of chords for A Minor (of which C is the relative major):

---

[5] In harmonic minor, the sequence of minor-major triads changes in that the sharped leading tone into the tonic alters the V to major and the vii° to diminished.

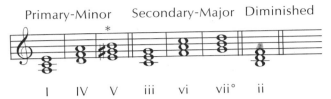

I IV V iii vi vii° ii

HARMONIC DEVELOPMENT

The earliest forms of harmony consisted of recurring patterns arranged among equal melodic voices. The composer's interest lay in the decoration of the melodic weave rather than the progression of the chord sequence. Though the twining of voices in any Baroque fugue or choral prelude forms complex harmonies, such harmonies are subordinated to contrapuntal considerations.

The rise of a Protestant middle class demanding music domestically accessible and emotionally secular produced a new audience with a new aesthetic. Mathematical embellishment gave way to dramatic psychology.[6] A single line of melody could be costumed and characterized by harmonies whose progressions derived from the tendential resolution of the melody. In homophonic, as distinct from earlier polyphonic composition, harmonic structure ceased to be melodically dependent and became on occasion the melodic determiner.[7]

INTRODUCING HARMONIC CONCEPTS TO CHILDREN

Because of the many forms of musical reproduction available today, children are constantly exposed to harmonies. The child's interest in making harmony himself will develop gradually once he gains sufficient control over his voice to carry a melody and to exercise some rhythmic independence.

Schools generally introduce part harmony in the fourth grade. To help the child develop independence in carrying a part, the teacher can employ canons, rounds, chants, partner song combinations, original descants, primitive organum (part singing at intervals of a fifth), part singing at intervals of thirds and sixths, ethnic effects (such as Scottish and Indian "drone" chords of fifths, 1–5), as well as imitations of instrumental sounds. Countermelodic, descant, and harmonic intervals can also be translated from sign language to numbers, syllables, and ultimately to music notation. Procedures for accomplishing all these are explored in the sections that follow.

[6] Hauser, Arnold, *The Social History of Art*, Alfred A. Knopf, Inc., New York, 1952, vol. II, pp. 573ff.
[7] Redfield, *op. cit.*, pp. 85–94. An example of melody dictated by harmony is "I Love You, Porgy" from George Gershwin's "Porgy and Bess," built on a sequence of ninth chords, i.e., a I^9 to a vi^9 to a IV^9 to a V^7 to a I. See also Ernst Toch, *The Shaping Forces of Music*, Criterion Music Corp., New York, 1948, p. 64. Compare the Mozart Piano Sonata recordings of Glenn Gould with those of Lili Kraus. Gould plays the homophonic Mozart in the style of the polyphonic Bach, at best a "left-handed compliment" to Mozart.
*Cf. footnote, 5, p. 139.

Canons and Rounds

Canons and rounds are melodies repeated in a delayed sequence to produce harmony. *Canons* in general consist of melodic repetitions, usually a measure later than the original voice, at the same, higher, or lower intervals. *Rounds* are a type of canon in which the delay spans a phrase and the melody is repeated identically.

To construct a simple round, ask the class to sing any four- or eight-line poem or nursery rhyme, such as "Humpty Dumpty," "Little Bo-Peep," or "Sing a Song of Sixpence," to a scale. After the children have achieved some facility, divide the class, one group to delay singing until the other starts its second line. When Group 2 starts, harmony in thirds will result. Rounds can be constructed using either ascending or descending scales.[8]

HUMPTY DUMPTY   Nursery Rhyme

Hump-ty   Dump-ty   sat on a wall,   Hump-ty Dump-ty   had   a   great fall,

All the King's hor-ses and all the king's men, Couldn't put Hump-ty to - geth-er a-gain.

SING A SONG OF SIXPENCE

Nursery Rhyme

Sing a song of   sixpence a   pock-et full of   rye

Four and twen-ty   black-birds, baked in a   pie.

FIGURE 7-4 Building Scale Rounds on Familiar Nursery Rhymes

[8]See p. 149, below.

Now divide another way. Have half the class sing the scale down while the other half sings up. This will give the children a sense of the charm of contrary motion.

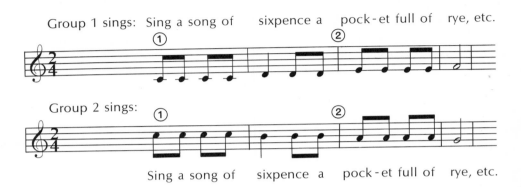

Partner Songs

Combining "Humpty Dumpty" with "Sing a Song of Sixpence" (Figure 7-5) will produce polyrhythms and a further sense of contrary motion:

FIGURE 7-5

Few songs are more familiar than the traditional rounds "Three Blind Mice" and "Frère Jacques." After being mastered separately, combine them to develop the tonal and rhythmic independence required for part singing, the boys singing "Three Blind Mice" as the girls sing "Frère Jacques" in the same key. The class will discover that although "Three Blind Mice" is in $\frac{6}{8}$ and "Frère Jacques" in $\frac{2}{4}$, they combine to reinforce each other tonally and rhythmically. Many canons and rounds capable of partnership will be found in any series of basic music for elementary schools.

Group 1 sings: "Three Blind Mice"
Group 2 sings: "Frère Jacques"

Three blind | mice | Three blind | mice | See how they | run, | etc.

Frè - re   Jac - ques   Frè - re   Jac - ques   Dor - mez   vous,   etc.

FIGURE 7-6

Combining Rounds with Other Songs

An example of canonic imitation is "The Lone Star Trail" against the descant "Leavin' Old Texas."[9] As indicated (Figure 7-7), rhythmic interest can be added in the last two measures if several children sing a "clip-a-clop-a" trail rhythm while others strike coconut shells or wood blocks as accompaniment.

Stephen Foster melodies, in particular "Oh, Susanna" and "Camptown Races," lend themselves to happy combination. "Old Folks at Home" keeps pleasant company to a whistled accompaniment of Dvořák's *Humoresque*.[10]

Adding a Drone Organ Point

To any song harmonized by I and V7 chords, the fifth step of the scale, common to both chords, provides pitch for a chant—as in Figure 7-9.

If the song has a swinging march tempo, like "Patsy," the low voice group (usually the boys) can imitate the sound of a tuba by singing "toom, toom," on each beat, alternating the pitches of the I (tonic) chord with those of the V7 (dominant) chord in succeeding measures as required. Ask the boys singing the tuba part to practice the descending sequence of I and V7 chords (steps 1–5 and 2–5) respectively by number, syllable (*do-so* for the I chord, *re-so* for the V7 chord), and pitch name (Figure 7-10).

Adding a Chordal Descant

Another form of harmony is the *chordal descant*. In "Patsy," for example, the children should locate the tones of the I (G) and V7 (D7) chords with the piano

[9]The earliest contrapuntal accompaniment to the chant of the early church service was called "plain song" or descant. Descant now indiscriminately refers to any contrapuntal melody above the melody.

[10]For other partner songs see Frederick Beckman, *Partner Songs* and *More Partner Songs*, Ginn & Company, Waltham, Mass., 1958.

THE LONE STAR TRAIL*
(Descant "Leavin' Old Texas")

American Cowboy Songs

Arr. by R. E. Nye

*For canonic imitation of upper part, second voice enters at beginning when first voice sings *leave*.
From This Is Music, Book 5, by W. R. Sur, Robert E. Nye, W. R. Fisher, and Mary R. Tolbert, © 1961,
1967, Allyn and Bacon, Inc., Boston, Mass. Used by permission.

Coconut shells or paper cups

Wood block

Selected voices

Clip - a clop - a - clip - a - clop - a, etc.

FIGURE 7-7

OH, SUSANNA

Group 1

Stephen Foster

Oh I come from Al - a - ba - ma with my ban - jo on my knee, etc.

Group 2   **CAMPTOWN RACES**

Stephen Foster

The Camp-town lad - ies sing this song, doo - dah, doo - dah,

Group 1 sings: "Old Folks at Home"
Group 2 whistles: *Humoresque*

Stephen Foster
Anton Dvořák

Way down up-on the Swan - ee Riv-er, Far, Far a - way, etc.

FIGURE 7-8

PATSY*

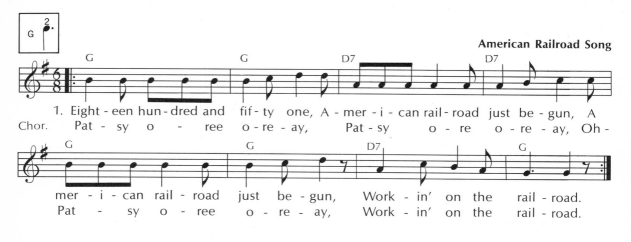

American Railroad Song

1. Eight-een hun-dred and fif-ty one, A-mer-i-can rail-road just be-gun, A
Chor. Pat-sy o - ree o-re-ay, Pat-sy o-re o-re-ay, Oh-

mer-i-can rail-road just be-gun, Work-in' on the rail-road.
Pat-sy o-ree o-re-ay, Work-in' on the rail-road.

Organ Point Chant

Work-in' on the rail-road. or Pat-sy o-ree, o-ree-ay.

Another harmonic part is created by singing the root tone of the chords as below:
Bass Part (voices, bells, piano, string bass or cello)

1. Eight-een hun-dred and fif-ty one, A-mer-i-can rail-road just be-gun, A-etc.

FIGURE 7-9

Toom toom toom toom   Toom toom   toom toom, etc.

FIGURE 7-10 Tuba Voice Part

*From This Is Music, Book 4, by W. R. Sur, R. E. Nye, W. R. Fisher, and Mary R. Tolbert, © 1961, 1967, Allyn & Bacon, Inc., Boston, Mass. Used by permission.

keyboard charts and Keyboard Scale and Chord Finder. Write the chords by syllable and music notation in scale relationships on a chalkboard music staff, as shown in Figure 7-11.

Sing these chord tones as arpeggios up and down going from I to V7 and back to I.

Two-tone chord descant

Eight - een hun - dred and fif - ty one, A - mer - i - can rail - road just be - gun, A - etc.

A more involved descant employing all the chord tones could go as follows:

Eighteen hun - dred and fif - ty one, A - mer - i - can rail - road just be - gun, A - etc.

Note that the descant is composed of the tones found in the harmonizing chords.

FIGURE 7-11   Building a Descant

Adding a Harmony Choir

A small group—containing a minimum of two voices in each range—can provide harmony by sustaining the tones of either I or V7 chords as a melody requires. (The V7 chord adds a note in the middle register for which either the middle voices must be added to or divided.) The choir should sing the song text, or a phrase selected from it, adding an introduction and Coda as in the example shown in Figure 7-12.

H—High voice
M—Middle voice
L—Low voice

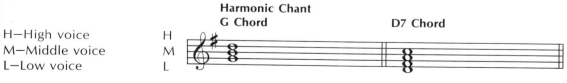

Workin' on the rail - road, Workin' on the rail - road

FIGURE 7-12   Building a Harmony Choir

A few chords can accompany a variety of songs, the choir singing the tonic when the teacher holds up one finger, and the dominant seventh when he holds up five. Of course, separate groups can be selected for each chord. (Bells may be added or substituted for voices.)

ADDING BARBERSHOP THIRDS BY FINGER HARMONY, ROUNDS, AND IMPROVISATION

The major third of the I chord (*do-mi*), the minor third of the ii chord (*re-fa*), the minor third of the vii° chord (*ti-re*), and the fourth of the IV chord (*do-fa*) can be cued by means of hand signals, the left hand representing the tonic third, and the movement of the right indicating whether the tones of the ii or vii° chord are above or below it. Thus the index and middle fingers of each hand touching at the same height require a I chord, Group 1 singing *do* and Group 2 *mi*. When the right hand moves up so that the right middle finger is at the space between the middle and index fingers of the left hand, Group 1 sings *re* and Group 2 *fa*. When the right hand moves down so that the right index finger is at the space between the middle and index finger of the left hand, Group 1 sings *ti* below *do* and Group 2 sings *re*. Finally, when only the right index finger moves up to the space between the left index finger and thumb, Group 1 sings *do* and Group 2 *fa*, an interval of a fourth. These positions are illustrated in Figure 7-13 in mirror image.

Left-hand fingers are stationary, right-hand fingers are moving:

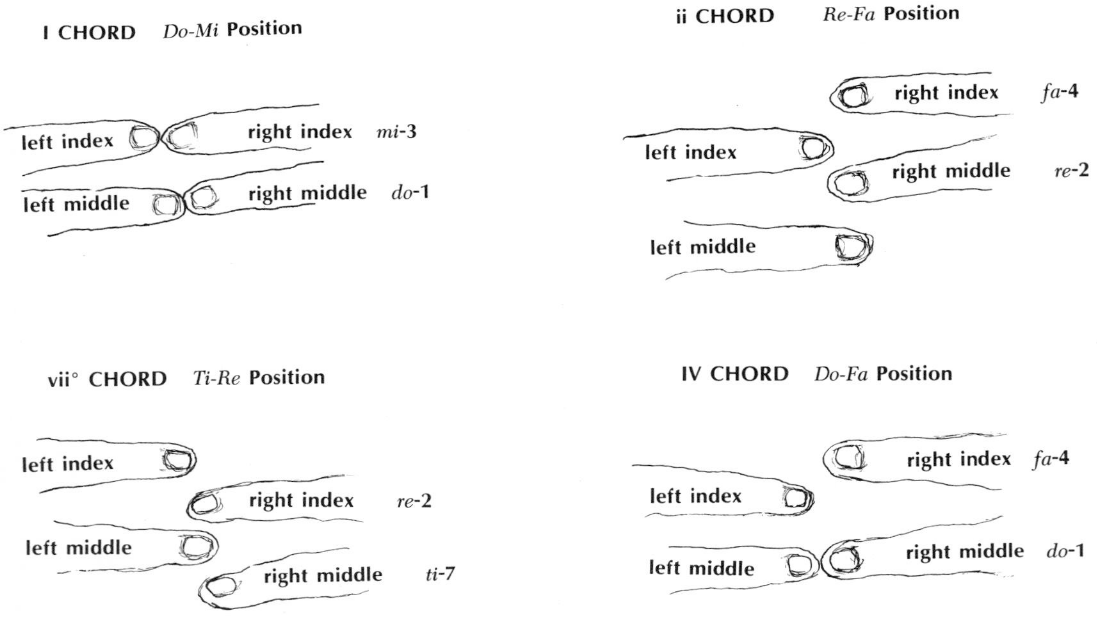

FIGURE 7-13 Finger Harmony

Practice these duads with syllables and scale numbers (1–3, 2–4, 7–2, and 1–4). Chart the numbers and syllables, placing roman numerals under the sequence (see Figure 7-14).

High voice:	3	4	2	3
Low voice:	1	2	7	1
Chord symbols:	I	ii	vii°	I

With Syllables

High voice:	*mi*	*fa*	*re*	*mi*
Low voice:	*do*	*re*	*ti*	*do*

Finally, write the notation for the duads:

FIGURE 7-14 Chord Numbers

To sing a scale round of thirds, direct half the class to delay starting the scale from *do* until the rest have reached its third step (see Figure 7-15).

FIGURE 7-15 Scale in Thirds

After the children have learned "Goodbye, My Lover, Goodbye," ask them to improvise a part a third above the melody by ear, singing the words, then analyzing the improvised new melody by number, syllable, and pitch name. Finally, write a notational chart of the descant melody on the chalkboard, as in Figure 7-16.

A bass part may be added by directing a group of boys to sustain the root tone of each chord as indicated, singing first text, then numbers, syllables, and pitch names. Singing root tones will develop their sense of interval relationships and improve their harmonic intonation, a prerequisite for skill in harmonizing.

Descant with numbers	5	5	5	3	3	5	5	3	3	5	5	5	6	5	4
Duration pattern	—	—	—	—	—	—	—	—	—	—	—	—	—	—	—
Melody line	3	3	3	1	1	3	3	1	1	3	3	3	4	3	2
Descant with syllables	*sol*	*sol*	*sol*	*mi*	*mi*	*sol*	*sol*	*mi*	*mi*	*sol*	*sol*	*sol*	*la*	*sol*	*fa*
Melody with syllables	*mi*	*mi*	*mi*	*do*	*do*	*mi*	*mi*	*do*	*do*	*mi*	*mi*	*mi*	*fa*	*mi*	*re*

GOODBYE, MY LOVER, GOODBYE

Happily, two beats to a measure
Added Descant

College Song

1. The ship is sail - ing down the bay, Good - bye my lov - er good - bye - ; We
2. Tho' now we sad - ly say a - dieu, Good - bye my lov - er good - bye - ; My

1. may not meet for ma - ny a day, Good - bye my lov - er good - bye - ;
2. heart will ever more be true, Good - bye my lov - er good - bye - ;

Bye - low, my ba - by, Bye - low my ba - by ba - by, good - bye my lov - er, good - bye.

Added bass part for boys: With numbers, syllables, and pitch names

Syllables *do, do,* etc.
Numbers 1, 1, etc.
Pitch D, D, etc.

sol
5
A

FIGURE 7-16

Adding a Drone in Open Fifths to Scottish, Indian, and Oriental Songs

Many Scottish, Indian, and Oriental songs lend themselves to rhythmic chanting on open fifths in imitation of the characteristic bagpipe, tom-tom, and koto. The drone of the bagpipe can be imitated by voice, piano, tuned bells, or a bow drawn across two open strings of violin, viola, or cello. The following notation (Figure 7-17, at foot) shows a bagpipe drone on open fifths for either voice, piano, viola, or cello; such a drone could accompany "The Campbells Are Coming."

THE CAMPBELLS ARE COMING*

With spirit   Scottish Folk Song

mf 1. Up - on the Lo - monds I lay, I lay, Up - on the Lo - monds I

lay, I lay, I look - éd down - to bon - nie Loch Lev - en And

saw   three bon - nie   pi - pers play.

Refrain

The Camp - bells are com - ing O - ho, O - ho! The

Camp - bells are com - ing, O - ho, O - ho! The Camp - bells are com - ing to

bon - nie Loch Lev - en The Camp - bells are com - ing, O - ho, O - ho!

*From Music For Young Americans, Book 5, © American Book Company, 1959. Used by permission.

Possible Drones for "Campbells"

FIGURE 7-17

In the Indian song in Figure 7-18, a chant on open fifths lends excitement.

HAPPY SONG*

Chant two-measure introduction and end with two-measure Coda

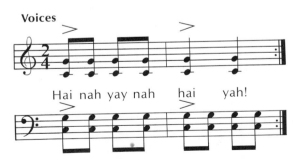

Piano with a large and small drum, rattles, or shakers

FIGURE 7-18

*From Together We Sing, Book 3, Follett Publishing Company, Chicago, Ill., © Janet E. Tobitt, 1955. Used by permission.

In traditional Japanese music a scale that sounds like the Aeolian mode is used in Gagaku, or noble music. The sound of the koto, a Japanese harp of thirteen strings frequently tuned to this scale, can be imitated by plucking the following melody (Figure 7-19) on any stringed instrument. Like much traditional Japanese music, the melody uses only the scale tones without accidentals.

ON YOSHINO MOUNTAIN

On Yo-shi-no moun-tain, far as we can see are the bloom-ing cher-ry

trees, But we don't know what lies be-hind the gray mist that cov-ers all.

Play pizzicato on D and A with first finger, one inch up from the peg box on the fingerboard on violin and viola, two inches up on cello.

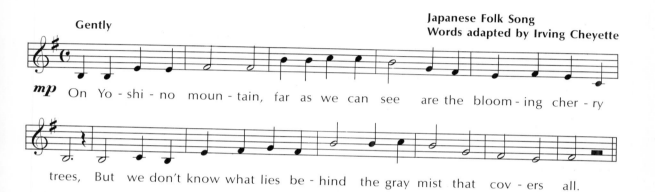

Tuning for Japanese 13-string koto

For the sound of Japanese instruments, play the melody pizzicato on violin with cello drone.

FIGURE 7-19

HAND HARMONIZING TRIADS

The sign language for duads, previously described (p. 148), can now be adapted for triads.[11] Hold both hands toward the class, the middle, ring, and little fingers touching, the index fingers and thumbs curling inwards, as in the mirror image in Figure 7-20.

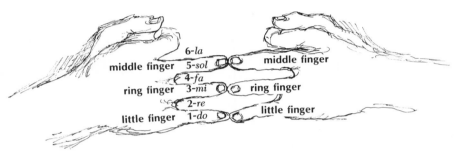

Left-hand fingers stationary, index finger held back by thumb

Right-hand fingers move, index finger held back by thumb

6-la
middle finger   5-sol   middle finger
4-fa
ring finger   3-mi   ring finger
2-re
little finger   1-do   little finger

FIGURE 7-20

Key to Hand Harmonizing

1. Left-hand little finger represents scale step 1 (*Do*)
    a. Space below little finger represents scale step 7 (*Ti*)
    b. Space above little finger represents scale step 2 (*Re*)
2. Ring or second finger represents scale step 3 (*Mi*)
    a. Space above ring finger represents scale step 4 (*Fa*)
3. Middle finger represents scale step 5 (*Sol*)
    a. Space above middle finger represents scale step 6 (*La*)

The left-hand fingers remain stationary; the right-hand fingers move to indicate chords.

Building Chords

Left-hand stationary fingers
Right-hand moving chord fingers

To build a I chord, let the opposite fingers of each hand touch

5   5
3   3
1   1

---

[11] See Irving Cheyette, *Songs for Camp and Campus*, Pro Art Music, Westbury, N.Y., 1960, for further uses of this system.

To build a IV chord, keep the 1 finger in place, move the other two fingers of the right hand up to spaces 4 and 6

6-*la*

4-*la*

1-*do*

To build a V chord, touch the middle fingers (5), move the other two fingers down to 2 and 7

5-*sol*

2-*re*

7-*ti*

To build a II chord, move all three fingers up into spaces 2–4–6

6-*la*

4-*la*

2-*re*

To build a iii chord, touch fingers 3 and 5, move the 1 finger of the right hand down to 7

5   5-*sol*

3   3-*mi*

1   7-*ti*

To build a vi chord, touch fingers 1 and 3, move the 5 finger of the right hand up to space 6

     6-*la*

5

3   3-*mi*

1   1-*do*

Hand Harmonizing Procedure

1. Divide the class into three voice groups: high, middle, and low

2. The high voices react to the movement of the top finger, the middle voices to the movement of the middle finger, and the low voices to the movement of the bottom finger

3. If their finger moves up a space, that voice group sings the next higher scale step; if their finger moves down a space, the voice group sings the next lower scale step; if the finger remains stationary, the voice group sings the same pitch. Practice singing sustained triads, using the chord sequence of any given song. In the key of the song to be harmonized, sing numbers, then syllables, then pitch names.

Humming Choir and Chanting Choir

After the class has sung a sequence of triads satisfactorily using numbers, syllables, and pitch names, ask them to try to imitate the sound of a string orchestra, humming the sequence on a sustained "hnnn" sound, the tongue behind the lower teeth and the lips open. Humming makes the head cavities resonate, thereby focusing the feeling of pitch and creating an acoustic standard toward which the class, as singers, can strive.

Hand Harmonizing Sequence of I, IV, V, I Chords

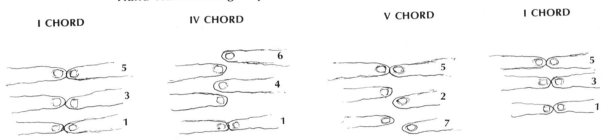

After these exercises, apply the chords to the harmonizing of a song such as "This Old Man," Figure 7-21.

THIS OLD MAN*

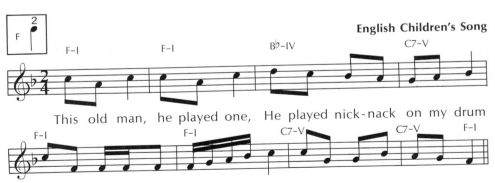

FIGURE 7-21

*From "Singing on Our Way" of Our Singing World Series, ⓒ Ginn and Company, 1949, 1957, 1959. Used by permission.

When a variety of songs have been harmonized in this fashion try some that require minor chords, such as Figure 7-22, "Sweet Betsy from Pike."

SWEET BETSY FROM PIKE

FIGURE 7-22

Songs with I, iii, IV, V7, vi Chords

Before harmonizing "Sweet Betsy from Pike," correlate the letter names of the chords required with the roman numerals of the finger patterns previously explained, directing the practice of the chords by hand signals. Relate chord roman numerals in each new tonality to pitch names, hand signals, scale intervals, and *sol-fa* syllables. Thus this chart might be constructed for the key of C:

		Pattern	Numbers	Syllables	Pitch names
C is I chord	High		5	*sol*	G
	Middle		3	*mi*	E
	Low		1	*do*	C

		Pattern	Numbers	Syllables	Pitch names
	High		5	*sol*	G
G is V chord	**Middle**		2	*re*	D
	Low		7	*ti*	B
			6	*la*	A
Am is vi chord			3	*mi*	E
			1	*do*	C
			5	*sol*	G
Em is iii chord			3	*mi*	E
			7	*ti*	B
			6	*la*	A
F is IV chord			4	*fa*	F
			1	*do*	C
			6	*la*	A
Dm is ii chord			4	*fa*	F
			2	*re*	D

DEVELOPING HARMONIC AWARENESS VOCALLY

After the class has practiced the chord sequence and learned "Sweet Betsy from Pike," choose a few voices to sing the melody while the class tries harmonizing on I chords. Ask the class to raise their hands when and if they think another chord is needed. Experiment, the harmony choir singing chords as the class directs by numbers or syllables, until all are satisfied that a particular chord sequence best harmonizes the song. Write the numbers and notation of the agreed chord sequence, according to the class advice, on the chalkboard as in Figure 7-23.

	High	5	5	5	5	6	5	6	5	5
	Middle	3	2	3	3	4	3	3	2	3
	Low	1	7	1	7	1	1	1	7	1
Add music notation after locating 1 or *do*										
Chord numerals		I	V	I	iii	IV	I	vi	V	I
Pitch names		C	G	C	Em	F	C	Am	G	C

FIGURE 7-23

Take a survey of the feelings and associations evoked by the I, IV, and V (major) and the iii, vi, and ii (minor) chords. Major chords should suggest gaiety and brightness; the minor chords, darkness and sobriety.

Adding Instrumental Color to Voices

Distribute flutophones, melody flutes, soda pop bottles tuned to scale, and other melody instruments capable of providing a harmonic background, each instrumentalist to harmonize "Sweet Betsy from Pike" by ear.

In songs in $\frac{3}{4}$ time, a guitar or banjo accompaniment can be imitated on the autoharp or harmolin by stroking its lowest strings on beat 1 of each measure and strumming its upper strings on beats 2 and 3. The harmony choir can produce a similar effect by the lower voices singing the first beat and the upper voices the others.

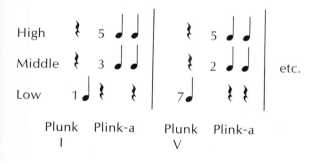

In lieu of the text, ask certain children to sing a chordal chant consisting of a reiterated phrase such as the title of the song.

Rhythm Chant:

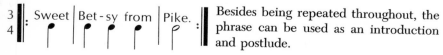

Besides being repeated throughout, the phrase can be used as an introduction and postlude.

MEMORIZING CHORD SEQUENCES FOR MAJOR AND MINOR SCALES IN UPPER GRADES

Ask the children to memorize the following sequences of chords for harmonizing ascending and descending scales.[12] Each chord can be cued by raising the appropriate number of fingers: one finger for a I chord, three fingers for a iii chord, four fingers for a IV chord, etc. The more familiar this sequence becomes, the more readily will the children be able to apply it to all keys. After the sequence has been memorized, many additional drill devices for tone improvement and diction should be tried. (See Chapter 5, "A Song to Remember.")

Ascending Scale

High	*sol* 5	*sol* 5	*sol* 5	*la* 6	*sol* 5	*la* 6	*ti* 7	*do* 8
Middle	*mi* 3	*re* 2	*mi* 3	*fa* 4	*mi* 3	*fa* 4	*sol* 5	*mi* 3
Low	*do* 1	*ti* 7	*do* 1	*do* 1	*do* 1	*do* 1	*re* 2	*do* 1
Chords	I	V	I	IV	I	IV	V	I

Descending Scale

High	*do* 8	*ti* 7	*la* 6	*sol* 5	*la* 6	*sol* 5	*sol* 5	*sol* 5
Middle	*mi* 3	*sol* 5	*fa* 4	*mi* 3	*fa* 4	*mi* 3	*re* 2	*mi* 3
Low	*do* 1	*mi* 3	*do* 1	*do* 1	*do* 1	*do* 1	*ti* 7	*do* 1
Chords	I	iii	IV	I	IV	I	V	I

Transposition by Voices

Try the scale chord sequence in the various major keys of songs the children have learned, in each case converting syllables and numbers into pitch names by referring to the scale ladder of the major scale.

---

[12] Of course this is only one of innumerable possible chord settings. See any book on elementary keyboard harmony, such as Irving Cheyette and Curt Shake, *Basic Piano for Classroom Teachers*, Theodore Presser Company, Bryn Mawr, Pa., 1953.

HARMONIZING THE MINOR SCALE[13]

Ascending Scale

High	mi 3	mi 3	mi 3	fa 4	mi 3	fa 4	si ♯5	la 6
Middle	do 1	ti 7	do 1	re 2	do 1	do 1	mi 3	mi 3
Low	la 6	si ♯5	la 6	la 6	la 6	la 6	ti 7	do 1
Chords	I	V	I	IV	I	VI	V	I
(Major Key)	vi	iii♯3	vi	ii	vi	IV	iii♯	vi

Descending Scale

High	la 6	si ♯5	fa 4	mi 3	fa 4	mi 3	re 2	mi 3
Middle	mi 3	mi 3	do 1	do 1	re 2	do 1	ti 7	do 1
Low	la 6*	ti 7	la 6	la 6	si ♯5	la 6	si ♯5	la 6
Chords	I	V	VI	I	vii°	I	vii°	I
(Major Key)	vi	iii♯3	IV	vi	v°♯	vi	v°♯	vi

As previously noted (p. 139), the chord sequence of a natural minor scale is the progression resulting from commencing with the vi chord of the relative major. Therefore, the hand signals for chords that harmonize the natural minor scale will be the same as those for the appropriate chords of the relative major scale, except the sequence will start with the vi chord of the relative major scale.

Hand Harmonizing for Minor Songs

Finger Patterns

left   **right**

The I chord is built on the sixth scale step of the related major scale and sounds minor (vi)

la 6
mi 3
do 1

[13] As with the major scale, there are many possible chord settings for the minor scale.
*Begin on *la* below *do,* high voice on *la* above *do.*

Finger Patterns

left right

The II chord is built on the seventh scale step of the related major scale and sounds diminished (vii°)

fa 4
re 2
ti 7

The III chord is built on the first step of the related major scale and sounds major (I)

sol 5
mi 3
do 1

The IV chord is built on the second step of the related major scale and sounds minor (ii)

la 6
fa 4
re 2

The V chord is built on the third step of the related major scale and sounds minor in natural minor, but major in the melodic and harmonic minor (iii #3)*

si #5
mi 3
ti 7

The VI chord is built on the fourth step of the related major scale and sounds major (IV)

la 6
fa 4
do 1

Relating Minor Chord Hand Harmonizing to a Song

Look at the song "Erie Canal" (Figure 7-24):

ERIE CANAL†

Rhythmically
I-Dm   IV-Gm   V7-A7   I-Dm
American Folk Song

mf   I've   got   a   mule,   her   name   is   Sal,   Fif - teen   miles   on   the

*The leading tone to the minor tone becomes #5 in the V chord.
†From *Making Music Your Own*, Book 5, © Silver Burdett Company, 1965. Used by permission.

FIGURE 7-24

The key is D Minor, therefore the key signature is that of the related F Major.

	Finger pattern		Syllable	number	Pitch
I Dm (vi of the related major)			*la*	6	D
			mi	3	A
			do	1	F
V A (iii of the related major with #5)			*si*	#5	C#
			mi	3	A
			ti	7	E
III F (I of the related major)			*sol*	5	C
			mi	3	A
			do	1	F
VI Bb (IV of the related major)			*la*	6	D
			fa	4	Bb
			do	1	F

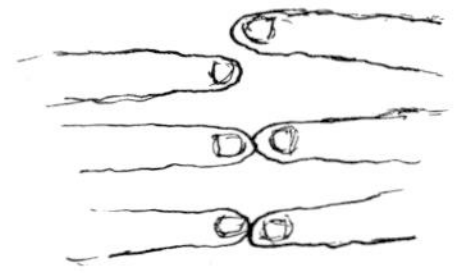

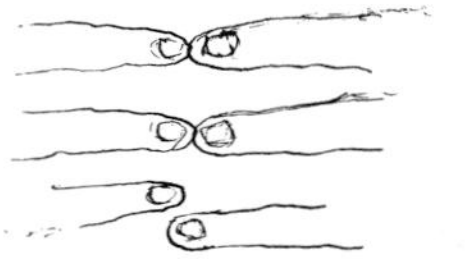

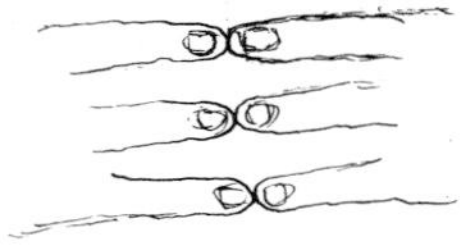

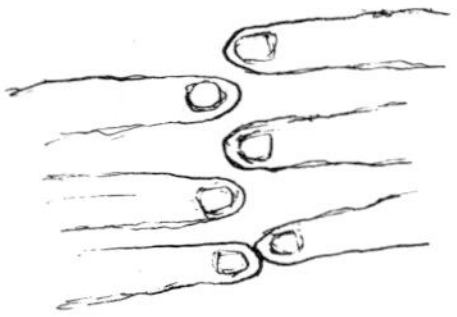

Practice the chords, dividing the class into range groups, each group following its part as directed by the movement of the appropriate finger in the sequence of chord signals. Chart the chords, the class furnishing chord, syllable, step, and pitch names.

Chords in D Minor											
6-*la*	6-*la*	6-*la*	5-*sol*	6-*la*	6-*la*	6-*la*	6-*la*	6-*la*	♯5-*sol*	6-*la*
3-*mi*	4-*fa*	3-*mi*	3-*mi*	4-*fa*	3-*mi*	4-*fa*	3-*mi*	3-*mi*	3-*mi*	3-*mi*
1-*do*	2-*re*	1-*do*	1-*do*	1-*do*	1-*do*	2-*re*	1-*do*	1-*do*	7-*ti*	1-*do*
I	IV	I	III	VI	I	IV	I	I	V	I

| Related Major | vi | ii | vi | I | IV | vi | ii | vi | vi | iii♯3 | vi |

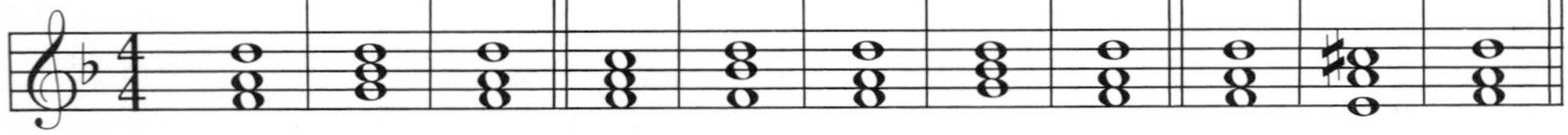

FIGURE 7-25

Eventually let the class attempt barbershop harmony, using chord chants, bass line additions, and descant following the procedures previously suggested for harmonizing in the major keys.

Tone bells, xylophones, Swiss bells, water glasses, bottle chimes, melody flutes, and recorders may all be added as instrumental coloring to reinforce the intonation of the voices. The autoharp provides an especially easy method of adding instrumental harmony.

If a string bass, cello, or viola are available, plucking their open strings in appropriate keys will make an excellent bass.[14]

SUMMARY

Sense of harmony is readily developed by activities proceeding from ear to voice to eye. The sequence of such activities should parallel the historical evolution of harmony: plain song; melody accompanied by a drone; melody accompanied by an organ-point chant; antiphonal song, group chanting and singing; organum in fifths; canonic imitation; combined melodies (polyphony); improvised descants; harmonizing in thirds; melodies accompanied by triads and sevenths.

The I, IV, and V7 chords possess universal appeal, as illustrated by their use as an accompaniment in folk music of all Western cultures.

A keener appreciation of the creative efforts of composers should result from direct experience working with harmonic materials.

[14] Cf. Chapter 8, Developing the Classroom Orchestra.

CHAPTER EIGHT

DEVELOPING A CLASSROOM ORCHESTRA

Nothing motivates greater musical interest than the desire to acquire instrumental skills. Obviously, to organize and direct instrumental activity, the teacher must possess some basic skills himself. At the very least he must know how to make, perform, and teach the simple homemade and manufactured instruments discussed in this chapter. Although there is no harm in being a virtuoso, the instrumental techniques required do not demand hours of laborious practice. A little effort should result in sufficient ability to accompany singing and rhythmic play.

One of the best ways to initiate interest is to bring older children to play instruments for the lower grades. The sight and sound of the instrument and the youth of the performer will impress upon the younger child that he too may someday similarly perform.

If possible, ask the student performers to play familiar melodies the class can accompany. Most elementary music series include transposed instrumental parts to accompany occasional songs. Non-transposing instruments such as violins, flutes, oboes, recorders, melody flutes, tonettes, flutophones, mouth harmonica, and melodica, can play directly from songbooks without special parts. If there are several instruments, ask the class to try to identify each by its sound without looking. Drawing pictures of instruments in music notebooks with appropriate captions, or pasting cut-outs, will provide a reference for future concerts. Comparing the youthful performance with a professional recording of the same work provides a means of stimulating critical standards.

OBJECTIVES FOR A CLASSROOM ORCHESTRA OF HOMEMADE AND MANUFACTURED STRING, WIND, AND PERCUSSION INSTRUMENTS REQUIRING SIMPLE TECHNIQUES

1. Enriching concepts of tone: by adding instrumental, rhythmic, contrapuntal, and harmonic accompaniment to their own voices, the class gains insight into the elements of musical sound: timbre, volume, duration, consonance, and dissonance

2. Muscular coordination: instrumental performance demands conscious and reflexive coordination to sense and communicate rhythm, to place and maintain pitch by fingering, embouchure, and kinesthetic control

3. Reading comprehension: to produce pitch and rhythm accurately from notation demands the ability to associate a given symbol with previous aural and kinesthetic experience

4. Scientific correlation: an orchestra provides opportunity for children to discover the physical principles on which musical instruments are based: the effect of the length, density, and tension of a string on pitch; the relationship of the length of a confined column of air to pitch; the effect of the strength of stroke and density of material on percussion dynamics; the mathematical relations of fundamental and partial tones

5. Discovering talent: some children possess talent, others do not. The same may be said of teachers

6. Cooperation: ensemble participation develops social as well as musical skills[1]

SUGGESTED PROCEDURES FOR TEACHING TONETTE, FLUTO-PHONE, AND OTHER SIMPLE PIPES

Explain the mechanics of the instrument by showing the class the correct position of the hands, the numbering system of holes and corresponding fingering; the syllabic and alphabetic names of each pitch produced within its range; and finally the relationship of the range of the instrument to the music staff. Create large posters similar to Figure 8-1 and the figures that follow.

1. Sing a song employing few notes. "Merrily We Roll Along" has only three.

2. Demonstrate the fingering of the melody while singing, as a substitute for

[1]"Casals speaks of the orchestra and of the soloists . . . as 'the family'—a confraternity of kindred souls . . . it is not a democracy, but rather is it a tyranny. Casals' authority is rarely questioned and it is exercised in an atmosphere of mutual respect and understanding." Bernard Taper, "A Cellist in Exile," *The New Yorker*, February 24, 1962, p. 97.

MERRILY WE ROLL ALONG

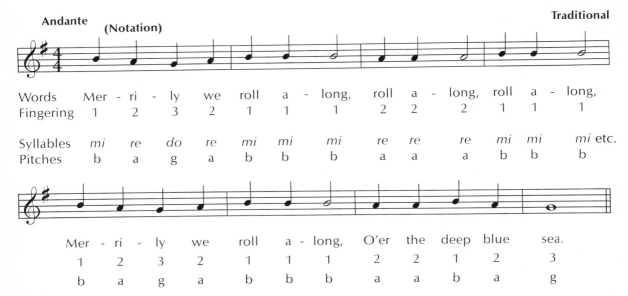

FIGURE 8-1

the text, (a) fingering number; (b) *sol-fa* syllables; (c) pitch names; and (d) rhythm names; that is, quarter, quarter, etc.

3. As the class attempts to play the melody, point on successive repetitions to the finger numbering, pitch name, and notation on the chart. (In instrumental classes, always intersperse ensemble performance with solo instruction. To help soloists maintain rhythm, ask the class to accompany by singing pitch name or fingering number.)

4. Practice rhythmic patterns by singing, playing, and verbally reading their notation. The learning sequence—from voice to hand to eye; from hearing to playing to seeing—is the most efficient method of teaching instrumental skills.

5. Transpose the key of the melody on successive repetitions so as to include the instrument's entire range. For instance, begin "Merrily We Roll Along" on C in A Minor, then on D in the Locrian mode.[2] Transposing the melody into major and minor keys will demonstrate differences in modality.

6. After the melody as transposed has been mastered, attempt to play the range of the instrument (from high D to low C in the case of the tonette or flutophone). Play various songs employing the full range. In each case, before playing, have the class finger the melody as described in paragraph 2 above. (A fingering chart for pipe instruments occurs later in this chapter, p. 173.)

[2]See Chapter 6, p. 130, "Counting Song."

SIMPLE WIND INSTRUMENTS

Pop Bottle Band

Figure 8-2 shows a series of pop bottles filled to produce a tuned scale. The arrow indicates the approximate length of the air column inside each bottle, and the horizontal line the approximate water level.

FIGURE 8-2

Before teaching the simple wind instruments, illustrate the principle of resonators by creating a scale of tuned pop bottles (wash them well before using).

1. Place eight empty pop bottles in a row

2. Tune the bottles to a C scale by adding water with a watering can or small spout teapot. Blow across the mouth of the bottle, its edge being placed under the lower lip, to determine if it resonates at the desired pitch. A little practice is required to produce a tone

3. When the complete bottle scale is tuned, tape the number of the scale step or the pitch name to each bottle

4. Let various children attempt to blow tones

5. Set up a tuning committee with a circulating membership of two children to tune the scale before each music class

6. Use the bottles in the same fashion as tone bells, each child with a bottle blowing his tone in the proper time and rhythm in appropriate sequence during the performance of a song

7. For song accompaniment in Grades 5 and 6, combine bottles 1–3–5 to blow a I chord, 4–6–8 to blow a IV chord, and 5–7–2–4 to blow a V7 chord

The children will discover that the higher the tone, the smaller the amount of water and corresponding change in air column required to alter pitch. This is because the air column in the bottle vibrates geometrically, rather than merely arithmetically, faster when confined in a shorter and narrower area. Similarly, on string instruments, the higher the pitch, the shorter the distance between stops.[3] The sound of a bottle band is similar to that of the old circus steam calliope.

Common or Transverse Flute (Fife)

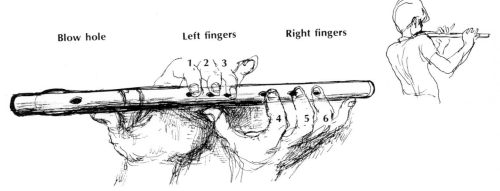

Blow hole   Left fingers   Right fingers

Its range is eleven tones (D to G) in the scale of D Major

Note: Octave tones are overblown. To produce high D (fourth line) leave the first finger hole open, closing all other fingers. Models for making transverse flutes may be purchased in many of the five-and-dime department stores.

FIGURE 8-3

The wind whistles and moans as it passes over sharp-edged rocks or hollow reeds and logs. A man can produce a similar sound by blowing against the edge of a sharp or hollow object. Imitating the wind, ancient man discovered how to produce sound by blowing across the end of a simple hollow tube. The descendant of that tube is the glorious modern instrument—the flute, a mechanical marvel of keys, springs, and pads, capable of producing music of whirlwind rapidity.[4]

[3] Ferguson, Donald N., *A History of Musical Thought,* Appleton-Century-Crofts, Inc., New York, 1959, p. 189.
[4] *Ibid.,* p. 186. See also "Lucretius, *De Rerum Natura,*" in *The Stoic and Epicurean Philosophers,* p. 148, Modern Library, New York, trans. H. A. J. Munro: ". . . The country people hearing far and wide, what time Pan, nodding the piny covering of his head half a beast's, oft runs over the gaping reeds with curved lip, making the pipe without ceasing to pour forth its woodland song." See also Ernle Bradford, *Ulysses Found,* Harcourt, Brace and World, Inc., New York, 1963, Chapter 18.

Children will discover that producing a tone on a simple transverse flute is as easy as producing a tone by blowing across the neck of a soda pop bottle. These flutes have a range from D below to G above the staff in the key of D Major.

The Shepherd's Pipe

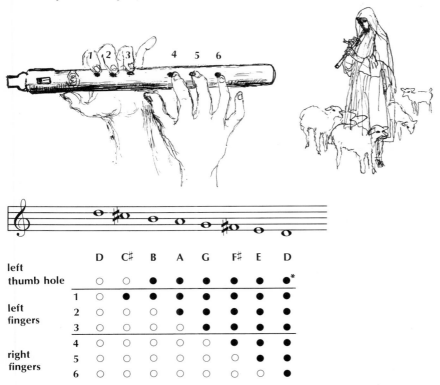

		D	C♯	B	A	G	F♯	E	D
left thumb hole		○	○	●	●	●	●	●	●*
left fingers	1	○	●	●	●	●	●	●	●
	2	○	○	○	●	●	●	●	●
	3	○	○	○	○	●	●	●	●
right fingers	4	○	○	○	○	○	●	●	●
	5	○	○	○	○	○	○	●	●
	6	○	○	○	○	○	○	○	●

Note: The shepherd's pipe is built in the key of D Major.

FIGURE 8-4

From immemorial times, shepherds have played simple pipes to quiet their flocks and pass the hours. It has been assumed that the earliest pipes had but one hole, and the first melody was probably an attempt to imitate the song of the cuckoo, an interval of a falling third.[5] Three-hole pipes may still be found among primitive peoples.[6] Shepherd's pipes with six holes in front and a thumb hole in back are the forerunners of the recorders and the whole gamut of plastic and steel tube pipes now produced for school use.

[5]Claiborne, Robert W., *The Way Man Learned Music,* Haddon Craftsmen Press, Camden, N.J., 1927, p. 22.
[6]*Ibid.,* p. 28.
*An open circle indicates hole to be left open; a filled circle, hole to be covered by one finger.

Pandean Pipes (Pipes of Pan)

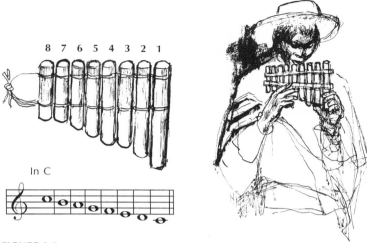

FIGURE 8-5

The invention of the Pipes of Pan is attributed to the Greek god Pan, god of the woods and mountains, and protector of shepherds. The pipes are considered by music historians to be among the most ancient instruments.[7] Instead of placing several holes in one pipe to produce various tones, individual pipes are bound together, each sounding a different pitch of the scale and each higher pitch requiring a shorter tube.

Pipes may be built in any desired key. Blowing obliquely across the open end of the pipe, much like blowing across the open end of a soda pop bottle, produces tone.

Melody Wind Instruments

[7] Ferguson, *op. cit.,* pp. 188–192. See also footnote 4, this chapter, p. 170.

		D	C#	C	B	Bb	A	Ab	G	F#	F		E	Eb	D	C#	C
left thumb		O	O	●	●	●	●	●	●	●	●		●	●	●	●	●
left fingers	1	O	●		●	●	●	●	●	●	●		●	●	●	●	●
	2	O				O	●	●	●	●	●		●	●	●	●	●
	3	O			●			O	●	●	●		O	●	●	●	●
right fingers	4	O						●		O	●		●	●	●	●	●
	5	O								●			●	●	●	●	●
	6	O												O	●	●	●
	7	O											●		◑		●

FIGURE 8-6 **Fingering Chart for Flutophone, Tonette, Song Flute, Ocarina**

The most commonly used simple wind instruments in the schools are the tonette, song flute, flutophone, melody flute, and, with increasing popularity and richer tone color, the soprano recorder. The fingering for these melody wind instruments is almost uniform, except that the recorder and melody flute have a pitch range of two octaves rather than the ninth of the others.

The mouth harmonica is a reed instrument still very popular with upper elementary grade children. The melodica is a comparative newcomer to the schools and is described under its illustration (p. 205). Fingering charts for all these instruments will be found in this chapter.

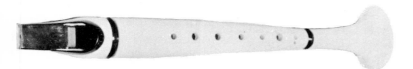

Tonette

Flutophone

Song Flute

FIGURE 8-7 *(Courtesy of Peripole, Inc.)*

Melody Flute in C or in D

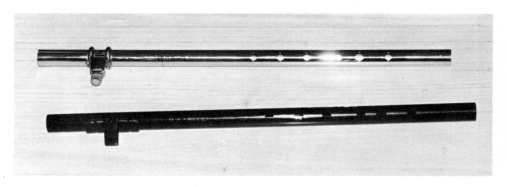

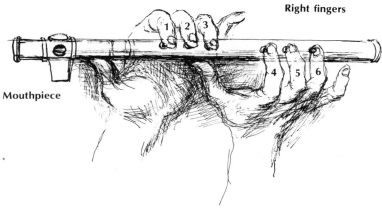

FIGURE 8-8 **Fingering Chart for Melody Flute**

Blow very easily for tones in the lower octave and only a little harder to play the upper octave.

HOMEMADE INSTRUMENTS

FIGURE 8-9

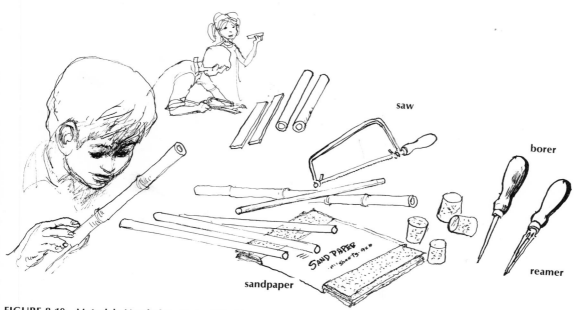

saw

borer

reamer

sandpaper

FIGURE 8-10 Materials Needed to Make Wind Instruments

Obtain:

1. Half-inch bamboo garden stakes in sufficient quantity to make the instruments desired
2. Dowel sticks ($\frac{1}{2}$ in. in diameter) for end plugs
3. Corks, which may be purchased in hardware shops
4. A fine saw
5. A borer
6. A reamer
7. Sandpaper

With these materials, and specifications from the Educational Department of Peripole, Inc., it is possible to make a transverse flute, a shepherd's pipe, and Pipes of Pan.[8] To produce pitches from G below the staff to E (first line) on the Pipes of Pan, 8-inch tubes are needed; for tones from F (first space) to F (fifth line), 5-inch tubes. Corks and end plugs fit in each pipe. Use cord to bind the pipes together.

In lieu of providing your own materials, "musikits" and "sound kits" can be procured from Peripole. As Figure 8-9 above indicates it is also possible to secure materials for making cigar-box ukuleles, xylophones, bongo drums, tub and conga drums, and larger instruments (see Chapter 9).

Along with the materials, the manufacturer provides directions for construction. A word of caution: try to obtain a completed instrument to use as a standard for the one being constructed.

FIGURE 8-11   Musical Water Glasses

[8]*Musikits and Sound Kits,* Peripole, Inc., 51–17 Rockaway Beach Blvd., Far Rockaway, N.Y., 11691, and also Marcelle Vernazza, *Making and Playing Classroom Instruments,* Fearon Publishers, Inc., 828 Valencia Street, San Francisco 10, Calif., 1959.

Younger children will enjoy playing tuned water glasses by striking the top of the glass with a teaspoon or wooden xylophone mallet. Glasses are tuned like pop bottles, except that the greater the amount of water the lower the pitch. To make the scale, tune bottom *do* to middle C on the piano, then relate *re* and *mi*. When the class understands the principles involved, add glasses for the remainder.

Indicate the scale number, *sol-fa* syllable, and pitch name of each tone by either water paint or gummed label. A drop of blue in the water of pitch 1, green or yellow in 3, and red in 5 makes a I chord easily identifiable. Generally, use large glasses for the lower pitch and smaller glasses for the higher, taking density of glass into account. A little experimentation will make children expert in arranging a scale. Organize a tuning committee with a circulating membership to tune the glasses before music class, or else create a permanent scale to be part of each grade's music corner.

MANUFACTURED RHYTHM INSTRUMENTS

The list following Figure 8-12 provides helpful suggestions for playing various rhythm instruments. Each number in the list corresponds to the number of the appropriate instrument in the figure. Companies manufacturing the instruments are listed in Appendix I.

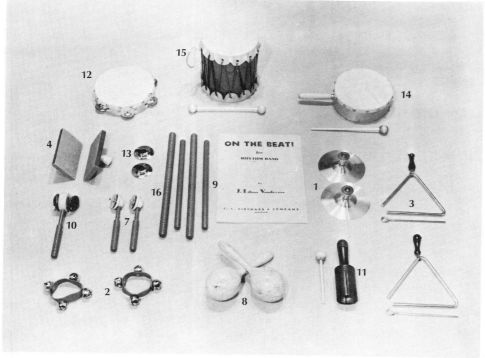

FIGURE 8-12 (*Courtesy of Peripole, Inc.*)

1. *Brass cymbals:* Strike together lightly with a sidewise motion. Crash as needed for accent
2. *Sleigh bells:* Shake with the right hand in pulse or melodic rhythm
3. *Triangle:* Play rapid trills on the arch, single tones on the lower bar
4. *Sandpaper blocks:* Scrape together in pulse or melodic rhythm
5. *Swiss bells* (not shown): Swing backward and forward
6. *Clapper* (not shown): Shake rapidly in a forward-backward motion for sustained tones, once for a single tone
7. *Clog:* Hold in a vertical position in the right hand, striking the palm of the left hand with the clog head
8. *Maracas:* Hold one in each hand, shake to fast rhythms
9. *Rhythm sticks:* Hold in each hand, striking tips together
10. *Castanets:* Hold in the right hand and strike against the left palm for a single stroke, or shake in desired rhythm
11. *Wood block:* Tap with mallet for pulse or melodic rhythm
12. *Tambourine:* Shake with the right hand for sustained tones. For single tones, strike with the knuckles of the left-hand fingers
13. *Finger cymbals:* Wear on the thumb and middle finger and strike together
14. *Hand drum:* Hold in the left hand and strike with either a stick or with the knuckles of the right-hand fingers
15. *Tom-tom:* Play similarly to the hand drum, striking with either a mallet or the knuckles of the right hand
16. *Corrugated rhythm sticks:* Play by rubbing against each other or tapping

Ask the children to suggest how the sound effects provided by these instruments should be employed for song and dance accompaniment. Other suggestions for their use in creative activities will be found in Chapters 4 and 9.

MANUFACTURED MELODIC PERCUSSION INSTRUMENTS

An orchestra of simply played melodic percussion instruments greatly increases the children's interest in learning to read music.

Individual Tone Bells: Resonator or Swiss

Bells, set on resonating boxes and arranged in a chromatic scale, help to develop pitch and rhythm sense. A set of tuned resonator bells usually consists of either twenty bell bars, each on an individual resonator box, to be played by a group of children, or a glockenspiel arranged chromatically to be played by one child. In sets with separate bars only those required should be removed from the case.

Distribute individual bells to eight children to form a scale octave. After each child has sung his bell's pitch, ask the class to sing a musical phrase from a familiar melody by numbers and syllables. The bell players should then attempt to play the phrase. Start with two-tone motives, then gradually expand the number of tones. When the class has developed some expertise, let children attempt to locate the phrase in

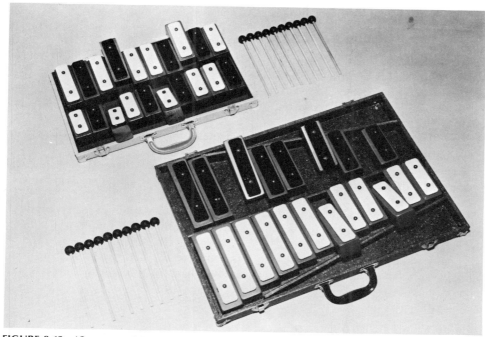

FIGURE 8-13 (*Courtesy of Peripole, Inc.*)

the song score from which it was taken. Once the players learn their bell's scale step number, they can identify its sound by number and syllable, as melodies are learned, and provide instrumental accompaniment.

At the side of the chalkboard, string a set of tone bells together by a piece of cord. Next to the bells draw a chart of scale numbers and syllable letters as in Figure 8-14.

Numbers   **Bells**

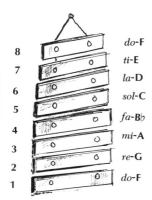

8 *do*-F
7 *ti*-E
6 *la*-D
5 *sol*-C
4 *fa*-B♭
3 *mi*-A
2 *re*-G
1 *do*-F

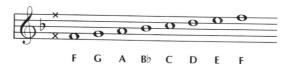

F   G   A   B♭   C   D   E   F

FIGURE 8-14   Scale in F

1. Sing melodic motives with a neutral syllable. One child should then attempt to play the motives, singing numbers, syllables, and pitch names on successive repetitions.

2. If a flannel board with a music staff is available, ask another child to notate each motive by placing note heads on the staff.

3. Using other bells selected from the case, see if a third child can construct a scale in another key and write the appropriate sequence of pitch names on the board.

4. If an Electronic Music Board is available, ask the child to write the pitch names on it, so that an immediate playback is available (see Appendix I).

If bells are set in I, IV, and V7 chord arrangements, cue the respective players by merely holding up the number of fingers corresponding to the chord desired (see below).

For ear training, match vocal pitch to bell, or let the class attempt to play motives by ear. Bells are especially useful as a means of participation for the child who cannot sing satisfactorily.

Bells come in various sizes. Large sets comprise the octave and a fifth, from middle C to G above the staff. Smaller sets, about half the price of the larger ones, contain the octave commencing on middle C.

Building Chord Bells

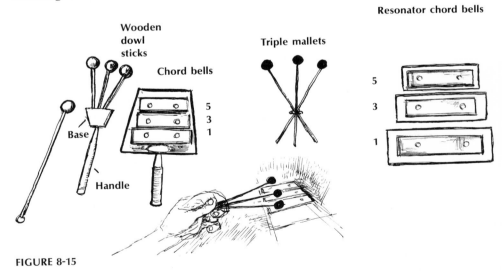

FIGURE 8-15

Bells in tonic (1–3–5), dominant (5–7–2), and subdominant (4–6–8) triads may be constructed in any key by tying tone bars together to a rack with string, or by fastening resonator bells together with strong rubber bands. To play the chord, place a rubber band at the center of the handles of three mallets whose heads are spread to the distance needed (as in Figure 8-15 above). The children can make triple mallets and chord racks in shop class.

Chords may also be played by asking different children to simultaneously strike the appropriate bells. Apply the suggestions for harmony choirs found in Chapter 7 (p. 147) in this way.

Tuned Swiss Bells

F   G   A   B♭   C   D   E   F

FIGURE 8-16 (*Courtesy of Peripole, Inc.*)

These delightful individual bells in sets consisting of an octave in the key of F are designed to permit younger children to perform on instruments comparable to tuned resonator bells. Besides being imprinted with both scale number and pitch name, each bell is a different color, corresponding to the color of the note and number of the pitch in a special music book. Thus, by pairing color, nursery and kindergarten children can recognize their cues even before they can read, the vivid correlation of color, pitch, and number making tangible the idea of melodic sequence.

All procedures suitable for individual tone resonator bells can be applied to Swiss bells as well. Swiss bells provide chord accompaniments in the following combinations:

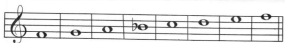

I   IV   V7
F   B♭   C7

"Build a Tune" Tone Bars

FIGURE 8-17

These music building blocks consist of metal bars in eight different colors, each color denoting a different step of the octave of a major key. The child arranges the bars on a rack by copying the color sequence of a colored melody sheet. Playing the bars from left to right produces the melody. Encourage the child to experiment in constructing new tone sequences, and to record them in crayon, using the manufacturer's music sheets as a model. The tone bars are packed in a fitted, slotted box so that they may be quickly identified and easily withdrawn. Installed in a classroom music corner, tone bars will help children develop ability to discriminate pitch.

Key to Figure 8-18

1. *One-octave Diatonic Song Bells:* Diatonic song bells consist of bars (1 inch wide) comprising an octave in the key of C, played with hard mallets, widely spaced so that children can find and strike the bars easily.

2. *Diatonic Bells of Wider Range* (not shown): Tuned from C to G above the staff in the key of C, these bells increase the class's reading ability by permitting obbligatos and descants beyond the range of the voice.

3. *Chromatic Bells:* Chromatic bells whose arrangement of black and white bars duplicates an octave and major third on the piano keyboard provide greater key flexibility than diatonic bells. Some sets have tone bars, others are equipped with a resonator box. Others, using marimba tubes, play an octave lower.

4. *Wide Range Chromatic Bells:* These have a range of an octave and fifth.

Key to Figure 8-19

1. *Diatonic Stair Bells:* A staircase frame conveys concepts of high and low. Each bar is stamped with pitch name and scale step number, some sets coloring the steps differently as well.

2. *Chromatic Stair Bells:* These bells include the chromatic octave scale, making modulations possible in all keys.

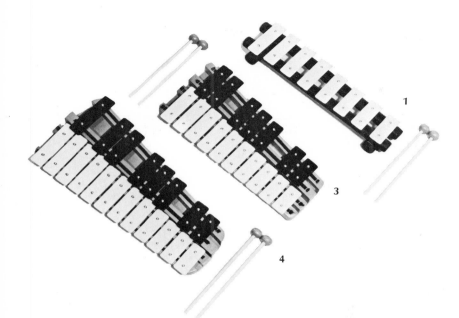

FIGURE 8-18   (*Courtesy of Peripole, Inc.*)

FIGURE 8-19   (*Courtesy of Peripole, Inc.*)

Xylophones

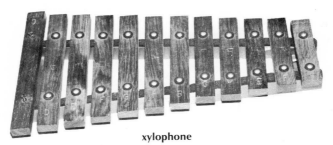

xylophone

FIGURE 8-20

Diatonic and chromatic xylophones are available in the same ranges as song bells. Although pitch letter is imprinted, numbering the bars from 1 to 8 in chalk reinforces the relationship of pitch name to number and facilitates locating melodies learned by number.

Melody Chimes

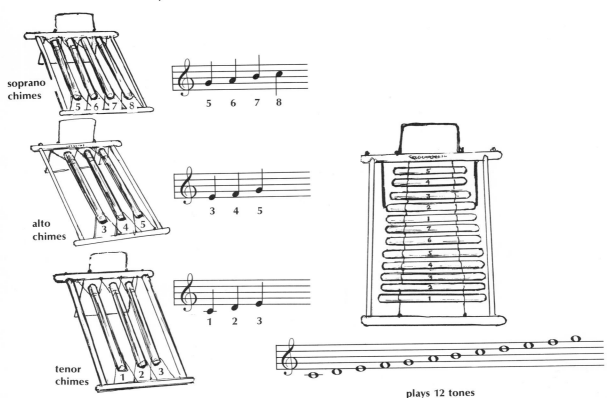

plays 12 tones

FIGURE 8-21

Another form of tubular bell, melody chimes, is sold in three- and four-tone sets, in octaves and octaves-and-fifths, and in chromatic scales. Simple melodies can be played on the three- or four-tone chimes by combining the soprano, alto, and tenor sets into full scales, a different child playing each set. Thus one child should play bells 1, 2, 3; another bells 3, 4, 5; and a third bells 5, 6, 7, 8. After the class has sung the numbers of the tones of the scale while the players accompany by striking their bells in sequence, let a similar attempt be made with a familiar melody. Locating melodic sequence on the bells should not be too difficult if the melody has been learned by number as well as by text.

THE STRING FAMILY: THE PRINCIPLE OF VIBRATION AND RESONANCE

In primary grades, try making simple string instruments by stretching rubber bands of differing widths lengthwise around various-sized juice cans, one end of which is open. When the band is plucked at the open end, the can will resonate.

If the children stretch a rubber band (approximately $\frac{1}{8}$ in. in diameter) along the length of a small can (to permit play in the rubber band), they will discover that tightening heightens pitch. With a little practice, the children should be able to graduate tension to play a scale. By adding different sized rubber bands to the same can, they can create a tuned scale that illustrates the effect of size and material on resonance and dynamic intensity.

Convert a small open cardboard box, wooden cigar box, or pint-sized milk carton into a resonator. The class will recognize the effect of tension, length and thickness of string, and resonating medium, on loudness and timbre.

INITIAL PROCEDURES FOR TEACHING AUTOHARP, FRETTED STRING INSTRUMENTS, AND PIANO IN CLASS

1. Acquaint the children with the mechanics of the instrument: where to put the hands, how to strum or strike strings or keys

2. Notate the chords most frequently used in accompaniment on a permanent poster visible to the entire class

3. Practice playing the chords on the instrument

4. Practice the rhythmic swing of the accompaniment (is it a pulse of twos or threes?), and strum or strike accordingly

5. Choose a song to sing, adding the instrumental accompaniment

The Autoharp

The autoharp resembles the sounding board of the grand piano and zither. Above bass and treble strings tuned chromatically, a crossbar contains a series of bars and buttons lettered according to chord. To play, select a chord by depressing the appropriate

FIGURE 8-22 The Autoharp (*Courtesy of Peripole, Inc.*)

button with the left hand, then strum with the fingernails of the right hand, or a felt or plastic plectrum. Music for the autoharp will usually contain chord letters above the text.

The five-button autoharp contains the C, G7, F, C7, and B♭ chords. The chords of the twelve-button autoharp, sufficient to accompany songs in a wide variety of keys, are as follows:

Major Chords	Minor Chords	Seventh Chords
B♭	Gm	A7
F	Dm	C7
C	Am	E7
G		G7
		D7

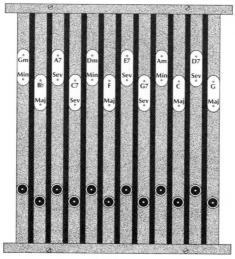

FIGURE 8-23 Autoharp[9] (Twelve-chord Practice)

[9] Practice charts for class use are available in quantity from National Autoharp Sales, 560 31st, Des Moines, Iowa. They are also found in the back inside covers of the This Is Music Series, Allyn and Bacon, Inc., Boston, and in the autoharp accompaniments of the Birchard Music Series.

The Psaltery

FIGURE 8-24   The Psaltery

The psaltery is a zither-type instrument that resembles an autoharp without bar or chord buttons. Tuned chromatically in two or more octaves, melodies may be played in any key. The melody is plucked with a plectrum held between the index finger and thumb of the right hand, while the instrument rests on either the lap or a desk. Usually the pitch name of each note will appear imprinted at the bottom of the psaltery under its respective string, the string being easily tuned by a key that turns the tuning pegs to which the strings are attached. Chords may also be plucked by the fingers of the right hand as on a harp. Easily mastered, with a sound similar to the harpsichord, the psaltery is especially popular in the southern Appalachians. Like another plectrum instrument, the rectangular dulcimer, it will frequently be found providing accompaniment for folk music.[10]

THE FRETTED STRING INSTRUMENTS

Simple chording is easily learned on the fretted instruments: ukulele, banjo, guitar, and mandolin. These instruments are especially useful in teaching since skill in their performance transfers readily to the bowed string instruments: violin, viola, cello, and bass.

The ukulele is small enough to be introduced in both its forms (the two-string melody and four-string chording ukuleles) in the third grade. The less manageable mandolin, banjo, and guitar should await the physical maturity of children in the upper grades.

Procedure for Teaching the Fretted String Instruments

1. Demonstrate proper position: the instrument is held against the body by the right forearm and stroked with the right hand, a felt plectrum being used on the ukulele, a plastic one on the banjo, guitar, and mandolin.

[10] The psaltery, one of the most popular of Elizabethan instruments, is frequently mentioned in the King James Version of the Bible (cf. Psalm 108; the words "psalm" and "psaltery" are derived from the same Greek root). It is not the only Elizabethan tradition preserved in Appalachia. See A. J. Toynbee, *A Study of History*, abridged D. C. Somervell, Oxford University Press, Fair Lawn, N.J., 1947, pp. 148–149.

2. Demonstrate tuning the instrument.

3. Illustrate 2 large posters—the first showing the range of the instrument in relation to its fretboard, the second a chord chart (see appropriate charts below). Demonstrate that pitch can be raised by stopping strings between frets with the fingers of the left hand. Shifting the fingers successive frets toward the player shortens the string and raises the pitch. Call attention to the correlation between the familiar scale ladder and the fretted fingerboard, each fret stop changing pitch a half step.

4. Harmonize a suitable song by a I chord, pointing on the chord chart to its location on the fretboard. Teachers usually start in the key of G on the ukulele, mandolin, and guitar, and in the key of C on the tenor banjo. By reference to fingering diagrams, most chords can be easily mastered.

5. Using the same procedure, add the V7 chord of the same key. Introduce new chords gradually, each with a new song and separate diagrams of its fingering.

6. Make a series of diagrams showing the fingering of the I, IV, and V7 chords in the keys of C, F, G, and D Major, and perhaps in D and G Minor, the chords most frequently used to harmonize songs sung in school. (To simplify the technical problems of changing key, use a tuning bar, which enables the player to use the same finger pattern for all keys, the bar changing the key to which the instrument is tuned.)

Peripole Duobass

FIGURE 8-25   *(Courtesy of Peripole, Inc.)*

This simple instrument has been designed to enable children to use a string instrument without requiring them to solve difficult technical problems. About 5 feet high, it has two strings capable of being pitched in combinations of D up to G, G to C, or C to F, *sol-do* being a standard interval for bass strings. The playing range of each string is an octave. Like other string instruments, intervals are measured by depressing a string above a given fret, each successive fret by which the length of a string is reduced raising the pitch a half step. If both strings of an instrument, pitched as indicated above, are stopped at the same fret, either by use of the fingers or a sliding bar (*capo*), the standard 1:4 bass note interval will be produced in the key of the fret.

The duobass is meant to be played *pizzicato* (by plucking) rather than *arco* (by a bow), and constitutes the bass section of the classroom orchestra. Suitable for melodic and countermelodic accompaniments as well as percussive rhythms on bass chord roots, it is also ideal for demonstrating the principle of the fingerboard and the effect on pitch of length, tension, and thickness of string.

The Two-string Ukulele or Pianolin

FIGURE 8-26   The Pianolin

The chart below is for a D scale. The Pianolin can also be tuned to C and G for a C scale, using the same fingering.

Chromatic Syllables					Fingering Pitch					D Major Scale				
Scale Ladder						**Frets**								
Low *do*	D	A	*sol*		Open *do*	D	A	*sol*		*do* Open D	A *sol*			Open
di			*si*		1 *di* D♯		A♯	*si*						
re			*la*		1 *re* E		B	*la*		*re* 1 E	B	*la*		1
ri			*li*		2 *ri* F		C	*li*						
mi			*ti*		♯2 *mi* F♯		C♯	*ti*		*mi* 2 F♯	C♯	*ti*		2
fa			*do*		3 *fa* G		D	*do*		*fa* 3 G	D	*do*		3
fi			*di*		♯3 *fi* G♯		D♯	*di*						

Like violins and violas, the strings of the ukulele are tuned a fifth apart, C and G to produce a C scale, or D and A to produce a D scale, the fretboard being of sufficient length to permit a chromatic octave to be played on each string. As with the other fretted string instruments, each fret constitutes a half step of the scale. To dampen, depress the string in the space above the fret desired. Strings are plucked by a felt plectrum or the right thumb. Playing a chromatic octave on a string is a convenient way to demonstrate scale construction, especially if the class sings along repeating the scale with syllables, fingering numbers and pitch names. Relating a scale ladder diagram to the fretboard will make evident that the board is only a scale ladder on which strings have been stretched. Comparable fingerboards are found on the mandolin, guitar, banjo, violin, and viola, so that although the position of the hands may change, the fingering remains the same.

MORE COMPLEX STRING INSTRUMENTS

The Four-string Ukulele

The A string of a four-string "chording" ukulele is tuned to A 440, the A above middle C on the piano. D is a fifth below A, F♯ a major third above D, and B a step above A. To stroke the strings, use a felt plectrum, or the upper joint of the index finger of the right hand. After a little practice, the stroke will seem natural.

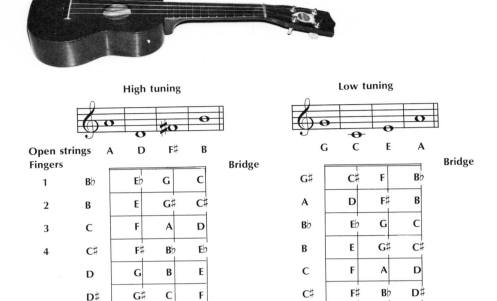

FIGURE 8-27

Chord Diagrams for Ukulele*

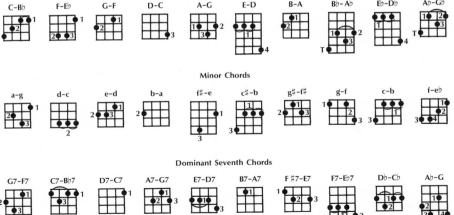

FIGURE 8-28 **Different Tunings for the Four-string "Chording" Ukulele**

*Note that two chord names are indicated for each diagram. The chord to the left is for a ukulele using high tuning, the chord to the right for one using low tuning.

To obtain a given chord, pluck the strings while depressing them with the left-hand fingers between the metal frets indicated in Figure 8-28. Try to memorize a few chords at a time. Many modern songbooks conveniently indicate a change in chord by placing the new chord name above the staff at the appropriate point. Popular sheet music frequently contains chord charts similar to those given below.

Shift to higher notes by moving the left hand toward the body along the fingerboard. Relate the tones produced to the music staff.

The Tenor Banjo

FIGURE 8-29   The Tenor Banjo (*Courtesy of Vega Instrument Co., Inc.*)

In tuning the tenor banjo, tune the strings from left to right as the instrument faces the player, from low to high:

String No.

4	3	2	1
C	G	D	A

The A string is tuned to A 440, D is a fifth below A, G is a fifth below D, and C is a fifth below G.

As on other fretted instruments, the space between each fret on the fingerboard constitutes a half step, the first fret on the C string producing C♯, the second fret D, and so forth.

To finger chords, as indicated in Figure 8-30, simply depress the strings between the designated metal frets. Try to memorize only a few chords at a time. A very limited chord repertoire will enable the player to accompany most songs. Although the banjo is most often used for chord accompaniments, melodies can be played easily with a plastic or celluloid plectrum. The fingering on the tenor banjo is exactly the same as that of the cello in terms of finger stretch and left-hand position.

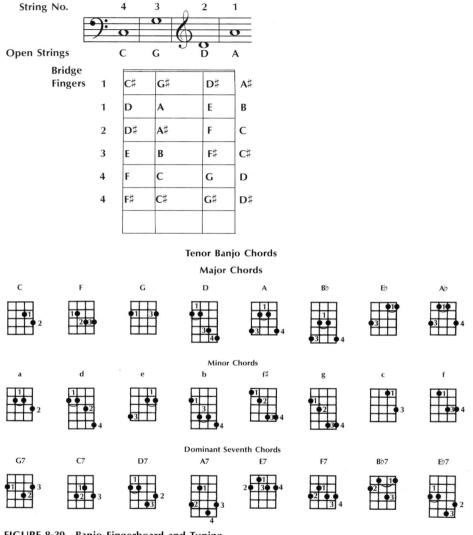

String No.	4	3	2	1
Open Strings	C	G	D	A

Bridge Fingers

Fingers				
1	C#	G#	D#	A#
1	D	A	E	B
2	D#	A#	F	C
3	E	B	F#	C#
4	F	C	G	D
4	F#	C#	G#	D#

Tenor Banjo Chords

Major Chords

C F G D A Bb Eb Ab

Minor Chords

a d e b f# g c f

Dominant Seventh Chords

G7 C7 D7 A7 E7 F7 Bb7 Eb7

FIGURE 8-30 Banjo Fingerboard and Tuning

The Six-string Guitar

From left to right, facing the instrument, the six-string guitar is tuned as follows:

String No.	6	5	4	3	2	1
	E	A	D	G	B	E

String 1 is tuned to E above middle C on the piano
String 2 is tuned a fourth lower to B just below middle C

FIGURE 8-31   The Six-string Guitar (*Courtesy of Vega Instrument Co., Inc.*)

String 3 is tuned to G a third below B
String 4 is tuned to D a fourth below G
String 5 is tuned to A a fourth below D
String 6 is tuned to E a fourth below A

Most guitar plectra are of celluloid and are held between the thumb and index finger. Some plectra are of metal and fit on the right thumb. Strum the strings with the fingernails of the right hand, alternating with the thumb plectrum (if used), always plucking the lowest pitched string first. A sliding bar (capo) fastened across the strings permits chords a half step higher to be played in each position with the same finger pattern.

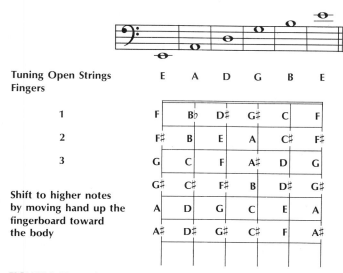

Tuning Open Strings	E	A	D	G	B	E
Fingers						
1	F	B♭	D♯	G♯	C	F
2	F♯	B	E	A	C♯	F♯
3	G	C	F	A♯	D	G
	G♯	C♯	F♯	B	D♯	G♯
Shift to higher notes by moving hand up the fingerboard toward the body	A	D	G	C	E	A
	A♯	D♯	G♯	C♯	F	A♯

FIGURE 8-32   Guitar Fingerboard

Guitar Chording

Fingering is shown in Figure 8-33 below. Dots indicate strings depressed between metal frets, open circles indicate open strings. Thus, to play the C chord, depress the second string B with the first finger at the first fret, and the fifth string with the third finger at the third fret, then strum the stopped strings and the open strings G and E. The lowest tone, stopped by the third finger, provides the root C of the chord. A little practice, memorizing but a few chords at a time, will make chording seem quite simple and will create sufficient skill to play most chords indicated in songbooks and popular songs.

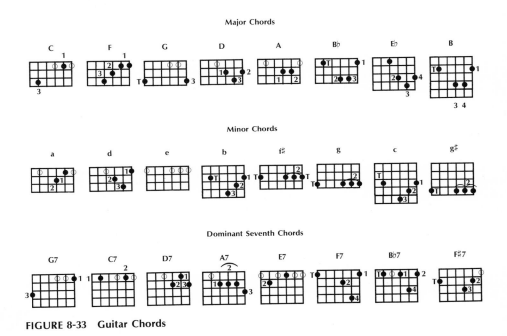

FIGURE 8-33   **Guitar Chords**

The Mandolin

Tune the strings from left to right, from low to high, facing the instrument.

String No.	4	3	2	1
	G	D	A	E

The A string is tuned to A 440, E is a fifth above A, D a fifth below A, and G is a fifth below D.

FIGURE 8-34   Three Styles of Mandolins: (1) Barrel Back, (2) Flat Back, (3) Banjo Mandolin

Since the mandolin utilizes double strings, there are four sets of strings, each set tuned to the same pitch. Each fret constitutes a half step in the scale. The fretboard spacing is exactly the same as that of the violin and the fingering is identical. A plastic or celluloid plectrum is used to play melodies; chords are strummed. Don't try to memorize more than a few chords at a time.

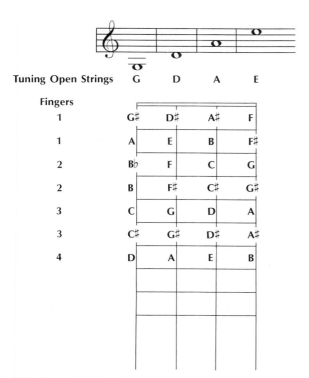

Tuning Open Strings	G	D	A	E
Fingers				
1	G♯	D♯	A♯	F
1	A	E	B	F♯
2	B♭	F	C	G
2	B	F♯	C♯	G♯
3	C	G	D	A
3	C♯	G♯	D♯	A♯
4	D	A	E	B

FIGURE 8-35   Mandolin and Violin Fingerboard

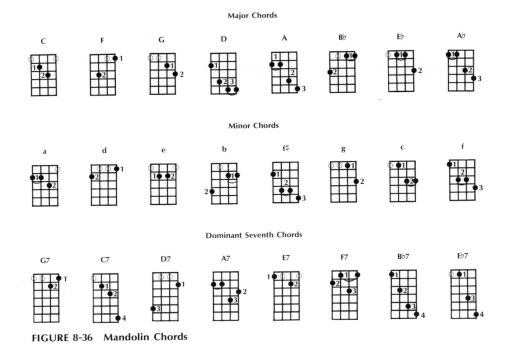

FIGURE 8-36   Mandolin Chords

THE BOWED NONFRETTED STRING FAMILY

The bowed non-fretted string family, consisting of the violin, viola, violoncello, and bass, should not be introduced until the upper grades, and then only after fretted instruments have been explored. Since there are no frets with which to measure exact half steps, scale pitch, determined by the placement of the fingers on the fingerboard, must be found by experiment. If the child sings the pitch he is trying to play, he will know when his fingers find its location. The fingering system of the mandolin is the same as that of the violin and viola; the fingering system of the banjo the same as that of the cello.

An easy way to remember the order of open strings of the bowed string family of instruments is to relate them to the extended fingers of the left hand pointing toward the floor, as in Figure 8-37 (in mirror image). Ask the children to pretend the fingers of their left hand are the strings of the various instruments, then to pluck the imaginary strings in unison, singing the "open" notes.

Always relate the pitch diagram to the music staff above it.

To play pizzicato on the violin place the right thumb against the side of the fingerboard, with the fingernail about 2 inches below its top, and pluck the string with the first finger of the right hand.

To stop the strings, place the left hand under the neck of the violin with the thumb about 1 inch from the scroll and the first finger opposite the thumb. Depress

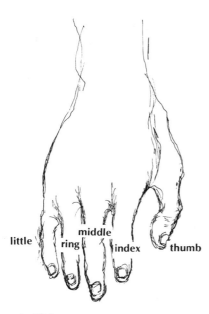

little   ring   **middle**   index   thumb

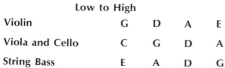

	Low to High			
Violin	G	D	A	E
Viola and Cello	C	G	D	A
String Bass	E	A	D	G

Violin Fingerboard and Tuning Chart

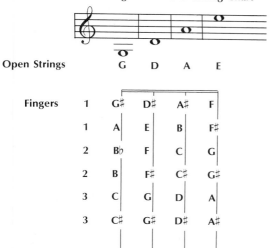

Open Strings	G	D	A	E
Fingers 1	G♯	D♯	A♯	F
1	A	E	B	F♯
2	B♭	F	C	G
2	B	F♯	C♯	G♯
3	C	G	D	A
3	C♯	G♯	D♯	A♯

FIGURE 8-37   String Family (*Photograph Courtesy of Bowmar Records*)

the string with the tips of the fingers. Notice that each finger can control both a flat and natural, or natural and sharp pitch. The violin is suitable for either melodic or harmonic use.

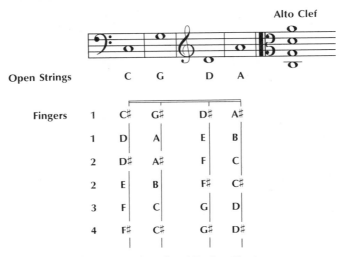

FIGURE 8-38 Viola Fingerboard and Tuning Chart

Pizzicato and stops are played on the viola as on the violin, although the fingers of the left hand must stretch further since the instrument is larger.

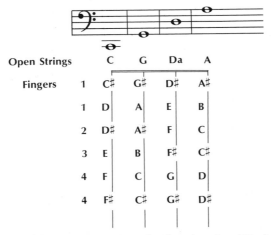

FIGURE 8-39 The Violoncello Fingerboard and Tuning Chart

To play pizzicato on the cello, pluck the string with the first finger of the right hand, resting the right thumb against the right side of the fingerboard about 3 inches below its top, palm facing down.

The strings of the cello are dampened by the left-hand fingers, the left-hand thumb resting under the neck about 4 inches from the scroll, and the left-hand palm facing down toward the fingerboard. The thumb acts as a guide for the middle finger. Depress the string with the tips of the fingers.

The viola, cello, and string bass should be used in the classroom orchestra primarily to provide the bass note of chords.

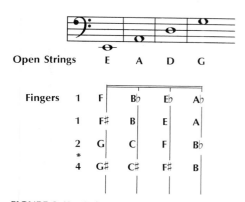

FIGURE 8-40   String Bass Fingerboard and Tuning Chart

To play pizzicato on the string bass, place the right-hand thumb against the right side of the fingerboard about 4 inches below its top and pluck the string with the first finger of the right hand.

To stop the strings with the left-hand fingers, place the left-hand thumb behind the neck of the string bass about 6 inches from the scroll, the thumb serving as a guide for the second finger. Depress the string with the ball of the fingers. Half-step interval stopping occurs between the position of the first and second or second and fourth fingers.

LATIN AMERICAN PERCUSSION

Chapter 4, Developing Concepts of Rhythm, suggested the value of making Latin American instruments. However, manufactured instruments do have the charm of producing a professional sound comparable to that heard by the child on recordings. Because such instruments require precise coordination, they are best reserved for the upper grades. Each number in the list following Figure 8-41 corresponds to the number of the appropriate instrument in the figure.

*Because of the long stretch between half-step stops, the third finger is not used.

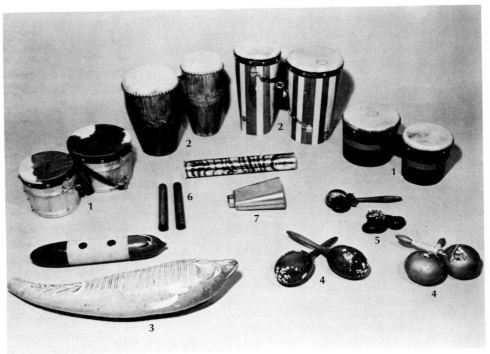

FIGURE 8-41 Latin American Instruments (*Courtesy of Peripole, Inc.*)

1. Bongo Drum: Generally played by holding the drum between the knees and beating the drumhead with the fingers of both hands

Characteristic rhythms are

2. Conga Drum: This narrow, barrel-shaped drum is suspended from the left shoulder by a strap, and produces a deep resonant tone when played with the fingers of both hands. The drumhead may be goat or mule skin

Characteristic rhythms are

3. Guiro: Usually made from carved cedar wood or a cowhorn, the guiro is shaped like a hollow gourd that has been scored or serrated, and is played with a scratcher, a thin piece of metal

Characteristic rhythms are

4. Maracas: Made from gourds, coconuts, or shaped wood, maracas are played in pairs: the smaller maraca being held in the right hand and the larger one in the left hand. To play, shake with a minimum movement using the wrist as a pivot. Music for the maracas is written as shown below, the upper line being the music for the right hand and the lower line the music for the left hand

Characteristic rhythms are

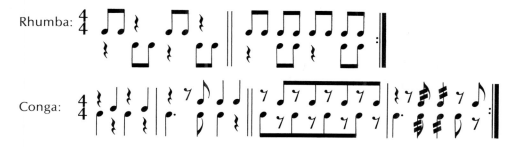

5. Castanets: Castanets on handles are easier to manage than those without. To play, strike the head against the palm of the hand. Rotating the wrist produces a roll effect for sustained tones. Playing finger castanets is much more difficult. Held by string looped around the middle finger of each hand, the two sides of the castanet are struck against each other by the fingers and thumb in appropriate rhythms such as

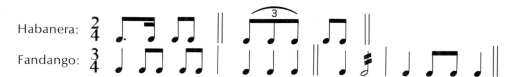

6. Claves: Claves pronounced "clah-ves" are made from seasoned hardwood, which results in a peculiar hollow tone. One stick, supported between the thumb, first

finger, and heel of the palm of the left hand, is struck at its midpoint by the stick in the right hand

Characteristic rhythms are

7. Cowbell: Cowbells produce a dull, metallic tone when struck with a mallet. Different sounds can be produced by striking at top, center, or bottom. To muffle the tone, a piece of adhesive tape may be fixed inside. Cowbells are made in various sizes—each producing a different pitch—and usually play melodic rhythms. A roll sound can be produced by striking the inside of the bell rapidly with a metal rod or large nail.

Characteristic rhythms are

COMPLEX PIPES

The Recorders

The recorder, created during the Renaissance, is one of the few wind instruments retaining its original design and performing technique. Its repertoire by many great composers includes solo and ensemble chamber music, as well as music for vocal accompaniment. Probably the easiest of all woodwind instruments to play, the recorder has a range, except for the contrabass, of a little over two octaves. A combination, or "consort," of recorders consists of the following:

Sopranino, the smallest in size and highest in pitch, built in F
Soprano, a fourth below the sopranino, built in C
Alto, an octave below the sopranino, built in F
Tenor, an octave below the soprano, built in C
Bass, an octave below the alto, built in F
Contrabass, an octave below the tenor, measuring $4\frac{1}{2}$ feet, built in C

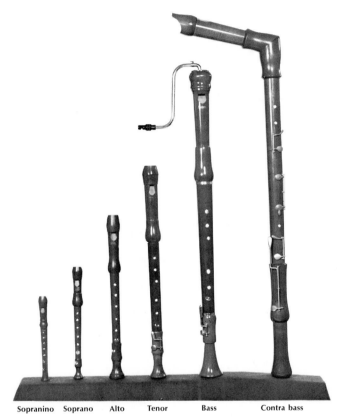

Sopranino Soprano Alto Tenor Bass Contra bass

FIGURE 8-42 A Consort of Recorders (*Courtesy of Melody Flute Co.*)

The sopranino, alto and bass, in F, must transpose their parts to play with instruments on the key of C.

Because of moderate cost and ease of performance, the most common recorders are the soprano, alto, and tenor. The bass and contrabass rarely perform except ensemble, and even then the tenor is frequently substituted. There is much highly embellished virtuoso literature for the soprano (descant) recorder, preferred by beginners, which is the coloratura of the recorder choir. However, most solo recorder music, and the lead part of most ensemble works, is composed for the alto. The soprano sounds an octave higher than its notation is written. The same is also true of the bass when playing music written in the bass clef.

The recorder is a truly professional instrument, yet sufficiently simple that upper grade children can acquire the skill to play some of the finest musical literature.

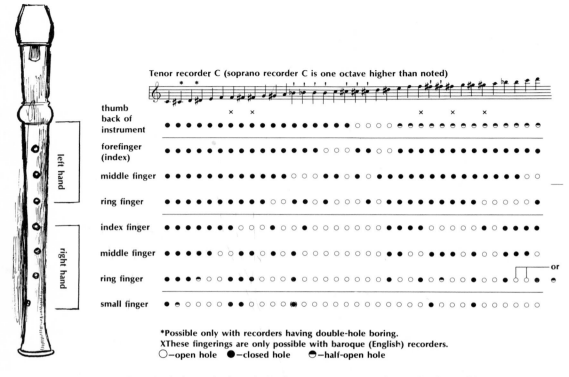

*Possible only with recorders having double-hole boring.
XThese fingerings are only possible with baroque (English) recorders.
○—open hole   ●—closed hole   ◗—half-open hole

From Melody Method, Melody Flute Company, Laurel, Maryland. Used by permission.

FIGURE 8-43   **Fingering Chart for Recorders**

The Mouth Organ or Harmonica

Ten-hole harmonica

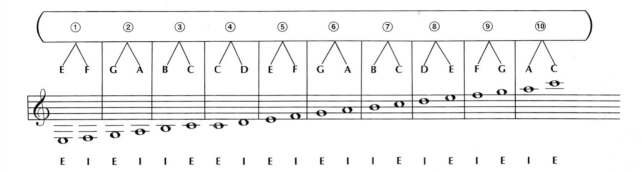

The letter E means exhale or blow breath into the hole indicated.
The letter I means inhale or draw breath in at the hole indicated.
The blown or inhaled breath vibrates the reed inside the harmonica.

FIGURE 8-44   The Ten-hole Harmonica Chart

KEYBOARD INSTRUMENTS

The Melodica

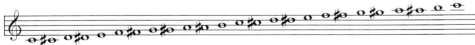

FIGURE 8-45   The Melodica (*Courtesy of M. Hohner, Inc.*)

The melodica produces a sustained reed tone sounding much like the piano accordion. It employs the piano keyboard principle, but sound is produced by blowing into a mouthpiece and depressing the keys. (If several children use the same instrument successively, the mouthpiece should be removed and washed, or individual mouthpieces provided for each child.)

The breath activates the reeds as a bellows does an accordion. The melodica can serve as a melody instrument or can play chords as accompaniment. Method books are available from the manufacturer, the Hohner Instrument Company.

Many of the methods suggested for teaching the piano keyboard are also applicable to teaching the melodica:

1. Acquaint the children with the arrangement of white and black keys

2. Copy the fingering chart on a poster or the chalkboard

3. Demonstrate each hand's fingering pattern: the index finger being given the number 2, the middle finger 3, the ring finger 4, and the little finger 5. Identify the respective notes played by each finger. Sharp notes are played by the most convenient finger according to the flow of the melodic line

4. Teach the scale by means of a simple three-note melody such as "Merrily We Roll Along." When the first three notes of the scale are mastered, shift the melody so that it commences on the next step of the scale and includes the fourth. By this means finally encompass the octave

5. Teach the upper octave before the lower. When both have been mastered, let half the class play the upper octave and half the lower in unison enriching the sound

6. Assign part of the class to play chords in accompaniment while the remainder play the melody

7. Use the melodica to reinforce the singing of part songs and descants. It is especially effective imitating bagpipe drone

The Piano Accordion

The piano accordion can be an effective accompanying instrument since it is easily portable and provides a sustained, reed-organ tone. It is extremely popular among Central European nationalities, who favor it as a solo instrument. The music educator cannot ignore the accordion, and should learn to play it if possible.

Besides the right-hand keyboard, played as is the piano, the accordion has a bass keyboard, invented by the English physicist, Wheatstone. This consists of a system of buttons that enables the player to produce, on the smallest accordions, the twelve major chords, and on the largest one hundred twenty, the latter being the full range of major, minor, dominant seventh, and diminished chords.

Playing the bass keyboard involves a touch system of key relationships based on the cycle of fifths. It therefore requires a knowledge of the basic fundamentals of key and chord relationships.

Figure 8-47 illustrates the construction of the bass buttons and their relationship to the cycle of keys.

FIGURE 8-46 The Piano Accordion (*Courtesy of M. Hohner, Inc.*)

Piano Accordion Bass Keyboard Chart

1. Starting with the C row (the heavy circle) and proceeding downward on the keyboard as the instrument is held (to the left on the diagram), the first adjoining row is in the key of F (one flat)

2. The next is in B♭ (two flats), then E♭ (three flats), A♭ (four flats), and D♭ (five flats)

3. To simplify the key pattern, the next row is changed enharmonically to F♯ (six sharps) which, on a modern keyboard instrument (because of equal temperament), is the same as G♭ (six flats)

4. Similarly, the key of B (five sharps) is enharmonically the same as C♭ (seven flats)

5. Starting with the C row, by moving upward on the keyboard (to the right), the first adjoining row is in the key of G (one sharp); the next is in D (two sharps); the A (three sharps); E (four sharps); B (five sharps); F♯ (six sharps); and C♯ (seven sharps). Here again an enharmonic change is made to the flat equivalent of A♭ (four

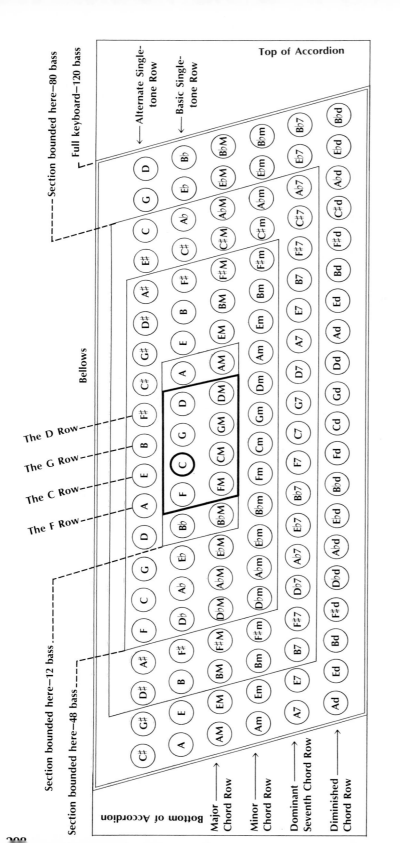

Top of Accordion

Section bounded here—80 bass
Full keyboard—120 bass
Section bounded here—48 bass
Section bounded here—12 bass

Bottom of Accordion

Alternate Single-tone Row
Basic Single-tone Row

Bellows

The D Row
The G Row
The C Row
The F Row

Major Chord Row
Minor Chord Row
Dominant Seventh Chord Row
Diminished Chord Row

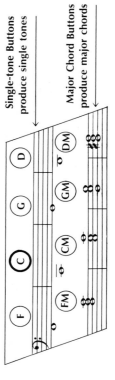

How these basses are written in music

Single-tone Buttons produce single tones

Major Chord Buttons produce major chords

Basses in heavy outline above

F	C	G	D
FM	CM	GM	DM

Single-tone Buttons played with 2nd finger

Chord Buttons played with 1st finger

FIGURE 8-47   Bass Keyboard Chart

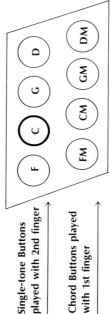

236

flats), which is the same as G♯ (eight sharps). Remember that on the accordion flat keys run downward from C, sharp keys upward. The dominant key is always to the immediate right of the tonic, the subdominant to the immediate left.

Since the key relationships of the buttons remain the same for both dominant and subdominant, namely, the dominant immediately above the tonic and the subdominant immediately below, the student learning to play in one key can automatically transpose to all keys merely by shifting key position.

A few moments' study of Figure 8-47 will explain why accordionists believe the bass keyboard to be a harmony manual. To the child studying this instrument, key relationships reveal themselves through sight, touch, and sound, and involved harmonic problems become kinesthetically clarified.

BASIC PIANO KEYBOARD HARMONY (TO BE USED AS A SUPPLEMENT TO THE KEYBOARD SCALE AND CHORD FINDER)

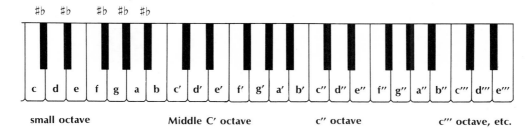

FIGURE 8-48 Shortened Piano Keyboard

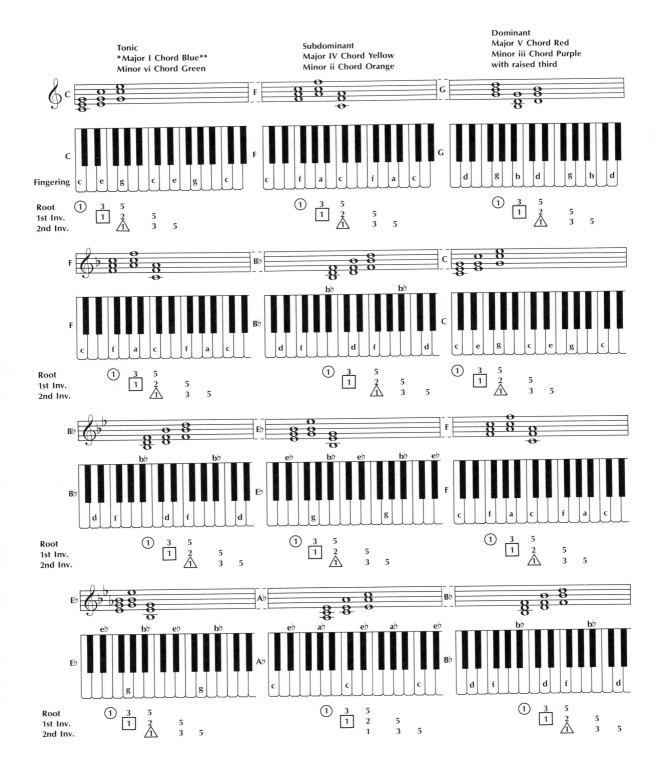

210

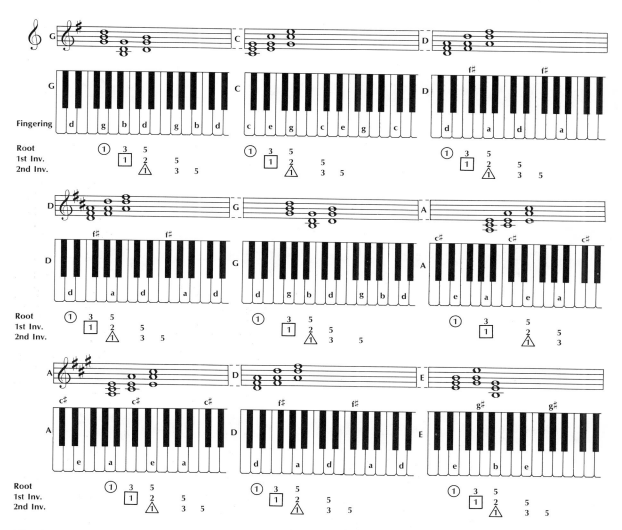

*To change any major triad to its tonic minor (same root), lower the third of the chord a half step. The finger pattern remains the same whether in major or minor.

**Color designations refer to the Keyboard Scale and Chord Finder, see Chapter 6.

FIGURE 8-49 Chord Notation and Right-hand Fingering

BASIC CHORDING AT THE PIANO

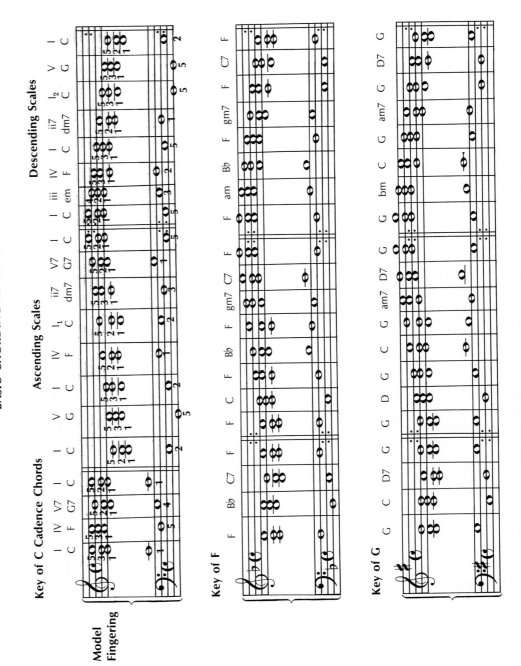

212

Key of Bb

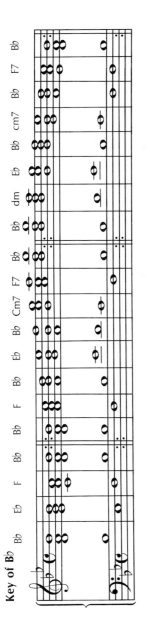

Key of D

Accompaniment Styles

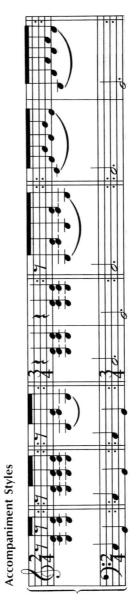

From Songs for Camp and Campus, Irving Cheyette, Pro Art Music Co., 1960, slightly modified.

FIGURE 8-50

213

Key To Figures

1. Establish right-hand finger patterns for major and minor chord triads most commonly used in school music books: major chords in C, F, B♭, E♭, G, D, A; minor chords in A, D, E, F, C, G. Each column of Figure 8-49 shows major chord triads built on the root, third and fifth in the keys indicated (see the chart footnote for the construction of minor chords). The music notation is read vertically, the fingering chart horizontally.

2. Use the Keyboard Scale and Chord Finder to locate the root (point of arrow on finder) in a given tonic (*do*) on a keyboard chart. In Figure 8-49:

Root Positions are identified by a circle ○

1st Inversion Positions by a square □

2nd Inversion Positions by a triangle △

Chords are said to be *inverted* when they are built on the third or fifth of the chord. Practice on the keyboard in various octaves. Note that the basic fingering position remains the same regardless of the key. To add a bass, play the root of the chord an octave below the right hand with the little finger of the left hand.

3. I–V–I: After the basic positions of the tonic chord triads and their inversions have been established, combine them with the comparable positions of the related dominant or V chord triads. (Third column in Figure 8-49.) By relating the tonic and dominant finger positions, the finger pattern for dominant-tonic chord resolutions can be established in all keys. Use the same finger for the common fifth scale step of both chords. For smooth progressions use this sequence:

	I	V	I
Root Position	○	□	○
1st Inversion	□	△	□
2nd Inversion	△	○	△

Add the root of the I and V chords in the left hand by skipping from the fifth (little finger) to the thumb (one) (see Figure 8-50). Establish the feeling of the left-hand finger pattern. In the right hand note the pivotal position of the common tone. When finger patterns are secure in each hand, combine the movement of both hands

4. I–IV–I: Keep the common tone (root of I) in the same pivotal finger in moving from the I to the IV chord and back (column 2 in Figure 8-49). Establish the feeling of the pattern in the fingers so that it can be duplicated without the keyboard, or merely imagined. For smooth progressions use this sequence:

	I	IV	I
Root Position	○	△	○
1st Inversion	□	○	□
2nd Inversion	△	□	△

Practice chord roots playing bass in the above keys separately with the left hand, moving from the fifth to second finger and back. Remember that in minor keys the IV chord is also minor, reducing the interval of the third in that chord a half step. Relate the Finder to help identify chords quickly by color (see column headings)

5. I–IV–V–I: Establish the right- and left-hand patterns separately. When these movements have been learned try to put them together, always remembering to keep common chord tones in the same finger. For smooth progressions through I–IV–V–I stay in the same octave using this sequence:

	I	IV	V	I
Root Position	○	△	□	○
1st Inversion	□	○	△	□
2nd Inversion	△	□	○	△

A little practice in both major and minor keys with the Keyboard Scale and Chord Finder should develop some facility in the recognition of chords and their harmonic relationships.

SUMMARY

Learning to play simple string, wind, and percussion instruments heightens the young child's musical interest. Once motivated to learn simple music notation, he may be inspired to study more complex instruments in the upper grades. Individual instrumental study also improves class performance since singing and rhythmic activities can be enriched by sound effects provided by the children themselves (see Chapter 9).

Children will recognize that music notation provides a blueprint for performance. The unusually gifted child should be encouraged to continue his instrumental study in advanced grades. Although music aptitude tests have value, nothing supersedes instrumental achievement as a test of musical talent. The requirements of practice challenge all facets of a child's personality, thus determining whether aptitude will be buttressed by the interest and perseverance necessary to achieve genuine musical success.

CHAPTER NINE

DEVELOPING THE INNATE CREATIVITY OF CHILDREN

Creativity is not taught, only guided. A child is prompted to sing original tunes to himself, to build mud pies, to create patterns of design, to move rhythmically to organized sound, to create rhymes and games, or simply to build blocks, by a drive instinctive, yet distinctively human.[1] The aborigine beating rhythms on a tree trunk and Stravinsky composing a symphony manifest the same demiurge, the same need to creatively communicate. Although both seek to organize the medium of sound into an expressive pattern of tone, rhythm, and dynamics, Stravinsky has the advantage of three thousand years of evolving musical techniques.[2] The "message" of music

[1] This is acknowledged even in cultures officially committed to materialist interpretations. A paper delivered at the Seventh International Congress of Anthropological and Ethnological Sciences, Moscow, U.S.S.R., 1964, included in its enumeration of the distinctive attributes of man, "primate—who thinks and communicates in symbols—finds satisfaction in singing and carving distorted figurines—whose very tools are aesthetic—" Quoted in Earl W. Count, "Whence Mankind?", *The Key Reporter,* xxx: 2 (1965).
[2] Cf. Henri Bergson, *The Two Sources of Morality and Religion,* trans. R. A. Audia and C. Brereton, Holt, Rinehart and Winston, Inc., New York, 1935, pp. 73, 93ff.

may be as esoteric as that devised by contemporary atonal serial systems, or as exoteric as the simple form and melodic structure of folk music.

The essence of so-called progressive education is to motivate learning by tapping the child's instinctive creative impulse.

The creative impulse is within the child himself. No educational discovery of our generation has had such far-reaching implications. It has a two-fold significance; first, that every child is born with the power to create; second, that the task of the school is to surround the child with an environment which draws out his creative power.[3]

This theory of learning is especially applicable to aesthetics, the subject matter of which is the discipline of creativity itself.

Music education should be planned, not in terms of technique and drill, but in terms of self-expression, emotional release, and the creative impulse.[4]

Creativity cannot be summoned by announcing: "We are now going to become creative," or, "We'll now have a unit on creativity"; it must be inspired.[5] The teacher must stimulate the child to synthesize his experience, while educating him to judge that synthesis.[6] Musically, the creative synthetic process can be fostered by demonstrating the manipulation of basic musical elements, by stimulating the child's sensory apparatus and imagination, and by relating the written symbols that represent music to the child's musical experience. Although technical requirements should not be allowed

[3]Rugg, H. O., and Ann Schumaker, *The Child Centered School,* Harcourt, Brace & World, Inc., New York, 1928, p. 228.

[4]Mursell, James L., and Mabelle Glenn, *The Psychology of School Music Teaching,* Silver Burdett Company, Morristown, N.J., 1938, p. 21.

[5]Even the best intentions must be supplemented by ingenuity, as indicated by the complaint of this harassed teacher:

I gave her her fourth lesson today, and, so far as the rules of composition and harmony are concerned, I am fairly well satisfied with her. She filled in quite a good bass for the first minuet, the melody of which I had given her, and she has already begun to write in three parts. But she very soon gets bored, and I am unable to help her, for as yet I cannot proceed more quickly. It is too soon, even if there really were genius there, but unfortunately there is none. Everything has to be done by rule. She has no ideas whatever—nothing comes. I have tried her in every possible way. Among other things, I hit on the idea of writing down a very simple minuet, in order to see whether she could not compose a variation on it. It was useless. "Well," I thought, "she probably does not know how she ought to begin." So I started to write a variation on the first bar and told her to go on in the same way and to keep to the idea. In the end it went fairly well. When it was finished, I told her to begin something of her own—only the treble part, the melody. Well, she thought and thought for a whole quarter of an hour and nothing came. So I wrote down four bars of a minuet and said to her: "See what an ass I am! I have begun a minuet and cannot even finish the melody. Please be so kind as to finish it for me." She was positive she couldn't, but at last with great difficulty—something came, and indeed I was only too glad to see something for once. I then told her to finish the minuet, I mean, the treble only. But, for *home work* all I asked her to do was alter my four bars and compose something of her own. She was to find a new beginning, use, if necessary, the same harmony, provided that the melody should be different. Well I shall see tomorrow what she has done.

W. A. Mozart, letter to his father, May 14, 1778 (308a) in *Some Musicians of Former Days,* trans. Romain Rolland, Holt, Rinehart and Winston, Inc., New York, 1915.

[6]Foster McMurray, "Pragmatism," in *Basic Concepts in Music Education,* National Society for the Study of Education, Chicago, Ill., 1958, pp. 51–52.

to impede expression, the child must be convinced that technical competence will enhance his satisfaction and that such competence can be acquired by diligent and logical application.

Recent theory differentiates between educational systems in terms of creativity.

The Open and Closed System in Education:

1. The Open System is a stimulating system of relationships which accepts uniqueness in perception and in thinking . . . [it] permits originality, experimentation, initiative, and invention; it constitutes the propitious environment for creativity.

2. The Impersonal Closed System is concerned very little with originality or invention by the student. It is concerned mainly with acquiring a body of knowledge, memorizing of facts, and finding answers to problems—all of which are already known to someone else.

Creativity must be thought of as a process of planning, experiencing, acting by the person who is creating the product. . . . It is rarely that from the product, one can infer or imagine the process, the struggle, the imagination, frustrations, endurance that went into the product. The reports of creative persons rather consistently imply that the process that produces a novel product is based on wide and deep knowledge and experience, in addition to skills, persistence and hard work. Creativity as process is important not because the product of each moment is such a gem but because the process is the essense of life itself.[7]

To create a musical composition requires mastery of the skill, insight, and information of a musically literate person. Thus the process of composition provides a means of challenging the class to acquire and synthesize the skills and information detailed in the preceding chapters. The combining of skills to achieve specific goals produces "insight," the ability to see means in terms of ends.

What belongs in general education is that kind of knowledge which is sometimes called "insight." Insight is learning characterized by intellectual grasp, or understanding, or the ability to perceive relations, and is different in kind from skills which require long habituation in muscular and eye co-ordination.[8]

Theory is proved by experience through experiment:

There are ways of building interest through pupil performance that do not involve the inept creation of music which is poor in quality. Performance on instruments can be used to teach facts from physics concerning how tones are produced, or to teach facts about orchestral coloring, or about types of intervals and their sounds, or about theory of composition or rules of harmony. Pupil activities involving the use of instruments and of singing in order to clarify theory, or as a means of lending a sense of reality to the intellectual and aesthetic STUDY of music, are altogether different in educational intent and in theoretical justification from playing or singing indulged in merely as an enjoyable sport. When pupils are encouraged to try their hand at producing musical sounds in an experimental attitude, then the level of interest is likely to be high and the learning good, no matter how unskilled the performance.[9]

[7] Anderson, Harold H., "Creativity and Education," in *College and University Bulletin* XIII:14, (May 1, 1961, special issue), N.E.A. Washington, D.C.
[8] McMurray, *op. cit.,* p. 57.
[9] McMurray, *ibid.,* p. 51.

Experiment permits the gestation of information, not merely the ingesting.

The alternative in teaching theoretical or cognitive materials is to introduce them within a situation of first-hand experience with the raw materials of sound. Procedurally, the idea is to begin with sounds, either musical or non-musical; to introduce theory as an intellectual instrument for doing something to or with the original raw materials; to conclude with further experience of music, changed in some way by cognition. In short, the teacher should introduce theory as a means to reconstruct first-hand experiences. . . . Let music become known for its sounds and its felt qualities.[10]

The musically literate individual recognizes music because he not only *hears* but *listens*, and reads music because he is able to translate visual symbols into sounds. Therefore, the creative challenge cannot be confined to composing music, but must also include communicating music by notation. The learning of notation is thus integrated into the creative process and gains meaning for the child by reason of that process. As Mursell has emphasized, teaching music notation is important, but equally so is making such teaching part of a larger musical context.

The standard notation, in spite of its many anomalies, is our best and most adequate means of symbolizing musical concepts. The familiar "sol-fa syllables," with "movable do," constitute another symbolic device, and a very useful one, for it represents key relationships and tonality trends with unique clarity and directness. These are working conceptual tools for coping with and grasping the expressive organization of the ordered world of sound. . . . It is altogether necessary that these symbols be learned. Otherwise, musical development is bound to remain at a low level, and musical apprehensions to be vague, crude, relatively incoherent. . . . They must be taught always in terms of their musical meanings and in application to musical situations and experiences, never merely in terms of verbal definitions and arithmetical designations. . . . Thus it is the musical content of the program that determines the presentation of musical concepts. Music is chosen for its own intrinsic worth, not for the sake of illustrating or teaching the so-called fundamentals.[11]

The procedures that follow are not designed to be carried out in a single music lesson or even over a specific period of time. Rather they typify a method, whose rudiments, applied in the first grade, are capable of continual refinement as the student matures. After orally creating simple rhymes and one-sentence melodies to be interpreted, dramatized, and rhythmically orchestrated, the student should gradually achieve the capacity to satisfy the complex creative demands summarized at the close of this chapter.

[10]McMurray, *ibid.*, p. 56. Cf. Arthur Schopenhauer, "On Education," in DeWitt Parker (ed.), *Schopenhauer Selections*, Charles Scribner's Sons, New York, 1928, p. 425ff. Schopenhauer's essay was written in 1851. How new is progressive education? Read Plato's *Republic*, Chapter VI. What is the Socratic Method? Is it "progressive"? In Anderson's terminology, is the system of education outlined in the *Republic* that of an "open" or "closed" society? Is it possible to teach the ideas of a "closed" society with progressive methods, and the ideas of an "open" society by rote? Germany, in the period immediately preceding the rise of Adolf Hitler, was reputed to have the most efficient public school system in Europe. Is the "open" system of education "efficient"?
[11]James L. Mursell, "Growth Processes in Music Education," in *Basic Concepts in Music Education, op. cit.*, p. 153.

INSPIRING CREATIVE ACTIVITY

One of the most exciting holidays for children is Halloween, which provides opportunities for masquerading; for games such as ducking for apples; for fearsome sounds and movements; for stories of witchcraft; and for colorful displays of art, dance, poetry, and music. To persuade the child to express this holiday in an original song is comparatively simple. Later the song can be dramatized rhythmically, scored for simple instruments, and analyzed for musical values capable of being translated into notation. Composing a song, then learning the symbols to express it, permits the child to experience the transmutation of ideas and feelings into music and the transcription of that music into signs that are meaningful to others.

Motivation

Choice of subject: Halloween

Through direct questioning, such as: "What holiday comes toward the end of October?"; "What do children like to do on Halloween?"; "What kinds of objects do we associate with this holiday?"; "What kinds of games do we play on Halloween?", list on the board words and phrases elicited from the class describing the holiday: goblins, owls, the wind, trick-or-treat, witches, scarecrows, masks, ducking for apples, sudden scary noises, pumpkin faces in the window, broomsticks, and so forth. The children will recollect poems and songs as well as personal incidents. To excite their imagination decorate the room with Halloween masks, pictures, costumes, pumpkins, and the like.

Selection

Ask the class to create the first line of a poem utilizing some of the listed words. If necessary volunteer a first line to establish the mood, beat, and eventually meter, then encourage the children to substitute one of their own.

Assume a first line:

Halloween will soon be here.

Recite this in unison to establish the beat, meter, and rhythm, marking the sequence of strong and weak pulsations:

Hal - low - een will soon be here.

The swing of long, short-long, short-long, short-long, can be symbolized musically by four three-beat measures, the first beat of the measure falling on the stressed syllable.

This can be demonstrated by conducting the line to a triangular pattern in $\frac{3}{4}$, down, right, up for each measure as follows:

```
  1   2   3   1   2   3   1   2   3   1   2   3
3 Hal - low-een will  soon be     here.
```

Ask the class to count in a pattern of threes as the line is recited; then reverse the procedure, the class reciting as the pattern is counted.

The meter signature $\frac{3}{4}$ placed at the beginning of the first line will indicate that the rhythm swings in three beats, each of which can be represented by the lower symbol. The second line must end in a word that rhymes with "here" (but there is nothing to prevent the use of non-rhyming free verse), must include one or more "Halloween" words, and must fit the first line's rhythmic framework of long-short motives of threes. After obtaining and listing suggested rhymes for "here" (such as "year," "fear," "tear"), encourage attempts at a second line. Write each suggestion on the board for rhythmic-metric analysis by the class. Hopefully, a child may suggest:

It is a scary time of year.

This fits the pattern of threes quite well.

```
It  is   a   scar - y   time  of   year.
 1   2   3   1   2   3   1   2   3   1   2   3
```

Recite the couplet while conducting in threes: down on 1, right on 2, up on 3.

Seek a third line that utilizes some of the descriptive words, but rhymes differently, analyzing each contribution for rhythm and pulse.

Assume, after consultation with the class, the following:

```
Witches on  broom  -  sticks, masked goblins too,
 1   2   3   1   2       3    1    2  3   1  2  3
```

and a fourth,

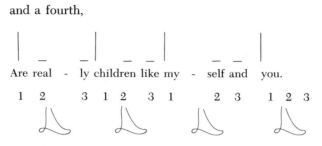

Are real - ly children like my - self and you.

  1   2   3 1 2   3 1   2   3   1 2 3

Now write the entire poem on the board leaving space between each line to add the metric pattern.

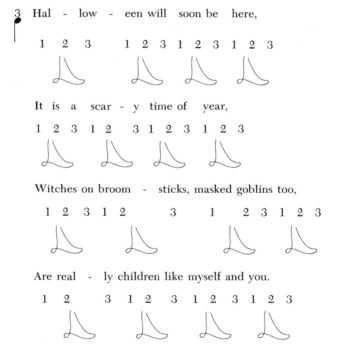

3 Hal - low - een will soon be   here,

   1   2   3   1 2 3 1 2 3 1 2 3

It is   a   scar - y time of   year,

1 2   3 1 2   3 1 2 3 1   2 3

Witches on broom - sticks, masked goblins too,

1 2   3 1 2   3   1   2 3 1 2 3

Are real - ly children like myself and you.

  1   2   3 1 2   3 1 2 3 1 2 3

Within the established framework of pulse and rhythm, add other Halloween verses.

NOTATION

If the class is not familiar with music notation, demonstrate the rhythmic flow explaining that simplified rhythmic symbols can be substituted for the conducting beats diagrammed below each line. According to this system, a sound lasting one count is symbolized by a *quarter note* ($\quarternote$), and a sound of two counts by a *half note* ($\halfnote$). A dot after a half note adds half its value again, producing the symbol for three counts ($\halfnote.$). Place duration lines under each note to reinforce its meaning.

Since the conducting beats are diagrammed below the text, notate the rhythm above it.

Excerpted Rhythm Chart

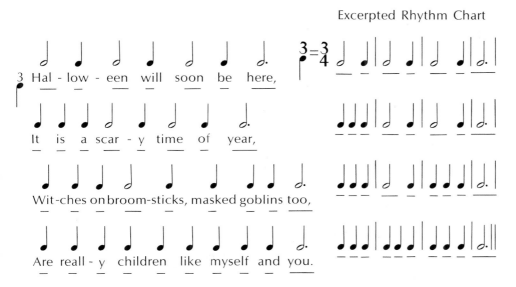

Alongside the text, notate the rhythm again, finishing with a double bar. The double bar signifies the end of a composition or section, much as a period marks the end of a sentence. Bar and measure lines divide notation so as to facilitate rhythmic pattern reading. Because the stresses of the Halloween song fall on the first beat of every three, the measure lines divide its notation into three-beat groups. The meter signature, $\frac{3}{}$, denotes this, showing that ($\bullet$), a quarter note, represents one beat, of which there are three to a measure. Since four quarters make a whole, a quarter note is also represented by the numeral 4, therefore the $\frac{3}{}$ meter can also be written $\frac{3}{4}$.

FINDING THE SONG'S EXPRESSIVE ELEMENTS

Read through the text again, underlining words that evoke images or create a mood. Their importance should be stressed in recitation or singing by changing pitch or intensity.

Halloween will soon be here,

It is a scary time of year,

Witches on broomsticks, masked goblins too,

Are really children like myself and you.

Ask a child to try to express through recitation the feelings evoked by the text. Chart his expression, showing word duration by length, pitch by vertical placement, and intensity by thickness of line. The class should accompany each reading by tracing the pitch movement of each phrase from left to right in front of their chest. Compare the chart of one child's reading with another, and let the class decide which is the most expressive.

Expression and Duration Chart

Hall - o - ween will soon be here,

It is a scar - y time of year,

Wit - ches on broom - sticks masked gob - lins too,

Are real - ly children like my - self and you

When the expression and duration chart is completed, the song's pattern of rhythmic beats, word duration, expression, and relative pitch movement will be symbolically represented on the board. This pattern can be reflected in the text by coloring the expressive words.

SELECTING TONALITY AND MODE

Ask the children to listen carefully to the major scale in the key of C and its tonic triad played on the piano or bells, the scale notes being C, D, E, F, G, A, B, C; the chord tones C, E, G. Then play the C Minor scale and tonic triad, the scale notes being C, D, E♭, F, G, A♭, B♭, C, the C Minor chord C, E♭, G.

The class must choose the scale that best fits the feeling of the text. Assuming the natural minor scale is selected, as well it may be, write its scale ladder containing numbers, syllables, and pitch names on the board next to the text.

6—— *la* —— C

—   ——   —

5—— *sol*—— B♭

—   ——   —

4—— *fa* —— A♭

3—— *mi* —— G

—   ——   —

2—— *re* —— F

—   ——   —

1—— *do* —— E♭

7—— *ti* —— D

—   ——   —

6—— *la* —— C

Establish tonality by having the class sing the scale's ascending and descending steps from the board chart of the scale ladder, first by number, then syllable. The class should also sing the C Minor triad to establish the sound of the tonic.

Now direct their attention to the chart of expressive feeling, asking one child to recite the text according to the chart's inflection, while the rest listen carefully to determine where his voice rises and falls. Find volunteers to propose and sing a melody for the first line, reminding them to stay within the tonality of the chosen scale. Help them by sounding a C Minor chord on the piano, bells, or autoharp before each attempt.

Try to fit each child's proposed melody into the scale ladder, asking the class to sing the suggestion first by text and then by appropriate numbers of the scale ladder. When a melody for a line has been accepted, write its scale numbers above the corresponding words, as illustrated below. Thus complete each successive line, listening to all proposals and letting the class make the final decision. Always relate each proposed melody to the scale ladder to measure the intervals: singing text, then numbers, then syllables.

6	7	1	2	3	4	3			
Hal - lo -	ween	will	soon	be	here,				

3	3	3	6	5	4	4	3		
It	is	a	sca - ry	time	of	year,			

6	6	5	4	3	2	2 1	7	
Witch -	es	on	broom - sticks,	masked	goblins	too,	

4	3	2	6 3	1	2 1	7	6
Are	real - ly	child - ren	like	my - self	and	you.

Transferring the Melody to the Piano Keyboard

After a song's melody has been selected, see if the children can find middle C on their piano keyboard charts. Pick out the notes of the melody on the scale ladder by measuring whole and half steps. Then, using middle C as a base, relate the intervals to the keyboard. Now sing the melody using the letter names of the notes read from the scale ladder. If appropriate, demonstrate minor scale construction at the keyboard using the Keyboard Scale and Chord Finder (see Chapter 6).

Some teachers have found it desirable to mimeograph reproductions of the piano keyboard on ordinary 8 x 11 notebook paper for the children to keep in their looseleaf music notebooks. On these paper piano keyboards the children can write the scale numbers, syllable names, and pitch names to help them identify relationships within the major and minor scales. A separate page should be used for each scale.

MUSIC NOTATION

The desirability, indeed the necessity, for developing symbolic concepts by means of direct experience of that which is symbolized cannot be overstressed.

It is highly desirable that as many concepts as possible be identified by means of symbols which are connotative of the concept. Many such symbols are expressed through words but not necessarily so. In the case of music there are many musical concepts which are expressed through musical symbolisms, [notation] of one kind or another. One of the principles of good pedagogy is to differentiate between the concept and the symbol. Such differentiation is made all the more difficult if the fundamental concept is vague, incorrect or misleading.[12]

Ask the class to attempt to devise a system of writing their song so that other children in other rooms of the school, or in other parts of town, will be able to sing its text, rhythm, and melody exactly. Experiment to see how much can be conveyed by writing the appropriate pitch number or letter name over each syllable.[13] Analysis will demonstrate that while such information as the words, the rhythm, and the interval can be shown by numbers combined with an expressive inflection chart, both are not sufficient to convey the song's pitch range and key.

Explain the convenience of the music staff: a music ladder on which notes are placed on both the lines and spaces, each line and each space representing a particular pitch in scale sequence. Sharps and flats need be shown only once, at the beginning.

Draw a music staff, using the five fingers of the hand (see Chapter 3), adding the G clef sign that marks G on the treble staff. In order to identify the notes of the song, notate the C Minor scale, including the necessary B♭, E♭, and A♭. Then delete the accidentals and substitute the initial key signature (Figure 9-1).

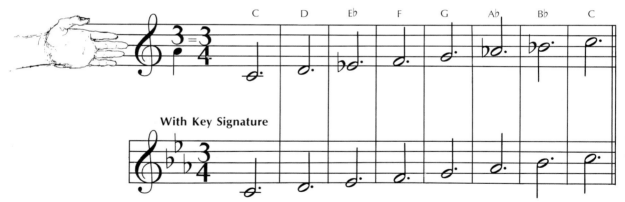

FIGURE 9-1 Hand Staff with Key Signature

Demonstrate that music notation permits the exact indication of melodic line (sequence of pitch), rhythm (sequence of quarter notes, half notes, and dotted half notes), motives and rhythmic patterns (sequence of notes between bar lines), and the relation of words to notes.

[12] Thurber Madison, "New Concepts" in *Basic Concepts in Music Education, op. cit.,* p. 8.
[13] The ancient Greeks used this system. As a result, no one today can be certain of the pitches represented and so the debates of musicologists rage. See Curt Sachs, *The Rise of Music in the Ancient World, East and West,* W. W. Norton & Company, Inc., New York, 1943, pp. 198ff.

OUR HALLOWEEN SONG

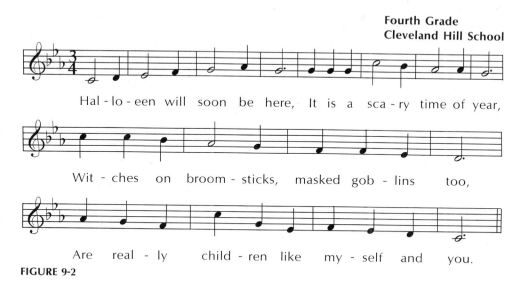

**Fourth Grade
Cleveland Hill School**

Hal - lo - een will soon be here, It is a sca - ry time of year,

Wit - ches on broom - sticks, masked gob - lins too,

Are real - ly child - ren like my - self and you.

FIGURE 9-2

Write the entire song with key and meter signature on the music staff as in Figure 9-2.

Terms of Tempo

Just as a fixed system of *sol-fa* syllables aids in communicating exact pitch to others, so the use of precisely defined words indicating the speed of music facilitates expressing ideas of tempo. Show the class a metronome. As the children sing their song, set its beat to approximate their tempo. The class will probably discover that the metronome is set at 72, which means there are 72 beats of the song to the minute (24 measures if the song is in $\frac{3}{4}$). If the metronome is marked with the Italian terminology as well as numbers, the class will find that 72 is encompassed in the word "Andante" near its upper, slower end, just below "Moderato." Therefore, above the key signature write: "Andante Moderato ♩ = 72." This signifies that each quarter note symbolizes a sound having the duration of $\frac{1}{72}$ of a minute.

Terms of Mood

As yet, there are no signs to indicate the kind of sound the singers should strive for to express Halloween's mood and excitement. The song is about mysterious happenings occurring during the dark hours of the night. Perhaps if the tempo words are amplified to read "Andante Moderato Misterioso," the singers will realize how they must make the audience feel.

Since this is a song about the mysterious, and the mysterious is frequently hushed, the singers should give the impression of walking on tiptoe. This effect can also be indicated on the score by adding the Italian music term for softly, *piano*. However, the song is not to be sung at exactly the same degree of softness all the way through. There must be indications to sing a little louder or a little softer at certain times. This information is conveyed by such Italian music terms as *crescendo* (to grow louder) and *decrescendo* or *diminuendo* (to grow softer). Because changes must be made at precise moments, these terms are usually abbreviated: *p* for piano, *cresc.* for crescendo, *decresc.* for decrescendo, *dim.* for diminuendo. Crescendo, diminuendo, and the limits of each, may also be indicated by expanding or narrowing horizontal Vs: < >. Because notes are written in the center of the score, dynamic indications are placed beneath the note heads to facilitate reading. Notes that are to be given special accent or stress are shown by crowning them with a horizontal or vertical dart (> \/).

That part of the song to be sung very softly should be marked by the Italian term *pianissimo*, abbreviated *pp*. For moderately loud, the Italian word is *mezzoforte* (half-loud), abbreviated by the letters *mf*. If all these indications of expression are added appropriately to the music score, it will appear as in Figure 9-3.

OUR HALLOWEEN SONG

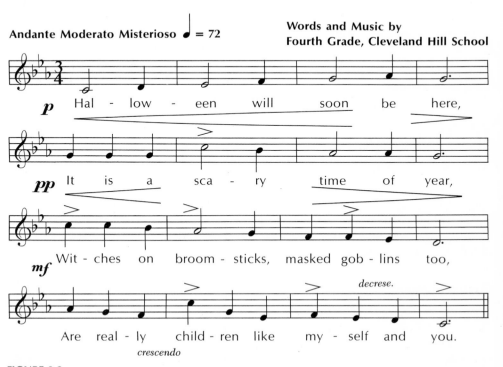

FIGURE 9-3

Sensing the Beats

Demonstrate to the class that within every group of three beats between measure lines a stronger accent falls on the first beat than on the second or third. This strong beat can be sensed, otherwise a beat of three could not be distinguished from any other. Sing the song, asking the class to clap hands on the strong beats.

Select a child to be a masked "goblin," hopping only on the strong beat. Represent this beat by writing a dotted half note on a rhythm chart at the side of the board:

1. ♩ Goblin Rhythm

Sing the song again, this time asking the class to clap each beat. Ask a second child to be the "witch on the broomstick," tiptoeing the pulse beat rhythm of 3 while the goblin hops on the strong beat. On the board, under the dotted half note, add the three quarter notes for the witch:

2. ♩ ♩ ♩ Witch's Rhythm

Sing the song a third time, this time asking the class to clap the rhythm of the melody line as it appears in the rhythm chart derived from the duration value of the words. This rhythm consists of combinations of quarter, half, and dotted half notes.

A third child can play a "scarecrow," teetering the melody rhythm while the others step the strong beat and the pulse beat. When all three actors move, the three rhythms will be seen in combination. Let the actors march across the front of the room together in their respective rhythms while the class sings the song, one-third tapping the strong beat, one-third the pulse beat, and the remainder the melody rhythm. The rhythm chart on the board will now show the three types of rhythm in each line of music:

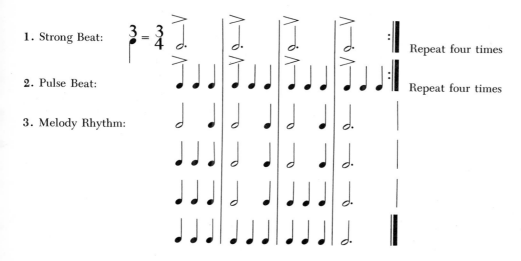

1. Strong Beat: Repeat four times

2. Pulse Beat: Repeat four times

3. Melody Rhythm:

Sensing the Phrase Line

To develop sense of phrase, ask the children to rotate their right arm, starting toward the left, in tight spirals to the pulse beat as they sing. At each temporary pause (the end of a phrase) they must reverse direction, as must the three actors the direction of their steps.

Phrases can be symbolized as follows:

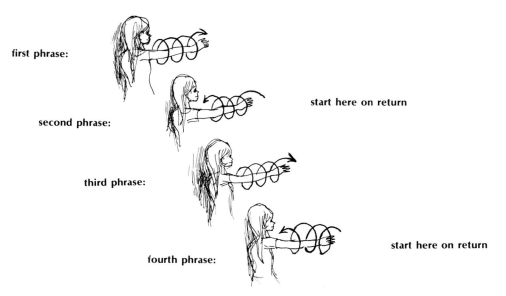

first phrase:

second phrase:

start here on return

third phrase:

fourth phrase:

start here on return

Adding Rhythmic Sound Effects

Ask the class to listen to various rhythm instruments to determine those best representing the rustle of wind through trees, the tapping of a witch's cane, the hooting of an owl, the tinkling of a door bell rung for trick-or-treat, or any other distinctive Halloween sound. Probably a wood block will be selected to represent the tapping cane, sandpaper blocks the sighing wind, a triangle or two-tone bells for the door bell. Distribute three of the instruments, changing performers on repetition, assigning to each a different song rhythm: strong beat, pulse beat, or melody rhythm.

Divide the class into three groups, each group, while singing, to tap a different rhythm, as the three actors dance their respective steps in character. Use the rhythm instruments to add a four-measure introduction and four-measure coda, the latter subsiding in a gradual decrescendo.

Adding Harmonic Background

Owls hoot on a falling minor third, simulated by singing "Whoo-oo" on the C Minor duad, E♭ to C, fourth space to third space on the staff. Children will be delighted to be "owls" accompanying the song by shifting pitch on the first beat of each measure:

A second motive can be based on the syllabic rhythm of the first word of the song: "Halloween." Motive 2 should be repeated in two-measure sequences sung against the "Whoo-oo":

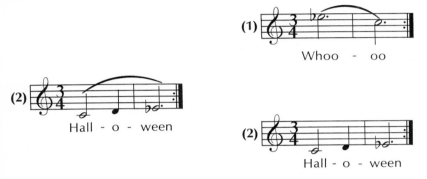

Practice these motives a few times, half the class singing each. Select a few children to sing motive 2 against a small group singing motive 1, while the rest sing the text. Both motives can also be used as a four-measure introduction, the owls singing the first two measures alone.

Adding Simple Melodic Instruments

Instead of simulating the hooting of an owl by voice, the falling third can be played by any of the melody flute family: the tonette, flutophone, song flute, or recorder, an octave lower. The Halloween motive sounds well if played by melody bells, xylophone, or tuned water glasses. An interesting calliope effect results from soda pop bottles tuned to the C Minor scale. Let the children tune the bottles themselves. With a little practice a tone is easily produced by blowing across the edge of the bottle opening, placed under the lower lip.[14]

The full scale can be tuned, one child to a bottle, by each player singing a note of the scale, then matching his bottle's tone by adding or removing water. After this has been done, line up the performing children so that the scale sounds from low to high, left to right, as the children face the class. Before the bottle band attempts to play the song, rehearse it vocally, each member singing his bottle's tone at the appropriate points of the melody in proper pitch and rhythm. After a few renditions by this

[14]See Chapter 8, p. 169.

vocal calliope, ask the class to sing the song by numbers, syllables, and text to a bottle-band accompaniment.

The bottle band will create a bit of laughter at first as the players find difficulty sounding their bottles promptly, but it also provides excellent ear training. Moreover, a child who develops skill blowing across the neck of a soda pop bottle will have acquired the embouchure to play a flute or fife. A simple instrument band also has the advantage of employing the vocally shy and persuading them that music making requires performers of diverse abilities.

Correcting Errors in Singing and Playing

At least as many singing and playing errors are due to faulty conception of pitch, rhythm, tempo, or dynamics as are due to lack of muscular coordination.

To overcome error, it is not sufficient for the learner to know what is wrong. *He needs to know what is right.* . . . The second grade children deliver a tune vaguely because they have only a vague apprehension of it. And as to the "uncertain" singer, his difficulty is an inadequate comprehension of the singable contour of the melody, not an inability to duplicate separate tones on order.[15]

For this reason, always have children listen to correct renditions of the music causing difficulty, and let the vocally adept sing along with those less able.

McMurray describes the method by which the mature performer perfects his conception of performance:

A concert artist's way of producing tones is his nearest approach to the physical creation of an artistic object, the ideal of which has already been created in his mind as a standard to guide performance. Before he can create a good sound, he must know what to listen for; he must have a prior ideal construct against which to measure his produced patterns of sound and such familiarity with the perfection of aesthetic content that he can tell how much of it he is realizing, and how much correction of the initial production is needed to bring the total to an acceptable level of realization. During the years of preparation, his ability to construct for himself an ideal of aesthetic content to be realized keeps changing and improving as his technique changes and improves. Nevertheless, this slowly forming ideal must always *"precede"* his capacity to realize it. If it did not, then he would not know in what direction to find improvement. . . . In his practice, each effort must be listened to and judged for its quality; judgment, which is an intellectual act, depends upon having ideas, and the ideas, in addition to those about technique, must include ideas about ultimate aesthetic content. He must know what the composer intended, or at least, what the composer ought to have intended. To know this, he must know what music means. To be a first rate performer is to be able to find or to understand the fullest range of meaning potential in music.[16]

The performer must master each of the elements involved in his performance, concentrating most on those that elude him, whether tonal, rhythmic, or dynamic.

[15] Mursell, *op. cit.*, p. 151.
[16] McMurray, *op. cit.*, p. 46.

EVALUATION

Sing other Halloween songs. Analyze them for "mood" words, accents, and expressive elements to see if the composer has caught the spirit of the text. Many creative activities that the class enjoyed can be adapted to preparing other songs, for instance: dramatizing strong beat, pulse beat, and melody rhythm; scoring for rhythm and melody instruments; analyzing musical phrases; adding harmonic chants and countermelodic descants based on the harmony underlying the melody; adding introductions, codas, and new verses.

Tape Recording

Make a tape recording of the class's performance of the song with its introduction, coda, vocal, and instrumental accompaniment. By analyzing tone quality, mood, and expression, the children can judge the extent of their achievement. One of the most salutary means of creating critical standards is surprise at success or failure. In the latter, most likely case, the children invariably comment, "Do we sound like *that?*" and listen more carefully to their performance in the future.

Notebooks

Upon completion of a creative song project, in addition to the song, the class's notebooks should contain copies of the various rhythm charts; scale ladders of the major and minor scales; a piano keyboard chart with scales and chords indicated; a glossary of music terms under such headings as Dynamic Terms, Tempo Terms, Expressive Terms; pictures representing activities related to the song; illustrative drawings; and, for later investigation, a bibliography of works concerning the song's subject—in this instance, Halloween.

Recorded Music

Having expressed their feelings about Halloween in music, the class will be intrigued to listen to similar symphonic evocations:

A Night on the Bare Mountain, Modest Moussorgsky
La Danse Macabre, Camille Saint-Saëns
"Hobgoblin" from *Symphonic Sketches*, George Chadwick
Halloween, Morton Gould
Todtentanz, Franz Liszt
Symphonie Fantastique, Hector Berlioz
Till Eulenspiegel, Richard Strauss
Halloween, Charles Ives

List of Procedures in a Creative Music Lesson

1. Choose subject
2. Select mood words
3. Create first line
4. Choose new words to rhyme with last word of first line
5. Analyze metric pulse of first line
6. Ask the class to read the verse, accenting the words that create poetic meter
7. Place a vertical line in front of accented words to separate into metric measures
8. Ask the class to read the poem aloud after completing the entire verse. Inflections should be charted on the board, perhaps in colored chalk
9. Extract and chart verse rhythm
10. Discuss mood, and analyze the modality that best fits the mood of the particular poem
11. Create the tune in the mode selected, following the expressive inflection chart
12. Draw the scale ladder on the board with numbers, syllables, and pitch names
13. Analyze the melody in terms of numbers related to the scale ladder
14. Relate the scale ladder to the keyboard, symbolizing the half and whole steps
15. Develop notation; derive the music staff from the fingers of the left hand, and draw it on the chalkboard
16. Place the melody on the music staff, adding terminology indicating tempo, dynamics, expression; harmonize and score for rhythm and melody instruments
17. Introduce additional songs concerning the same subject, adding scoring for rhythm and melody instruments; dramatize
18. Tape-record performance for evaluation
19. Present recorded music inspired by the same experience

DEVELOPING CREATIVE ACTIVITIES USING CONTEMPORARY MUSICAL TECHNIQUES

The suggestions that follow are not arranged by grade level, but depend upon the musical maturity of the children. Obviously the more complex the technique, the greater the physical, intellectual, and emotional maturation needed for mastery. The teacher is the best judge as to when each activity is most appropriate.

Discovering Sound Sources

Create an orchestra for sound painting, making children aware of the variety of techniques available to produce sounds from objects struck, plucked, blown, shaken, and scraped. Building instruments will illustrate the effect of size, density, and tension of medium on resonance, intensity, and pitch.

Struck objects often possess varied timbres depending on the type of mallet used.

Struck Objects

Pieces of pipe of various metals
Nails of various sizes
Mixing bowls
Pots and pans and their covers
Glasses, with or without water
Bottles, with or without water
Clay pots, empty and filled
Spoons
Cardboard cartons
Wood cigar boxes
Coconut half shells

Strikers

Nails
Dowl sticks
Wooden mallets
Rubber mallets
Metal rods
Spoons

Plucked Objects

Rubber bands
Stretched wires

Resonators

Cigar boxes
Cardboard cartons

Blown Objects

Pop bottles filled with varying amounts of water
Bird whistles and signal whistles
Grass held between thumbs to form a reed
Straws snipped at the top to form a double reed
Buzzing the lips into a small cardboard tube
Buzzing the lips on a brass instrument mouthpiece
Buzzing the lips and hissing
Whistling
Filling balloons with air, then letting the air escape

Shaken Objects

Small jars or cans filled with sand, dried peas, cherry pits, rice
Rattles made by nailing bottle caps to dowl sticks or ping-pong paddles
Tambourines made by stitching together two facing aluminum pie pans containing bottle caps or pebbles. (Use an awl to puncture holes in the rims of the pie pans)
A collection of large nails fastened together with colored string

Scraped Objects

An old washboard
A many-notched dowl stick
A many-notched dried gourd
A many-notched piece of pipe
A heavy comb

Scrapers

A piece of heavy wire
Fingers
A thin nail
A spoon

CREATIVE ACTIVITIES EMPLOYING SOUND PAINTING

Primary Grades

New Sound Sources for a Sound Painting: Music Concrète
Source of Inspiration: Coming of spring
Motivation: Questions relating to rebirth of nature and children's activities in spring: budding of trees; return of birds; first flowers; daffodils, crocuses, hyacinths; watering lawns; planting seeds; flying kites; buying new automobiles; children's outdoor games; cleaning porch furniture; washing windows; strong March winds
Selecting Sounds: Rustle of tree branches; bird songs; water running from hose; honking auto horns; calls for hide-and-seek, calls for flying kites; scraping of brushes cleaning furniture
Organizing Sounds: Ask children to create their own story about the coming of spring. Use voice, as well as homemade and rhythm instruments to illustrate appropriate sounds. Organize the sounds in a sequential pattern with a time limit for each
Recording Sounds: Record the sequential pattern on a tape recorder
Playback: While a child recites his story, play the taped recording. Use the recording also as a sound effects accompaniment to the singing of a spring song. Once aware of the possibilities, children will find many ways to enhance musical activities with appropriate sound effects.

1. Sing a familiar melody, such as "Mary Had a Little Lamb":

Nursery Rhyme

1. Mar - y had a lit - tle lamb, lit - tle lamb, lit - tle lamb,

Mar - y had a lit - tle lamb, its fleece was white as snow.

2. While the class sings the melody, accompany by shifting the tones to various octaves in the manner indicated below. Ask the class to describe how the accompaniment differs from the singing.

2. Mar - y had a lit - tle lamb, lit - tle lamb, lit - tle lamb,

Mar - y had a lit - tle lamb, its fleece was white as snow.

3. Play the melody in a minor mode, then ask the class to sing the melody in the same fashion. Can they describe what has occurred?

3. Mar - y had a   lit - tle lamb, lit - tle lamb,   lit - tle lamb,

Mar - y had a   lit - tle lamb, its fleece was white as   snow.

4. Play the melody in waltz time $\frac{3}{4}$. Ask the class to sing it, then to describe and analyze the effect.

4. Mar - y   had a   lit - tle   lamb,   lit - tle   lamb,   lit - tle   lamb,

Mar - y had a   lit - tle lamb, its fleece was white as snow.

FIGURE 9-4 Expanding Tonal and Rhythmic Spectrum: New Concepts of Melody Construction Employing Displaced Octaves

Improvising Irregular Rhythms in a Chance (Aleatory) Arrangement

1. Write a list of children's names on the board

Beat:
Rhythm:

```
  |   |
John Jones

  |        |
Ma - ry Fla - her - ty

  |        |
Jo - ce - lyn Hun - ter

  |        |
Vi - vi - an Kon - fed - er - ath
```

2. Above each name indicate the pulse beat by a vertical line as the name is pronounced
3. Under each name indicate the duration value of the sound, divided according to the pulse beat
4. Beside each name notate its rhythm

5. After each child has pronounced his name, ask him to clap his name's rhythm as he taps the pulse beat

6. Write the rhythms of all names across the board, in the sequence of the class seating, without bar lines:

7. Set a pulse beat. Ask each child to clap the rhythm of his own name as notated on the board when it occurs in the sequence

8. Now place bar lines in a meter of twos, then in a meter of threes, followed by alternating meters of twos and threes. When bar lines are added, place an accent over the first beat. Tap each pattern as illustrated with accent

9. Instead of having each child clap his name's rhythm when it occurs, let him play it on a rhythm instrument

10. Ask the children to find all similar rhythms. They will discover which names have the same duration value, and the importance of accent in establishing meter

11. Make a score composed of the various rhythm patterns constituting a beat

12. When the notation of a rhythm is designated, all children with either first or last names in that duration pattern must play the rhythm on their instruments. Mix up the sequence. The children will recognize the element of chance in its organization

13. In the upper grades, the same procedure can be followed to create a serial tone row. Assign a chromatic scale tone to each of twelve children to sing, or to play on a tone bar, in the rhythm of his name. The sequence of tones should be organized haphazardly rather than scaled chromatically. After the initial tone row is sounded, play it in retrograde motion (backwards), each child playing the tone in the rhythm of his name

Polyrhythms

1. Combine the singing of "Three Blind Mice" with "Frère Jacques"
2. As they sing, let the children establish the beat pulse by toe tapping

3. Next, ask half the group to clap the rhythm of "Three Blind Mice," while the remainder tap the rhythm of "Frère Jacques"

4. Distribute to a child in each group a different rhythm instrument to add color

5. Notate in $\frac{4}{4}$ and $\frac{6}{8}$ respectively a rhythm chart of the songs:

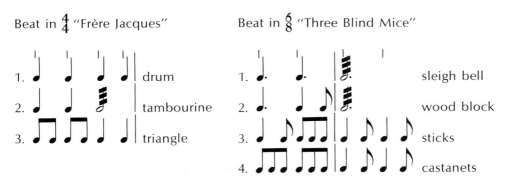

Beat in $\frac{4}{4}$ "Frère Jacques"   Beat in $\frac{6}{8}$ "Three Blind Mice"

1. drum   1. sleigh bell
2. tambourine   2. wood block
3. triangle   3. sticks
                 4. castanets

Play the various rhythms utilized in each song. Locate the text related to each rhythm set, outlining the syllabic duration. Relate the duration outline to the rhythmic notation

6. Assign each of the indicated rhythms above to a specific rhythm instrument, being careful to instruct the player that he is to play his rhythm only when required by the song

7. Demonstrate that it takes two measures of the $\frac{6}{8}$ of "Three Blind Mice" to give the same four pulses that occur in the $\frac{4}{4}$ of "Frère Jacques." Therefore, performing the notation of item 1 in the $\frac{6}{8}$ list above will sound the same as performing the notation of item 2 in the $\frac{4}{4}$ list. The difference between the two rhythms becomes more apparent in the more complex rhythms of item 3 in the $\frac{4}{4}$ list and items 3 and 4 in the $\frac{6}{8}$ list. The distinction between "twoness" and "threeness" will be more readily perceived by children in the upper grades who have more experience in singing partner songs

IN UPPER GRADES: DEVELOPING AN AWARENESS OF CONTEMPORARY TECHNIQUES OF MUSIC COMPOSITION

1. Use a familiar melody such as "Frère Jacques" for illustration. Sing it through. Alter it dynamically with an echo effect on repeated measures, alternating ensemble with solo voice

2. Make the following alterations singing or playing to illustrate changing modality (see Figure 10-6):

    a. minor mode (2a)

    b. pentatonic (2b)

    c. whole-tone scale (2c)

    d. Phrygian mode (2d)

3. a. Alteration by displaced octaves

    b. Alteration in serial row

4. Alteration by changing meters

5. Retrograde motion (backwards)

6. Inversion (the relative pitch of the original melody reversed)

7. Retrograde inversion (the pitch of the retrograde version of the melody reversed)

8. Contrapuntal combinations of the original, utilizing inversion, retrograde, retrograde-inversion variations

The simplest of these alterations illustrated in item 2 below can be introduced in the primary grades. The more complex variations should await suitable maturity in the upper grades.

FRÈRE JACQUES

1. Original Melody

FIGURE 9-5 Illustrations for Developing Awareness of Contemporary Techniques in Composing Music

MAKING A SCHOOL SOUND STUDIO

The child's developing interest in science in the upper grades can be used to motivate the building of a "sound studio," in a corner of the music room or classroom, housing the raw materials employed to make musical sounds. Through experimentation with the materials listed below, the class can investigate the nature of sound (periodicity, amplitude); the nature of media (membranes, woods, metals, strings, plastics); characteristics of timbre; and the physics of conductivity and resonance.

Kits are available to make melodic and rhythmic percussion, string, and wind instruments. Students with sufficient interest should try to compose music utilizing the instruments and techniques outlined in this section.

SOUND KITS FOR THE SOUND STUDIO

The materials for a sound studio may be procured from Peripole, Inc., which provides many models from which to choose, including a manual giving directions for construction and a list of suggested activities. An illustrated catalog describing these sound kits is available free, as well as an excellent film on *The Magic of Music: The Nature of Sound.*[17]

Percussion

  I. Woods

    A. Sound from solid wood cylinders

      Materials: solid wood cylinders: 3 mallets (1 hardwood, 1 softwood, 1 hard rubber); 2 double-felted and indented wood strips to act as an adjustable supporting frame

      Constant factor: diameter

      Variable factor: length

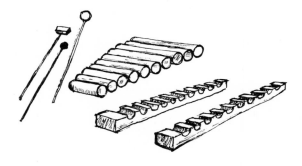

---

[17] Perry, Mack, "Sound in the Science Program," in *Catalogue and Program of Activities,* Peripole, Inc., Far Rockaway, N.Y.

Or
Same materials
Constant factor: length
Variable factor: diameter

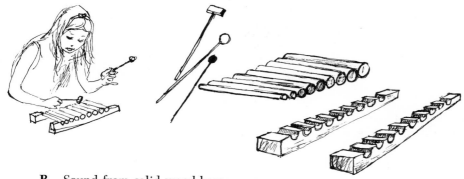

B. Sound from solid wood bars
Materials: solid wood bars of either pine, bass, or maple; 3 mallets as above;
2 felted wood strips to act as an adjustable supporting frame
Constant factors: length and thickness
Variable factor: width

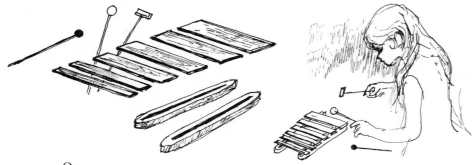

Or
Solid wood bars of equal width and length but variable thickness

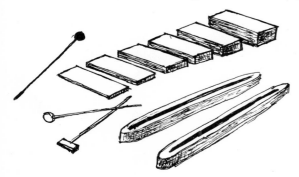

Or
Solid wood bars of equal width and thickness but variable length

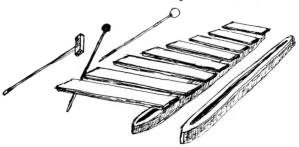

II. Metals or Plastics

    A. Sound from hollow metal cylinders: brass, steel, aluminum; or hollow plastics

        Materials: hollow metal or plastic cylinders; 4 mallets (1 hardwood, 1 softwood, 1 rubber, 1 nickel-plated steel); 2 double-felted and indented wood strips to act as an adjustable supporting frame

        Constant factors: wall thickness and length

        Variable factor: diameter

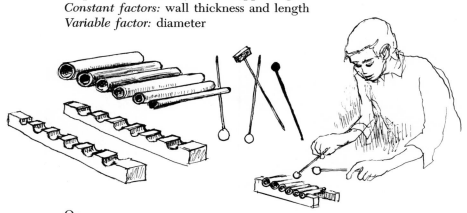

Or
Same materials of equal wall thickness and diameter but variable length

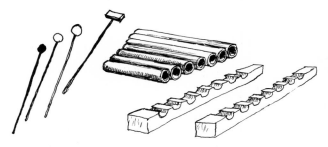

Or
Same materials of equal length and diameter but variable wall thickness

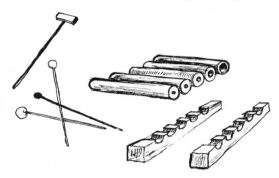

B. Sound from flat metal bars: brass, aluminum, or steel; or flat plastic bars
Materials: flat metal or plastic bars: 4 mallets as above, 2 felted wood strips
for supporting frame
Constant factors: width and thickness
Variable factor: length

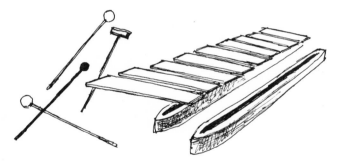

Or
Same materials of equal length and thickness but variable width

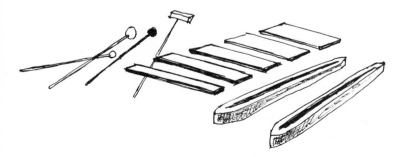

Or
Same materials of equal length and width but variable thickness

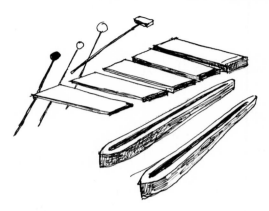

C. Sound from solid metal cylinders of brass, aluminum, or steel, or solid plastics
Materials: solid metal or plastic cylinders with mallets and indented wood strips for supporting frame
Constant factor: diameter
Variable factor: length

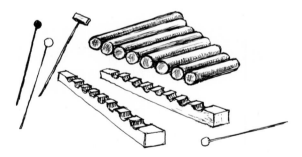

Or
Same materials of equal length but variable diameter

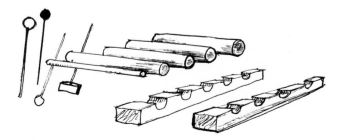

III. Sound from Steel Gongs
Materials: large steel gongs, 2 mallets (1 soft tympani mallet, 1 hard felt)
Constant factors: alloy and thickness
Variable factor: diameter

IV. Sound from Cowbells
Materials: 2 cowbells; 2 mallets (1 rubber, 1 wood)
Constant factors: alloy and thickness
Variable factor: overall size

V. Sound from Wood-resonating Chamber
Materials: wood-resonating chamber with two tynes, 2 softwood mallets, 2 rubber mallets
Constant factor: resonating chamber
Variable factor: length of tynes

VI. Sound from Drums of Odd Shapes
Materials: Y-shaped pipe; "elbow"-shaped pipe; 2 skin drumheads; special pegs to attach skins to pipes; 3 mallets (1 hardwood, 1 softwood, 1 felt-wrapped)
Constant factor: drumheads
Variable factors: odd shapes

VII. Sound from Fibre Cylinder Drum Shells
Materials: fibre cylinders in assorted heights and diameters; skin drumheads; special tacks to attach skins to cylinders; 3 assorted mallets as above
Constant factor: thickness of shell
Variable factors: diameter, height

Wind: Breath-supported

I. Voice
Materials: assorted-size megaphones
Constant factor: technique of voice production
Variable factors: Length and diameter of megaphones

II. Natural Horn from a Cow (Shofar)
Material: a cowhorn with fitted mouthpiece
Constant factor: type of horn
Variable factor: method of blowing into cowhorn (embouchure)

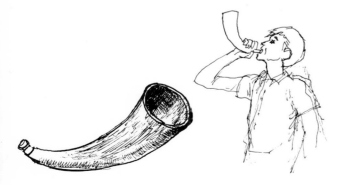

III. Bottles and Jugs
Materials: bottles of graduated sizes from gallon downward
Constant factor: breath control
Variable factors: sizes of bottles and jugs, water level

IV. Slide Whistles
Materials: slide whistles of varying sizes
Constant factor: playing technique
Variable factors: design and construction

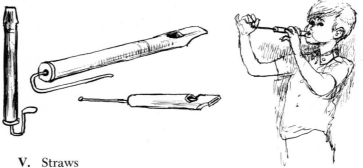

V. Straws
Materials: sets of various length straws
Constant factor: wall thickness
Variable factors: diameter and length

VI.   Flutes, Fifes, Recorders
    Materials: assorted instruments
    Constant factor: stopping of holes to alter pitch
    Variable factors: design and construction

VII.   Balloons
    Materials: assorted-size rubber balloons
    Constant factor: technique of sound production by controlling emission of confined air
    Variable factor: size of balloons

VIII. Simple Reeds and Accessories
Materials: assorted reeds, 2 round whistles, 2 sleeves, 3 mouthpieces, 2 rubber bulbs
Constant factor: method of blowing
Variable factor: type of reed

IX. Mouthpieces for Single-reed Woodwind Instruments
Materials: assorted mouthpieces for single-reed woodwind instruments
Constant factor: method of blowing
Variable factors: type of mouthpiece, density of reed

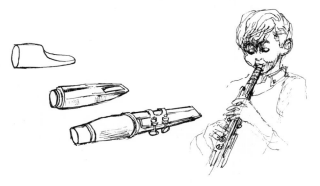

X. Double Reeds
Materials: oboe or bassoon reeds to attach to small diameter pipes
Constant factor: method of blowing
Variable factors: size and thickness of reeds

binding   reeds

XI.   Brass Mouthpieces
   Materials: assorted mouthpieces from cornet, trumpet, French horn, trombone, tuba
   Constant factor: method of blowing
   Variable factors: size and cup shape of mouthpiece

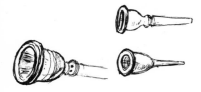

Strings

I. Three Sound Boxes, Rectangular, Square, and Tapered, as Amplifiers
   Materials: rubber bands of assorted size and width
   Constant factors: length and thickness
   Variable factor: width
   Square Sound Box

Or
Same materials
Constant factors: width and length
Variable factor: thickness
Rectangular Sound Box

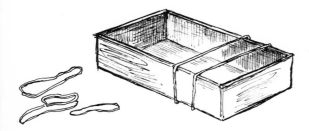

Or

Same materials

Constant factors: length, width, and thickness

Variable factor: amount of tension applied

Tapered Sound Box

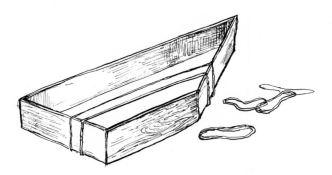

CONSTRUCTING MUSICAL INSTRUMENTS

Many children are manually oriented and enjoy making musical instruments. Through the use of musikits it is possible to procure all the needed parts to make a variety of string instruments, such as

1. Quadrilin: a type of violin without a sound box
   Materials: neck, bridge, strings, tuning pegs, bow
   Constant factors: bowing technique, fingering
   Variable factors: type of string, diameter, tension

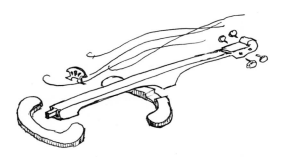

2. Ukulele
   Materials: neck, bridge, tuning pegs, pick, sound box, strings
   Constant factors: strumming technique, fingering
   Variable factors: type of string, diameter, tension

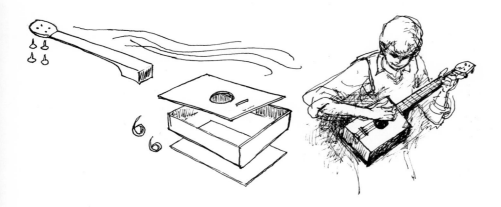

3. Violin
   Materials: sound box, neck, bridge, strings, tuning pegs, mute, bow
   Constant factors: bowing technique, pizzicato, fingering
   Variable factors: type of string, diameter, tension

4. Viola
   Materials: sound box, neck, bridge, strings, tuning pegs, mute, bow
   Constant factors: bowing and pizzicato technique, fingering
   Variable factors: type of string, diameter, tension

5. Banjo
   Materials: sound box, neck, bridge, strings, tuning pegs, plectrum
   Constant factors: plectrum technique, fingering
   Variable factors: type of string, diameter, tension

6. Guitar
   Materials: sound box, neck, bridge, strings, tuning pegs, plectrum
   Constant factors: plectrum technique, fingering
   Variable factors: type of string, diameter, tension

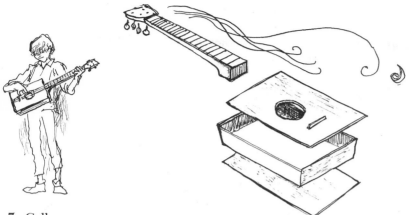

7. Cello
   Materials: sound box, neck, bridge, strings, tuning pegs, mute, bow
   Constant factors: bowing, pizzicato, fingering technique
   Variable factors: type of string, diameter, tension
8. String Bass
   Materials: sound box, neck, bridge, strings, tuning pegs, mute, bow
   Constant factors: bowing, pizzicato and slap pizzicato, fingering
   Variable factors: type of string, diameter, tension

cello

string bass

9. Duobass: a two-string triangular-shaped instrument
   Materials: comes completely assembled
   Constant factors: bowing, pizzicato and slap pizzicato, fingering
   Variable factors: type of string, diameter, tension

10. Boom Bass (Caribbean Calypso instrument)
    Materials: a metal washtub; a sawed-off broomstick; a heavy steel wire or gut string bass G string
    Procedure: drill a hole through one end of the broomstick and make an incision in the other. Drill a hole in the center of the washtub. Fasten a clothespin to one end of the string or wire and, overturning the washtub, pass the string through the hole with the clothespin underneath to hold the string in place. Pull the free end of the string through the hole in the broomstick and tie in place. Erect the stick on the tub by forcing the incision in the other end of the stick over the rim on the base of the tub. Place one foot on the tub and pluck the string with the opposite hand. To raise pitch, use the free hand to increase tension on the string by pulling the top of the stick farther from the hole in the tub.
    Constant factor: size of tub
    Variable factors: type of string, tension, diameter

pull for tension of string

string through hole in stick

hole in broomstick

bass G string

notched broomstick over rim

rim

pin

tub

SUMMARY

Art, like science, consists of symbolic depiction. The purpose of science is to affect the depicted; the purpose of art, to affect the depictors. To understand science or art requires knowledge of the characteristic mode of abstraction. The scientist must comprehend mathematics in the context of experiment, the musician, notation in the context of composition.

Enacting the process of composition in the classroom and then discovering a means of conveying that composition's pitch, rhythm, meter, mode, tonality, dynamics, expression, phrasing, harmony, style, quality, and color engages the child in an attempt to manipulate the diverse musical concepts discussed in earlier chapters. To aid him all methods for developing the necessary concepts and skills may, as appropriate, be employed.[18]

Every music lesson should arouse curiosity, demand creativity, utilize skill, and grant satisfaction. An additional bibliography of works concerning creative music teaching will be found in Appendix I. It is hoped that the procedures outlined will stimulate the teacher to formulate his own plans rather than restricting him to a rigid method.

[18]See Abraham Schwadron, *Aesthetics, Dimensions for Music Education,* Music Educators National Conference, Washington, D.C., 1967, Chapter IV, "Teaching Suggestions," pp. 109ff.

CHAPTER TEN

DEVELOPING LISTENING SKILLS

A prerequisite for musical growth is the ability to differentiate those significant constituent elements that determine music's expressiveness, its appeal, and its beauty.[1] Since the distinction between uneducated and educated listening parallels that between associative and conceptual thinking, educated listening requires an awareness of the elements of the music heard.[2]

Dewey aptly points out:

No whole is significant to us except as it is constituted by parts that are themselves significant apart from the whole to which they belong, . . . no significant community can exist save as it is composed of individuals who are significant.[3]

Music is more satisfying, both to hear and to perform, if its rhythmic organization, its key relationships, its phrase structure, and its melodic and harmonic textures are

[1] Mursell, "Growth Processes in Music Education," in *Basic Concepts in Music Education,* National Society for the Study of Education, Chicago, Ill., 1958, p. 150. See also Meyer W. Isenberg, "The Emphasis on Music and Fine Arts in General Education," *Journal of General Education,* XI:1 (January, 1958), pp. 51–55.
[2] See Chapter 1.
[3] Dewey, John, *Art As Experience,* G. P. Putnam's Sons, New York, 1934, p. 204.

understood. The act of discovering the constituent elements of a given composition and their relations is the process of rational appreciation.[4]

The work of art is a communicable, not a private expression. . . . Elements of feeling . . . are either vague, when directly linked with the sensuous medium or else definite, when this linkage is mediated by *ideas* through which the medium is given content and meaning. . . . Without thought our experience falls asunder into separate bits and never attains to unity. . . . The life of thought and the life of feeling have a common root; they are both parts of the one life of the mind and so cannot be foreign to each other. . . . To love without understanding is, to the thoughtful lover, an infidelity to his object.[5]

Children are not animals or phonographs, though on occasion they may be as noisily predictable. They are musical by neither reflex nor instinct, nor can they be made so by mere repetition of exercises. Children want to *understand* their musical experience. Understanding requires musical literacy, that is, familiarity with a large repertoire of music as performed, and with the symbolic system that is the blueprint of that performance.

TONE

The most pleasurable of musical elements is *tone*.[6] Lovely tone is even more instinctively attractive to the ear than melody.[7] Most people would rather hear a great artist sing a scale than a poor one sing an entire recital.

Generally speaking, beautiful tone is free, resonant, expressive, and idiomatic to the character of the voice or instrument that produces it. Appropriate tone quality, especially in vocal music, should be inferred from the text. A Halloween song about witches and goblins will demand a breathy, spooky tone, inappropriate to a sea chanty like "Blow, Boys, Blow," which requires one more robust and full-bodied.[8]

[4] Much of what follows may seem elementary to those students already musically trained. It is often true, however, that a person may study an instrument for a number of years and nevertheless not possess a clear and accurate understanding of the fundamentals of music. For that reason even such students may wish to give this chapter careful attention.

[5] Culled from Parker, DeWitt, *Principles of Aesthetics,* Appleton-Century-Crofts Inc., New York, 1920, pp. 12, 13, 60.

[6] Mursell, James L., *The Psychology of Music,* W. W. Norton & Company, Inc., New York, revised, 1941 pp. 13–14.

[7] Though not to John Keats,

Heard melodies are sweet, but those unheard
Are sweeter; therefore, ye soft pipes, play on;
Not to the sensual ear, but, more endear'd,
Pipe to the spirit ditties of no tone:

Presumably, Keats would be pleased by the school bands that comply literally with the last part of his request. The "Ode on a Grecian Urn" offers the bandmaster a comparable justification to that of the football coach: "I'm not building musicianship, I'm building character."

[8] William Sur, et al. (eds.), This Is Music Series, Book IV, Allyn and Bacon, Boston, 1961, pp. 67, 166.

Only from sense data (obviously no primary sensation such as sound can be experienced vicariously) can the child develop a standard for judging tone. That standard, unless counteracted by the educator, will be the aesthetic of the jukebox, the television set, and the radio. Therefore, music played in the classroom must be selected for excellence of tone and played on equipment of highest fidelity.

MELODY: PITCH AND INTONATION

Even in the rise and fall of birdsong, man strives to hear a melodic line, to contrive from the succession of notes an ordered sequence, a recognizable musical idea. (*Aleatory* music, consisting of tones selected by chance, presents a comparable challenge, but its devotees are denied the bird watcher's beneficial exercise.) Tones not perceived in a temporal unity, which seem discontinuous and lacking in coherence, are not heard as a melody.

A melody is set by the tonic note, to which an expectancy of return is set up as a tension of attention. The "form" of the music becomes form in the career of the listening. Moreover, any section of the music and any cross-section of it has precisely the balance and symmetry, in chords and harmonies, as a painting, statue or building. A melody is a chord deployed in time.[9]

Popular music is popular precisely because the repetitious motives of the simple melodic line become quickly familiar. Conversely, contemporary serious music is unpopular largely for the lack of such repetition.

One of the factors distinguishing music from noise is the element of *pitch*—the regular, organized recurrence of vibrations at a fixed rate of speed. The middle C of the piano, that of the Western tempered scale, is customarily fixed at 256 vibrations per second; the A above middle C to which orchestras tune is customarily at 440 vibrations per second. (Any such pitch-vibration correlation is entirely the product of convention. The late conductor Serge Koussevitsky tuned the Boston Symphony to a more vibrant A of 443 vibrations per second.) More vibrations than customary raise (sharp) the pitch, and fewer make it lower (flat).

Sharping or flatting a pitch is known as *intonation*. The Western tradition prefers pitch intonation as close as possible to the pitch "point" of the familiar tempered diatonic or chromatic scale. Performing off pitch is considered to be "out of tune."

RHYTHM

Rhythm has a dual nature. Music, except, for example, cantillation, possesses a continuous *beat*, likened to the pace of marching men. It is the beat that the conductor directs and the listener taps. Related to but independent of beat is *melodic rhythm*, consisting of the impulses formed by the various long and short notes of a melody.

[9]Dewey, *op. cit.*, p. 184.

In the song "Yankee Doodle" the melodic rhythm moves in part exactly twice the pace of the beat.

Melodic Rhythm: Fath'r and I went down to camp, along with Captain Good - win,

Beat:

The beat and melodic rhythm of "America" are identical until the words "'tis of thee":

Melodic Rhythm: My country! 'tis of thee

Beat:

Further rhythms are created by the performer's *accent* or *stress*, and by the listener's subconscious emphasis of those tones longest apprehended.

Rhythms, like melodies, can be combined into patterns which, when familiar, give pleasure.

TEMPO

The rate of speed of a given composition is called its *tempo*. Tempo is of such importance in determining mood that Wagner and Berlioz declared it the first requisite of proper performance.[10]

The performer can determine appropriate tempo from stated indications and by musical analysis. Composers usually state tempo in Italian terminology for speeds ranging from *vivo* (very fast) to *largo* (very slow). The composer may also provide a metronomic marking. The metronome, invented by Mälzel, a contemporary of Beethoven, is a clocklike mechanical device for equating Italian tempo terminology with the corresponding rates of speed per beat. Each click represents a beat within a measure. Thus, a metronome marking—such as M.M. (Mälzel metronome) $\downarrow = 60$—at the beginning of a composition tells the performer to set the metronome indicator at 60. If he follows the metronome's sixty evenly spaced clicks per minute, he will play at the exact speed desired by the composer. (There are now electrically operated metronomes that blink as well as click.)

In analyzing music for tempo, such elements of musical structure as the frequency of harmonic changes are strongly indicative. Generally speaking, rapidly changing tonal multiplicity is difficult for an audience to comprehend, therefore, the greater the frequency of chord changes, the slower the tempo. Song texts also provide tempo clues. The words "Hickory, Dickory, Dock" suggest a fairly steady walk, while those of "Silent Night," though in the same meter, are obviously to be sung more slowly.

[10] Wagner, Richard, *On Conducting,* William Reeves, London, 1919, p. 20.

METER

As has been stated, a regularly recurring beat exists in almost all music. It serves as punctuation, organizing the long and short notes of melody into twos or threes or combinations thereof.[11] In the music score, the notes comprising such groupings are enclosed by two vertical lines called *measure bars*. This organization by beat is called the *meter*, shown on the score by a symbol, placed at the beginning of a musical selection, that looks like a fraction without a line through it:

$$\frac{6}{8} \quad \frac{4}{4} \quad \frac{3}{2} \quad \frac{12}{8}, \text{etc.}$$

This symbol is called a *time* or *meter signature*.

The lower numeral in the signature indicates a certain note value, for example, $2 = \text{half note}, 4 = \text{quarter note}, 8 = \text{eighth note}$. The upper numeral indicates the number of these notes or their rhythmic equivalent needed to complete a measure. Thus, $\frac{2}{4}$ indicates that two quarter notes, or their equivalent in notational duration, will complete one measure. A very common error made in describing the nature of a meter signature is to say that the upper numeral states the number of beats in a measure and the lower numeral the kind of note that receives one beat. Actually the number of beats in a measure is determined by the tempo of a composition. For example, a $\frac{2}{4}$ marked largo may have four beats in a measure, while a $\frac{2}{4}$ marked presto may have only one. "Silent Night" is marked $\frac{6}{8}$ and has six beats to the measure, but "When Johnny Comes Marching Home," also at $\frac{6}{8}$, has only two. The number of beats in a measure cannot always be determined from the meter signature alone. An examination of the music itself is frequently necessary.

DYNAMIC INTENSITY

Music, like speech, receives much of its interest from changes in loudness and accent. A musical performance lacking in dynamic contrasts would be of no more interest than a lecturer's monotonous drone. The character of the music determines the intensity of each musical phrase. The intensity desired by the composer dictates his choice of voices or instruments, affecting the volume of tone produced. Thus, to ascertain dynamics properly, dynamic symbols must be supplemented by analysis of the score's changing instrumentation.

EXPRESSIVE INFLECTION

Related to dynamics, *expressive inflection* refers to the emotional quality of vibrato (quivering of tone) as well as to the dynamic rise and fall within each musical phrase.

[11] $\frac{5}{8}$ and $\frac{5}{4}$ consist of a group of three notes alternating with a group of two, or vice versa.

The earliest form of Western music notation denoted not individual pitch, but the changing dynamic intensity of traditional religious text settings the singer was presumed to know. This expressive inflection of text, known as *cantillation*, constituted Egyptian, Vedic, Hebrew, and Gregorian chant (the last being the earliest form of Christian liturgical music, which evolved from the preceding Hebrew).

The symbols used in the Middle Ages to express cantillation were called *neumes*. The composer today also uses terms and symbols to indicate appropriate inflection.

Expressive inflection should reflect the demands of the score. As a general rule, rising melodic lines presage rising dynamic intensity, while falling melodic lines presage the reverse. All dynamic symbols should be regarded as merely suggestions to the final arbiter, the performer. For this reason, inflection is frequently referred to as "performer's phrasing" or "nuance." It is the very breath of performance, for without it music has no more vitality than a metronome.

MODE, SCALE, AND TONALITY

A string of a given length vibrates at a certain rate per second, called its *frequency of vibration*. A string half as long vibrates twice as fast and sounds a higher pitch. A string twice as long as the first vibrates at half the frequency and sounds a lower pitch. This tonal interval, called an *octave*, is in some cultures divided into as many as twenty-two separate pitches. The Western musical system divides the octave into twelve equi-distant intervals called *half steps*. This may be verified by examining the piano keyboard, which contains twelve keys—seven white and five black—between any tone and its octave. The reason for the use of twelve tones, a system devised in early antiquity, is that the instinctive steps of the human voice are the octave, the fifth, and fourth. These steps may be produced on a stringed instrument by stopping a string at a distance of one-half, two-thirds, and three-fourths its length respectively. The lowest common denominator of 2, 3, and 4 is 12. Therefore, the necks of ancient lutes were divided into twelve equal parts to enable the player to produce these tones from one string.[12]

Since any pipe or string when played automatically resonates or vibrates over its full length and smaller portions of its length, each tone consists of a *fundamental* or *primary tone* and a succession of *overtones* of diminishing strength. The order of the first overtones of any tone are the octave, the fifth (such as the interval C–G), the double octave, and the major third (such as the interval C–E) above the double octave. (Overtones are discussed in Chapter 7.)

An ascending or descending arrangement of tones within the octave is called a *scale*. The twelve-tone arrangement is called a *chromatic scale*. Skipping every other

[12] Early scales were constructed by using twelve equidistant holes (on pipes) or fretmarks (on string instruments). While such a system produced accurate octaves, fifths, fourths, and minor thirds (ten-twelfths of a string), the other equidistant points produced microtones; that is, steps less than a half tone apart. Because of this, the arithmetic progression of twelfths was replaced by a geometric progression, a string stopped at a fifth of its length producing a major third (an interval of two whole steps) and at a sixth of its length a minor third (an interval of one whole and a half step).

tone in the chromatic scale creates a series of whole steps: a *whole-tone scale*. A pentatonic scale has five tones. Its sound may be demonstrated by playing the octave using only the black keys of the piano. Oriental and other musical cultures have scales that utilize smaller intervals than the half step.

MODALITY

In Western music, the primary method of constructing an octave scale consists of an ascending or descending arrangement of eight half and whole tones, called *diatonic*.[13] This scale may be arranged to sound major, minor, modal, each having a distinctive, easily recognizable quality based on the distribution of the whole and half steps within the octave.[14]

TONALITY

The tone first in the scale gives its pitch name to the scale's "key" and is called its *tonic*. The fifth tone is called the *dominant* because it is the strongest overtone of the tonic after the octave. With the third ascending note of the scale, these tones are often referred to as the *tonic triad* or key center. As previously stated, the tones of the major tonic triad are the principal overtones of the tonic tone, and all the tones of the major scale of a given tonic are overtones of either that tonic or the dominant.

The scale steps, depending upon their position within the scale, seem to require the playing of other tones. This tendency, called *resolution*, becomes stronger when tones are combined in chord groups.

Since melodies in traditional Western music are organized around a given key center, concluding on the first step of the key, or within the tonic triad, creates a feeling of finality lacking in varying degrees with other steps. The indecisiveness of the latter results from the demand of tendential resolution for the tonic triad.[15]

The organization of scales may be illustrated by the use of ladder diagrams. (Musical illustrations of songs in various modes are found in Chapters 5, 6, and 7.)[16]

Needless to say, these are not all the scales employed for music. A composer or a people may utilize any combination of intervals within the octave, as for instance the three steps in the Chinese song, "Trot, Pony Trot," or the seventeen in the Balinese and the twenty-two in the Hindu octave.[17] Obviously the latter two scales cannot be played on Occidental instruments designed to perform Occidental intervals.

[13] The word "octave" is derived from the Greek *okto* meaning eight.
[14] Piston, Walter, *Harmony*, W. W. Norton & Company, Inc., New York, 1941, Chapter I. Also, cf. Chapter 6.
[15] Redfield, John, *Music, A Science and An Art*, Alfred A. Knopf, Inc., New York, 1927, pp. 71ff.
[16] See Chapters 5 and 7 for ear training in chordal harmony.
[17] The pitch of the Western scale is itself subject to aesthetic variation and thus to Oriental subdivision. See Charles Shakford, "Some Aspects of Perception," Part I, *Journal of Music Theory* (November, 1961), pp. 162–202; Part II (Spring, 1962), pp. 66–90; Part III (Winter, 1962), pp. 295–303; Yale University School of Music Publication, New Haven, Conn.

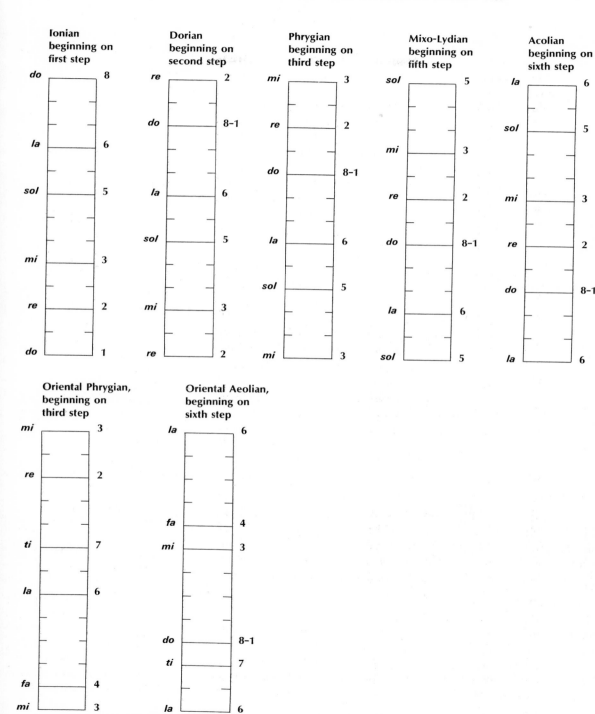

FIGURE 10-1 Pentatonic Scales in Occidental and Oriental Cultures

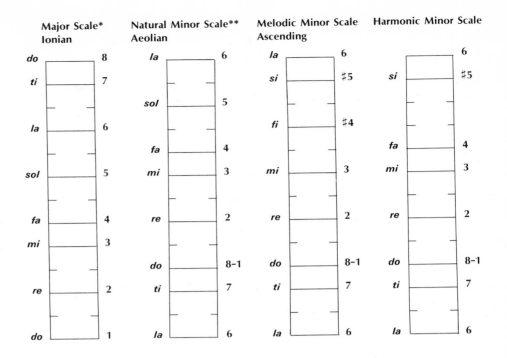

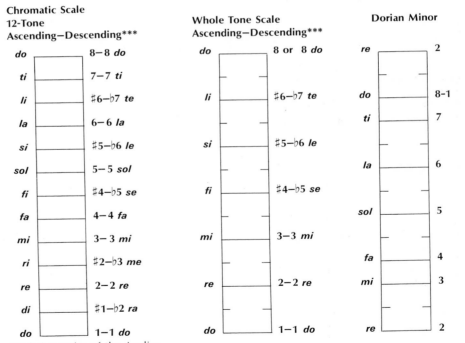

*Relative major of the Aeolian.

**Relative minor of the Ionian.

***Note: Denoting the same pitch differently ascending and descending is called an *enharmonic change.* Thus ♯1 may be ♭2, *di* ascending may be called *ra* descending, in the same scale or melody line.

FIGURE 10-2 Traditional Scales Employed in Occidental Music

Other Modal Scales Employed In Early Musical History and Occasionally Used Today

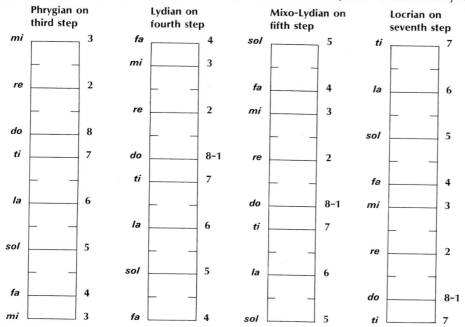

Phrygian on third step

mi	3
re	2
do	8
ti	7
la	6
sol	5
fa	4
mi	3

Lydian on fourth step

fa	4
mi	3
re	2
do	8-1
ti	7
la	6
sol	5
fa	4

Mixo-Lydian on fifth step

sol	5
fa	4
mi	3
re	2
do	8-1
ti	7
la	6
sol	5

Locrian on seventh step

ti	7
la	6
sol	5
fa	4
mi	3
re	2
do	8-1
ti	7

Exotic Scales of Eastern European Countries (Rumanian, Hungarian, Ukrainian, Balkan)

Modified Phrygian on third step (Gypsy Scale)

mi	3
ri	♯2
do	8-1
ti	7
la	6
si	♯5
fa	4
mi	3

Modified Dorian on second step

re	2
do	8
ti	7
la	6
si	♯5
fa	4
mi	3
re	2

Modified Aeolian on sixth step

la	6
si	♯5
fa	4
mi	3
ri	♯2
do	1
ti	7
la	6

North African and Near Eastern Scales (Egyptian, Tunisian, Iranian, Israeli)

Modified Phrygian

mi	3
re	2
do	8-1
ti	7
la	6
si	♯5
fa	4
mi	3

Modified Lydian*

fa	4
mi	or (3)
ri	♯2
re	2
do	8
ti	7
la	6
sol	5
fa	

*In Modified Lydian either *Ri* (♯2) or *Mi* (3) maybe used.

FIGURE 10-3

269

Hans Barth and David Barnett constructed a piano with a double keyboard capable of subdividing the octave into quarter-tone steps. At least this instrument has the advantage of fixed and certain intervals, envied by string players struggling to find the quarter tones, half sharp (⁺), and half flat (♭), demanded by some modern quasi-Oriental composers. Even if the string player succeeds, his audience is likely to believe him amusical rather than amusing. The traditional octave is so ingrained in the Western tradition, any other seems a violation not merely of convention but of nature.

HARMONY

Earliest music was *monodic*, having a single melodic line. However, hearing men's and women's voices singing in unison, composers discovered that the addition of the octave added color to the tone. Then in about the ninth century smaller intervals were added. First women with heavier and men with lighter voices sang a middle part beginning a fifth above the first step of the key, creating a harmonic effect called *organum*.[18] During the medieval period parts at the third and sixth intervals above the melodic line were created. The invention of the *round* or *canon* in Renaissance music required the addition of a second melodic line directly imitating the first, but starting a measure or phrase after the original. This was followed by canons imitating by organum at the fifth step, creating the fugual forms of Baroque music. Slowly, other voices at the third, seventh, ninth, and eleventh interval from the root tone were introduced until there were as many as six tones in a chord.[19] Although each additional tone was a third higher than the next lower tone in the chord, the overtones of these added tones became successively closer, and the chord, therefore, successively more dissonant, especially in its inversions.[20]

Harmony is the subtle combining of diverse tones, rhythms, and melodies creating a new unity from many voices. Understanding the harmonic structure of a musical work requires an advanced stage of musical training. Various writers have attempted to describe the effects of harmonious sound. Pratt suggests that:

Each interval . . . has its own unique formal character. . . . The fifth is hollow, flat, and a bit commonplace; the major third, lively, rich, compact; the major seventh, raspy, bitter, disjointed.[21]

Erskine describes the effect of harmonic resolution thus:

Some chords and sequences of chords make upon us an unfinished impression—they ask a question. Other chords and cadences satisfy with an answer. Out of question and answer come

---

[18] This effect can be illustrated quite easily by having boys sing "America" in the key of C and girls sing the same song in the key of G.

[19] Redfield, *op. cit.*, pp. 74ff.

[20] Thus the ninth is only a whole tone higher than the octave of the root of the chord, and the eleventh only a half tone higher than the octave of the third of the chord. Therefore when a chord is *inverted*, its lower tones being transposed above the remaining tones of the chord, these smaller intervals are reinforced.

[21] Pratt, Carroll C., *The Meaning of Music*, McGraw-Hill Book Company, New York, 1931, p. 7.

the subject matter of music, and also its language, and at last its form. The simplest form of question in music is the dominant seventh chord; the most complete answer is the major triad.[22]

To understand Pratt's analysis, using the Keyboard Scale and Chord Finder, place the indicator for tonic 1 (*do*) on C of the piano and listen to the sound of the intervals C–G for the fifth; C–E for the major third, and C to the B above for the major seventh. Now play a C Major chord, indicated by blue on the chord finder, followed by the G7 chord, which is in red, thus demonstrating Erskine's analysis as well.

TIMBRE

Timbre (pronounced taḿ-br) is a French word referring to the quality of sound. The use of the word "quality" in this sense does not refer to value in terms of beauty, but rather to the distinctive elements that help to identify the kind of voice or instrument producing the sound.[23] A child's voice differs from that of an adult, a man's from a woman's, strings from wind instruments, and percussion from any other. Among children's voices, differences between high tones that are reedy and high tones that are flutelike are immediately apparent. Within adult female voices there are distinctions between sopranos and altos. Sopranos are subdivided into coloratura, lyric, dramatic, and mezzo, while the lower alto voice is called contralto. Adult male voices are classified as lyric and heroic tenors, baritones and basses.

Musical instruments may be acoustically divided into string, woodwind, brass, and percussion families, each member of each family having a distinctive, identifiable timbre. Thus a cultivated listener should be able to distinguish the sound of the violin, viola, violoncello, and string bass, and an expert musician, not only the sound of those instruments, but the sound of their particular strings. Similarly, among woodwinds, the difference in sound between the edge-tone instruments of piccolo and flute, the double-reed instruments of oboe, English horn, bassoon, and contrabassoon, and the single-reed instruments of clarinet and saxophone can be distinguished. With sufficient sophistication, the particular member of the clarinet family such as the E♭ sopranino clarinet, B♭ soprano, E♭ alto, B♭ bass and contrabass can be recognized, likewise the characteristic quality of the soprano, alto, tenor, baritone, and bass saxophone.

Brass instruments contain even greater refinements of timbre. Cornet, trumpet, and fluegelhorn are all soprano brass instruments but they differ in their construction, variations in shape of tubing and mouthpiece producing tones of distinctly differing quality. There are also qualitative differences among the alto instruments: alto horn, mellophone, and French horn; tenor instruments: trombone, tenor horn, baritone, and euphonium; and between bass tubas and sousaphones.

The sound of pitch and non-pitch percussion instruments can be distinguished

[22] Erskine, John, *What Is Music?*, J. B. Lippincott Company, Philadelphia, 1944, p. 13; for ancient attitudes toward the effect of harmony see Curt Sachs, *The Rise of Music in the Ancient World, East and West*, W. W. Norton & Company, Inc., New York, 1943, pp. 108, 248.

[23] The distinctiveness is created by the differing overtones produced by any vibrating instrument such as a person's vocal chords.

and each group in turn classified according to material: wood, metal, membrane, or their combination. Among pitch producers are the piano, xylophone, glockenspiel, chimes, tympani, and celeste. The non-pitch percussion, called by the professional *traps*, includes snare drum, tom-tom, cymbals, bass drum, triangle, wood block, sandpaper block, whip, whistles, tambourine, castanets; and the Latin American cowbell, guiro, maracas, temple blocks, and claves; all of which are used to enhance rhythmic effect and tonal color.

Great enjoyment can be derived from the ability to identify voices and instruments, to determine whether the source of a given sound is a coloratura or dramatic soprano, an oboe or a flute.

STYLE

Style is the name given to the sum of those distinctive characteristics of musical expression that can be ascribed to a given age, composer, or performer.[24] Style is seldom the creation of any individual. It is rather a product of period and circumstance. The composer absorbs as part of his sensibility the conventions of his age, its idioms and its demands. He is the inheritor of the techniques of musical expression of his immediate predecessors, who have educated his audience and created their expectations. Both composer and audience are affected by contemporary intellectual movements and aesthetic fashions, such as Neoclassicism in the eighteenth century, Romanticism in the nineteenth, and Technological Eclecticism in the twentieth. Though each composer seeks to assert his individuality, he is at the same time confined by the limitations of his patron, be it church, court, impressario, or audience. Music is much more of a social art than painting or literature, and the larger the scale of composition, the more dependent on patronage is the composer for performance. The rise of extremely personal and experimental music in the United States bears a direct relationship to the increased support of composers by universities and foundations expecting neither pleasure nor profit from the result. Of course, the more of such music performed, the more will the public become conditioned to accept and eventually demand it.

On less sophisticated levels, all nations and races have particular rhythmic, scalar, and harmonic idioms, easily recognized in popular and folk music. Thus, it is relatively simple to distinguish Latin American, Hungarian, Russian and Near Eastern music, as it is to identify spirituals, Calypso, rock-'n-roll, and jazz. The ethnic scales of various nationalities are discussed in Chapter 6. Song sources and recordings are found in Appendixes I and III.

The ability to identify the styles of composers and nationalities, their characteristic forms, rhythms, harmonies, and melodic designs, gives the keenest pleasure to the initiated.[25]

[24] See Paul Shrecker, *Work in History*, Princeton University Press, Princeton, N.J., 1948, pp. 56ff.
[25] See Herman Scherchen, "The Musical Past and the Electronic Future," *Saturday Review*, XLVII:44 (October 31, 1964), pp. 63–65.

STRUCTURES OF MUSICAL FORM

Modern composers have expanded both the aural spectrum and the aural aesthetic. The former has been accomplished by the inclusion of nontonal sounds and tonal sounds of nontraditional pitch, the latter by discarding traditional musical forms. Because music is an art that occurs in time, musical form must by definition consist of repetition of an aural sequence in various guises. Since the beginning of the twentieth century, and at an accelerated pace since the end of the First World War, the trend of modern serious composition has been to change the traditional nature of the repeated aural sequence and the basis on which such repetition occurs. The abandonment of traditional concepts of melody, key, and pitch has deprived the audience of its accustomed cues to recognition, and assaulted its accustomed criteria of sensibility.

Composition since the First World War may be classified into four major schools, by no means mutually exclusive: the ethnocentric, electrocentric, equicentric, and merely eccentric.

The *ethnocentric* group—including Bartók (Hungarian), the early Stravinsky (Russian) Janáček (Czech), Orff (German), and Ives (American)—generally an earlier generation than the composers of other schools, were primarily concerned with expanding the range of musical technique, especially in the areas of rhythm and polytonality, in order to convey a sense of regional color.

The *electrocentric* composers, under the impetus of Edgar Varèse, have sought to substitute modern electronic devices for the traditional orchestra, the theory being that since to the modern audience music is produced by amplification of a recording device, the means of generating the recording is aesthetically irrelevant. This development in music is comparable to a similar trend in film. A film may consist of photographs of living actors, photographs of drawings representing living actors (animation), or drawings imprinted on the film itself. Varèse and his disciples compose on the recording tape itself. The orchestra is a vestigial and unnecessary intermediary.

The *equicentric* group are devotees of the serial technique developed by Schoenberg. Serial technique substitutes for the traditional concept of theme and key, that of a twelve-tone row, each tone of which is of equal importance. A row is subject to repetition by various well-defined means borrowed from traditional forms of composition: inversion, attenuation, retrograde motion, retrograde inversion, and the like. While the older practitioners of this system, Schoenberg, Berg, and Stravinsky, combined technical brilliance with a flair for emotional chromaticism, the later serialists such as Webern tend to an abstract brittleness.

The merely *eccentric* composers elevate aesthetic anarchy to doctrine. Dignified by the pseudo-academic description of "aleatory music," they create "chance noise." In effect, Stockhausen and Cage argue that the expectant audience is the true composer. Therefore silence is as valid a musical instance as any other.[26]

The intellectual apprehension of musical forms can be among the highest satisfactions derived from listening to music. Broudy goes so far as to say:

[26] See generally, Leonard Bernstein, *The Joy of Music,* Simon and Schuster, Inc., New York, 1959, pp. 180ff; Jacques Chailley, *40,000 Years of Music,* Farrar, Straus & Giroux, Inc., New York, 1964.

In music, as in all art, form makes or breaks the work with regard to both the composer and the listener. Unless the listener detects form, he is limited to the most rudimentary level of appreciation, namely, the apprehension of the aesthetic qualities of isolated tones and phrases. Hence . . . the ability to detect form is the heart of musical education.[27]

And Hartshorn reinforces this thesis by adding:

An understanding of form becomes the master key to an understanding of how music communicates. What a piece of music means may not be the same for all people, and it may not have identical meaning for the same person who experiences it at two different times. In music education, more important than "what" music means is "how" it means it; for, in developing an understanding of how music communicates, the student is dealing with the content of music itself.[28]

PLANNING LISTENING LESSONS

The musical experience is threefold: 1) creating, 2) performing, 3) listening. Listening becomes skilled when sensory experience is oriented by rational discrimination based on knowledge of musical creation and performance. Since creation and performance are related to other forms of endeavor, the cultivated listener will apply knowledge of the other liberal arts, as well as of the techniques of music, to inform his appreciation.

Prepare a class for listening by presenting relevant data through oral and written program notes designed to direct attention to specific aspects of composition and performance. However, it is important to introduce such information only after the class has had the opportunity to enjoy the work simply on a sensory basis. A lesson plan for instructed listening should include the following steps:

1. Initial sensory enjoyment of the piece as pleasurably organized sound. Analyze repetitions for
    a. Dynamics (loud and soft passages)
    b. Tempo and beat (contrasts in speed)
    c. Meter (pulse and accent)
    d. Rhythms within pulse
    e. Qualities (voices or instruments performing melodic line)
    f. Modality (major, minor, or modal)
    g. Mood (gay, somber, light and airy, heavy and dark, martial, funereal)
    h. Accompaniment (polyphonic, harmonic)
    i. Form (motives, phrases, periods, sections)
    j. Style characteristics (period, nationality, ethos, composer)
    k. Character (legato, staccato, dancelike)

[27] Broudy, Harry S., "Realism," in *Basic Concepts in Music Education,* National Society for the Study of Education, Chicago, Ill., 1958, p. 71.
[28] Hartshorn, William C., "Music for the Academically Talented," *Music Educators Journal,* XLVII:1 (Sept.-Oct., 1960), pp. 33-36.

2. Activities to enhance listening
  a. Sing themes
  b. Dramatize character of music through bodily movement: dancing, swaying, tapping, clapping, imitating natural or mechanical rhythms
  c. Accompany with rhythm instruments to aid analysis of changing motives, phrases
  d. Accompany as capable with melodic instruments
  e. Illustrate with drawings inspired by listening
  f. In upper grades emulate the conductor by attempting to read score and determine the conducting beats.
3. Library and homework
  a. Research biographical material concerning composers and performers
  b. Correlate music with other classroom activities and subject matter
  c. Locate the region from which the composer drew inspiration: for example, locate site of Ferde Grofé's *Grand Canyon* suite, *Mississippi* Suite; Copland's *Appalachian Spring, Billy the Kid, Rodeo*
  d. Read poems and stories that inspired musical compositions: *The Sleeping Beauty, The Magic Nutcracker, Hansel and Gretel*
  e. Present reproductions of art conveying mood similar to that of music, for example, Remington's paintings of Western scenes for *Grand Canyon* suite
4. Symbolize musical forms by line drawings

  a. Binary $\boxed{A}$ — $\bigcirc\!\!B$

  b. Ternary $\underrightarrow{\text{Intro}}$ $\boxed{A}$ bridge $\bigcirc\!\!B$ bridge $\boxed{A}$ $\underleftarrow{\text{Coda}}$

  c. Rondo $\boxed{A}$ – $\bigcirc\!\!B$$\boxed{A}$ – $\triangle\!\!C$ – $\boxed{A}$ – $\diamond\!\!D$ – $\boxed{A}$

  d. Fugue

S   subject at fifth

A   subject at fifth—counter melody

T   subject at tonic—counter melody

B subject—counter melody

  e. Theme and variations

Theme	Embellishment	Diminution	Augmentation	Modality	Inversion
1	2	3	4	5	6

SAMPLE LISTENING LESSON

The following third grade lesson plan uses the Andante from Haydn's "Surprise" Symphony to illustrate theme and variation:

1. Play the Andante movement

2. Can the class explain the reason the symphony is nicknamed "Surprise"?

3. Locate Austria and the city of Vienna on a map of Europe

4. Discuss Franz Josef Haydn, born in 1732, the same year as George Washington

5. Demonstrate the use of folk themes derived from his farm boyhood (see Source Materials in Appendix III)

6. Teach the class to sing the opening theme of the Andante on a neutral syllable "loo" from a previously prepared theme chart

7. Play the recording again and ask the children to raise their hands every time they hear the theme, even when changes occur in rhythm or modality

Another day, before listening to the symphony, play, and ask the class to sing, "Twinkle, Twinkle Little Star" in the key of C. Make the following variations on successive repetitions, asking the class to try to explain the changes (Figure 10-4).

1. Notate each variation on the chalkboard adding its appropriate form symbol as indicated in Figure 10-4, numbering the variations consecutively

2. Play the variations at random. See if the children can identify them, indicating the answer by showing the right number of fingers for the variation played

Now relate the forms of variation of "Twinkle, Twinkle Little Star" to the Haydn Andante.

1. Point to the similarity between the rhythms and phrases of the two pieces

2. On repetitions of the Andante, see if the class can identify its variations by the number or symbol of the analogous variations of "Twinkle, Twinkle Little Star," writing the sequences of variations as they listen

3. Focus attention on the parts played by different instruments:

    a. Violins—melody

    b. Flutes—embellishment

    c. Oboe—melody

    d. Cellos—low voices

The sequence of prominence of each of these instruments in the orchestration of the symphony can be symbolized by its letter in the above list.

4. Focus attention on the A and B sections of the theme. Ask the children to symbolize the sequence of the sections by letter

5. Add a rhythm score based on strong beat, pulse beat, and melodic rhythm. Let the children select the instruments to be used

6. Teach an Austrian folk dance and a minuet, in anticipation of hearing the Minuet from the same Haydn symphony (see Appendix I)

THEME AND VARIATIONS ON "TWINKLE, TWINKLE LITTLE STAR"

LISTENING TO CONTEMPORARY MUSIC[29]

In an attempt to reflect the relationship of man to modern technology, contemporary composers are expanding the aural spectrum to include new sound sources and techniques.

New Sound Sources

Musique Concrète: employs noises of indefinite pitch, which are either literal sounds such as auto horns, airplane engines, factory noises, grunts, groans, shouts; or mechanical sounds, recorded on tape and then organized into some free form structure. (*Ballet Mécanique,* Georges Antheil, Columbia ML 4956.)

Electronic Music: called "sound painting" by one of its exponents, Henri Pousseur, employs sound produced by electronic devices. Just as ballet and opera music evolved into a form aesthetically valuable in itself, so electronic music has become emancipated from its original function providing background for radio and television programs. (*Poème Electronique,* Edgar Varèse, Columbia MS 6146, or *Sounds of New Music,* Folkways, FX 6160.)

Expanded Tonal and Rhythmic Spectrum

1. *Melody:* is no longer limited to the traditional contiguity of closely related intervals within a framework of diatonic or chromatic harmony. Tendential resolution and other evidence of traditional aesthetic progression are eliminated by melodic intervals that leapfrog octaves. (*Complete Music,* Anton Webern, Columbia K4L 232)

2. *Serial Tone Row:* developed by Arnold Schoenberg about 1923 as a technique to free music from dependence upon key (see Figure 9-5).[30] A *tone row* is a set or series of twelve tones of the chromatic scale, in which, as the result of not being related by any concept of key, each tone has equal value. For development, a row is varied by any of forty-eight variations, based upon the following prime forms:

    a. Original series or set
    b. Retrograde: series played in reverse or backward
    c. Inversion: intervals are inverted
    d. Retrograde-Inversion: series played backwards and inverted

Each of these prime forms may be transposed to any of the eleven other tones or steps of the chromatic scale. Of course, there may also be rhythmic alterations of the prime forms for additional variation. (*Chamber Concerto for Violin, Piano and Thirteen Winds,* Alban Berg, Columbia M2S 620)

3. *Improvisation:* a technique originally popular in Baroque and Classical periods,

---

[29] For an excellent bibliography of recordings, together with descriptions of contemporary techniques and procedures for teaching children to create compositions and to participate in rhythmic bodily expression using contemporary musical idioms, see *Experiments in Musical Creativity, A Report of Pilot Projects,* Contemporary Music Project, Music Educators National Conference, Washington, D.C., 1966.

[30] Page 241.

now employed in both jazz and non-jazz idioms. Improvization requires the development of free fantasias or rhapsodies around a given theme. (*Dialogues for Jazz Combo and Orchestra*, Dave Brubeck, Columbia CS 8257; *Time Cycle*, Lukas Foss, Columbia MS 6280)

    4. *Unusual Scales:*

      a. Pentatonic: five-tone scales occur both in Occidental and Oriental music: Occidental, scale steps 1, 2, 3, 5, 6; Oriental, scale steps 6, 7, 8, 3, 4; or Javanese, whole-tone scale steps 1, 2, 3, ♯4, ♯5

      b. Modal Scale: ancient scales whose structure resembles a major scale played commencing with a scale step other than the first. Debussy and Ravel frequently employed Dorian, Phrygian, and Mixo-Lydian scales

      c. Whole-tone Scale: one beginning on C, the other on C♯. Since scale steps are uniform, a scale beginning on D has the same intervals as that beginning on C (*Piano Preludes*, Vol. 1, Claude Debussy, Columbia ML 4977)

      d. Scales built on intervals of thirds, fourths, fifths

    5. *Unusual Harmonic Patterns:*

      a. Traditional triadic harmonic structure of chords in two keys (*Appalachian Spring*, Aaron Copland, Columbia MS 6355)

      b. Quartal and quintal harmonies based on intervals of fourths and fifths (*Mathis der Maler*, Paul Hindemith, Columbia MS 6562)

      c. Harmony by various intervals: two-tone chords built on seconds, thirds, fourths, fifths, sixths, or sevenths, combined to form unusual progressions (*Mikrocosmos* Volumes I, II, III, Béla Bartók, Columbia ML 5082, ML 5083, ML 5084)

      d. Polyharmony and Polytonality: combining chords from two or more keys (*Les Choephores*, Darius Milhaud, Columbia MS 6396; *Halloween*, Charles Ives, Cambridge 804; *Le Sacre du Printemps*, Igor Stravinsky, Columbia MS 6319)

      e. Pandiatonic Harmony: chromatic additions to triads to form tone clusters, created by imposing neighboring triads one on the other: that is, combining F and G Major chords. A favorite device of Henry Cowell and Charles Ives (Symphony No. 4, Charles Ives, Columbia MS 6775; *Advertisement*, Henry Cowell)

    6. *Unusual Rhythmic Organization:*

      a. Rhythmic Drive: rhythmic force rather than melodic or harmonic interest constitutes the motivating element of form and structure (*Le Sacre du Printemps*, Stravinsky, Columbia MS 6319)

      b. Syncopation: shifting rhythmic accents off the beat and frequently changing meters, showing strong influence of jazz idioms

      c. Irregular meters, frequently changed, organized in phrase lengths rather than in traditional duple or triple measures

      d. Unmetered music organized around speech phrases or cantillation (Cantorial singing and choral speech. *Cantorial Jewels*, Columbia ML 4805; *Pierrot Lunaire*, Arnold Schoenberg, Columbia M2S 679)

      e. Polyrhythms: combining multi-meters, $\frac{2}{4}$ with $\frac{6}{8}$, $\frac{2}{4}$ with $\frac{3}{4}$, a favorite device of Charles Ives

    7. *Cacophony*

    Mention should be made of the current *avant-garde* musical fad, cacophony, defined by Webster's dictionary as "a combination of discordant sounds." The rationale of its musical creation is that such sounds reflect the world and that what exists is by definition beautiful. Traditionalists, on the other hand, trace the word to the ancient Greek word *kakos,* meaning bad or evil, and react accordingly. In speech, cacophony refers to "an uncouth or disagreeable sound of words, proceeding from the meeting of harsh letters or syllables." (Aristophanes parodied sententious Greek verse by a chorus of frogs croaking "koax, koax—Brekekekex, koax.") By analogy, cacophonous music "has a harsh sound, is discordant and unmelodious."

Modern cacophony is produced by combining a sequence of sound effects on electronic tape; in the orchestra it is produced by using the extreme ranges of musical instruments (string instruments played on the short string in back of the bridge; brass instruments overblown; percussion, especially hardware, pounded fortissimo; woodwinds honked; and every variety of noise, including grunts, howls, groans, and shrieks added). Suggestion of fixed pitch is avoided. By its nature, cacophonic music cannot employ traditional music notation. Each composer invents his own symbolic system, which may include traditional terminology but seldom a music staff. Performers must be taught interpretation by the composer himself or else have specific written instructions. For the listener conditioned to the tonality, consonance, and resolving dissonances of conventional music, deliberate cacophony makes deafness desirable. The composer of cacophonic music insists, however, that traditional sounds have been fully exploited and that expansion of the aural spectrum is now needed.

At present, the cacophonists have few adherents. However, it is hardly fair to judge an artistic movement by less than its best. As yet no cacophonous work has exploded a hydrogen bomb, man's loudest, most symbolic, and most aesthetic sound, since inevitably unique in each listener's experience. Until a philanthropic foundation enables some advanced composer to make this ultimate demonstration of his art, musicologists must withhold definitive judgment as to its merits.

The following are some general rules and some of the music signs and symbols that are employed by contemporary cacophonous composers.[31]

1. Pitch is frequently left to the judgment of the performer

2. The music staff may consist of a single line

3. A note on the line represents any pitch in the middle register of the instrument

4. A note above the line calls for a pitch above the middle register

5. A note below the line calls for a pitch below the middle register

6. Highness and lowness above the middle register may be indicated by added leger lines:

[31] See "Mid Century Music," special issue of the *Selmer Bandwagon,* XIII:5 (November, 1965); also *New Sounds for Woodwinds,* Bruno Bartolozzi, Oxford University Press, London, 1967.

7. Rhythms are notated as in traditional music, except that a stopwatch is sometimes employed. In such instances the conductor indicates the start and cutoff of sound
    8. Scoring for instruments:

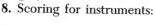 Keyboard

Woodwinds

Brass

Strings

Damped note on piano, hold string inside piano while playing corresponding key

Make any noise performer wishes

An example of one measure from a score for a contemporary piece of cacophonous music is illustrated below.

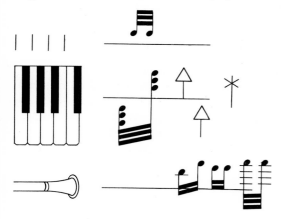

NEW PERFORMING TECHNIQUES

The composer is concerned with the organization of melody, harmony, rhythm, dynamics, and form, and with the kinds of sounds produced by instruments and voices. The twentieth century is an age of musical innovation, demanding new means to perform new sounds. Jazz musicians especially have been the source of many of the brass, woodwind, and percussive techniques listed below.

Before presenting recorded music, list on the board the distinctive instruments to be heard and describe any novel techniques of performance.

Strings

Glissando: a chromatic slide resulting from pressing one finger up or down a string while bowing. If the string is not depressed to the finger board, natural harmonics are produced as the nodal points are passed

Sul ponticello: bowing near the bridge to create a glassy, almost screeching effect

Sul ponticello pizzicato: plucking the string near the bridge, making a banjolike sound

Col legno: playing with the stick instead of the hair of the bow. Drawing the stick across the string produces an eerie sound; bouncing the stick on the string produces a buzzing as of insects

Tremolo: rapidly bowing over the fingerboard near the tip of the bow creates a shimmering effect; near the bridge a scratchy, glassy effect

Slow vibrato: alternately shading on and off pitch by quarter tones creates "bent" pitch, a characteristic of Oriental music

Trills: trills on successive diatonic or chromatic steps create a fluttering effect

Thrown spiccato: bouncing the bow in a definite rhythmic pattern creates a jigging effect as of tap dancing

Bowing behind the bridge: produces a howling, shrieking effect of nonperiodic vibrations, a noise like chalk scraping on a blackboard, only worse

Brasses

Flutter tonguing: a trilling of the tongue in the mouthpiece, creating a rough, jazzy tone

Various mutes: "wah-wah" mutes; plastic straight mutes; hard hat mutes; each creates different tone colors. A muted effect is also created by placing a hand or small megaphone in the bell of the instrument

Bent tone: depressing the valve part way on a trumpet depresses the tone, creating the effect of a crooner's quarter tone

Extremely high range: creates a sense of emotional climax because of the shrieking sound, particularly when combined with

Glissandi or smears: a chromatic slide up or down

Woodwinds

Flutter tongue: as above, especially effective in a flute's low register, producing a sound like the "crooing" of pigeons. In high registers creates a rough shriek

Slap tonguing on reeds: a percussive, slapping sound produced when the tongue hits and withdraws from a vibrating reed. Especially effective on low register saxophones

Glissandi: the famous opening of *Rhapsody in Blue* illustrates the glissando on a clarinet

Subtone: an amplified tone produced by a clarinet placed inside a large megaphone with holes in the sides to permit the player's hands, the mouthpiece protruding from the top

Bent tone: as on brasses, altering pitch a quarter tone downward. On woodwinds accomplished by releasing lip pressure on the reed

Prepared Piano

A *prepared piano* is a piano whose strings, according to the pianist's whim, have been impeded by various objects: paper clips, inner tubes, pieces of metal, and the like. Of course, any object placed on a string alters the tone quality

Plucking strings: instead of playing the keyboard, the performer lifts the lid of the piano and strums *glissando* across the strings, or plucks tones like a harp. Another method is to select chords on the keyboard with one hand, put down the damper pedal, then strum the chord strings inside the piano with the other

Massive tone clusters: producing the sound of rolling thunder or breaking surf by either rolling or crashing the arm down; for the effect of chimes, striking the high tones with the right fist

Glissando: running the keyboard with the backs of the fingers

Percussion

Anything that will clink, clank, or clunk, thump, scrape, or squeal, becomes a fit instrument for the creation of sound. Spike Jones "played" tuned bedsprings, oxygen tanks, even a bleating goat

Electronic Amplification

Not only guitars are being amplified, but also bowed string instruments. One violin can now sound as loud as a hundred, and as bad

Electronic Alteration of Tempo

Playing a record at a speed different from that at which recorded will demonstrate possible alterations of pitch, rhythm, and quality

Spoken Voices

A speaking chorus may employ non-pitched vocal techniques utilizing either conversational inflection or varied speech levels at high, middle, and low registers, with glissando slides from one to another:

Here comes John, he can't swim.

A Checklist for Listening Activities in Upper Grades[32]

This type of checklist might be mimeographed for use in the upper grades to help focus children's attention on musical elements as they listen.

[32] See F. A. Viggiano, *Music Listening Evaluation Form*, William C. Brown Company, Inc., Dubuque, Iowa, 1961. Also, Melvin Berger, *Instrumental Music in Perspective*, Sam Fox Publ. Co., Inc., New York, 1963.

Title of Piece: **Composer:**
Place an X next to the word that best fits what you hear.
   I. Meter: A feeling of twos............A feeling of threes............
  II. Rhythm: Simple............Complex............
 III. Melody: Smooth legato............Jerky staccato............Short motives............Long
          line............
  IV. Harmony: Pleasantly consonant............Harshly dissonant............Cacophonic............
   V. Form and Structure: Binary A B............Ternary A B A............Fugue............Rondo
          A B A C A D A............Theme and Variations............Waltz............March............
          Minuet............Gavotte............Laendler............Scherzo............Nocturne............Bal-
          lade............Other............
  VI. Texture: Monodic (single melody)............
          Homophonic (melody with harmonic accompaniment)............
          Polyphonic (several intertwined melodies)............
          Harmonic (melody less important than harmony)............
 VII. What performing group do you hear?
          Solo with accompaniment of Piano............Orchestra............Other............
          Orchestra............Chorus............Band............Jazz Band............
          Solo Voice: Soprano............Alto............Tenor............Baritone............Bass............
          Solo Instrument: Strings: Violin............Viola............Cello............Bass............Harp
          ....Guitar............Banjo............Mandolin............
          Woodwinds: Piccolo .... Flute .... Oboe .... Bassoon .... Clarinet
          ....Saxophone............Recorder............
          Brass: Trumpet............Trombone............French Horn............Tuba............Baritone
          ....
          Percussion: Tympani .... Chimes .... Celeste .... Bells .... Others
          ....
VIII. What is the mood of the music? Martial............Funereal............Dancelike............
          Fairylike............Other............
  IX. How would you use such music? In church............As dance music............As movie
          background music............In a theater............For solemn occasions such as a cor-
          onation or funeral............For pleasurable listening............
   X. What is the scale primarily? Major............Minor............Modal............
  XI. When do you think this music was composed?
          About the time Columbus discovered America (Renaissance)............
          About the time of the Mayflower (Early Baroque)............
          About the time of George Washington (Rococo-Classic)............
          About the time of Abraham Lincoln (Romantic)............
          About the time of the Spanish American War (Late Romantic)............
          About the time of the First World War (Impressionist)............
          About the time of the Second World War (Modern)............
          Recently (Contemporary)............

Such a checklist can serve as the basis for further discussion, and can be added to music
notebooks as a reminder of compositions studied.

OUTLINE OF DEVELOPMENT OF MUSICAL FORMS AND TYPES OF ORCHESTRATION

A record collection should include music in various forms and illustrate different types of orchestration. The following brief outline can serve as a checklist. Before buying a professionally prepared program of recordings from a record company analyze its content carefully. (A suggested list of source recordings and a teacher's and children's bibliography will be found in Appendix III.)

I. Historical Periods
   A. Early Christian (A.D. 200 to 800) Monody, Plain Song
   B. Medieval (A.D. 800 to 1400) Ars Antiqua and Ars Nova
      1. Some Instrumental Forms
         a. 1200: Estampie, Danse Royale
         b. 1300: Rota, Saltarello
      2. Some Vocal Forms
         a. 800: Organum
         b. 850: Plain Song Tropes and Sequences
         c. 1100: Troubadours and Trouvere Monody
         d. 1200: Motet
         e. 1300: Ballade, Madrigal, Caccia, Ballata, Isometric Motet
   C. Renaissance Period (1400 to 1600)
      1. Some Instrumental Forms
         a. 1450: Danse Basse, Tourdion, Pavane, Galliard
         b. 1500: English Virginal School
         c. 1500: Ricercare, Canzona, Prelude
      2. Some Vocal Forms
         a. 1400: Motet
         b. 1450: French Chansons, Villota, Canzonetta, Balletto
         c. 1475: Polyphonic Lied
         d. 1525: Cathedral Anthem
         e. 1550: Italian Madrigal
         f. 1575: Verse Anthem
         g. 1575: English Madrigal
   D. Baroque Period (1600 to 1750)
      1. Some Instrumental Forms
         a. 1600–1700: Dance Suite, Sonata, Toccata, Prelude and Fugue, Choral Prelude, Trio Sonata, Concerto Grosso, Solo Concerto
      2. Some Vocal Forms
         a. 1600–1700: Opera (classical subjects), Oratorio, Cantata, Solo Song, Recitative
   E. Rococo Period (1725 to 1775)
      Generally considered a transition from the Baroque to the Classic Period
   F. Classic Period (1750 to 1800)
      1. Some Instrumental Forms
         a. String Quartet, Symphony, Serenade, Concert March, Concert Overture

    2. Some Vocal Forms
      a. Major works for soloists, chorus, and orchestra, Operatic reform toward dramatic emphasis, Operetta, Opera Buffa
  G. Romantic Period (1800 to 1890)
    1. Some Instrumental Forms
      a. Ballet and Ballet Suite, Symphonic Poem, Military March, Virtuoso Instrumental Solo Pieces, Virtuoso Concerti, Incidental Music for Theater (Suites)
    2. Some Vocal Forms
      a. Lieder, Music Drama (Wagnerian), Grand Opera (Verdi), Musical Comedy, American Minstrelsy
  H. Modern to Contemporary (1890 to present day)
    1. Styles: Neoclassicism, Neoromanticism, Impressionism, Gebrauchsmusik (functional music), Atonality, Polytonality, Twelve-tone Serial, Electronic, Random or Aleatory, Primitivism, Cacophonic
    2. Forms: Greater freedom breaking limited restrictions
    In opera moving to "verismo," Puccini, Leoncavallo, Gershwin
II. Types of Orchestration
  A. Solos
    1. Vocal
      a. Soprano: Coloratura, Lyric, Dramatic, Mezzo
      b. Contralto
      c. Tenor: Lyric, Heroic
      d. Baritone: Lyric, Heroic
      e. Basso: Contando, Profundo
    2. Instrumental
      a. Antique Instruments: Vielle, Portative Organ, Krumhorn, Cornette, Lute, Virginal, Antique Flutes, Recorder, Viola d'amore, Viola da gamba
      b. Modern Plectrum Instruments: Guitar, Banjo, Ukulele
      c. Modern Orchestral Strings: Violin, Viola, Cello, Bass, Harp
      d. Modern Woodwinds: Piccolo, Flute, Clarinet, English Horn, Bassoon, Oboe, Saxophone, Contrabassoon
      e. Modern Brass: Trumpet family—trumpet, alto horn, tenor trombone, bass trombone
      Cornet family—cornet, baritone-euphonium, mellophone, tuba-sousaphone
      Saxhorn family—fluegelhorn, French horn, tuben
      f. Percussion: Pitched—xylophone, marimba, chimes, bells, tympani, celeste, piano, temple blocks
      Non-pitched—side drum, tenor drum, bass drum, cymbals, tam-tam, gong, triangle, tambourine, wood block, slap stick, brushes, sandpaper blocks, whistles, etc.
      Latin American—maracas, guiro, claves, cowbells, rasp, bongo drums, conga drum, steel drums

B. Ensembles
1. Vocal: Duets, Trios, Quartets, Large Choruses
2. Instrumental: Duets—strings, woodwinds, brass, combinations
   Trios—piano with strings, woodwinds, brass, combinations (jazz)
   Quartets—strings, woodwinds, brass, combinations (jazz)
   Quintets—strings with piano, added viola or cello to quartet, added clarinet
     or flute to quartet, woodwinds with horn, brass groups, combinations
   Sextets—strings, woodwinds, brass, combinations
   Septets—strings, woodwinds, brass, combinations
   Octets—strings, woodwinds, brass, combinations
3. Larger Ensembles: Military Band, Concert Band, String Orchestra, Symphony Orchestra, Jazz Band (Dixieland), Swing Band (Large), Chamber Orchestra, Jazz Orchestra (with string section)

SUMMARY

Pleasure is derived from music to the extent that the listener is aware of its elements. He must be able to recognize tone, melody, contrasts in dynamics, the emotional rise and fall of expressive inflection, timbre, mood, scale, tonality, the structure of musical forms, style, rhythm, harmony, meter and tempo. It is the way in which the composer combines these elements that determines whether he produces great, good, or mediocre music, or merely noise.

CHAPTER ELEVEN

THE MUSIC TEACHER AS SUPERVISOR AND RESOURCE AND UNIT CONSULTANT

In many schools the music specialist serves not only as a teacher of music, but also as a supervisor of the music activity that is conducted by classroom teachers in self-contained classrooms. As supervisor, he must demonstrate model lessons the classroom teacher will implement, help prepare study units, and demonstrate music methods and materials in workshops sponsored by local school, county, and state teacher organizations.

Unfortunately, in too many schools, the arrival of the music teacher for a demonstration lesson (usually the only music lesson of the week) signals the departure of the classroom teacher for a coffee break. Thus what is really demonstrated to the class is that music must be unimportant. Having failed to interest the teacher, it will certainly not interest the class.

To prevent such occurrences the music specialist must plan to educate the grade teachers before attempting to educate their students. Each grade teacher should be made aware of

1. The general objectives of the total music program (see Chapter 2)

2. The specific objectives for each grade (see Chapter 2)

3. The activities to be carried out to achieve these objectives (see following outline)

4. The procedures to follow in teaching (see Chapters 2 to 10)

5. The materials to be used and their sources (see Chapter 2 and Appendix I)

6. The methods of evaluation of performance, objective tests, and behavioral attitudes (see Measurement and Evaluation in this chapter, pp. 327–336)

SOME PROCEDURES FOR SUPERVISION OF CLASSROOM TEACHERS

At the beginning of the school year, arrange separate meetings for each group of teachers at a given grade level. Distribute to each teacher the general music outline for the grade school as a whole and the specific plan book for the grade. Describe the details of the plan book, demonstrating teaching procedures briefly but with enthusiasm. Be sure to emphasize the particulars of lesson progression, namely, that after a song has been learned, rhythmic and instrumental accompaniment can be added, specific musical concepts listened for, and a new text or tune created.

Give the teachers plenty of time to ask questions, stressing that you are available for consultation. Prepare a brief questionnaire asking each classroom teacher to indicate how you may be of help. Request that the questionnaire be returned in sufficient time to permit you to plan your consultation schedule and research.

Questionnaire for Classroom Teachers

Name: Grade: Room:

I can play a little piano, autoharp, flutophone, recorder, other _____. (Please underline)

I would be willing to exchange teaching music with someone who would like me to teach _____

I would welcome assistance in securing materials for the following:

1. Unit plan for _____;

2. Music to accompany an assembly program on _____;

3. Music for recess recreation;

4. Foreign language songs in _____ (language);

5. Recordings to accompany dances for a unit on _____;

6. Recordings and filmstrips for illustrating _____ (story);

7. A music corner;

8. I need help in learning to play a flute-type instrument, plectrum instrument, autoharp, Latin American rhythm instruments, others. (Please underline)

9. My free time occurs:

10. My room is musically equipped with:

Series of books:

Piano_____Autoharp_____Rhythm Instruments_____Water glasses_____

Staff liner_____Tape recorder_____Other equipment (specify)_____.

AN OUTLINE GUIDE TO MUSIC TEACHING IN THE ELEMENTARY SCHOOL

	Singing	Rhythms	Focused Listening
GRADE 1	Activity songs; songs about family, play, pets, circus, school. Imitate sounds, birds, whistles, sirens, etc. Distinguish shouting voice from singing and speaking voice. Develop pitch sense, vocal quality appropriate to mood.	Dramatize songs with rhythmic play in fundamental movements: walk, run, jump, hop, skip, clap, bend, sway, pull, nod, tap. Develop sense of beat and accent. Use game and action songs.	Listen quietly. Attempt recognition of story, action, instrumentation, dynamics, pitch, rhythms, mood, beat, quality, mode. Alter familiar songs modally, rhythmically, or in tempo to create change of mood.
GRADE 2	Introduce music books. Teach how to find page and line, how to hold books when singing or playing. Sing phrases following music notation (rote to note). Emphasize vowel sounds, pronunciation, consonant endings. Attempt recognition of familiar songs sung by teacher to neutral syallable "loo." Develop awareness of major and minor modality.	Emphasize beat, accent, and duration values in fundamental movements. Accompany free rhythmic activities with singing, drumming, and listening to recordings. Utilize action and game songs in rhythmic play.	Develop ability to recognize duple and triple pulse. Describe complete phrase with hand and body movement. Teach recognition by ear of rhythmic and melodic patterns that are similar. By use of recordings, develop perception of mood quality. Introduce sound of violin, guitar, banjo, flute, trumpet, clarinet, male and female voices.
GRADE 3	Develop sense of inner hearing. Start a phrase and let children finish. Encourage solo singing. Use many rounds and canons, creating original canons with scale songs having familiar nursery rhymes as text.	More involved game songs, easier folk dances. More involved use of rhythm instruments and bells to accompany dance and game movements. Design movements to illustrate strong beat, pulse beat, melodic rhythm.	Introduce recordings of cello, viola, bass, French horn, trombone, tuba, oboe, bassoon, saxophone, melodic percussion; common instrumental dance forms; children's operas such as *Hansel and Gretel*. Correlate listening to appropriate art, poetry, and narration.
GRADE 4	Develop awareness of good vowel quality of musical sounds. Emphasize good diction, proper enunciation. Introduce some of the better Broadway show tunes, foreign language songs, partner songs, and rounds, finger harmony for I, IV, V chords. Harmonize chants, developing sense of the quality of primary triads in major and minor modality. Establish harmony and elementary choir (third and fourth grades)	Develop sense of fast $\frac{3}{8}$ and $\frac{6}{8}$ through folk dances, eurhythmics. Dramatize by free movement, rhythms heard in recordings. Develop feeling for phrase, cadence, and changes in form by folk dancing.	Correlate listening with units in social studies. Identify instruments (violin, viola, cello, flute, clarinet, trumpet, horn, melodic percussion) by sight and sound through live performances and recordings. Develop recognition of some of the simpler forms (march, waltz, and some folk dances), ethnic styles: Indian, spiritual, cowboy, etc. Encourage proper concert listening behavior.
GRADE 5	Sing two-part folk and art songs, descants, more involved partner songs, and rounds. Demonstrate harmonic quality of major and minor chords and scale modality. Introduce chromatic syllables and numbers in scale ladders. Develop small vocal ensembles, special elementary choir (fifth and sixth grades). Encourage solo singing of enlarged repertoire.	Develop recognition of duple and triple meter through square dancing and free bodily expression. Introduce Calypso rhythms employing Latin American instruments. Correlate folk dances with physical education and social studies.	Class study of performance on orchestral instruments: solo, duet, trio, quartet. Contrast band, orchestra, and dance band instrumentation. Arrange trips to live concerts. Identify all string, woodwind, brass, and percussion instruments by sight and sound. Correlate study of music styles with geography and social studies. Recognize some operas, such as *Aida, Carmen, Madam Butterfly, Merrymount*; some ballet suites, such as *Rodeo, Swan Lake*, and *Nutcracker*.
GRADE 6	Sing two-and three-part folk and art songs, Broadway show tunes. Encourage small ensembles and solos. Create special choir. Emphasize learning to discriminate between major and minor harmonies. Employ descants, partner songs, original musical plays.	Develop more refined feeling for phrase. Utilize accent and melodic rhythm in varied meters. Conduct slow six-eight as well as two-four, three-four, and four-four. Correlate square and round dances with social studies. Employ rhythmic sound effects for singing and dancing.	Emphasize listening to live performance in singing and playing. Arrange class visits by high school performers, concert artists where possible. Emphasize historical musical periods and styles. Further exercises on recognition of orchestral instruments by sight and sound. Contrast oratorio with opera. Visit live concerts of orchestras, bands, chorus, ensembles, and solo performances.

Creative Activities	Instrumental Activities	Symbolizing Pitch-rhythm Dynamics	Notation: Reading Writing
Play singing games. Relate music to fundamental movements and vice versa. Develop recognition of rhythms of familiar songs and actions. Imitate sounds. Illustrate songs, add sound effects. Dramatize narratives with drums and other rhythm instruments. Experiment at piano. Find sound pictures.	Accompany singing with piano, guitar, ukulele, melody flute, or recorder. Children should perform on rhythm band instruments, i.e., jingle sticks, triangle, tambourine, toy instruments, tone bells, stair bells, build-a-tune bells. Experiment with pentatonic scale on black keys of piano.	Illustrate notation syllables and interval numbers by body sign language. Draw scale interval numbers and pitch names on chalkboard. Add duration pattern of text under words. Illustrate movement of pitch by hand, and by lines on chalkboard.	Follow contour of melody line by hand movements. Extract intervals from familiar songs and relate them to sign language and music ladder. Relate singing of children's names to numbers on music ladder. Introduce concepts of high and low, loud and soft, beat and accent, quality and mood.
Make simple rhythm instruments. Create two- or four-line poems and improvise a tune for them. Write parodies to familiar tunes. Tune water glasses to scale for song accompaniment. Add tone bells and appropriate sound effects with mood recordings and rhythm instruments. Illustrate duple and triple meter with bodily movement. Relate graphic arts to song texts. Start music notebook.	Make bottle chimes, tuned glasses. Use drum sticks to play rhythms of familiar songs. Play organ point or pedal point for songs with I and V chord accompaniment on bells or piano. Play pizzicato open strings of string instruments. Experiment with two-string ukulele to build a scale in order to measure intervals.	Teach recognition of sign language for familiar songs. Illustrate duration values and accents from familiar songs. Introduce music ladder on chalkboard, relating it to sign language. Add numbers, syllables, and pitch names to music ladder, Describe change of pitch, using hand movements. Use rhythmic notation to illustrate duration patterns of words.	Introduce concepts of music staff, treble clef. Construct original sentence songs. Relate original and familiar songs to music ladder with number, syllables, and pitch names. Introduce vocabulary appropriate to tempo and dynamics as needed. Relate music ladder to music staff drawn from fingers of hand.
Create orchestrations with rhythm instruments and sound effects. Add percussion for game songs and dances. Add bass line using piano and cello pizzicato. Use organ points with bells where appropriate. Add materials to music notebook appropriate to study.	Let children try to accompany I chord and I, V, I chord songs on autoharp, piano, and pizzicato on the open string of string instruments. Teach melody flute, flutophone, etc., using familiar songs.	Teach the reading and writing of familiar rhythm patterns. Conduct movements for $\frac{2}{4}, \frac{3}{4}, \frac{4}{4}$. Write pitch line on chalkboard and measure against scale ladder. Relate scale ladder to step bells, xylophone, tone bells, frets on ukulele. Sing familiar songs with syllables, interval number names in various languages. Relate pitch names to music ladder.	Tune voices by singing scales and tonic chords using syllables, numbers, and pitch names. Let children write melodic line by number and pitch names. Demonstrate scale line and chord tone patterns in songs in books. Use scale ladder to measure intervals. Introduce piano keyboards as visual aid. Introduce Keyboard Scale and Chord Finder and relate to music ladder to demonstrate scale construction.
Create orchestrations by ear using rhythm and simple melody instruments: bells, flutes, etc. Compose complete song. Dramatize original songs by use of bodily movement. Encourage original responses in dance, singing, and playing. Create instrumental group to accompany singing and bodily expression. Play original melodies on piano and simple instruments.	Instruction on autoharp, ukulele, with chord letters. Tune bottle band. Add simple flute and orchestral instruments to singing and rhythms. Class instruction in piano, violin, cello, trumpet, horn, flute, clarinet, percussion. Introduce Latin American instruments for rhythm effects.	Introduce music terminology for dynamics, tempo, style. Develop ability to recognize melodic and harmonic sequences from familiar songs. Translate from ear to voice to eye scale sequences in major and I, IV, and V chords using numbers, syllables, and pitch names. Use piano keyboard as visual aid with Keyboard Scale Finder. Introduce abbreviation of syllables in English system, d, r, m, f, s, l, t, d.	Find do from key signature, interpret meter signature and tempo indication. Read major scale line beginning on do. Develop facility in reading scale line, beginning on other scale steps. Read major triads in given key by numbers, syllables, and pitch names.
Add harmony part to original and familiar songs. Add orchestral instrument accompaniment to singing and dancing. Create partner songs and rounds. Add harmony choir of voices and instruments. Create original dance movements. Create original musical play. Correlate music with social studies. Illustrate songs.	Use band, orchestral, and recreational instruments for classroom orchestra and for special assembly programs. Teach solo and ensemble performance. Add fretted instrument classes on ukulele, guitar, banjo. Arrange a piano accordion class for those interested. Class instruction on larger instruments: string bass, trombone, tuba, saxophone, double reeds (oboe and bassoon), French horn, viola.	Proper interpretation of music terminology: accents, slurs, staccato, legato style. Skill in interpreting numbers, syllables, and notation for I, IV, V7 chords instrumentally on tone bells or autoharp or vocally in harmony choir. Teach construction of major key signatures. Teach chromatic syllables.	Read new chromatic intervals with syllables. Sing related minor scales from music ladder, then from notation. Read easier songs in minor mode. Read second part independently. Read secondary chord intervals, II, III, VI chords. Practice writing syllables and pitch names after measuring intervals by number.
Create rhythmic accompaniments to Latin American dances and songs. Compose original songs with correct music notation. Create musical play. Correlate music with social studies, language arts, visual art, drama. Create "hootenany" sessions with own accompaniment on plectrum instruments. Create own dance movements for ballet, based on original songs or composed suites studied in listening lessons.	Combine percussion, recreational, band, and orchestral instruments in a classroom orchestra to accompany singing and dancing. Encourage participation in a school orchestra and band. Help organize hootenany group of recreational instruments. Develop solo and small ensemble programs for classroom, assemblies, PTA, and community organizations.	Teach sight reading by syllables, numbers, pitch names. Introduce key signatures in minor and relate to piano keyboard and scale finder. Interpret entire musical page rhythmically, melodically, and expressively.	Develop tonal memory. Try to sing songs from memory with numbers, syllables, and pitch names. Read parts independently and in small ensembles. Develop special choir for the talented. Emphasize proper interpretation of music tonally, rhythmically, and expressively. Introduce great staff, bass clef.

OUTLINE FOR CLASSROOM TEACHERS

In the preceding outline, the activities and methods described in this book are summarized by grade. Fleshing out the outline becomes the responsibility of the music specialist. The resulting plan book may be organized for each week, month, or the full year. The greater the detail, the stronger the feeling of security in teaching, and the more effective the learning.

A plan book is also an invaluable aid to a substitute teacher, especially one called in on short notice.

A SAMPLE LESSON PLAN FOR SECOND GRADE

Month of September

I. Objectives
   1. Encourage wholehearted, joyful participation in music activities
   2. Review singing of favorite first grade songs
   3. Improve tone quality of singing
   4. Develop muscular coordination by rhythmic activities and playing of instruments
   5. Focus listening to pitch, intensity, mood, beat, meter, duration
   6. Introduce composer of the month, Johannes Brahms, through song and recording.

II. Procedures
   1. Set up music corner with needed materials
   2. Employ as many suggested activities and procedures from the general outline for each song as time and interest permit. Don't hesitate to amplify the general outline with your own ideas.

III. Materials (the songs referred to will be found on pp. 295–297)
   1. Songs: Review from Grade 1, "Frère Jacques" and "If You're Happy." New songs: "Oranges and Lemons" and "Lullaby"
   2. Recording of "Lullaby," Johannes Brahms, RCA-Victor (L100) *Discovering Music Together*, Book 1, Follett Publ. Co., Chicago
   3. Instruments: autoharp, resonator bells, rhythm instruments, scarves, ball, jump rope, water glasses (see Chapters 2, 3, and 8)
   4. Visual Aids: scale charts (ladder) for pentatonic and major scales, flash cards for rhythms, scale tone groups, tonic chord groups (see Chapters 2 and 3).

IV. Some suggested activities for "Frère Jacques"
   A. Without recourse to notation, solely by ear
      1. Sing to recall melody and words
      2. Teach as an echo song, stressing idea of loud and soft; class sings odd measures 1, 3, 5, 7; individual children answer as echo in measures 2, 4, 6, 8 (see p. 240).

3. Call attention to the similar melodic and similar rhythmic patterns in the song

B. Find the song in the book (see Appendix VII for additional sources)
  1. Ask children to locate the notation of the similar melodic and rhythmic phrases
  2. On repetitions in subsequent lessons, introduce devices suggested for altering the song by changes in modality, meter, and tempo, by inversion and retrograde motion (see Chapter 9, p. 240).

V. Activities for "If You're Happy"
  1. Sing to recall melody and words
  2. To teach feeling of mood, change words to "If You're Sad." Ask children to suggest how the music ought to be changed in consequence
    a. Sung more slowly?
    b. The quality of mode changed to minor?
    c. The rhythm and meter changed to a slow $\frac{3}{4}$?
  3. On repetitions in subsequent lessons, add rhythm instruments to appropriate parts of the song for rhythmic emphasis; add tone bells at appropriate pitches when clapping hands or shaking heads
  4. Call attention to tones that
    a. Remain the same
    b. Move stepwise
    c. Skip
  5. Find similar rhythmic patterns
  6. Play recording to compare children's performance with professional sound.

VI. Activities for "The Barnyard Song" (p. 41)
  1. Teach by focused listening. What does the cat sing at the end of the song?
  2. For each successive verse, ask the children to listen to the song of the hen, goose, duck. On repetitions of each verse, ask the children to complete the last two measures
  3. After a few repetitions let the class sing the first part of the song and the teacher the remainder. When the song has been thoroughly learned, let the class sing the entire song
  4. To evaluate individual voices, select soloists to sing the song of each bird or animal
  5. In succeeding lessons add instrumental rhythmic elements to imitate the sound of animals or birds: a quack by a serrated rhythm stick scraped with triangle beater; "swishy-swashy" by sandpaper blocks; a horse's neigh by sleigh bells (see Chapter 9, Adding Rhythmic Sound Effects, p. 230)
  6. Sing the pentatonic scale from a scale ladder by numbers and syllables
  7. See if children can recognize the song from the sequence of its sign language symbols
  8. Can the song be recognized from its tapped rhythm?

9. Sing excerpted tone groups on neutral syllable "loo" to which the class should respond with the appropriate text

10. Distribute tone bell bars of the pentatonic scale to six children. As the class sings, each child must play his bar when required by the melody

11. Draw duration patterns of the song text on the board

12. Bounce a ball in time to pulse beat; jump rope to strong beat

VII. Apply similar procedures to "Oranges and Lemons" and "Lullaby" below. (Additional sources for these songs are found in Appendix VII. See generally, Chapter 3, Teaching a New Song.)

VIII. "Lullaby"

1. After singing the song, play the recording. Focus listening on:
   a. Mood (quiet lullaby)
   b. Rocking motion of accompaniment
   c. Repetition of phrase forms
   d. Instruments playing the melody
   e. Dynamics

2. Dramatize by pretending to rock a cradle

3. Imitate the sound of the violin by humming with open lips. Let the class hum an accompaniment to the recording

IX. Evaluation
Try to spot individuals who need remedial help with pitch placement. Look for growth in interest through active participation in performance, responses to questioning, willingness to contribute. Encourage children to present related materials: pictures to illustrate songs, recordings from home for "Show and Tell" (a period during which the children describe to the class what they have brought and why they like it).

THE MUSIC TEACHER AS UNIT CONSULTANT

Subject matter in elementary schools is frequently organized into study units based on topics of especial appeal to children. Because of the breadth of such units, the classroom teacher will often seek help in finding related artistic materials. The music teacher will be called upon to suggest specific musical objectives, sources, teaching procedures, and methods of evaluation. Besides furnishing musical instruments, he may also be asked to give demonstrations and otherwise assist in the classroom.[1]

In the higher grades of most schools, units of instruction narrow to traditional subjects—languages, social studies, science, mathematics, music, art, physical education, home economics—encompassing a variety of teaching methods.

Regardless of unit form, relationships between subjects must be articulated if the work is to produce understanding rather than rote enumeration. Bruner emphasizes the need to structure the curriculum in order to clarify the unity of principle under-

[1] *The Unit in Curriculum Development and Instruction,* Bureau of Curriculum Research, 130 W. 55th Street, New York, N.Y. 10019, 1956.

IF YOU'RE HAPPY*

1. If you're hap-py and you know it, clap your hands (clap, clap). If you're

hap - py and you know it, clap your hands (clap, clap). If you're

hap - py and you know it, then your face will sure - ly show it, If you're

hap - py   and you know it, clap your hands   (clap, clap).

2. . . . tap your toe
3. . . . nod your head
4. . . . do all three

FIGURE 11-1

lying academic diversity.[2] Correlating the materials of various specialties requires faculty cooperation. It also means making use of the vast resources available for little or no fee from film distributors, educational agencies of foreign embassies, recording manufacturers and distributors, radio and television companies, and companies dealing in programmed instruction.

[2] Bruner, Jerome S., *The Process of Education,* Harvard University Press, Cambridge, Mass., 1960.
*From This Is Music, Book 2, by W. R. Sur, Mary R. Tolbert, W. R. Fisher, and Adeline McCall, © Allyn and Bacon, Inc., 1961, 1967. Used by permission.

ORANGES AND LEMONS*

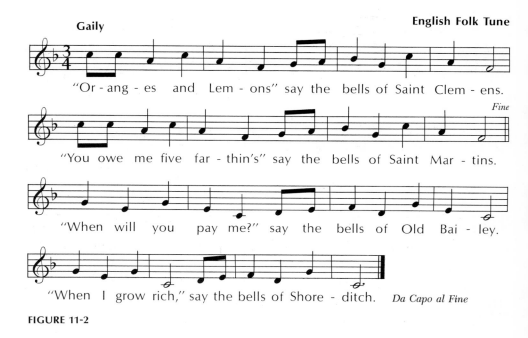

FIGURE 11-2

THE CORRELATED UNIT OF INSTRUCTION

In correlating varied subject matter for a unit, it is helpful to outline under topic headings the unit aims and the sequence of related teaching methods. For example:

I. Grade for which unit is intended

II. Title of unit

III. General and specific objectives

IV. Anticipated results in the acquisition of
1. Knowledge
2. Skills
3. Attitudes (standards and ideals)
4. Appreciation

V. Specific procedures to be followed:
1. Introduction
2. Activities to develop subject matter

*From "Singing Every Day" of Our Singing World series, © Ginn & Company, 1950, 1957, 1959. Used with permission.

LULLABY*

Gently   Johannes Brahms

1. Lul - la - by and good - night with ro - ses be - dight, with lil - ies be - decked, is ba - by's wee bed; Lay thee down now and rest, May thy slum-bers be blest, Lay thee down now and rest, May thy slum - bers be blest.

FIGURE 11-3

    3. Possible culminating programs
VI. Materials of instruction (here limited to music):
    1. Music materials: songs, recordings, dances, piano pieces, instruments
    2. Visual aids: slides, films, bulletin board, art, photographs, pictures drawn by children
    3. Teacher's bibliography: class readings (prose and poetry), methodological and resource materials
    4. Children's bibliography and reading assignments
VII. Evaluation of the unit by:
    1. Objective testing
    2. Recording class performances of music and recitations of poetry and prose
    3. Culminating assembly and PTA programs
    4. Exhibits of original works of art, creative writing, creative music, and dance
    5. Observation of attitudes toward learning

*From Songs for Camp and Campus, Irving Cheyette, © Pro Art Music Company, 1960. Used by permission.

The application of this outline to a unit of instruction as prepared by a group of second grade teachers and a music specialist follows:[3]

I. Unit for second grade
II. Title: The Zoocus, uniting children's interest in zoo animals and the circus
III. Objectives (general):
 1. To understand the circus as a social agency: what it does, how it travels, its various jobs, and the type of training required
 2. To understand zoo and circus animals: their appearance, care, and habits
 3. To develop interest in reading further materials about the circus and zoo
 4. To provide experience of formal rhythmic patterns and creative rhythmic responses; to develop creative expression in rhythmic activities through mimicry of circus performers and animals
 5. To develop appreciation of tonal beauty by singing, listening, playing, and responding rhythmically to music inspired by the circus and animals
 6. To create a repertoire of enjoyable songs inspired by animals and the circus: to acquaint the class with related musical literature
 7. To provide an opportunity to learn techniques of designing, making, and painting posters, scenery, clay figurines
 8. To develop the ability to combine art and narrative by making shoe box movies and paper bag puppets
 9. To develop artistic appreciation by the use of paintings inspired by animals and the circus
 10. To develop appreciation for the technique of the clown and other circus performers through a study of make-up, gesture, posture, mimicry, and by imitating circus feats in the gymnasium (use films and slides, and perhaps visit the circus)
 11. To develop appreciation of literature inspired by animals and the circus
 12. To present a culminating unit, The Zoocus, as an assembly or PTA program
IV. Results to be achieved (knowledge and skills):
 A. Nature Study
  1. Acquaintance with numerous animals, their habitat and habits
  2. Realization of the importance of good care for animal pets
  3. Increased accuracy of observation resulting in more accurate information
 B. Language Arts
  1. Increased desire to read; better comprehension producing a larger vocabulary
  2. Greater ease of verbalization and writing
  3. Improved ability to conduct interviews and library research including,

---

[3]"The Zoocus," curriculum unit prepared by a committee of classroom teachers, summer session course on Music for the Classroom Teacher, University of Buffalo, Buffalo, N.Y., 1961.

with the assistance of the librarian, discovering new materials, using references, and finding appropriate illustrations

4. Learning rules of conversational deportment

C. Arithmetic

1. Developing more accurate concepts of (a) proportion, (b) problem-solving methodology, (c) monetary values, and (d) measurements

D. Spelling

1. Learning to spell words of second grade level relating to the zoo and circus

E. Music and Physical Education

1. Learning by both rote and story-telling methods the songs in the basic music series and other unit sources
2. Developing skill in recognizing specific aspects of music to which attention has been focused, such as phrasing, instrumentation, melodic line, rhythmic flow, dynamics, tempo, etc.
3. Developing ability to respond to rhythms through bodily movement
4. Developing ability to dramatize unit materials through original rhythms
5. Developing skill in the use of rhythm instruments to enhance songs and dances
6. Developing sensitivity to qualities of sound
7. Developing ease in performance before an audience

F. Art

1. Improved skills in (a) coloring—both color relationships and techniques of application; (b) lettering—to letter posters and signs recognizably and artistically; (c) painting—color combinations, use of brushes, and mixing of colors; (d) muscle coordination—use of fingers in modeling; (e) making pictures tell stories

V. Attitudes and Appreciation

1. To be silent and attentive while others are talking
2. To willingly allow others to share in discussion
3. To cooperate in group work
4. To consider the opinions and feelings of others
5. To take pleasure in preparing and presenting things to the group
6. To question, to seek answers
7. To desire to learn
8. To develop a love and admiration for wild and domestic animals
9. To develop a spirit of neighborliness toward circus and zoo workers
10. To sense growth and accomplishment through success in some academic, musical, artistic, or gymnastic facet of the unit
11. To develop aesthetic interest beyond the confines of the unit
12. To be sensitive to aesthetic elements developed in the unit
13. To participate in musical activities, such as group and individual singing, playing rhythm instruments, dancing, marching, imitating animal movements, acrobatics

14. To appreciate the art of others
15. To enjoy personal creative work
16. To appreciate rhythmic movement through personal expression in acrobatics and dance

VI. Procedures
   A. Approach—Lively discussion
      1. Recall an earlier trip to the zoo (summer or fall)
      2. Recall individual experiences at the circus
      3. Individual reports based on questions stimulating further reading
         a. How do circus people usually travel?
         b. Do the circus trains look like passenger trains?
         c. How fast do they travel?
         d. Do families travel together?
         e. How long does it take to unload cars in each town where they stop?
         f. Who puts up the tents?
         g. Who feeds the animals?
         h. How are animals trained to do tricks?
      4. Collecting circus articles for exhibition
      5. Hopefully, as a result of their research and class discussions, the children will become interested in presenting an animal show, "The Zoocus," to which parents and friends will be invited
   B. Activities used to develop subject matter and test comprehension
      1. Read and retell the story
      2. Read and be able to answer questions about the story
      3. When the story is divided into parts, be able to put it in sequence
      4. Answer questions based on pictures of the circus

      Example: Find the animal that eats peanuts.
               Find the one that makes us laugh.
               Find the animal with the longest neck.

      5. Prepare and read a daily bulletin about The Zoocus
      6. Write notices for the billboards
      7. Read bits from the daily papers concerning a recent circus visit or zoo activities
      8. Dramatize readings about the circus
      9. Plan for a children's show, keep a diary of the discussions
      10. Compile an animal riddle book
      11. Compose talks to introduce Zoocus characters and acts
      12. Individually and in groups compose stories of four or five sentences about the circus animals and people
      13. Compose original poems
      14. Listen to poems and stories; develop appreciation of aesthetic elements
      15. Write a letter or jingle invitation to parents

16. Study art inspired by animals or the circus
17. Draw and letter Zoocus advertisements, posters, and billboards
18. Make and show puppets
19. Model animals and figures for a sand-table circus
20. Design costumes
21. Construct cages, backdrops, and tents in miniature
22. Make a shoe box circus movie from original drawings and paintings
23. Outline characteristics of various animals from study
24. Listen to music recordings inspired by animals and the circus
25. Performance
    a. Sing songs about animals, zoo and circus life
    b. Play rhythm instruments, organize a soda pop bottle band
    c. Play flute-type melody instruments, bells
    d. Create original songs based on original poems
26. Rhythmic activities
    a. Circus parade
    b. Acrobatics
    c. Song dramatizations
27. Talks based on slides, film strips, and films for the unit
C. Possible culminating program containing the following activities:
    1. The Circus Parade: the children pretend to be the animals and characters in the parade, preparing costumes and developing antics appropriate to the animal or character imitated
    2. Acrobatics: the children imitate clowns and acrobats to music
    3. Circus Band—Rhythm Band: soda pop bottles, filled with varying amounts of water to make the scale, simulate a calliope. Eight children, each blowing his own bottle tone at the proper time, play the song to accompany class singing. Other instruments such as bells, xylophone, melody flutes, assist
    4. Dancing bears: costume two boys to portray dancing bears by attaching papier-mâché heads to painted burlap sacks. Use appropriate recordings or music from the basic music series
    5. Dramatize and sing group songs and solos
    6. Feature the class talent: solo singers, instrumentalists, dancers, and small ensemble groups
    7. Devise a miniature circus on the sand table. The tent and cages are made of cardboard and chicken wire; the animals are modeled in painted clay
    8. Sideshow attractions
        a. A shoe-box circus movie
        b. A peepshow
        c. A puppet show dramatizing a circus story previously read in class
    9. Short talks illustrated with slides, drawings, and models presenting information gathered about the exhibited animals

        10. Dispense balloons, popcorn, pink lemonade, and other food made in home economics

VII. Materials of Instruction

    A. Music

        1. Circus parade recordings

            America's Favorite Marches (RCA LPM 1175)

            Favorite Marches, (RCA CAL 474)

            A Day at the Circus (Col. HL 9540)

        2. Piano pieces

            Rhythm and Action with Music, Katherine P. Norton, Oliver Ditson Co., Boston

            Circus Time Action Songs, Ruth Norman, Mills Music Co., New York

            Classroom Teachers Piano Book, Marjorie Hunter, Summy-Birchard Co., Evanston, Ill.

        3. Recordings for acrobatics

            RCA Elementary Music Album (E-71), vol. 1: Horses, Gnomes, Clowns, Dwarfs

            Circus Comes to Town, Young Peoples Records (713)

            Circus Music, Aaron Copland, Adventures in Music (RCA LE 1002), Grade 3

            "Captain Kangaroo," *Dance Along Zoo* (Col. HL 9520)

            March of the Toys, Victor Herbert, Adventures in Music (RCA LE 101), Grade 2

            Let's Play Zoo, Young Peoples Records (802)

            Circus Polka, Stravinsky (Bowmar Bol 51; Col. MS 6648)

        4. The Circus Band—rhythm band to accompany songs below

Series	Song Title	Book	Page	Publisher
This Is Music	The Music Man	2	52	Allyn & Bacon
	My New Red Drum	2	55	
	The Park with the Zoo	2	103	
	Jack Can I Ride	2	104	
	Funny Song	2	106	
	Carrousel	3	109	
	I Am a Gay Musician	3	58	
	My Friends in Orchestraville	3	49–61	
Together We Sing	We Play in Our Band	2	73	Follett
	The Circus Parade	2	60	
	The Tune the Calliope Played	2	62	
	Circus Riders	2	63	
	Circus Clowns	2	64	
	The Man on the Flying Trapeze	2	66	
	The Lost Balloon	2	67	
	Come to the Fair	2	112	
	The Merry Go Round	2	114	

Series	Song Title	Book	Page	Publisher
Our Singing World	The Circus	1	111	Ginn
	The Clown	1	112	
	The Lion	1	113	
	The Elephant	1	113	
	I Like Monkeys	1	114	
	The Seal	1	115	
	The Camel	1	115	
	Marching Song	3	164	
	Let's Play Band	3	165	
Music for Young Americans	Let's Have a Circus	2	57	American Book Co.
	The Ponies	2	58	
	The Lion Tamer	2	59	
	Clowns	2	60	
	Snake Charmer	2	61	
	The Circus Parade	2	62	
	Jumbo	2	63	
	The Merry Go Round	2	64	
	The Leader of the Band	3	132	
Music for Living	Our Ponies	2	90	Silver Burdett
	Here Come the Monkeys	2	98	
	Riding on an Elephant	2	99	
	Did You Ever	2	101	
	Merry Go Round	2	86	
	The Clown	2	94	
	The Man on the Flying Trapeze	2	95	
	Circus Parade	2	96	
Birchard Series	Jumbo Elephant	K	84	Summy-Birchard
	Under the Big Top	K	84	
	The Seal	K	86	
	The Clown	K	86	
	The Zoo	K	88	
	The Hippo	K	89	
	The Panther	K	89	
	The Monkey	K	90	

5. Recordings and piano selections for listening, creative work, and rhythmic activities

a. Recordings to accompany stories found in basic series

Series	Title	Book	Page	Record Company and No.
This Is Music	*The Tailor and the Mouse*	2	100–102	RCA Basic Record Lib. E78
This Is Music	*Peter and the Wolf*	3	62–64	RCA LM 1803
This Is Music	*The Carnival of the Animals*	3	84–90	RCA LM 2075
	Circus Polka (Stravinsky)			Bowmar BOL 51
	Under the Big Top (Donaldson, reverse side)			

b. Piano Pieces for listening, creative rhythms

Series	Title	Book	Page	Publisher
Music for Living	*The Elephant*	2	80 (Teachers)	Silver Burdett
Music for Living	*Galloping Horses*	2	96	
Birchard	*March*	2	187 (Teachers)	Summy-Birchard
Music for Living	*The Orchestra*	Music in Early Childhood	72	Silver Burdett
Music for Living	*The Ringmaster*	Music in Early Childhood	43	Silver Burdett
Birchard	*A Lively Tune*	1	121	Summy-Birchard
Birchard	*Waltz Melody*	1	125	Summy-Birchard

6. Supplementary Songbooks for the Zoocus Unit
   a. *Music in the Zoo,* Goldberg-Edwards, Mills Music Co., New York, 1955.
   b. *The Animal Alphabet,* Percy M. Young, Mills Music Co., New York, 1953.
   c. *Zoo Nonsense Songs,* Kent, Mills Music Co., New York (rhythmic movement and percussion), 1958.
   d. *Circus Time,* Ruth Norman, Mills Music Co., New York (finger plays and rhythmic games), 1952.
   e. *Sing with Action,* Rita Kiltz and Hazel Neff, Schmitt, Hall & McCreary, Minneapolis, Minn. (Circus and Animal Unit), 1958.
   f. *Singing Fun,* Lucille Wood and Louise Scott, Webster Publ. Co., Pasadena, Calif., (Circus Unit), 1954.
   g. *Animal Folk Songs for Children,* Ruth P. Seeger, Doubleday & Company, Inc., Garden City, N.Y., 1950.
B. Visual aids for the Zoocus Unit
   1. Animal stories, 6 film strips, Jam Handy Organization, 2821 E. Grand Blvd., Detroit, Mich.
   2. Films about zoo and circus:

Title	Publisher	Rental Source	Fee	Length
Circus Animals	United World Films	Syracuse University	$2.00	11 min
Circus Boy	United World Films		7.00	46 min
Circus Day In Our Town	Encyclopaedia Britannica		3.00	16 min
Circus People	Academy		2.00	11 min
Animules (how to create animals out of wire, paper, paint)	International Film Bureau		3.00	11 min
Animals of the Zoo	Encyclopaedia Britannica		2.00	11 min
Animals in Winter	Encyclopaedia Britannica		2.00	11 min

Many university audio-visual departments provide a film rental service to the public schools in their area. Inquire at the nearest university or look under rental film services in the yellow pages of the telephone directory.

C. Children's books and stories illustrated with filmstrips and recordings:

Title	Author	Publisher	Source
Andy and the Lion	James Daugherty	Viking Press	Picture Book Parade, Weston Woods, Conn., 1938 (1952)
The Biggest Bear	Lynd Ward	Houghton Mifflin	
The Camel Who Took a Walk	Jack Tworkov and Roger Duvoisin	E. P. Dutton	(1951)
The Circus Baby	The Petershams	Macmillan	(1950)
Peter and the Wolf	Sergei Prokofiev		Jam Handy Organization, 2821 E. Grand Blvd, Detroit, Mich.
The Three Bears	Fairy Tale		
Let's Go to the Zoo			
Animals Get Ready for Winter			

D. Children's bibliography

Animal Friends and Adventures, J. Morris Jones, (ed.), Childcraft Series, Field Enterprises Educational Corp., Chicago, Ill., 1966

The Story of Babar, The Little Elephant, Jean de Brunhoff, Random House, Inc., New York, 1957

Chanticleer and the Fox, Geoffrey Chaucer, adapted Barbara Cooney, Thomas Y. Crowell Company, New York, 1958

The Bears on Hemlock Mountain, Alice Dalgliesh, Charles Scribner's Sons, New York, 1952

The Happy Lion, Louise Fation, McGraw-Hill Book Company, New York, 1954

The Wolf and the Seven Little Kids, Grimm and Carl, Charles Scribner's Sons, New York, 1960

Animals of the Bible, Dorothy Lathrop, J. B. Lippincott Company, Philadelphia, 1937

Horton Hatches the Egg, Dr. Seuss, Random House Company, New York, 1940

E. Books to be read to children

Just So Stories, Rudyard Kipling, Doubleday & Company, Inc., Garden City, N.Y., 1946

The Jungle Books, Rudyard Kipling, Doubleday & Company, Inc., Garden City, N.Y., 1948

The World of Pooh, A. A. Milne, E. P. Dutton & Co., Inc., New York, 1957

The World of Christopher Robin, A. A. Milne, E. P. Dutton & Co., Inc., New York, 1958

This Singing World, Louis Untermeyer, Harcourt, Brace & World, Inc., New York, 1926

Animal Tales, Ivan T. Sanderson, Alfred A. Knopf, Inc., New York, 1960

  F. Teacher's bibliography

   World Book Encyclopedia, Field Enterprises Educational Corp., Chicago, Ill., vols. A-1 and C-3 for information about animals and circus life

   Compton's Pictured Encyclopedia, F. E. Compton and Company, Chicago, Ill., vols. 3, 24.

   Britannica Junior, Educational Department, Encyclopedia Britannica, Chicago, Ill.

   Circus! From Rome to Ringling, Marian Murray, Appleton-Century-Crofts, Inc., New York, 1956.

   Ways of the Circus, George Conklin, Harper & Row, Publishers, Incorporated, New York, 1921

   Book of Zoography, Raymond L. Ditmars, J. B. Lippincott Company, Philadelphia, 1934

   How to Put On an Amateur Circus, Fred A. Hacker, F. S. Denison, Chicago, Ill., 1923

   The Animal and Its Environment, L. A. Borradaile, Hodder & Stoughton, Ltd., London, 1923

   Our Very Own Circus, I. Underwood, Unit 68, Teachers College Press, New York.

   The Animal Family, Randall Jarrell, Pantheon Books, a Division of Random House, Inc., New York, 1965

VIII. Evaluation of the Unit

  While extensive formal testing is not suitable in the second grade, a few tests during the course of the unit will provide a cursory check on the accretion of information. The best measure of the unit's success is that of each child's participation in the culminating program.

  Encourage the children to measure their performance, tape-recording musical portions of the program and photographing the displays to help class evaluation. The children will be pleased to discover their growing skill and understanding. To evaluate individual success the teacher must appraise increased skill in describing acquired information, manipulating material, singing, coordinating rhythms, recognizing musical elements, and adjusting to the group.

CURRICULUM UNITS PREPARED BY MUSIC SPECIALISTS

  The Zoocus typifies a unit prepared by classroom teachers with the aid of a music specialist. What follows is a music unit prepared for general use by music specialists after consultation with classroom teachers as to the interest of particular grades. The actual teacher of such a unit must clearly understand its objectives and procedures, available materials, and appropriate methods of evaluation.[4]

[4]"Music of Mexico," curriculum unit prepared by a committee of music teachers, summer session course on Improvement of Instruction in Music Education, State University of New York at Buffalo, Buffalo, N.Y., 1963.

I. Unit for Grade 5
II. Title: The Music of Mexico
III. Specific Objectives
1. Skills to
   a. Improve tone quality
   b. Read melody and harmony parts independently
   c. Interpret typical Mexican rhythms through dance and with Latin American orchestral and recreational instruments. Perform folk dances
   d. Be able to recognize the ethnic characteristics of Mexican music
   e. Sight read Mexican vocal and rhythmic instrumental music
2. Habits of work, stress
   a. Independent library research, especially in the light of the individual student's contribution to the group effort
   b. Creative verbal expression
   c. Accurate evaluation of own and other's work
   d. Cooperation
3. Information to be gathered
   a. Miscellany of Mexican songs reflecting work, play, national customs, holidays
   b. Music evincing typical Mexican rhythmic patterns
   c. The role of music in Mexican life
4. Attitudes to be developed
   a. Greater understanding of United States–Mexican relations, and the reciprocal influence of national art forms
   b. Appreciation of Mexican music and dance
5. Result to be achieved
   The unit should increase knowledge and appreciation of Mexico's contribution to music and the other fine arts
IV. Types of Activities
1. Develop a repertoire of songs sung in English and Spanish for unison and part singing
2. Accompany recorded, and class' performances with manufactured and home-made rhythm, melody, and orchestral instruments, especially emphasizing instruments characteristic of Latin America
3. Utilize Latin American rhythms for rhythmic activities. Perform folk dances
4. Compose poems, dances, and songs derived from Mexican forms
5. Dramatize songs and narratives, devising musical settings employing native rhythms
6. Make, collect, and demonstrate Mexican instruments
7. Investigate Mexican festivals, legends, and customs
V. Kinds of Experiences to be Stressed
1. Musical: the unit's purpose is to teach music. Therefore, musical experience must be stressed and related activities relegated to a secondary position
2. Sociological: amplify studies of food, clothing, shelter, transportation, holidays,

customs, occupations, religion, and folk superstitions of the Mexican people with appropriate songs and dances

3. Correlation:
   a. Language arts: oral and written reports on independent research
   b. Arts and handicrafts: making of instruments for class performance. Illustrate songs and dances, portray a fiesta

VI. Materials Needed and Their Sources

1. Teachers books

   Creative Rhythmic Movement for Children, Gladys Andrews, Prentice-Hall, Inc., Englewood Cliffs, N.J., 1954, pp. 111–119 (directions for making rhythm instruments).

   Hi, Neighbor!, Book 4, with recording, UNICEF, United Nations, New York, pp. 32–37. Background information about Mexican crafts, holidays. The Educational Department, Mexican Embassy, Washington, D.C., provides literature on Mexican history, and tourist information rich in cultural background

2. Song sources from basic series and possible enrichment activities

   a. Birchard Series, Book 5, Summy-Birchard

Jesusita de Chihuahua, p. 128	Percussion accompaniment, dance directions given
Fiesta Time (Jarabe Tapatia), p. 130	Improvise a hat dance
Little Dove, p. 132	Improvise rhythmic accompaniment
Morning Song, p. 121	Autoharp accompaniment

   b. This Is Music, Book 5, Allyn & Bacon

Marvelous Mountains, p. 177	Antiphonal calls, sing in Spanish
La Jesusita, p. 178	Castanets, tambourine, flutes
Las Mañanitas, p. 179	Small woodwinds, bells
Jarabe, p. 180	Chording, voices and instruments
In Old Mexico, p. 181	Accompany with rhythm instrument
Piñata Song, p. 185	Christmas song, bells

   c. Growing with Music, Book 5, Prentice-Hall

Pajara Pinta, p. 54	Violin or flute obbligato
To Bethlehem, p. 204	Duet, voices and flutes
With One Peseta, p. 97	Chording, voices and instruments

   d. Music for Young Americans, Book 5, American Book Co.

Adelita, p. 62	Duet, triangle and bells
Christmas in Mexico, p. 76	Carol, bells and flutes

   e. Music for Living, Book 5, Silver Burdett Co.

Fiesta, p. 188	Maracas, claves, tambourine
Mexican Hat Dance, p. 194	Improvise dance, recorded in series

    f. Discovering Music Together, Book 5, Follett Publishing Company, Chicago Ill.

La Raspe, p. 136	Tambourine, flutes on upper voice part
Serenade, p. 64	Chording song, duet in thirds; autoharp
Jarabe Tapatio, p. 30	Chording song, sing in Spanish

    g. Making Music Your Own, Book 5, Silver Burdett Company, Morristown, N.J.

My Ranch, p. 166	Woodblocks, bridle bells, autoharp
Stars of Heaven, p. 169	Descant for bells, flutes, chording
De la Locomotora, p. 170	Autoharp in habañera rhythm, maracas

    h. Exploring Music, Book 5, Holt, Rinehart and Winston, Inc.

La Raspa, p. 146	Recorded dance in fifth grade album
Duermete, Niño Lindo, p. 208	Xmas carol, triangle on first beat with melody flutes
Pretty Piña, p. 147	Chording song, varied meters, wood block and castanets

    i. Music Through the Year, Follett Publishing Company, Chicago, Ill.

Break the Piñata, p. 57	Chording song, improvise duet
Sweet Oranges, p. 56	Xmas carol, chording song, bells

Many additional Mexican folk songs will be found in Book 6 of each of the series listed above

3. Instruments: guitar, castanets, claves, tambourine, maracas, guiro, conga and bongo drums. Ukulele and autoharp may be substituted for guitar. Make homemade rhythm instruments to substitute for above

4. Tuning instruments: pitch pipe, step bells, piano, autoharp, melody flutes

5. Recordings

    a. Bowmar Educational Records, 10515 Burbank Blvd., North Hollywood, Calif.

They Came Singing (B 513 LP)

Children's Songs of Mexico (B106), three ten-inch records, 78 r.p.m.

Mexican Folk Dances (B207), three ten-inch records, 78 r.p.m.

    b. CBS Records, 51 West 52 Street, New York

"Chiapanecas," Follett Music Series Recordings (L52)

Songs of the World, "Carmen Carmela," Luboff Chorus, (C2L13)

Twelve Songs of the Mexican Revolution "La Cucaracha," (WL 161)

Music of the Bullfight "Pasodobles," (LF 18018)

    c. RCA Victor Educational Services, Dept. 390, Camden, N.J.

Mexican Folk Songs (LPM 1077)

> *El Salon Mexico,* Aaron Copland (LM 1928)
>
> The World of Folk Dances Series (LPM 1621, LPM 1619, LPM 1623)
>
> **d.** Hi, Neighbor! Record Series, UNICEF, United Nations, New York
>
> El Hijo Desobediente, Record 4 (XTV 68798)

6. Visual aids

  a. Map of Mexico

  b. Filmstrips, Stanley Bowmar Co., 10515 Burbank Blvd., North Hollywood, Calif.

  Small Town in Mexico (#5742)

  Mexico (#4184)

7. Children's resource materials may include instruments, pictures, souvenirs, recordings, tourist posters, and magazines

8. The Mexican Embassy will provide additional resource materials: a brief history in pictorial magazines; lists of recordings; lists of available music, slides, and films

9. Pan-American Union, Washington, D.C., will provide materials concerning any of the member states of the Organization of American States

VII. Evaluation

Although testing for knowledge of Mexico falls within the scope of social studies and is the responsibility of the classroom teacher, evaluation of musical growth during the unit should be undertaken by the music specialist in the following ways:

  1. Make tape recordings of performance to evaluate improvement in vocal tone and expressiveness, and instrumental skill

  2. Test knowledge of terminology, symbols, notation

  3. Observe attitudes and behavior patterns

  4. Evaluate independent research projects

  5. Evaluate individual performance by students

Conclusion

This unit attempts to provide a variety of materials and resources related to social studies. Both the maturation and the musical capabilities of students must be considered in selecting materials. It is difficult to incorporate every possible activity in a general outline. The teacher should use his imagination and creativity to adapt this sketch to the needs and interests of his class.

A UNIT PLAN FOR UPPER GRADES ON NEGRO AFRO-AMERICAN MUSIC[5]

This unit, utilizing an ethnic approach to the teaching of music, is also the work of a group of music specialists.

[5]"Negro Afro-American Music," curriculum unit prepared by a committee of music teachers, summer session course on Problems in Music Education, State University of New York at Buffalo, Buffalo, N.Y., 1965.

I. General Objectives

The general objective of this unit is to analyze the impact of Negro Afro-American music, since its introduction in the eighteenth century, upon the popular, jazz, folk, and gospel music of America. The plan of study will include singing, dancing, playing, listening, creative activities, and individual research. Note that a code to the basic song series mentioned will be found on pp. 316–317.

II. Specific Objectives: types of activities to be employed

    1. Categorizing various types of Negro music; learning songs from each group

    2. Learning to play characteristic instruments: drums, banjo, guitar, and home-made percussion instruments such as bones, spoons

    3. Analyzing syncopation: clapping, finger snapping, rhythmic combinations using hands and feet, shuffling

    4. Listening to authentic recordings and live performances for characteristic rhythmic patterns, forms, and types of improvisation

    5. Improvising words and rhythms and incidental exclamations: creating percussion scores, vocal and rhythmic backgrounds

    6. Studying African backgrounds, biographies of Negro leaders, economic and social conditions in Africa and America

    7. Reporting current events pertaining to Negro culture: performances of Negro artists, analyzing the portrayal of Negro characters in literature

    8. Creating notebooks to include spirituals (categorized as to their use and function), assignments, newspaper clippings, and any pertinent material brought to class

III. Information to be covered

    A. African heritage of the Negro

        1. Sense of rhythm

        2. Monotonous expression of voice (chants)

        3. Strong tendency to imitate

        4. Strong religious feelings (voodooism)

    B. Types of songs that the Negro has developed in America

        1. Spirituals

            a. Call and response

            b. Melodic spiritual

            c. Rhythmic spiritual

        2. Shouts and Jumpin' or Pattin' Juba

        3. Folk blues

        4. Work songs

        5. Creole Negro music

    C. Characteristics of Negro singing

        1. Syncopation

        2. Frequent use of minor mode

        3. Use of pentatonic scale

        4. Response singing

        5. Improvisation

        6. Slurring or sliding of voice

       7. Coarse and gutteral voice quality

   D. American music that shows Negro influence

       1. Minstrel show

       2. Songs of Stephen Foster

       3. Dvořák's *New World Symphony* and Violin Sonatina

       4. Gershwin's *Rhapsody in Blue, American in Paris, Porgy and Bess*

       5. Nathaniel Dett's *Juba Dance*

       6. W. C. Handy's *St. Louis Blues*

   E. Negroes prominent in the entertainment field, and concert artists

       1. Marian Anderson

       2. Nat "King" Cole

       3. Duke Ellington

       4. Sammy Davis, Jr.

       5. Ella Fitzgerald

       6. Louis Armstrong

       7. Errol Garner

       8. Johnny Mathis

       9. Leontyne Price

      10. William Warfield

IV. Materials

   A. Song sources

       1. The *Call and Response Spiritual* is often considered a chant in which the melody or "call" is slow and sustained with long phrases, and the "response" is syncopated and segmented. Responses are usually sung with a rapid tempo and are characterized by a fiery spirit:

Title	Book	Page	Publisher
It's Me, O Lord	6	114	Ginn
When Moses Smote the Water	5	83	Ginn
Mary and Martha	5	135	Allyn & Bacon
Kum ba Yah	5	163	Allyn & Bacon
When the Saints Go Marchin' In	4	22	Allyn & Bacon
Don't Stay Away	5	70	Follett
Go Down Moses	6	52	American Book Co.
Listen to the Lambs	6	196	American Book Co.
Swing Low, Sweet Chariot	6	89	Silver Burdett
Rise Up Shepherd and Follow	6	146	Silver Burdett
Goin' to Ride Up in the Chariot	5	84	Ginn
Ain't Gonna Grieve My Lord	5	128	Prentice-Hall
This Ol' Time Religion	ANS	99	Crown

       2. The *Rhythmic Spiritual* has a fast tempo. Its rhythm features a swing that stimulates body responses. The melodic line is of secondary importance and is often segmented and syncopated:

Title	Book	Page	Publisher
Little David Play on Your Harp	5	71	Follett
Shout All Over God's Heab'n	6	117	Ginn
Ol' Ark's a'Moverin'	5	96	Prentice-Hall
Zion's Children	5	104	Allyn & Bacon
He's Got the Whole World in His Hands	5	21	Allyn & Bacon
Rocka My Soul	4	22	Allyn & Bacon
Golden Harp	5	6	American Book Co.
Two Wings	5	64	American Book Co.
Joshua Fought the Battle	5	98	American Book Co.
Then I'm Goin' Home	5	12	American Book Co.
The Old Ark	4	90	American Book Co.
Get On Board	5	68	Summy-Birchard
Ezek'el Saw the Wheel	5	126	American Book Co.
Soon A Will Be Done	ANS	109	Crown
O Lord I'm Hungry	ANS	154	Crown
Ain't That Good News	ANS	195	Crown

3. In the *Melodic Spiritual,* the tempo is slow and the phrase line long and sustained:

Title	Book	Page	Publisher
My Lord What a Morning	5	106	Allyn & Bacon
Steal Away	6	84	American Book Co.
Let Us Break Bread Together	4	146	Summy-Birchard
Deep River	7	65	American Book Co.
He Never Said a Mumblin' Word	ANS	103	Crown
Walk My Lonesome Valley	ANS	108	Crown
There Is a Balm in Gilead	ANS	128	Crown
Jacob's Ladder	6	169	American Book Co.
Were You There	ANS	105	Crown

4. *Pentatonic*—Negro pentatonic scales avoid the fourth and seventh steps of the major scale. They also employ notes foreign to the conventional major and minor scales:

Title	Book	Page	Publisher
Shortnin' Bread	6	89	Ginn
All Night, All Day	3	27	Allyn & Bacon
Mister Rabbit	4	17	Silver Burdett
Git on Board	4	76	Silver Burdett
Swing Low, Sweet Chariot	6	6	Silver Burdett
Plenty Good Room	4	147	Summy-Birchard
Yes He Knows	7	70	American Book Co.
Ezek'el Saw the Wheel	5	126	American Book Co.
Little David Play On Your Harp	5	71	Follett
Ol' Ark's a'Moverin'	5	96	Prentice-Hall
Roll, Jordan, Roll	ANS	199	Crown
Soon A Will Be Done	ANS	109	Crown

5. *Work Songs,* designed to establish rhythmic group action, or to lighten individual daily tasks, date primarily from the Reconstruction Period:

Title	Book	Page	Publisher
This Train	5	95	American Book Co.
Cotton Needs Pickin'	4	180	American Book Co.
Heave That Cotton	4	190	American Book Co.
John Henry	5	144	Silver Burdett
Boll Weevil Song	5	89	Silver Burdett
Choppin'	5	65	Silver Burdett
Drivin' Steel	5	96	Silver Burdett
Workin' on the Railroad	4	109	Summy-Birchard
Trampin'	5	71	Follett

6. The *Blues* are basically sad, earthy, and intensely emotional. Usually sung as a solo, they are rarely without instrumental accompaniment. The melodic line is characterized by the flatted third and seventh and the form is twelve measures—A, A, B.

Title	Book	Page	Publisher
Wayfaring Stranger	5	86	Allyn & Bacon
Remember Me	5	4	American Book Co.
Down by the Riverside	7	68	American Book Co.
Lord, Lord, Lord	7	37	Summy-Birchard
Sometimes I Feel Like a Motherless Child	ANS	146	Crown
Nobody Knows the Trouble I've Seen	ANS	116	Crown

7. *Social Folk Songs* filled the needs of the ordinary people for music for leisure hours, dances, parties, and other social events:

Title	Book	Page	Publisher
There's a Little Wheel	6	35	American Book Co.
There's a Meeting Tonight	5	8	American Book Co.
Somebody's Knocking	7	70	American Book Co.
Supper on the Ground	4	52	Silver Burdett
Dark Green Shawl	4	92	Silver Burdett
Let Us Cheer the Weary Traveler	Look Away	28	Cooperative Recreation Service
The Grey Goose	Look Away	45	Cooperative Recreation Service
Green Trees	Look Away	44	Cooperative Recreation Service

8. The *Shouts and Jumpin' Juba* songs were considered "runnin'" as opposed to "settin'" spirituals. They call for clapping, stamping, and shuffling to accompany religious excitement:

Title	Book	Page	Publisher
Shout and Sing	5	73	Allyn & Bacon
I'm Gonna Sing	5	96	Allyn & Bacon
There's a Little Wheel a'Turnin'	5	85	Ginn
Going to Shout	6	193	American Book Co.
Shout All Over God's Heab'n	6	117	Ginn
Get on Board	5	68	Summy-Birchard
Ain't That Good News	ANS	195	Crown
Every Time I Feel the Spirit	Look Away	22	Cooperative Recreation Service

9. *Creole* Negro Music reflected the influence of Louisiana Creole masters—"crooning" melodies and story texts using words in French dialect:

Title	Book	Page	Publisher
M'sieu' Banjo	5	62	Allyn & Bacon
Come Dance O Me	4	4	Silver Burdett
Creole Waltz	5	54	Follett
Ay, Ay, Ay	8	214	Follett

10. Another source of Negro musical influence was the *minstrel show*. This was an imitation by the white man of the Negro manner of singing and dancing—a "take off" on his way of life. The minstrel show is one of the few entertainment forms that is truly American in origin (another is the beauty pageant). Song sources and unit suggestions can be found in:

Music Americans Sing—Unit IV—Silver Burdett
Living with Music—The Music of Stephen Foster, p. 43—M. Witmark & Sons

B. Recordings

Spirituals, Tuskegee Institute Choir (Westminster WN 18080)
Spirituals, Marian Anderson (RCA Victor LM 2032)
Spirituals and Blues, Josh White (Elektra EKL 193)
Spirituals to Swing, Carnegie Hall Concerts (Vanguard VRS 8573–8524)
Clara Ward and Her Gospel Singers at the Village Gate (Vanguard VRS 9135)
Cowboy Songs and Negro Spirituals, Voice of Carl Sandburg (Decca DI 9105)
Negro Folk Music of Alabama (secular), Ethnic Folkways Library (P 417)
Southern Folk Heritage Series (Atlantic 1346)
Negro Prison Camp Work Songs, Ethnic Folkways Library (P 475)
Negro Religious Songs and Services, from the Archive of American Folk Song, Library of Congress (AAFS L10)
Afro-American Blues and Games Songs, Library of Congress (AAFS L4)
We Shall Overcome—Songs of the Freedom Riders, (Folkways FH 5591)
Bless This House—Negro Spirituals, Mahalia Jackson (Columbia CL 899)
Swing Low, Sweet Chariot, Paul Robeson (Columbia ML 2038)

Literature Recordings

Great Negro Americans, Alan Sands (World Specialties, Inc.)
The Glory of Negro History, Langston Hughes (Folkways FP 752)
Anthology of Negro Poets (Folkways FP 91)
Poems, Langston Hughes (MGM E3697)
Poetry of the Negro, read by Sidney Poitier and Doris Belack (Glory GLP 1)
Anthology of Negro Poets in the U.S.A. for 200 Years (Folkways FL 9792)

C. Audio-visual Aids

Rhythm of Africa, Film Images, 1860 Broadway, New York 10023, 1947, (17 min)
Rhythm of the Drum, UMTV, 1960 (30 min)
To Hear Your Banjo Play, Brandon, 200 W. 57 Street, New York 10019, 1947, (20 min)
Work Songs and Shanties, University of Michigan TV, 310 Maynard Street, Ann Arbor, Mich., 1958, (30 min)

V. Teacher References

Burk, Cassie, Virginia Meierhoffer, and Claude Phillips, *America's Musical Heritage,* Laidlaw Brothers, Publishers, River Forest, Ill., 1942

Chase, Gilbert, *America's Music,* McGraw-Hill Book Company, New York, 1955, Chapter 12

Courlander, Harold, *Negro Songs, History and Criticism,* Columbia University Press, New York, 1963

Fisher, Miles Mark, *Negro Slave Songs in the United States,* Cornell University Press, Ithaca, N.Y., 1943

Howard, John Tasker, *Our American Music,* Thomas Y. Crowell Company, New York, 1939, pp. 415–428

Jackson, George Pullen, and J. J. Augustin, *Negro Spirituals,* Columbia University Press, New York, 1943

Music of the World, N.B.C. Inter-American University of the Air, Southern Music Publ. Co., Inc., New York, 1944, Handbooks 2, 3, 4

Nathan, Hans, *Dan Emmett and the Rise of Early Negro Minstrelsy,* University of Oklahoma Press, Norman, Okla., 1962

Negro Folk Music of Alabama, Introduction, Text, and Notes of Recordings, Folkways Records and Service Corp., 121 W. 47 Street, New York, 1950

Richardson, Allen L., and Mary E. English, *Living with Music,* M. Witmark & Sons, New York, 1956, pp. 43–49

Work, John W., *American Negro Songs and Spirituals,* Crown Publishers, Inc., New York, 1940

Code to Basic Series Song Sources Mentioned in this Unit

Allyn and Bacon: This Is Music Series, Allyn and Bacon, Inc., 150 Tremont St., Boston 11, Mass.
American Book Co.: Music for Young Americans Series, American Book Company, N.Y.

American Negro Songs: American Negro Songs and Spirituals, Crown Publishers, Inc., N.Y.

Follett: Together We Sing Series, Follett Publ. Company, Chicago

Ginn: Our Singing World Series, Ginn and Company, Boston

Look Away: Cooperative Recreation Service, Delaware, Ohio

P.H.: Growing with Music Series, Prentice-Hall, Inc., Englewood Cliffs, N.J.

S.B.: Music for Living Series, Silver Burdett Company, Morristown, N.J.

Summy-Birchard: Birchard Music Series, Summy-Birchard Company, Evanston, Ill.

The units of instruction given above typify various approaches to organizing such lessons. Possible topics are only limited by the ambition of the teacher and the proprieties of the school administration. Regardless of approach, the teacher's aim should always be to promote the recognition of musical elements and the enjoyment of musical experience. As stressed earlier, music can be enjoyed without knowledge; but music never leads to knowledge without joy.

WORKSHOPS FOR THE MUSICAL PREPARATION OF THE CLASSROOM TEACHER

Frequently, especially in lower grades, teaching music is the responsibility of the general teacher. Since aesthetic attitudes develop early, the effect of the general teacher's approach may be lasting, though not necessarily beneficial. The most common source of difficulty is hesitancy and rigidity, born of inadequate preparation. Such deficiencies can be eliminated by teacher training designed to develop the following skills:[6]

1. Knowledge of the content of musical literature (see Appendix III)
2. Some theoretical knowledge of musical elements (see Chapter 10)
3. Musical skills:
   a. Proper use of the voice (see Chapter 3)
   b. Limited facility on a keyboard instrument (see Chapter 8)
   c. Facility with some melody flute instrument (flutophone, recorder, tonette); (see Chapter 8)
   d. Facility with the autoharp or harmolin (see Chapter 8)
   e. Limited facility with a string accompaniment instrument such as ukulele, guitar, or banjo (see Chapter 8)
   f. Proper use of the pitch pipe
4. A large repertoire of songs for many occasions (see Appendix I)
5. Knowledge of suitable recordings for a given grade. In higher grades, sufficient knowledge to correlate music with other subjects (see Chapter 10 and Appendix III)

[6]Boyd, Silas, *The Music Preparation of General Elementary Teachers in State Supported Colleges and Universities,* doctoral dissertation, Indiana University, Bloomington, Ind., 1961. See also Jessie Fleming, "A List of Desirable Musical Experiences for Elementary School Children, in the Maryland Public Schools," *Journal of Research in Music Education,* I:1 (Spring, 1953), pp. 59–67.

6. Knowledge of related materials: books of folk songs, folk dances; songs in foreign languages; filmstrips and films (see Appendix I)

7. Knowledge of basic methods of teaching music, including those concerned with the proper development of children's voices (see Chapters 2 through 6).

The extent of the general teacher's preparation depends upon the amount of music education incorporated in college elementary education courses, the in-service assistance available from clinics, workshops, extension courses, and refresher classes, and such teaching demonstrations as may be made by a music consultant. Unfortunately, many elementary education teacher programs contain only one or two music courses. These attempt cursorily to survey the fundamentals of music, its history and literature, and also to provide some acquaintance with methods and materials for the elementary grades. Such preparation is inadequate to develop either self-confidence or musical ability. However, textbooks devoted to the musical preparation of classroom teachers have rapidly increased in recent years. This may presage an improvement in the courses offered.

There seems to be agreement that courses or workshops for the classroom teacher should encompass mastery of the following skills:

Vocal Abilities[7]

1. To sing children's songs properly with good projection and adequate range, good diction, breath support, and phrasing

2. To sing at sight melodies employing scale and chord skips within the diatonic harmony appropriate for the grade

3. To acquire a repertoire of songs suitable for specific grades

4. To sing a harmony part to a melody sung by others

5. To sing melodies, and ascending and descending chromatic scales, using *sol-fa* syllables, numbers, and pitch names

6. To sing major and minor intervals within the diatonic scales

7. To be able to sing chord intervals employed in the harmonization of a scale, such as ascending scale chords: I, V, I, IV, I, vi, V7, I, and descending scale chords: I, iii, IV, I, ii, I, V7, I

Keyboard Skills[8]

1. To demonstrate an understanding of the piano keyboard, identifying all keys on the piano

2. To be able to play melodies found in any basic music series

3. To play and recognize scale intervals by ear

4. To play and recognize by ear, I, IV, and V7 chords in major and minor keys through three sharps and three flats

[7] See Chapters 3, 5, 6, and 7.
[8] See Chapter 8.

5. To be able to identify by ear the appropriateness of I, IV, and V7 chords to harmonize a melody

6. To apply chords at the keyboard so as to harmonize a melody, and be able to play melody and harmony simultaneously

7. To be able to play chords for marching, skipping, running, and other fundamental rhythms

8. To be able to use the pedals correctly

Instrumental Skills[9]

1. To make simple rhythm instruments

2. To demonstrate and perform rhythm band instruments

3. To know how to use rhythm band instruments for adding sound effects to accompany singing and/or dancing

4. To acquire skill in performing simple flute instruments

5. To play tone, orchestra, and Swiss bells and the xylophone

6. To play either the autoharp, harmolin, ukulele, guitar, or banjo

7. To construct scales with water glasses, soda pop bottles, and bottle chimes

Rhythmic Skills[10]

1. To be able to sense and step strong beat, pulse beat, and melodic rhythm, and to be able to appropriately add instrumental rhythmic accompaniment and bodily movement to songs

2. To demonstrate an understanding of those time signatures in duple, triple, and compound meters found in school song series

3. To be able to read at sight rhythms found in any series of basic music books for the elementary grades

4. To acquire a repertoire of action and game songs, and of folk dances appropriate for given grade levels

5. To be able to symbolize duration patterns under the text of songs, identifying beat, demonstrating duple and triple meter, and showing accents and bar line division

6. To be able to translate duration patterns into music notation

7. To be able to use a small drum for "drum talk," enabling the children to identify the rhythms of familiar songs and to interpret them with appropriate bodily movement

Song Leading Skills[11]

1. To use proper patterns for conducting two-, three-, four-, or six-beat measures

2. To be able to cue in singers with the left hand on an upbeat when necessary

[9]See Chapter 8.
[10]See Chapter 4.
[11]See Chapters 3 and 4.

3. To be able to properly indicate entrance and release beats

4. To be able by conducting gesture to indicate style (staccato-legato), tempos, and variations in dynamics

5. In setting tempo and dynamic level to understand the proper relationship of conducting and piano accompaniment

6. To understand the effect of personal attitude on the part of the conductor in engendering enthusiasm for singing, and encouraging confidence in performance

Theoretical Music Skills[12]

1. To demonstrate an understanding of music notation symbols

2. To understand the terminology employed to indicate tempo, dynamics, styles, and expression

3. To understand the time signatures employed in basic song series

4. To understand key signatures; to be able to find the proper key at the piano keyboard and with the pitch pipe

5. To understand the construction of major and minor scales and recognize mode by ear and from score

6. To be able to construct major, minor, pentatonic, and chromatic scale ladders

7. To be able to identify from notation, scale intervals by number, syllable, and pitch names

8. To be able to notate music on the staff

9. To be able to identify by quality of sound soprano, alto, tenor, baritone, and bass voices; orchestral and rhythm band instruments

10. To develop an understanding of the ranges of voices and their distinguishing qualities

11. To be able to recognize by ear major, minor, diminished, and augmented intervals

12. To be able to employ in the upper grades barbershop and finger harmony using the I, IV, and V7 chords, the class being divided into low, middle, and high voice parts on the respective chords

13. To recognize by ear music indicative of various historical periods

14. To recognize by ear easier musical forms such as the march, waltz, minuet, polka, and folk dances

Teaching Skills[13]

1. To exercise good taste and judgment in the selection of songs for given grades

2. To be creative in presenting new songs to children and in enhancing familiar songs by dramatization and sound effects

3. To understand various methods of presenting songs: by story, rote, and focused listening

[12] See Chapters 4, 6, 7, and 10.
[13] See Chapters 3 and 9.

4. To learn how to handle the physical materials needed, such as staff liner, flannel board, pitch pipe, and phonograph

5. To be able to interpret moods of songs through voice, physical attitude, and gesture

6. To develop criteria for making judgments as to the usefulness of music materials

7. To know some of the literature for teaching elementary music

8. To seek opportunities to observe creative music teaching by specialists

9. To be familiar with techniques for applying creative processes to song writing, rhythmic activities, instrumental accompaniment, harmonizing, dramatization, and listening activities

Cultural Skills[14]

1. To know something about various musical periods in history and be able to correlate this information with related fields

2. To be aware of "permanent" music through sensible listening

3. To understand the development of nationalistic music and to be able to relate folk music and dances, foreign language songs and serious foreign compositions to social studies

4. To know something about the differences between folk music and art songs; how vocal music developed into the larger forms of opera, oratorio, mass, and cantata

5. To know something about the elements of music and to be able to speak intelligently about children's performance and recorded music

6. To know something of the motivations of musical enjoyment

METHODS OF TEACHING CLASSROOM TEACHERS

Teacher education institutions responsible for the preparation of classroom teachers may find the above outline too idealistic. However, comprehensive reading, guided listening, independent research, laboratory experience with instruments, and a stimulating faculty can do much to make it practicable.

Colleges have operated too long under the assumption that learning occurs only in the classroom. Future classroom teachers will accomplish much of the necessary learning on their own initiative if courses are organized as laboratory workshops in which theoretical information is taught as an outgrowth of experience in the classroom. Oral and written reports, reading and listening, should stem from the requirements of eventual teaching.

The bibliography in Appendix VI should assist in the preparation of such courses.

[14] See Chapter 10.

PROGRAMMED INSTRUCTION IN MUSIC EDUCATION[15]

Programmed instruction is designed to enable the student to acquire information or skill on his own with little assistance from the teacher. Such instruction, to be effective, should possess the following characteristics:

1. A logical, graduated sequence, adequate to the work involved, but within the student's competence
2. A mode of presentation that requires a response by the student at each step
3. An immediate check on the accuracy of each response

Materials may be programmed into a teaching machine. This involves the preparation of films, slides, or tape recordings, expert technical knowledge, and considerable expense, but has proven efficient on an experimental basis. The techniques of programmed instruction, however, may also be adapted for use on the equipment readily available in the audio-visual room of any school.

Materials can be mimeographed from lesson plans; tapes and transparencies prepared, photographs assembled. The important element is the imagination and creativity of the teacher in analyzing teaching aims and devising the most effective methods of achieving them.

Advocates of programmed instruction have shown that learning time can be decreased considerably. The small steps and immediate checks on accuracy decrease the probability of failure, fear of which is a major deterrent to learning. Such instruction is especially helpful in teaching specifics, since the student sets his own pace and must constantly evaluate his progress. Many skills usually taught by frequent drill or rote can be organized for self-instruction.

Some of the arguments leveled against programmed instruction are that it discourages divergent thinking and creativity; denies learning by discovery and intuitive insight; eliminates exploration of errors as a learning procedure; and fails to take account of differences in learning styles and theories.

Program Construction

The procedure usually followed in developing a program is based on good lesson planning:

1. Choose the subject
2. Define the specific objectives
3. Select the type of approach
4. Put the material to be learned into proper sequence
5. Construct small step items in frames
6. Evaluate and revise the program as needed

Informational materials are usually organized in double frames, the problem be-

[15] Evans, James L., *Principles of Programmed Learning,* Teaching Machines, Inc., New York, 1961. Also David Cram, *Explaining "Teaching Machines" and Programming,* Fearon Publishers, San Francisco, Calif., 1961; Robert Glazer, *Teaching Machines and Programmed Learning II,* N.E.A., Washington, D.C., 1965; and B. F. Skinner, "Teaching Machines," *Scientific American,* CCV:5 (November, 1961).

ing posed in the left frame with room for an answer. The right frame contains the answer covered or folded over. Upon completing the problem frame, the student checks his response against the answer frame.[16]

Programmed instruction is suitable for three areas of the music curriculum: (1) fact identification; (2) acquisition of muscular skills; and (3) cognition, relating music symbols to sounds and sounds to symbols.

1. Fact Identification: music signs and symbols, items in music history, form, biography, as in the following examples:

a. Signs

Problem frame	Answer (frame folded under)
1. The sign for a sharp is _____	sharp ♯
2. The sign for a flat is _____	flat ♭
3. The sign for a natural is _____	natural ♮

b. Terminology of dynamics

1. The Italian term for singing or playing softly is _____	piano
2. It is abbreviated as _____	*p*
3. To play or sing loudly is written in Italian as _____	forte
4. It is abbreviated as _____	*f*

c. Music form

Problem	Answer (frame folded under)
1. A song with two different themes is in _____ form	binary or AB form or two-part form
2. A song with theme A, Contrasting theme B, Return to theme A is in _____ form	ternary or three-part form

[16] Carlsen, James C., "The Role of Programmed Instruction in the Development of Musical Skills," in *Comprehensive Musicianship,* Contemporary Music Project, Music Educators National Conference, Washington, D.C., 1965.

Learning is reinforced whenever a written response can be combined with an aural experience. Thus questions about dynamic terminology can be coupled with a tape of illustrative sounds; questions about form with a tape of illustrative works.

2. Muscular Skills

A mirror shows the student what he is doing. For comparison, a projector or slide viewer illustrates the correct movement or position. Thus, a series of frames may be prepared in sequence demonstrating specific fingering patterns for playing a recorder or other flute-type instrument. This can be done in several ways.

> **a.** The student sits in front of a mirror with a study guide, which poses a sequence of questions. Each question demands a specific muscular response. He checks his response against a filmstrip or slide, which depicts the proper action. A film can be explained by a sound track, a slide by a written statement. The student practices the correct form by looking into the mirror, and checks his movement against the illustration.
>
> **b.** The student writes answers to a sequence of problems about fingering patterns, the correct fingering being indicated in the right-hand-side frames. Thus, for flutelike instruments:

Problem	Answer

1. To finger B
Fill in holes to be ○ 1
closed   Thumb ○   ○ 2
  ○ 3
  ○ 4
  ○ 5
  ○ 6
  ① 7
	close thumb hole and first
	hole ● 1
	Thumb ● ○ 2
	  ○ 3
	  ○ 4
	  ○ 5
	  ○ 6
	  ① 7

Of course, only concepts can be taught in this fashion. To achieve skill, the student must attempt to play the tone on the instrument and compare the result with a recording of the proper sound.

The identification of fingering patterns for scales and chords on the piano can be taught by the sequence of questions on page 325. However, such questions teach mere theory. The student must then attempt to play, and correct his attempt by example.

3. Cognition: relating music symbols to sounds and sounds to symbols. This involves the preparation of tapes, slides, or filmstrips containing:

> **a.** tonal melodic, intervallic, harmonic, and rhythmic patterns that the student must first identify, then represent symbolically
>
> **b.** symbols to be identified, then demonstrated vocally or instrumentally

In each case the student checks his answer against a tape or slide depicting the correct form.

Problem	**Answer**
1. Fingers on the left hand are numbered 	
2. Fingers on the right hand are numbered 	
3. Scale steps are played from ———— — ————	**finger to finger**
4. Chord skips are played by ———— ————	**skipping fingers**

Example: Identifying scale step patterns

The taped sequence contains the sound of the tonic to establish tonality, followed by tonal groups in a sequence:

a. Scale steps 1–2–3 sung or played

b. Student writes 1–2–3

c. Slide or film strip projects 1–2–3 as correct answer

Or conversely

a. Slide projects on screen

b. Student sings or plays 3–2–1 or *mi-re-do*

c. Tape plays correct sequence of 3–2–1

Using the Electronic Music Board for Immediate Playback

A valuable aid which, like tape, also provides immediate playback, is the Electronic Music Board. With a prepared list of tonal or rhythmic patterns, the student sings the requested pattern, then checks his response against the Music Board by touching the board with the electronic stylus, thereby triggering the playing of the correct phrase. For instance:

Visual Stimulus	**Student Response Vocally**	**Music Board Check**
	*do-mi-sol* or C–E–G	first for tonic for proper pitch, then singing pattern

Using Prepared Tapes for Feedback

The above illustration would also be suitable for a tape recording enabling the student to check his response against the correct taped response.

The following example illustrates the sequence of steps in a rhythmic problem:

a. Establish beat and tempo by metronome set at $\quarternote = 72$

b. Flash card, prepared slide, or film depicts

c. Student taps or vocally responds with rhythmic pattern

d. Student checks against correct taped response

Although programmed instruction requires the teacher to spend considerable time and effort preparing materials in logical sequence, it does enable students to learn on their own. Furthermore, the accuracy of the learning is immediately evaluated, reducing the need for further testing.[17]

---

[17] An excellent description of the application of programmed instruction to music education, including a bibliography of recent materials, is found in Don Metz, Paul Eickmann, and Donald Shetler, "A Resource Guide to Pupil-Controlled Instruction," mimeographed form, Eastman School of Music, Rochester, N.Y., 1966. See also Robert J. Hutcheson, Jr., "Programmed Instruction in Music Education," in *Missouri Journal of Research in Music Education*, II:1 (Autumn, 1967), pp. 9–52.

MEASUREMENT AND EVALUATION IN MUSIC EDUCATION

The major function of testing is to provide evidence upon which to make judgments. Most tests purport to measure either aptitude or achievement, though the distinction between the two is not subject to precise definition. Traditionally, musical aptitudes were considered to be innate responses to given sensory stimuli. Recent studies have indicated, however, that most so-called aptitudes include learned responses, and to such extent should be measured as achievement. Nevertheless, aptitude tests still claim to measure innate capacity or talent. Achievement tests, by contrast, seek to measure learned responses resulting from the acquisition of information, skills, attitudes, standards, and habits.[18]

Tests in music education are used to provide diagnostic or prognostic evidence on:

1. The achievement of general or specific objectives, or conversely, individual or group needs

2. The accuracy of learning

3. The efficiency of teaching

4. The weaknesses or strengths of individuals or groups

5. Guidance to be provided for pupils by parents, teachers, and administrators

6. The organization of music curricula to meet needs of a varied school population, that is, talented and interested, interested but not talented, neither talented nor interested

7. The relative musical potential of performing groups in a school system, as well as in comparison to national norms

8. The selection of students to be given school-owned instruments for study

SOME CRITERIA FOR CONSTRUCTING TESTS

In constructing tests Whybrew suggests a few basic principles:

1. List the specific objectives of instruction, or the specific responses the test is to measure: information, skills, perception, interpretation, attitudes

2. A test should reflect the emphasis placed on the subject matter. Major areas of instruction should receive a proportionate share of testing

3. Know the purpose for which the test is to be used. Some tests are constructed for grading the learning of specifics, others are constructed for diagnostic purposes, to discover weaknesses and the need for remedial work

4. Make sure conditions are suitable. Factors such as seating, materials, lighting, and time limits at the time a test is given may influence test results

5. Problems should range in difficulty. Some items should be sufficiently easy for all to answer, some sufficiently difficult to pinpoint those with optimum knowledge or ability

[18] Whybrew, William E., *Measurement and Evaluation in Music,* William C. Brown Company, Inc., Dubuque, Iowa, 1962, Chapters 8, 9, and 10.

6. Arrange test items according to degree of difficulty, proceeding from easy to difficult. This way, poorer students may at least complete some items, while better students can advance as far as they are able

7. Avoid ambiguous questions. Use vocabulary suited to grade level, without providing unintended clues. Make clear the specific type of answer requested

8. Determine the criteria to be used in test scoring. Objective tests, usually limited to simple item-by-item responses, are easier to score than essays. Although an essay test may call for objective information, factors such as spelling, grammar, verbal expression will also affect grading. A method frequently used to grade a large number of essay tests is to prepare in advance a list of specifics to be covered by each answer, then to examine the extent to which the student has encompassed and organized such specifics. When scoring essays, to better enable the examiner to maintain a constant standard for each question, grade each question in all papers, rather than grading test papers separately in their entirety.

SOME DEVICES FOR MEASURING MUSICAL APTITUDE EMPLOYED IN STANDARDIZED TESTS[19]

1. *Pitch discrimination:* sound two pitches in succession. The second sound is to be identified as either higher (H) or lower (L) than the first. Start with wide intervals, move to closer intervals

2. *Time discrimination:* with an instrument that sustains tone (violin, recorder), play two tones on the same pitch. Use a stopwatch or the second hand of a watch to measure time. Ask pupils to indicate if the second tone is longer (L) or shorter (S) than the first tone

3. *Rhythm discrimination:* play a rhythm pattern, which is repeated in exact or altered form. Ask pupils to indicate if the second pattern is the same (S) or different (D)

4. *Loudness discrimination:* play two tones at the same pitch. Alter the repeated tone in intensity, either louder or softer. Ask the pupils to indicate whether the second tone is louder (L) or softer (S) than the first

5. *Timbre (quality discrimination):* sing two tones on the same pitch with identical or altered vowel sound. Ask pupils to indicate if the quality of second tone is the same (S) or different (D)

6. *Tonal memory:* play a sequence of three tones, preferably neither scalic nor within normal chord intervals. On the repetition of the sequence alter one of the three

[19] Lundin, Robert W., *An Objective Psychology of Music,* The Ronald Press Company, New York, rev. ed., 1967, Chapter 12.

tones. Pupils must indicate which of the three tones has been altered. Increase the sequence to groups of four, five, and six tones

7. *Tonal movement:* play a sequence of three or four tones that requires a concluding tone to create a feeling of tendential resolution. Students are to indicate if the final tone should resolve up (U) or down (D)

1.   U   2.   D   3.   D   4.   U   5.   D

8. *Interval discrimination:* play an interval of a major third followed by an interval of a major second. Pupils are to indicate whether second interval is larger (L) or smaller (S). Vary the intervals on the scale and also whether the low or high pitch is played first

TESTS FOR MEASURING MUSICAL IMAGERY AND SENSITIVITY[20]

1. *Melodic taste:* select a number of unfamiliar four-measure melodies. Substitute two slightly incongruous measures for the final two measures of each. Play each melody twice, first with the original measures then with the incongruous substitution (see example below). Students are to indicate their preference (1 or 2).

2. *Pitch imagery:* mimeograph a series of tone sequences either by number, syllable, or pitch. As each tone sequence sounds, the student must indicate whether the printed version is the same (S) or different (D).

Written	Sounded	Answer
Do - Re - Mi	Do - Mi - Fa	D
or		
1 - 2 - 3	1 - 3 - 4	
or		

[20] Gordon, Edwin, "Testing Today," Bulletin 11, *The Musical Aptitude Profile,* Houghton Mifflin Company, Boston, 1965.

3. *Rhythm imagery:* compose rhythm patterns using the same method as that described for pitch.

Written	Sounded	Answer
♩. ♪ ♩ ♩	♩ ♩ ♩ ♩	D
♩ ♫ ♩ ♩	♩ ♫ ♩ ♩	S

4. *Chord imagery:* play a major triad followed by a second major or minor triad. Pupils are to indicate whether the second triad is major (M) or minor (m).

5. *Musical memory:* play a series of four-measure melodies. On successive repetitions either:

    a. Change key
    b. Change rhythm
    c. Change one or more notes in the melody
    d. Keep the melody the same

Students must tell what has happened with each alteration: (K) for key change; (R) for rhythm change; (N) for note change; (S) for same.

6. *Pitch recognition:* sound a given pitch from a song. Children are to count how many times this pitch occurs during the playing of the song. Use a number of different songs and different pitches.

7. *Rhythm recognition:* from a given song select a rhythm pattern, say in ¾ | ♩. ♪ ♩ | Ask children to count the number of times this pattern occurs.

MUSIC ACHIEVEMENT TESTS

1. *Sight reading (pitch recognition):* notate a series of four-measure melodies, each containing one measure with an inaccurately notated pitch. Play the melody correctly. The pupils are to put a circle around the incorrect measure.

2. *Sight reading (rhythm recognition):* notate a series of four-measure melodies, each containing one measure with inaccurate rhythm but correct pitch. Play the melody correctly. The pupils are to put a circle around the inaccurately notated measure.

3. *Sight reading:* prepare a list of ten or more familiar melodies numbered from 1 to 10. Underneath, notate in a different sequence from the list the first phrase of each of the melodies. The pupils must identify each melody by the number of its title in the list.

1. America
2. America the Beautiful
3. Old Folks At Home
4.
5.
6. etc.

4. *Meter recognition:* prepare a sequence of measures in a given meter. The children are to add the meter signature:

5. *Rhythm recognition:* prepare a sequence of measures that can be organized within a meter signature, but leave out the bar lines. The children are to add bar lines.

6. *Musical forms:* from recordings previously heard, select representative examples of forms for identification: march, waltz, minuet, gavotte, etc.

7. *Musical styles and periods* (*upper grades*): from recordings previously heard, select a representative group to be identified as to particular periods, styles, national or ethnic character: Classic, Romantic, Baroque; Hungarian, Spanish, Italian folk dances or songs; spirituals, Calypso, American Indian, cowboy, etc.

8. *Instrument recognition:* from among recordings previously heard, select those from which instruments, voices, and small ensembles can be identified.

9. *Memory for music literature:* from recordings previously heard, select about ten, the titles and composers of which the children should be able to recall.

TYPES OF OBJECTIVE TESTS

True-False (use + sign for true and 0 for false)

1. ....To raise the pitch of a tone a half step, place a sharp in front of it.
2. ....A flat sign (♭) raises the pitch a half step.

Matching Test

1. ....America
2. ....Swing Low, Sweet Chariot
3. ....Yellow Bird
4. ....Tenting Tonight
5. ....La Paloma

    a. Negro Spiritual
    b. Civil War Song
    c. Mexican Song
    d. Calypso Song
    e. Patriotic Song

Multiple Choice

1. ....*Rhapsody in Blue* was composed by
    a. Ferde Grofé   b. Irving Berlin   c. George Gershwin

Completion

1. The themes of Haydn were often inspired by the (folk) (music) of his native Austria.

Identification (brief description)

1. Violin: (possible answer) A bowed string instrument held under the chin. It is the soprano string instrument in the orchestra. It has four strings tuned in fifths, E, A, D, G.

MUSIC SYMBOLS TESTS

1. Name pitches on the staff below

2. Identify major and relative minor key signatures

Major
Minor

3. Add the key signature called for

Eb   C Minor   G   A   Ab   D   etc.

4. Indicate the Italian terms and abbreviations for the following:

softly: fast:
loudly: slow:
moderately soft: walking time:
moderately loud: moderately fast:

5. Translate these terms into English and show abbreviation:

piano:
forte:
mezzopiano:
mezzoforte:

6. Write the music symbols that represent these words:

staccato   legato   tie   accent
hold   sharp   flat   cancel
bar line   double bar   repeat sign

7. Reverse 6, show the symbol and ask for its definition.

SOME STANDARDIZED MUSIC APTITUDE AND ACHIEVEMENT TESTS

Achievement tests are generally devised by individual teachers, who base them on materials taught in class. Aspects of talent, however, are generally measured by standardized music aptitude tests. In evaluating the success of the music program, standardized achievement tests have the value of providing norms for various age and grade levels for the purposes of comparison. Standardized tests have been validated, are generally reliable, accurately and scientifically constructed, and easily administered and scored.

MUSICAL APTITUDE TESTS[21]

1. *Musical Aptitude Profile*, Edwin Gordon, Houghton Mifflin Co., Boston, 1965. Measures basic musical factors classified into three main divisions: tonal imagery, rhythm imagery, musical sensitivity

  a. Subtests for tonal imagery: melody and harmony
  b. Subtests for rhythm imagery: tempo and meter
  c. Subtests for musical sensitivity: phrasing, balance, and style

2. *Revision of Seashore Measures of Musical Talents*, Carl E. Seashore, Joseph E. Saetveit, and Don Lewis, Dept. of Education, RCA Manufacturing Co., Camden, N.J., 1940. Measures discrimination of pitch, loudness, time, rhythm, timbre, tonal memory

3. *Kwalwasser-Dykema Music Tests*, Manual of Directions for Victor Records, Carl Fischer, Inc., New York, 1930. Measures discrimination of pitch, intensity, time, rhythm, timbre, tonal memory, tonal movement, melodic taste, pitch imagery, rhythm imagery

4. *Drake Musical Aptitude Tests*, Raleigh M. Drake, Science Research Associates, 57 W. Grand Avenue, Chicago 10, Ill., 1932. Measures musical memory, interval discrimination, retentivity, and musical intuition

5. *Tilson-Gretsch Musical Aptitude Test*, Lowell M. Tilson, Fred Gretsch Mfg. Company, 60 Broadway, Brooklyn, N.Y. 11211, 1941. Measures discrimination of pitch, intensity, time, tonal memory. Available with test operator as a service from the Gretsch Manufacturing Company

6. *Musical Aptitude Test*, Harvey S. Whistler and Louis P. Thorpe, California Test Bureau, 5916 Hollywood Blvd., Los Angeles 28, Calif., 1950. Measures rhythm recognition, pitch recognition, melody recognition, pitch discrimination, and advanced rhythm recognition

7. *Wing Standardized Tests of Musical Intelligence*, Herbert Wing, National Foundation for Educational Research, 79 Wimpole Street, London, W.1, England, 1948. A battery of seven tests dealing with

  a. chord analysis
  b. pitch change
  c. memory
  d. rhythmic accent
  e. harmony
  f. intensity
  g. phrasing

Used from age seven up. Norms available from age eight up

---

[21]Colwell, Richard, *Elementary Music Achievement Test Manual* for EMAT, Follett Publishing Company, Chicago, 1965.

8. *Kwalwasser Music Talent Test,* Jacob Kwalwasser, Mills Music Co., 1619 Broadway, New York 10019, 1953. A recorded test that takes only ten minutes to administer. Form A consists of fifty three-tone patterns that on repetition are altered in one of the following respects: (a) pitch, (b) time, (c) rhythm, (d) loudness. Form B consists of forty items that present the same features but in somewhat simplified form

MUSIC ACHIEVEMENT TESTS

1. *Elementary Music Achievement Test,* Richard Colwell, Follett Publishing Company, Chicago, Ill., 1966

Part 1 measures pitch, interval, meter discrimination

Part 2 measures auditory-visual transfer in pitch, rhythm, feeling for tonal center in cadences and phrases; major and minor mode recognition in chords and phrases

2. *Kwalwasser-Ruch Test of Musical Accomplishment,* Bureau of Educational Research, University of Iowa, Iowa City, 1924. Measures:

a. Knowledge of musical terms and symbols

b. Recognition of syllable names from notation

c. Detection of pitch errors in notation of a familiar melody

d. Detection of time errors in a familiar melody

e. Knowledge of pitch and letter names of bass and treble clefs

f. Knowledge of time signatures

g. Knowledge of key signatures

h. Knowledge of rest values

i. Knowledge of note values

j. Knowledge of familiar melodies from notation

3. *Torgerson-Fahnestock Music Tests,* T. L. Torgerson and E. Fahnestock, Public School Publ. Company, Bloomington, Ill., 1926

Part I measures knowledge of note and rest values; time signatures, pitch and syllable names, marks of expression, repeat bars, major and minor key signatures, natural and harmonic minor scales

Part II includes writing syllable names from oral dictation; writing time signatures; detecting pitch and time errors in notation; writing notes of the staff from dictation

4. *Beach Music Accomplishment Test,* F. A. Beach and H. E. Schrammel, Bureau of Educational Measurement, Kansas State Teachers College, Emporia, Kansas, 1930. Measures knowledge of music symbols, direction of melody, correction of notation, melody recognition, syllables, composers, performers

5. *Knuth Achievement Tests in Music,* William E. Knuth, Educational Test Bureau, Minneapolis, Minn., 1936. Measures ability to recognize certain rhythmic and melodic elements in music notation. The examiner plays a series of four-measure phrases. From four examples of notation for each phrase, each example differing only in the last two measures, the subject must choose that actually played

6. *Gildersleeve Music Achievement Tests,* Glenn Gildersleeve, Teachers College

Press, Columbia University, New York, 1929. Two tests of equal difficulty, using the same techniques. Tests measure the following abilities:

a. Recognition of compositions played by the examiner
b. Detection of changes in pitch, meter, key signature, and meter signature
c. Writing key signatures; locating *la* in six different keys; knowledge of use of accidentals, note values, time signatures, and ability to transpose a phrase from the treble to the bass clef
d. A multiple-response test, containing fifteen main questions, which cover in some detail instrumentation, theory, history, and harmony
e. Recognition of compositions from the score

7. *University of Oregon Musical Discrimination Test,* Kate Hevner and John Lansbury, University of Oregon, Oregon. Consists of a recording of a series of forty brief musical selections. Each selection is played in two versions, one correct, the other altered in either rhythm, harmony, or melody. The pupil must indicate which version he prefers, and whether the rhythm, harmony, or melody has been altered

KEEPING STUDENT RECORDS

Music teachers, like others, are usually required to grade achievement and are frequently hard put to know what criteria to employ to evaluate each child's ability. For this reason it is advisable to make a cumulative music profile chart on which each

Student Name: Instrument Studied:
Address:

	Singing Skill	Rhythms	Instrumental Activities	Listening Attitude	Creative Ability	Aptitude Tests	Achievement Tests
First Grade							
Second Grade							
Third Grade							
Fourth Grade							
Fifth Grade						Pitch Rhythm Intensity Timbre	
Sixth Grade							Reading Theory Literature Information

Remarks:

FIGURE 11-4 Cumulative Music Profile Record

child's musical development over the years can be recorded. Grades may be recorded either quantitatively with numbers or letters, or qualitatively with anecdotal comments, or both. A chart also provides a useful record for guidance in the upper grades. An example of such a chart is shown in Figure 11-4.

KEEPING INVENTORY RECORDS

In order to facilitate finding music materials and equipment, and to know their condition and the amounts available, it is important that the music teacher keep accurate records. Administrative officers must also be informed at budget time, usually early spring, of replacement needs. Examples of such inventory cards follow:

Music Series

Title: Publisher: Date Acquired:

Price: Tchrs Book: Student Book:

Address:

      Quantity: Condition: Location:

Kindergarten
Book 1
Book 2
Book 3
Book 4
Book 5
Book 6

Recordings

Individual recordings should be housed in a central location. Each record jacket or album should be numbered. Records should be stored standing on edge rather than flat in a file cabinet, preferably closed to keep out dust. Cross-reference inventory cards should be kept for each recording.[22]

One card might list:

1. Title
2. Composer
3. Performer

4. Character: i.e., symphony
5. File No.
6. Publisher
7. Record No.   Price

[22] Excellent cards for recording inventories of instruments, recordings, music, uniforms; filing folders with inventories for choral and instrumental music; and student record cards are all available from the Southern Music Company, San Antonio, Texas.

A second card in a different color might list:

1. Composer
2. Title   etc.
3. Performer

A third card in a different color might list:

1. Character
2. Title
3. Performer   etc.

Cross referencing enables the teacher to find a recording by either title or composer, or to find examples of a particular musical form: suite, opera, etc.

Cards should also be made for the albums of music series, particularly for listening lessons.

Choral Music

Choral octavo numbers should be housed in individual envelopes, each numbered for ease of location and filed numerically. Inventory cards in duplicate or triplicate should be filed, listing:

1. Title   4. Performing Time   7. Grade
2. Composer   5. Setting   8. Quantity
3. Publisher   6. Address   9. Price

The second card in a different color would list composer at 1, and a third card would have character or setting at 1. Setting refers to SA or SSA, etc.[23]

Orchestra and Band Music

Cards similar to those for choral octavo music should be filed, listing:

1. Title   4. Address   7. Instrumentation
2. Composer   5. Character   8. Price: Score, Parts
3. Publisher   6. Performing Time

Parts
.............Piano
.............1st Violin
.............2nd Violin
.............Viola   etc.

Orchestra and Band Instruments

A depreciation and location card should be kept for each instrument. The depreciation record should be used to substantiate an annual allocation of funds equal to

[23] Soprano, Alto, or First Soprano, Second Soprano, Alto.

the annual recorded depreciation so that, when necessary, money will be available to replace worn-out instruments. Depreciation record cards may be secured from the Conn Instrument Company, Elkhart, Ind.

School No.:		
Instrument:	**Make:**	**Serial No.:**
Purchased from:		**Price:**
Equipped with.........case.........crooks.........Ligature.........Reed case.........Key.........mouthpiece.......		
lyre.......bow.......cap.......strap.......chin rest.......piston wiper.		
Condition at purchase:		
Repairs: Date		Cost:
Issued to	Date	Returned

Rhythm Instruments
Sets:

School No.:

Manufacturer:

Address:

Instruments	Quantity	Condition	Unit Price	Located
Tambourines				
Cymbals				
Sandpaper blocks				
Rhythm sticks				
etc.				
Latin American				
Maracas				
Claves				
Gourds				
etc.				
Melodic Percussion				
Xylophones				
Tone bars				
Orchestra bells				
Step bells				
etc.				
Orff				
Metalophones				
Drums				
etc.				
Autoharps				

SUMMARY

The elementary school music specialist must acquire the following skills: skilled performance in at least one medium of musical performance; accompaniment ability in several media of musical performance; knowledge of music history related to the periods studied in elementary school; knowledge of music theory and the ability to relate it to music performance; knowledge of learning theory and its relationship to physical, emotional, and intellectual growth; knowledge of theories of motivation and the ability to implement them by a variety of teaching methods; the ability to develop curriculum plans and units of instruction; and the ability to organize in-service workshops for general classroom teachers, to stimulate them to achieve the skills and interests necessary to provide a sound music program for the school system.

CHAPTER TWELVE

CHANGING CONCEPTS OF MUSIC EDUCATION

The science of aesthetics is an attempt . . . to obtain a clear general idea of beautiful objects, or judgments upon them, and the motives underlying the acts which create them—to raise the aesthetic life, otherwise a matter of instinct and feeling, to the level of intelligence, of understanding. . . . Our understanding will be complete if our idea includes all the distinguishing characteristics of art, not simply enumerated, but exhibited in their achieved relations.[1]

The trouble with some art writings, and most so-called aesthetics and treatises on art in the abstract, is that they seldom if ever betray that the author has "lived" the work of art. They are the outcome of reading and cogitation. They remind one of those voluminous and tangled bills of fare presented in Paris restaurants for greenhorns to puzzle over until in despair they cry out, "Give me something to eat, any darned thing."[2]

[1] Parker, DeWitt, *Principles of Aesthetics*, Appleton-Century-Crofts, Inc., New York, 1927, p. 3. See also Jeanne G. Faulkner, "Taste, Music and Education," A survey of comments on taste in general, musical taste, and how it relates to music education, is found in *Missouri Journal of Research in Music Education*, II:1 (Autumn, 1967), pp. 84–113.

[2] Berenson, Bernard, *Aesthetics and History*, Pantheon Books, a Division of Random House, Inc., New York, 1954, pp. 28ff.

Music education must concern the consumer rather than the producer of music. Fewer than 1 percent of American high school students turn to music as a career, but 100 percent turn to it on radio, television, phonograph, and juke box. An audience captive if not captivated in public buildings and conveyances is assailed by background music designed to be absorbed rather than heard. "Hear ye, hear ye" has become obligatory in far more places than court.[3]

Music education must now provide the means of curbing the tyranny of much quantity and accessibility of sound with criteria of quality and selectivity. Not only must young people be required to learn the skills which will transmit the accomplishments of the past, but they must also learn that standards are civilization's defense against barbarism.[4]

The aesthetic level of popular music and other such aural sedatives will improve only in response to a more discriminating mass demand. Thus a major purpose of music education in a democratic society must be to help each member of the common audience develop, within the limits of his capacity, the ability to choose music wisely. Choice presupposes judgment, and judgment necessitates philosophy, a standard of taste.

. . . criticism . . . fails to accomplish its full office if it does not indicate what to look for and what to find in concrete aesthetic objects. . . . A philosophy of art . . . makes us aware of the function of art in relation to other modes of experience and . . . indicates why this function is so inadequately realized, and . . . suggests the conditions under which the office would be successfully performed.[5]

[3]"My feelings are so strongly engaged as a victim of the practice in controversy that I had better not participate in judicial judgment upon it." Mr. Justice Frankfurter, *Public Utilities Commission v. Pollak*, 343 US 451, 1951, p. 467 (upholding the right of the commission to broadcast music on buses in Washington, D.C.).

[4]Whitner, Mary Elizabeth, "Why Music Is Indispensable," *Music in the Senior High School*, Music Educators National Conference, Washington, D.C., 1959, Chapter 1, p. 19. See also Francis H. Horn, "Music for Everyone," *Music Educators Journal*, XLII:4, (February–March, 1956), pp. 27–29; and Foster McMurray, "Pragmatism," in *Basic Concepts in Music Education*, National Society for the Study of Education, University of Chicago, 1958, p. 41.

[5]Dewey, John, *Art as Experience*, G. P. Putnam's Sons, New York, 1934, p. 11. Cf. Paul Schrecker, *Work and History*, Princeton University Press, Princeton, N.J., pp. 56ff.; Thomas Munro and Herbert Read, *The Creative Arts in American Education*, Harvard University Press, Cambridge, Mass., 1960. Classic and influential works on aesthetics include: Plato, *The Symposium, Phaedrus*; Gottfried Lessing, *Laocoön*; Immanuel Kant, *Critique of Aesthetic Judgment*; Friedrich Nietzsche, *The Birth of Tragedy*; Clive Bell, *Art*. See also George Santayana, *Selections*, Charles Scribner's Sons, New York, 1953, pp. 27ff., 212ff., 711ff., 769ff.; René Wellek, *A History of Modern Criticism*, Yale University Press, New Haven, Conn.; or any of the numerous works of Sir Herbert Read, such as *Education through Art*, Pantheon Books, a Division of Random House, Inc., New York, 1945; *The Grass Roots of Art*, George Wittenborn, Inc., New York, 1955; *The Forms of Things Unknown*, Horizon Press, New York, 1960.

The standards of taste that have framed the curricula of public schools in the United States have almost invariably mirrored contemporary current social aspirations. During periods of political and economic stability, traditional disciplines have been emphasized, while in periods of crisis, curricula have been revised by the introduction of new subject matter and educational techniques.

Current professional and general education journals illustrate the anxiety of music educators to maintain the educational status of music in the revision of general education that has accompanied the advent of the atomic age. Such articles adduce a miscellany of reasons for the continuance of music in the curriculum: music is alleged to serve as a humanizing force in a nation of technocrats, as a buttress for individuality in an age of conformity, as a therapeutic escape mechanism, as an instrument for international diplomacy, and as a force for domestic egalitarianism.[6]

The belief that music needs justification as an expedient for achieving non-musical goals is at least as old as another, though more theoretically atomic age, the Greek. Both Greeks and Egyptians attributed to their respective gods of wisdom, Apollo and Thot, extraordinary musical ability. To the Greeks, however, music was preeminent among the arts, not only because it could induce given emotional states in the listener, but because it was believed able to impress upon the mind the cosmic order of the universe. This power, the "ethos" of music, judiciously used by the teacher, rendered music the primary means in Greek pedagogy for crystallizing desirable emotional and ethical faculties in the young.[7] Unfortunately, neither ancient nor modern history lends

---

[6]See Harold C. Youngberg, "The Music Program in the Senior High School," *California Journal of Secondary Education,* XXXIV:4 (April, 1959), pp. 241–246; Wolfgang Kuhn and June K. M. Fee, "Basic Education in Art and Music," *California Journal of Secondary Education,* XXXIV:4 (April, 1959), pp. 223–229; Edwin C. Mustard, "An Administrator Looks at Music in the Junior High School," *Music Educators Journal,* XLIII:1 (September–October, 1956), pp. 40–42.

[7]The two most influential Greek writers on the educational value of music are Plato and Aristotle. Plato's discussion of music, which occurs in nearly all his works, is briefly summarized in Paul Henry Lang, *Music in Western Civilization,* W. W. Norton & Company, Inc., New York, 1941, pp. 14ff. Aristotle's theories are concisely set forth in his *Politics* 8: 1339 (a) ff., The Basic Works of Aristotle, R. Mckeon (ed.), Random House, Inc., New York, 1941. For a more controversial view than Lang's, see Curt Sachs, *The Rise of Music in the Ancient World, East and West,* W. W. Norton & Company, Inc., New York, 1943, pp. 248ff. Sachs is criticized in Egon Wellesz (ed.), *Ancient and Oriental Music,* Oxford University Press, London, 1957, in the article by Isobel Henderson. Pythagorean number theory, which inspired Plato's ideas on music, can be found in S. Sambursky, *The Physical World of the Greeks,* The Macmillan Company, New York, 1961, pp. 52ff. As a legacy of these ideas, music was considered a branch of mathematics until the end of the eighteenth century, and is still, heretically, in the twentieth. See Joseph Schillinger, *The Mathematical Basis of Art,* Philosophical Library, Inc., New York, 1948, and *The Schillinger System of Musical Composition,* Carl Fischer, Inc., New York, 1946. Plato studied under the Pythagoreans; George Gershwin studied under Schillinger. Do the analogues and *Rhapsody in Blue* have mathematical principles in common? Compare Descartes, *On the Direction of the Mind;* Maurice Goldblatt, *A Newly Identified Head of Leda by Leonardo Da Vinci,* The Citadel Press, New York, 1961; Isaac Newton, *Observations on the Prophesy of Daniel,* James Nisbet, London, 1831; Boris Pasternak, *Dr. Zhivago,* Pantheon Books, Inc., New York, 1958 (conclusion, section 12); Martin Foss, *The Idea of Perfection in the Western World,* Princeton University Press, Princeton, N.J., 1946, pp. 58ff. Have the Dialogues, the Bible, the Mona Lisa, survived because of their mathematical content?

much support to the theory that music, or any other art, of itself inculcates particular moral or political attitudes.[8]

Aside from its putative civic virtues, music by definition possesses attributes peculiar to a medium of humanly created and organized sound. Music is an art. As an art, it is apprehended through an individual's sensory organs. The study of such apprehension is the psychology of music. Music education employs both the art and psychology of music to achieve pedagogic goals.

Music has been defined as an expression of emotion utilizing sound as its medium, organized in a significant, objective form for purposes of heightening experience.[9] The elements music employs are pitch, intensity, timbre, rhythm, meter, harmony, and form.

Pitch, as the highness or lowness of a tone, relates to the frequency of vibration of a medium. *Intensity* or *dynamics*, the loudness or softness of a tone, is the result of the amplitude or width of the vibration or resonation. *Timbre* or quality of sound is illustrated by the difference in vowel sounds in human voices (for example, ē–ō), or the difference between a trumpet and a violin playing the same pitch with the same intensity. *Rhythm* is the onward flow of sound organized into varying durations by stresses and pauses at recurring intervals. *Meter* or pulse refers to the organization of rhythm into a feeling of "twoness" or "threeness," commonly thought of as two-beat or three-beat measures, or their compounds. The contrast between the two-beat measure of the march and the three-beat measure of the waltz is quickly recognized. *Harmony* refers to the combinations of pitches sounding simultaneously to produce a feeling of consonance or dissonance, pleasing or otherwise to the ear. *Form* refers to the organization of sounds into motives, phrases, and their combinations to make identifiable groups.[10]

Progress in apprehending music . . . is significantly related to formal training, interest, attitude and to verbal intelligence . . . learning to listen is (a) learning to perceive the details of rhythm, harmony and form, (b) giving names to these perceptions, (c) building these percepts into more complex and well-defined wholes (concepts), and (d) using these concepts as the framework for comprehending new musical experience.[11]

[8] Rather, the causal relation seems to be the reverse. Assuming a reasonable state of material welfare, the arts have tended to flourish when the balance or absence of strong political forces has alleviated the pressure of the state upon the individual: for example, classical Greece, Renaissance Italy, Elizabethan England, Pre-Bismarck Germany. Cf. Alfred Zimmern, *The Greek Commonwealth*, Random House, Inc., New York, 1956, p. 215, and *passim;* Jacob Burckhardt, *The Civilization of the Renaissance in Italy*, Phaidon Press, Ltd., London, 1950, pp. 81ff. There is as much difficulty in ascribing political, intellectual, or ethical content to music generally as there is in ascribing such characteristics to any piece of music in particular. Non-Jewish musicians were, of all German artists, the most receptive to Nazi ideology; see William L. Schirer, *The Rise and Fall of the Third Reich*, Simon and Schuster, Inc., New York, 1960, p. 242; Ned Rorem, *The Paris Diary of Ned Rorem*, George Braziller, Inc., New York, 1966, p. 14; Anthony Burgess, *A Clockwork Orange*, Ballantine Books, Inc., New York, 1963.
[9] Parker, *op. cit.,* pp. 155–157.
[10] Hamilton, Clarence, *Sound and Its Relation to Music*, Oliver Ditson Company, Philadelphia, 1902.
[11] Mueller, Kate Hevner, "Studies in Musical Appreciation," *Journal of Research in Music Education*, IV:1 pp. 2–25.

Physiological reactions to the elements of music occur whether the person apprehending is musical or unmusical, and regardless of his enjoyment of the experience. The mere presence of sound affects the listener. Mursell, in speaking of the musical education of children, states:

Musical structure sets up expressive demands because we feel and apprehend it through the responses of our bodies. Music is not tonal geometry. If we only *hear* music, we never fully apprehend it. Music enters into us, possesses us, permeates us, and molds and modifies all our physical responses. . . . Expression in music is a translation into tone of the bodily apprehension of the music. The human body is the basic musical instrument. We are responsive to music because of the nature of our bodies.[12]

Although the precise nature of physiological reactions to music is in dispute, there is general agreement that music will increase or decrease muscular tension (according to tonal intensity and pitch), increase bodily metabolism, accelerate respiration and decrease its regularity, produce a marked but variable effect on the volume, pulse, and pressure of the blood, lower the threshold for sensory stimuli (the threshold varying according to mode), and affect internal glandular secretions.[13] Some psychologists believe that it is a combination of these physiological factors that causes music to produce emotional responses in the listener. Anciently, music was thought to have demonstrable physiological effects, the Greeks particularizing to the point of prescribing the Phrygian mode as a cure for sciatica.[14]

Simple sounds in and of themselves may cause pleasure or pain as may other simple sensory perceptions. Reactions to sound may also be affected by the environment of the listener. In a dark alley on a moonless night following footfalls are disturbing, an innocuous sound in broad daylight. To bolster his morale, the night pedestrian whistles a familiar tune. In either case, reaction to sound is affected by its non-aural context.

Since music is apprehended through the ear, the structure of the ear may determine the nature of the apperception.

From the evolutionary standpoint, the ear is the receptor organ most closely associated with the general orientation of the body. Originally it does not appear as an organ of hearing at all. . . . The neural connections of the ear are of special and direct importance in giving the sense of balance, of up and down, of direction, upon which controlled bodily movement depends. And thus music is an art which employs a medium—aural experience—associated with unique intimacy with our feeling of bodily movement and control.[15]

[12] Mursell, James L., and Mabelle Glenn, *The Psychology of School Music Teaching,* Silver Burdett Company, Morristown, N.J., 1931, p. 259–260.
[13] Diserens, Charles M., and Harry Fine, *A Psychology of Music,* College of Music, Cincinnati, Ohio, 1939, p. 253.
[14] Athenaious, 14:624; Homer and Pindar refer to staunching songs to clot blood. Cf. Egon Wellesz, *Ancient and Oriental Music, op. cit.,* fn. 14, p. 402.
[15] Mursell, James L., *The Psychology of Music,* W. W. Norton, & Company, Inc., New York, 1938, p. 19.

This characteristic of the ear indicates that considerably more than metaphor is involved in such expressions as "being carried away," "possessed," or "moved" by music. The feeling that music moves—up and down, forward and around, expanding and contracting—is based upon the association of musical stimuli with the ear's function of maintaining bodily equilibrium.

Rhythm is the element most directly involved in bodily reactions. Stetson's extensive experiments on reactions to rhythmic stimuli suggest that the listener's muscles empathically respond to the rhythms produced by a performer.

But one has as vivid and satisfactory sense of rhythm when one merely hears (or sees, or feels) the series. Where are the movements at the basis of such "sensory" rhythmic experience? The body is provided with muscles capable of producing rapid and varied movements not visible to ordinary observation; among those one looks most naturally to those organs which have to do with the production of rhythm. . . . But the most important rhythm-producing apparatus is the vocal apparatus. . . . The writer finds rapid series rhythmized by slight movements of the muscles of the tongue and perhaps of the throat, in conjunction with the expiratory muscles which mark the main accents. Every rhythm is dynamic; it consists of actual movements. It is not necessary that joints be involved, but changes in muscular conditions which stand in consciousness as movements are essential to any rhythm whether "perceived" or "produced."[16]

Response to melody and to pitch relationships is organic and kinesthetic. Melodies are congeries of pitches united by recognizable continuity rather than a mere series of discrete pitches apprehended separately.[17]

In Bingham's experiments, a number of subjects tapped an apparatus much like a telegrapher's key. The key was arranged so that any variation in the nature of the tapping could be measured and recorded. It was found that melody, unlike the effects of simply raising pitch and increasing tonal intensity, created a muscular tension that relaxed at the close of the perceived unity.[18]

That the urge for self-expression is innate has been amply documented by researchers in the field of child development.[19] The baby lying in his crib will sound

[16]Stetson, Raymond Herbert, "Motor Theory of Rhythm and Discrete Succession," *The Psychological Review*, XII:4 July, 1905, p. 255.
[17]Redfield, John, *Music, A Science and an Art*, Tudor Press, 1928, p. 91.
[18]Bingham, W. Van Dyke, *Studies in Melody*, monograph supplement 50 of *The Psychological Review*, Baltimore, 1910, pp. 1–88.
[19]Gesell, Arnold, *Infancy and Human Growth*, The Macmillan Company, New York, 1928. Cf. the following definition of man from a paper delivered at the Seventh International Congress of Anthropological and Ethnological Sciences, Moscow, U.S.S.R., 1964. "PRIMATE who formalizes his every biological process in rituals; regulates and channels his behavior via complex social 'institutions'; who thinks and communicates in symbols; who finds satisfaction in singing and in carving distorted figurines, and whose very tools are esthetic; the CREATURE whose mentation is such that, even primitively, he can worry as to whether the stars are friendly; who can become willing to die while supporting abstractions, or torture and kill another of his kind for the sake of the same abstraction; a PERSON who can be simultaneously a son, a husband, a father; a hunter who turns over his kill to someone else; an ANIMAL sensitive to absurdities; a LIVING ORGANISM who can commit suicide, and who can conceive of death yet deny its existence . . . " Quoted in Earl W. Count, "Whence Mankind?", *The Key Reporter*, XXX:2, (1965).

forth demands for attention. Suddenly recognizing his own voice, he will begin experimenting with the kinds of sounds he can produce. At a later stage of development, he will pound out rhythms with a spoon on the high chair as he waits for food. Still later he will begin to improvise melodies and to invent rhythmic movements and dances.

The growing child recapitulates musical evolution. It has been found that the improvised melodies of Viennese children between the ages of two and four were identical in form to the two-tone melodies that comprise the musical culture of the most primitive societies.[20]

Primitive man learned early how to use natural musical materials to aid his work, propitiate his gods, and frighten his enemies. He discovered the boom of a hollowed log, the rattle of dried gourds, and the twang of the bow string that varied according to tension. Birds could be imitated by voice or by blowing across a hollow reed; insects by blowing to vibrate a blade of grass held between thumbs; thunder by pounding taut skins stretched across a hollowed log. The last sound, varying with the depth and length of hollow and type of wood, could carry a signal a great distance. The pitch of a hollow reed could be varied and multiplied by combining reeds of different lengths.

As man developed language, he developed song. Rudimentary chants embodied a simple two- or three-note melodic line with a constantly reiterated rhythmic pattern. Frequently, melodies were the secret of an individual medicine man and his family; others the exclusive property of a clan or sex.[21]

To primitive man, as to the child, music was not isolated from the context of everyday living. His music was designed either to accompany a simple message, or to convey the impression of a particularly powerful emotion, but was always an integral adjunct of his daily activity. Gorer describes the motivation of African dancing:

Africans dance. They dance for joy, and they dance for grief; they dance for love, they dance for hate; they dance to bring prosperity and they dance to avert calamity; they dance for religion and they dance to pass the time. Far more exotic than their skin and their features is this characteristic of dancing . . . [22]

Similar to the easy rapport among small children, the art of primitive man is not so much personal as tribal.[23] The force of the emotion, moreover, creates an ambivalent attitude toward the role of the individual.

Preliterate peoples in general have one of two prevalent attitudes towards composition. Some of them consider it a craft, consciously practiced by the composer; others associate it with

---

[20]Sachs, *op. cit.,* p. 43.

[21]Claiborne, Robert W., *The Way Man Learned Music,* Haddon Craftsmen, Camden, N.J., 1937, pp. 22–23.

[22]Gorer, Geoffrey, *Africa Dances,* W. W. Norton & Company, Inc., New York, 1962, p. 213. Copyright 1935, 1949 by John Lehman, Ltd., Copyright 1962 by Geoffrey Gorer.

[23]Contrast the singing contest in Joyce Cary's *Mr. Johnson* with that in *Die Meistersinger.* See also Aristotle, *Politics,* 8:1342 (a) 20, *op. cit.*

the supernatural and believe the composer to be the tool of mysterious powers over which he has no control. Both attitudes are, of course, also found among members of Western culture.[24]

In an increasingly collective society, the state has assumed the obligation of educating its citizens, making a standardized curriculum inevitable and permitting little initiative or creativity on the part of teacher or pupil. Only the arts remain the constant affirmation of the individual human spirit. With the possible exception of the Bible, nothing of enduring aesthetic value has ever been designed by committee.

Music's capacity to bind the emotions creates a social mortar available to both statesman and tyrant. "La Marseillaise" did no more for Gambetta than Wagner did for Hitler. Whether "good fences" indeed make "good neighbors" is a political rather than an aesthetic problem.

FACTORS INFLUENCING DISCRIMINATION AND JUDGMENT

All music—popular, folk, chamber, symphony, opera, and oratorio—serves a purpose and satisfies a particular human need for communicating feeling from composer through performer to listener. Music, therefore, can be usefully categorized according to its purpose: (1) music for the feet, or motor music, most frequently called *dance music;* (2) music for the heart, or sentimental and *romantic music;* and (3) music for the head, or serious *intellectual music.*

To discriminate as to the value of the music in each of these categories involves many factors, not all of them aesthetic. In each category there is much "good" music. No one, however, can create a universally applicable definition of "good," since "good" means only that something is fit for a given purpose. "Good" music is that thought good by an individual at a particular time and place to achieve a given end.[25]

Obviously, music good for one use is not necessarily good for another, and one person's choice of the good in any category is not necessarily that of someone else. Even alumni of conservatories are not prone to lift their voices in Bach chorales while carousing at a college reunion. Chubby Checker's twist fans are not necessarily partial to the two-steps of Lawrence Welk. There is enjoyment to be had from the four great American B's of music, blues, barrelhouse, boogie, and bop, as well as from the four great European B's, Bach, Beethoven, Brahms, and Berg.

The definition of the good directs the attention of the music educator to forming a child's musical personality. The more sophisticated such musical personality becomes, the more complex will be the ends and the greater the musical data that inform the child's judgment of good music. The educator's objective is to enable each child to learn to use music of all varieties to achieve his goals and satisfy his needs.

The development of a catholic musical taste depends upon developing the child's interest, skill, and knowledge. More specifically, the child's choice of music will result

[24] Nettl, Bruno, *Music in Primitive Culture,* Harvard University Press, Cambridge, Mass., 1956, p. 19.
[25] See Aristotle, *Nichomachean Ethics,* 1139 (b) 14ff, *op. cit.*

from (1) his attitude toward music; (2) his standards or ideals developed from previous experience with music; (3) his knowledge of musicological, sociological, and biographical data associated with music; (4) his skill and ability as a performer or creator of music; (5) his associative and conceptual imagination; and (6) his emotional, mental, and muscular agility.[26]

Attitudes toward Music

An individual's attitude toward music is more important than any other factor in developing genuine discrimination. How he feels about the music will determine how he reflects upon it. If his initial attitude is averse he is not likely to change upon subsequent reflection. Moreover, he will not be inclined to repeat the unpleasant. If, on the other hand, his initial experience is a happy one, he will want to renew and contemplate the enjoyable.

If the teacher is to motivate positive musical attitudes he must be aware of individual differences among children, their family background and the environmental influences upon them, their likes and dislikes. Much of this information may be obtained from school records, visits with parents, and from skillful verbal or written questioning of the children during classroom periods.[27]

Standards and Ideals

A judgment is distinguished from an instinctive reaction or whim by the judge's conscious application of a standard. Aesthetic standards designed to discriminate between types of sense data can only be derived from experience; one cannot become a gourmet merely by reading a cookbook, or a violin virtuoso by simply scanning the score of the Paganini Variations. Even if, as Wordsworth claimed, the genesis of art stems from the "spontaneous overflow of powerful feelings . . . recollected in tranquillity," the feelings must be stimulated, experienced, and recognized before they can be recollected.[28]

The function of the teacher must be to order the sequence of experience from which the child's standards of beauty will be derived. He must whet the child's latent aesthetic appetite, not gorge it, and provide a diversified menu, not merely a pre-

[26] Leonhard, Charles, and Robert House, *Foundations and Principles of Music Education,* McGraw-Hill Book Company, New York, 1959. A table of skills, attitudes, and habits of the musically cultivated appears in Chapter 5, pp. 104–141.

[27] Thorpe, Louis P., "Learning Theory," in *Basic Concepts in Music Education,* National Society for the Study of Education, University of Chicago, 1958, p. 170.

[28] Wordsworth, William, "Poetry and Poetic Diction" (preface to *Lyrical Ballads*), *English Critical Essays, XIX Century,* Oxford University Press, London. Wordsworth has no doubt of the causal relation between art and experience. "But these passions, thoughts and feelings are the general passions, thoughts and feelings of men. And with what are they connected? Undoubtedly with our moral sentiments and animal sensations and with the causes which excite these; with the operations of the elements and the appearances of the universe; with the storm and sunshine, with the revolutions of the seasons, with cold and heat, with loss of friends and kindred, with injuries and resentments, gratitude and hope, fear and sorrow."

scribed regimen. Having tasted and been nourished by much, the child will soon realize that he can learn to discriminate among chefs as well as styles of cuisine, and derive satisfaction from knowledge of the chemistry, as well as the taste of food. The educated listener is a gourmand of sound, acquainted with the techniques of music, the chronology of musical style, and the biographical data of composers and performers. He can employ all facets of his knowledge and experience to stimulate his senses and nourish his mind. The creation of an educated musical character, of ingrained "musicality," is the goal of the music educator.[29]

SOCIOLOGICAL ASPECTS

All art is created within the matrix of a given society at a given time. A composer or performing artist is a human being subject to the emotional, mental, and physical vagaries human beings experience. His creative output will be influenced by contemporary social, political, and economic factors. The music of Bach differs from that of Cole Porter much as eighteenth-century Dresden differed from twentieth-century New York. Although Porter, with the advantage of history, knew the elements of Bach's style, to compose like Bach would have been no more possible for him than for the church choirmaster to have composed a cantata in honor of his appointment entitled "I Get a *Kirche* Out of You." Understanding creative genius requires understanding the creator, his aspirations and achievements, his philosophy and practice. The greater the insight into the human being, the greater the insight and understanding of his art.

Music always combines elements of the immediate acoustic environment of the composer (the rhythms and tonality of the speech, dance, and background sounds with which he is familiar), in a form dictated by his intellectual environment. The type of form constitutes his style: Medieval, Renaissance, Baroque, Classic, Romantic, Impressionist, Atonal, Contemporary Electronic. This is not to say that a composer may not evoke the style of another period as does Paderewski's Minuet in G, or Prokofiev's *Classical Symphony*, or the style of another composer as do the parodies of Hoffnung and Ibert.

New musical style can present an audience with as much difficulty as witnessing a play in a foreign language. The reason is much the same. To understand language requires unconscious anticipation of its formulas, enabling the listener to organize sounds and pauses into syllables, and translate combinations of syllables into words, phrases, and sentences. Music also has formulas which the audience understands and anticipates. The audience that can no longer anticipate ceases to understand. For this reason many modern composers contend they are creating for the next generation, since only to that audience will their music be sufficiently familiar to be comprehensible. Perhaps because music intoxicates like wine, many teacher education institutions

---

[29] Madison, Thurber H., "New Concepts," in *Basic Concepts in Music Education,* National Society for the Study of Education, University of Chicago, 1958, pp. 17–18.

believe it must be aged to be good, graduating audiences with a taste for no music less than fifty years old.[30]

There has been a legitimate fear on the part of recognized composers, asked to write music for schools, that audiences will misjudge the music on the basis of the likely inferior quality of the performance. Many school music directors, insulated from contemporary music in their own performing careers, are unacquainted with its idioms and, therefore, incapable of its interpretation. To overcome this reluctance and its cause, the Ford Foundation through the Music Educators National Conference endowed young composers-in-residence at a number of high schools in the United States. These composers, selected by a committee of distinguished American composers, spent a year living in the local community as a regular member of the school faculty for the purpose of composing music that the pupils are capable of performing. Needless to say, much of the music avoids nineteenth-century stereotypes and incorporates the twentieth-century's brash, dissonant, rhythmically irregular, twelve-tone atonality, polytonality, cacophony, and polymeter. Much of the output of these young composers is being published. Through performance of their music in school assemblies and public concerts, a contemporary and more receptive audience may develop. Hopefully, technological improvement in communication facilities and the increasing number of community organizations will also help reduce the time lag between musical composition, performance, and acceptance.

MUSICOLOGICAL ASPECTS

Skills

To appraise the skill of another adequately requires some ability to exercise the skill oneself. As McMurray accurately states:

There are at least two important reasons why some measure of instruction in performance skills in music should be included within *everyone's* formal education. In the first place, no one can be said to have discovered whether or not he has talent or liking for musical performance unless he has tried it. In the second place, it seems probable that learning to hear music in its full reality is made easier of accomplishment if accompanied by training in the making of music.[31]

Musical skills include the ability to read musical score; to perform with facility on a musical instrument; to sing easily with good tone quality; to coordinate muscularly so as to feel rhythm, meter, and the phrase of melodic line; to recognize emotional

---

[30] Harris, Roy, personal conversation with one of the authors, American Music Festival, State Teachers College, Indiana, Pa., Spring, 1947. For the formulary quality of language, see Schrecker, *op. cit.,* pp. 101ff. See also Contemporary Music Project, Music Educators National Conference, Washington, D.C., 1966.

[31] McMurray, *op. cit.,* p. 45.

expression in music as produced by changes in its various elements; to recognize and remember melodic style and form.

Imagery

One of the most life-creating elements of a work of art is imagery. Everywhere in art the tendency exists for *ideas* to be filled out, rendered concrete and vivid, through images. . . . Our demand for feeling in art also requires the image; for feelings are more vividly attached to images than to abstract ideas. . . . *We can preserve the feeling tone of a past event or an absent object only if we can keep a vivid image of it:* as our image of it becomes vague, our interest in it dissipates. . . . The ideas and images associated with a work of art depend very largely on the education, experience and idiosyncrasy of the spectator.[32]

Only if melodic, rhythmic, and harmonic imagery can be remembered can musical learning occur. It is the discovery of the possibility of classification and recognition that stimulates the child to explore and identify the elements which have given him pleasure. In this regard Schoen suggests that the musical audience may be divided into "internal" and "external" listeners.[33] The internal listener is able to analyze and distinguish elements of tone, melodic line, harmonic structure, musical form, rhythmic interest. He can "see with his ears and hear with his eyes," translate sound into a mental image of the score, and the sight of music notation into imagined sound. Through empathy, he will also respond to the kinesthetic tensions of the musical performer, as well as to the music's metric and rhythmic flow. Thus, three types of imagery are involved: aural, visual, and kinesthetic. The listener hears music's diverse elements, visualizes its notation, and feels not only its rhythmic surge but also the performer's placement of instrumental and vocal pitch, the musculature of bowing, blowing, fingering, or singing.

By contrast, music wafts the "external" listener into a realm of fantasy. It stimulates his imagination rather than his intellect, evoking association rather than analysis. Whereas all "internal" listeners will approximate the description of a given piece of music, because each is able to sift and classify his perceptions of identical sense data, no two "external" listeners respond similarly. For them music creates privacy, immerses them in a bath of personal emotion that momentarily relieves the

---

[32] Parker, *op. cit.,* pp. 74–76.

[33] Schoen, Max, *The Psychology of Music,* The Ronald Press Company, New York, 1940 pp. 114–126. Compare the Apollonian and Dionysiac of Nietzsche's *Birth of Tragedy.* A compendium of reactions to music will be found in Nicholas Slonimsky, *A Lexicon of Musical Invective,* Coleman-Ross, New York, 1953. See also James Joyce, *The Dead;* Aldous Huxley, *Antic Hay* (Chapter XIII); Leo Tolstoy, *The Kreutzer Sonata* (Chapter XXIII); Stendhal, *Rome, Naples, Florence;* Thomas Mann, *Doktor Faustus;* Josef Bor, *The Terezin Requiem,* Anthony Burgess, *A Clockwork Orange.* Listening to music made Lenin "tired." Would a better program of music education in Simbirsk have averted the Russian Revolution? See William Saroyan, "The Time of Your Life," in John Gassner (ed.), *Best Plays of the Modern American Theater,* Crown Publishers, Inc., New York, 1947, p. 58, (McCarthy's speech—but see Nick, p. 45). Compare Lenin, Franz Kafka (Max Brod, *Franz Kafka,* Schocken, New York, 1947, p. 116); and Bernard Shaw (St. John Irvine, *Bernard Shaw,* William Morrow and Company, Inc., New York, 1956, pp. 190ff).

weight of rational identity. Generally, all listening begins with an external or emotional response, and becomes more rationally analytical as the listener becomes musically educated.

CHANGING CONCEPTS OF MUSICAL LEARNING

Programs in music education in American schools have tended to reflect the psychological research of a given period, but have generally lagged behind educational theory. A study of music education basic series at various periods illustrates the changes in methodology and practice that have occurred.

Nineteenth-century music education was strongly influenced by the Pestalozzian theory of learning, which propounded this sequence of activities:

1. To teach sounds before signs and the child to sing before he learns written notes or their names;

2. To lead him to hear and imitate sounds, their resemblances and differences, their agreeable and disagreeable effect, instead of explaining these things to him—in a word, to make him active instead of passive in learning;

3. To teach but one thing at a time, rhythm, melody and expression to be taught and practiced separately, before the child is called to the difficult task of attending to all at once;

4. To make him practice each step of each of these divisions, until he is master of it, before passing to the next;

5. To give the principles and theory after the practice, and as induction from it;

6. In analyzing and practicing the elements of articulate sound in order to apply them to music; and

7. In having the names of the notes correspond to those used in instrumental music.[34]

Psychological theory of the early twentieth century was based on the conditioned reflex theory of learning and its law of repetition, recency, intensity, primacy, and satisfaction or dissatisfaction. These theories explained in Pavlovian terms the acquisition of vocal and instrumental skills, as in the following passage:

The more completely the various areas of expression are made an automatic process that will function quickly and accurately wherever conditions and consciousness give them their cue, the better has been the training. Only then can the mind be freed from hampering details and the person become an efficient executive with subordinates in the form of habits to carry out with little or no supervision whatever he commands.[35]

Music materials were built around exercises for developing specific musical skills, which were then related to more meaningful musical materials.

[34] Monroe, Will S., *History of Pestalozzian Movement in the U.S.,* C. W. Bardeen, Syracuse, N.Y., 1907, p. 145. See also Howard Ellis, "Lowell Mason and the Manual of the Boston Academy of Music," in *Journal of Research in Music Education,* III:1 (Spring, 1955).

[35] Michael V. O'Shea (ed.), *The Child: His Nature and His Needs, A Survey of Present Day Knowledge,* Chapter VII, E. A. Kirkpatrick, "The Child's Mastery of the Arts of Expression, Language, Drawing and Music," The Children's Foundation, Valparaiso, Ind., 1924, p. 155.

Subsequent research into the child's learning of aesthetics evolved a gestalt approach in which exercises, no longer isolated, were centered on the child's particular interests. Therefore a psychologist such as Mary Whitley, in teaching younger children, modified the Pestallozian approach by incorporating its tenets into types of creative play.

How Aesthetic Interest Develops
First, sensitivity or passive enjoyment of objects presented. This may be illustrated by the touching of smooth surfaces, of listening to rhythmic sounds, as well as of looking at beautiful forms and colors. Second, there is imitation, shown in children's repetition of sounds that please them and in the dramatic play, impersonating people they have seen. The third form is creative, shown in the inventive dramatic play, the construction of little melodies, the imaginative drawing. In little children's play we see all three forms in a preliminary stage of development only. So far as pure aesthetic feeling is concerned, they are not really disinterested in their enjoyment, but quite personal.[36]

DeWitt Parker's analysis of the aesthetic experience followed Whitley. According to Parker, five elements entering into every experience of art include:
1. Direct sensations of the media
2. Associated sensations
3. Associated ideas
4. Definite feelings of mental elements
5. Images from sense departments and associated ideas of images.[37]

Music series books for the elementary school of the 1930s and 1940s emphasized the necessity of providing total experience for the child, requiring that he synthesize disparate techniques. However, since musical learning involves the acquisition of muscular skills for performance, such methods also contain much material on habit formation and exercises for the development of motor skills. This is particularly reflected in the elementary instrumental methods.

The development of motor skills involves the modification of tendencies governing action. . . . It is a process of reducing purposive action to sensorimotor action. In this process the task drops out and the control action is taken over by habit. Other changes include the decline of perception; the elimination of irrelevant responses; a decrease in tensions and unpleasant feelings; and a stabilizing and consolidation of the total performance. There is also an increase in the speed and accuracy of the performance, and it is carried out with less fatigue. . . . Practice is essential for acquiring motor skills. To be most effective it should be conducted under conditions like those attending the use of the skill.[38]

[36]Whitley, Mary T., *A Study of the Little Child,* The Westminster Press, Philadelphia, Pa., 1932, p. 79.
[37]Parker, *op. cit.,* p. 53.
[38]Kingsley, Howard J., *The Nature and Conditions of Learning,* Prentice-Hall, Inc., Englewood Cliffs, N.J., 1946, p. 256.

At mid-century music education was devoted to the concept of recreation, avoiding any theory requiring the acquisition of reading skill for its own sake. Music series of this period contain little more than music literature, and lack specific reference to ear training, sight reading, and the development of tonal and rhythmic memory.

The interest of the atomic age in improved technical skills, scientific inquiry, and political usefulness has invested theories of music education with a new seriousness. Music is no longer thought to be useful merely as a group respite, but is now considered a medium for the development of the intellectual as well as the sensory and emotional character of the individual. Analytic discipline is again fashionable.

THE SPACE AGE AND RESEARCH ORIENTATION

The strong influence of scientific inquiry and research in all areas of education including music education, coupled with grants for such research from philanthropic foundations and federal and state agencies, has encouraged a new regard for music as an academic discipline. The development of state and regional research centers in music education; the creation of new professorships in universities headed by trained, research-oriented specialists; the growing list of articles and monographs designed to improve music educational practice, widely disseminated through abstracts in the *Journal of Research in Music Education,* provides evidence of music education's new academic dignity conferred by solvent interest.[39]

FOREIGN INFLUENCES

The creation of the International Society for Music Education, whose journal includes studies in comparative music education practices, teacher training, and musicology, has brought to the attention of music educators throughout the world the work of Carl Orff in Germany, Zoltán Kodály in Hungary, and Shinichi Suzuki in Japan. It has also served to bring to the attention of foreign educators new developments in American practice.[40]

The Orff System

The Orff system of music education is based on the program Orff developed at the Guentherschule, a school of gymnastics, dance, and music in Munich, Germany; and also on a series of radio broadcasts for and with children, which he condensed

[39] See *Journal of Research,* issued Spring, Fall, and Winter, Music Educators National Conference, Washington, D.C., particularly Bibliography of Research Studies; *Bulletins* issued by the Council of Research in Music Education, Dr. Richard Colwell, Director, University of Illinois at Urbana; *Bulletins* issued by the U.S. Office of Health, Education and Welfare, Washington, D.C., Dr. Harold Arberg, Director of Music Education Research.
[40] "Influences from Abroad," in *Perspectives in Music Education,* Source Book III, Music Educators National Conference, Washington, D.C., 1966, pp. 381–407.

into a five-volume series of books. The English adaptation with a Teacher's Manual
was prepared by Doreen Hall and Arnold Walter. The system involves the active
participation of children in singing, rhythmic movement, and the playing of rhythmic
melodic percussion instruments. The system is organized around the development of
scalic forms based both on familiar melodies and those created by children, to which
are added ostinato basses. Rhythmic perception is developed through the conversion
of speech patterns into rhythmic movement, which in turn are translated into patterns
for rhythmic and melodic percussion instruments. The rhythms are then evolved into
melodic and countermelodic materials created by the children. Harmony is introduced
by the addition of an ostinato-repeated bass figure.

The instruments employed in the Orff system include small tympani, triangle,
cymbals, wood block, jingles, rattles, tambourine, bass drum, and small drums; and
melodic percussion of soprano and alto glockenspiel, soprano and alto metalophone
(a heavier type of bells); soprano, alto, and bass xylophones; a bass two-string instrument
called a *bordun*, which may be played pizzicato, struck with a soft mallet, or bowed;
a viola da gamba of six strings played pizzicato; and water-tuned musical glasses played
with a hard mallet. The ranges of some of the instruments are shown in Figures 12-1

FIGURE 12-1   Ranges of Orff Melodic Percussion

FIGURE 12-2 Orff Instruments. From above left: Cymbal, Triangle, Wood Block, Glockenspiel, Tympani, Metalophone, Xylophone

and 12-2. The correlation of singing, rhythmic activities, and instrumental performance makes for an enriched musical experience.[41]

The Kodály Method

Zoltán Kodály's methods of instruction have revolutionized music education in Hungarian elementary education, where music is accepted as a major subject of child education. The instruction is carried on by music specialists as well as classroom teachers, the latter having been taught to teach the music program as part of their teacher education. At least one observer reports both classes of teachers as being uniformly enthusiastic.

The Kodály system employs native folk music and ethnic music of other cultures, beginning with pentatonic modality. Starting with the interval of the falling minor third, the call of the cuckoo, the interval is expanded to include the descending *mi-re-do* and the *la* above *sol* to provide the five-tone pentatonic scale. A series of figures like

[41] For a complete description of the Orff System see the Teacher's Manual for the Orff-Schulwerk Music for Children Series, Associated Music Publishers, New York, 1960. See also Carl Orff, "Orff-Schulwerk: Past and Future," in *Perspectives in Music Education*, pp. 386–394.

dancing dolls is attached to the staff notes, followed by hand signals taken from the Curwen hand signal system and modified to introduce chromatic tones for *fi* and *si* above *fa* and *sol*.

Rhythms are also built from speech patterns moved to free rhythmic improvisation and then to organized dance patterns. The recorder and percussion instruments also play an increasing role in the upper grades.[42]

Suzuki Talent Education

Shinichi Suzuki is the founder of a school for talent education that teaches the violin to very young children. His program starts with the playing of recorded string music in the home while a child is still a baby. At the age of three the child is brought to the music school, where both mother and child begin lessons, learning by rote and imitation a theme and variations on "Twinkle, Twinkle Little Star." The mother practices with the child daily. Notation is introduced after the child has acquired skill in playing by ear and can use the bow arm freely. A carefully graduated program of studies in group lessons eventually moves the children to performance of fine violin literature.[43]

Current Objectives

Current music education objectives are expanding beyond the traditional equating of music education with music performance. Many colleges and universities have instituted five-year teacher training programs leading to a master's degree, deemphasizing performance while demanding stronger undergraduate preparation in the liberal arts. Courses in music methodology now include—beside performance—music analysis, history, literature, and theory (basic musicianship); and music in society (the correlation of music with sociological, anthropological, philosophical, and psychological factors as evidenced by research studies).

The Music Educators Conference has proposed minimum goals of achievement in music education for all children graduating American high schools. While programs to achieve these results may be differently elaborated, they must begin in the elementary grades.[44] It is hoped that the pupil will have acquired the following skills: skill in listening to music; the ability to sing, to express himself on a musical instrument, and to read music notation. He should be able to understand the importance of design in music and be able to relate music to man's historical development, contemporary society, and to other areas of human endeavor. He should value music as

[42] Sandor, Frigyes (ed.), *Musical Education in Hungary,* trans. Cynthia Jolly, Corvina Press, Budapest, 1966; available through Alexandre Broude, Inc., 150 W. 57 Street, New York, N.Y. 10019. See also an American adaptation of the Kodály System in Mary Helen Richards, *Threshold to Music,* Fearon Publishers, San Francisco, Calif., 1964, and "The Legacy from Kodaly" in *Perspectives in Music Education,* pp. 402–407.
[43] The Suzuki Method has been adapted for American Schools by John W. Kendall in "Listen and Play," Summy-Birchard Company, Evanston, Ill., 1961.
[44] Ernst, Karl D., and Charles L. Gary (eds.), *Music in General Education,* Music Educators National Conference, Washington, D.C., 1965.

a means of self-expression, want to continue musical experience, and be able to discriminate between music of various types.

These objectives are reflected in the most recent basic music series for elementary schools. Moreover, as a result of publishers' including among their editors contemporary composers, the series and accompanying recordings contain, for the first time, besides traditional materials, contemporary works and types of creative activities.[45]

Current learning theories favor organizing education in evolving cycles, reiterating the subject matter in more complex contexts.[46] This process, which Bruner calls a "spiral curriculum," encourages children to discover relationships between prior knowledge and current learning.[47]

The best contemporary music books exhibit a multifaceted approach. In addition to song literature they provide materials for:

1. Instrumental performance
   a. Simple rhythm band and Latin American instruments
   b. Autoharp accompaniments
   c. Simple pipes
   d. Fretted instruments: ukulele, banjo, guitar
   e. Tone, Swiss, and orchestra bells, xylophone
   f. Transposed parts for orchestral instruments
2. Units relating to music: science, social studies, art, literature, and dance
3. Music Plays
   a. Traditional fairy tales set to music by distinguished composers
   b. Materials based on contemporary city and country life, giving the child opportunity to create music
4. Biographies of composers and performers related to their works
5. Complete sets of recordings for listening and for accompanying rhythmic, vocal, and instrumental activities
6. Reproductions of art masterpieces related to music
7. Instructions for free rhythmic play and formal dances
8. Materials to develop understanding of musical forms, styles, and periods: from folk song to opera, from folk dance to symphony and cacophony

Teachers manuals emphasize that participation in music making hopefully leads

---

[45] See *Making Music Your Own,* Silver Burdett Company, Morristown, N.J.; *Exploring Music,* Holt, Rinehart and Winston; *The Magic of Music,* Ginn & Company, Boston; *Discovering Music Together,* Follett Publishing Company, Chicago. *Avant-garde* composers such as Luening, Babbitt, and Ussachevsky serve as consultants in preparation of new series. See also *Experiments in Musical Creativity,* three pilot projects administered under the Contemporary Music Project for Creativity in Music Education, Norman Della Joio, chairman, Grant Beglarian, director; *Comprehensive Musicianship,* a symposium on the Foundation for College Education in Music, based on the seminar sponsored by the same Contemporary Music Project at Northwestern University, Evanston, Ill., April, 1965, through the Music Educators National Conference.

[46] Mursell, James L. "Growth Processes in Music Education," in *Basic Concepts in Music Education,* National Society tor the Study of Education, University of Chicago, 1958.

[47] Bruner, Jerome S., *The Process of Education,* Harvard University Press, Cambridge, Mass., 1960. See also C. A. Weber, "Do Teachers Understand Learning Theory?", *Phi Delta Kappan,* XLVI:9 (May, 1965), pp. 433–435; and W. C. Meierhenry, same issue, "Implications of Learning Theory for Instructional Technology," pp. 435–438, which is an excellent summary of current theories of learning.

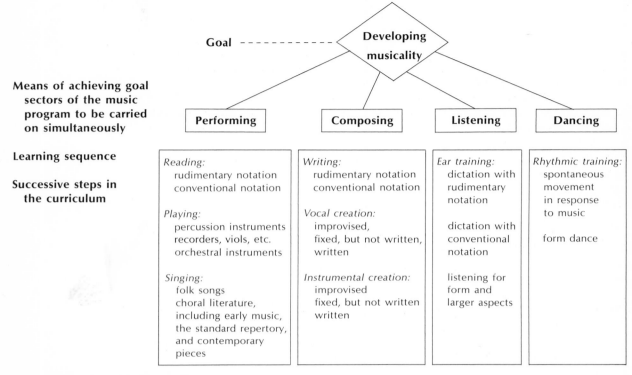

Goal ---------- Developing musicality

Means of achieving goal sectors of the music program to be carried on simultaneously

| Performing | Composing | Listening | Dancing |

Learning sequence

Successive steps in the curriculum

| *Reading:* rudimentary notation, conventional notation

Playing: percussion instruments, recorders, viols, etc., orchestral instruments

Singing: folk songs, choral literature, including early music, the standard repertory, and contemporary pieces | *Writing:* rudimentary notation, conventional notation

Vocal creation: improvised, fixed, but not written, written

Instrumental creation: improvised, fixed, but not written, written | *Ear training:* dictation with rudimentary notation

dictation with conventional notation

listening for form and larger aspects | *Rhythmic training:* spontaneous movement in response to music

form dance |

FIGURE 12-3　The Music Program[48]

to an understanding of man's musical motivation; the ability to recognize musical elements and structure; and skill in translating music symbolism (notation and terminology) into performance.

At a seminar at Yale University sponsored by the Office of Education of the Department of Health, Education and Welfare, the following statement on musical learning was proposed; it attempts to relate the gestalt theory of psychology, the grasping of unified aesthetic "wholes," to the development of the individual (see Figure 12-3 for procedure).

The development of musicality is the primary aim of music education from kindergarten through the twelfth grade. Musicality is universally understood by musicians, but it is a quality difficult to define. The analogous quality with respect to language would be verbal ability. Essentially it is the capacity to express accurately through pitch and time the *mental image* of a musical idea. Conversely it is *the capacity to grasp in its completeness and detail a musical*

[48]Palisca, Claude V. (ed.), *Music in Our Schools, A Search for Improvement,* Report of the Yale Seminar on Music Education, U.S. Department of Health, Education and Welfare, Washington, D.C., 1964. See also The Tanglewood Symposium, *Music In American Society,* Music Educators National Conference, 1967.

idea heard. It can be assumed that a degree of musicality is a natural attribute of everyone. . . . Since in most people this ability is only approximate, its cultivation is a continuous effort throughout a person's musical education. However, a basic musicality should be developed before the teaching of skills of reading, notation or composing is attempted. For all of these skills become mechanical and meaningless without it. As the *teaching of reading and writing music progresses,* corresponding progress should be expected in the ability to express and grasp musical ideas. With the growth of this capacity, greater attention can be given to the musical ideas themselves. . . . Musicality is developed through vocal and instrumental performance, bodily movement, attentive listening and ear-training, and vocal and instrumental creation, both improvised and written. These must be understood as components of a simultaneous and continuous process.

SUMMARY

The child's cultural development, like his physical development, undergoes phylogenetic transformation. Like primitive man, he is sensible to

Sounds and sweet airs that give delight and hurt not

but unless trained he matures into a Caliban rebuking in his popular music his educators,

You taught me language; and my profit on't
Is, I know how to curse.

From a mechanistic psychology of habit formation exemplified by Pestallozian exercises, music education theory has progressed to the developmental psychology of the Yale Report. Today the music teacher is encouraged to provide music of aesthetic value from which by analysis and experiment the child may gradually glean symbolic knowledge. This requires that the ear be tantalized before the voice and eye can be trained.

APPENDIX I

THE MATERIALS
OF TEACHING

The teacher is no longer a person whose main function is to impart information or even to demonstrate skills, since so many resources are available and conveniently organized in a variety of published forms. In the age of the mass media the teacher's functions shift to emphasis on SELECTION, EVALUATION, INTERPRETATION, APPLICATION, and INDIVIDUAL GUIDANCE.[1]

AUDIO-VISUAL

1. ALLEN, WILLIAM H., "Audio Visual Materials," *Review of Educational Research* (April, 1956), pp. 131–135.
2. DALE, EDGAR, *Audio-visual Methods in Teaching*, rev. ed., Holt, Rinehart and Winston, Inc., New York, 1954.
3. EBOCH, SIDNEY C., *Operating Audiovisual Equipment*, rev. ed., Chandler Publ. Co., Science Research Associates, Chicago, Ill., 1968.
4. Educators Progress Service, Randolph, Wis., offers: Educators Guide to Free Films; Guide to Free Tapes, Scripts, Transcriptions; Guide to Free Filmstrips.
5. KEMP, JERROLD E., *Planning and Producing Audiovisual Materials*, Chandler Publ. Co., Science Research Associates, Chicago, Ill., 1963.
6. LEVENSON, WILLIAM B., and EDWARD STASHOFF, *Teaching through Radio and Television*, rev. ed., Holt, Rinehart and Winston, Inc., New York, 1954.
7. MORLAN, JOHN E., *Preparation of Inexpensive Teaching Materials*, Chandler Publ. Co., Science Research Associates, Chicago, Ill., 1963.
8. National Tape Recording Catalog, 2d ed., Department of Audio-Visual Instruction, National Education Association, Washington, D.C., 1962, 1963.
9. SANDS, LESTER B., *Audio-visual Procedures in Teaching*, The Ronald Press Company, New York, 1956.

[1] Phenix, Philip, "Education and Mass Media," *Phi Delta Kappan,* XLIII:1 (October, 1961).

10. Stolurow, Lawrence, *Teaching by Machine*, Cooperative Research Program monograph, U.S. Office of Education, Washington, D.C., 1961.
11. Wittich, Walter A., and Charles F. Schuller, *Audio-visual Materials, Their Nature and Use*, rev. ed., Harper & Row, Publishers, Incorporated, New York, 1957.

AUDIO-VISUAL EQUIPMENT AND MATERIALS

Various machines are becoming increasingly available to the elementary school teacher. These include:

1. Phonographs and monaural or stereo recordings.

2. Tape recorders: may either be used to play commercially recorded sound tape or sound tape recorded by the teacher to evaluate student performance.

3. Video tape: a prepared tape, with or without sound track, to be played by video-tape projector.

4. Video-tape camera: available in some schools to make video-tape recordings of special activities.

5. Filmstrip: a prepared roll of film, usually 35mm, containing still pictures on a given subject. May be accompanied by a record, tape recording, or spoken narrative.

6. Color slides: a series of 35mm 2 x 2 slides organized around a particular subject and projected through a slide projector. May be accompanied by a record, tape recording, or spoken narrative.

7. Transparencies: a tissue-thin transparent acetate or plastic sheets on which the teacher can draw or print for projection.

8. Overhead projector: a machine with a light source that, passing through transparencies, projects an image onto a mirror which in turn focuses the image onto a screen.

9. Opaque projector: a machine suitable for projecting nontransparent printed materials onto a screen.

10. Slide projector: a manually or mechanically operated machine, which holds a tray of 2 x 2 slides and projects them onto a screen for viewing.

11. Slide viewer: a hand-held battery-operated machine into which individual slides may be placed for viewing. Excellent for teachers' use in selecting slides to be shown to a class.

12. Filmstrip projector or attachment: a piece of equipment that can be attached to some slide projectors so that the roll of filmstrip, attached to spools at top and bottom of the device, can be manually controlled to show one picture at a time.

13. Study prints: enlargements for individual use of materials originally designed for use by projector.

14. Movie films: prepared films with or without sound track about a given subject. Occasionally the sound track may be separately recorded on tape or disc.

15. Movie projector: built in various sizes to project 8mm, 16mm, or 35mm film. Some are built with speaker inside, others with separate speakers that can be placed at advantageous places around a room for better hearing.

16. Electronic Music Board: a portable chalkboard, 5 ft 10 in. long and 2 ft 6 in. high, with a lined music staff and a piano keyboard diagrammed at its left side. To the left of the piano keyboard diagram are knobs for sharping or flatting pitches. The range is from small A to A" (from A below middle C to A above the staff). Notation may be written on the chalkboard. When the chalkboard is touched on the lined music staff by an electronic stylus, it produces a reedlike tone for each pitch. If the stylus is held in one hand, the person holding it becomes a conductor of electrical current, and the free hand may be used to create the tone from the chalkboard. By using three or four fingers to touch the board, chords may be produced at their appropriate positions on the music staff. A volume control button alters dynamic level. This is an excellent device for teaching concepts of scale, tonality, key signatures, rhythm, part singing, and matching pitch. A manual accompanies the board, offering many aids for its use.

17. Electronic blackboard by wire: a system that transmits the teacher's voice and script over ordinary television lines from a central console to television screens in various classrooms. This enables an instructor to teach students simultaneously in widely separated rooms.

DISPLAY MATERIALS: CHALKBOARD SUPPLIES

1. Teaching Materials Service, 914 North Avenue, Beloit, Wis. (blackboard drawing set).
2. Time-Saving Specialties, 2816 DuPont Avenue S., Minneapolis 8, Minn. (blackboard marking set, cleaning solvent).
3. Lea Audio-Visual Service, Albert Lea, Minn. (bulletin board styx, adhesive wax).
4. Ronald Eyrich, 1091 North 48 Street, Milwaukee 8, Wis. (magnets, $\frac{3}{4}$ x $\frac{1}{4}$ in., strong enough to hold lightweight objects to steel chalkboard or metal display surface).
5. E. J. Blosser Co., 2239 Oros Street, Los Angeles, Calif. (Add-a-Panel flannel board).
6. John C. Winston Co., 1010 Arch Street, Philadelphia, Pa. (coheragraph).
7. Self-Teaching Aids, 9616 S. Normandie Avenue, Los Angeles 44, Calif. (Flannaroll screens).
8. Follett Publ. Company, 1010 W. Washington Blvd., Chicago, Ill. (Kling-Tite paper surfacing).
9. Match-a-Tach, 26 E. Person Street, Chicago 11, Ill. (magnetic display boards with numbers, letters, objects).
10. Oravisual Company, Inc., 321 15th Avenue, S., St. Petersburg, Fla. (Oravisual folding flannel board and display tripod).
11. Demco Library Supplies, 2120 Forden Avenue, Madison 4, Wis. (pegboards and pegboard hardware).
12. The Judy Company, 310 North 2nd Street, Minneapolis 1, Minn. (visual manipulative aids, flannel-board kits for music).

GENERAL CURRICULUM BUILDING

1. ANDERSON, DAN W., JAMES B. MACDONALD, and FRANK B. MAY, *Strategies of Curriculum Development* (works of Virgil E. Herrick), Charles E. Merrill, Inc., Englewood Cliffs, N.J., 1965.
2. BRUNER, JEROME S., *The Process of Education*, Harvard University Press, Cambridge, Mass., 1960.
3. CRONBACH, LEE J., et al., *Text Materials in Modern Education*, University of Illinois Press, Urbana, Ill., 1955.
4. *Curriculum Publications Catalogue*, Portland Public Schools, Portland, Ore., 1961–2.
5. DOLL, RONALD C., *Curriculum Improvement: Decision Making and Process*, Allyn and Bacon, Inc., Boston, 1964.

6. *Free and Inexpensive Learning Materials,* Division of Surveys and Field Services, George Peabody College for Teachers, Nashville 5, Tenn.
7. GRUBER, HOWARD E., GLENN TERRELL, and MICHAEL WERTHEIMER (eds.), *Contemporary Approaches to Creative Thinking,* Atherton Press, New York (paper back), 1966.
8. SAYLOR, J. G., and WILLIAM M. ALEXANDER, *Curriculum Planning for Modern Schools,* Holt, Rinehart and Winston, Inc., New York, 1966.
9. SCHAIN, ROBERT L., and MURRAY POLNER, *Where to Get and How to Use Free and Inexpensive Teaching Aids,* Teachers Practical Press, Atherton Press, New York, 1965.
10. SHORES, LOUIS, *Instructional Materials,* The Ronald Press Company, New York, 1960.
11. SMITH, JAMES A., *Setting Conditions for Creative Teaching,* Allyn and Bacon, Inc., Boston, 1967.
12. *The Unit in Curriculum Development and Instruction,* Bureau of Curriculum Research, 130 West 55 Street, New York, 1956.
13. World Book Encyclopedia, Merchandise Mart, Chicago, Ill., offers free: (1) literature for children; (2) primary grade activities; (3) teaching aids for elementary grades; (4) developing research skills.

CATALOG SOURCES FOR RECORDINGS, TAPES, AND FILMSTRIPS

1. Children's Reading Service, 1078 St. Johns Place, Brooklyn, N.Y. 11213
2. Teacher's Record Catalog, 274 Madison Avenue, New York, N.Y. 10015
3. Children's Music Center, Inc., 5375 West Pico Blvd., Los Angeles 19, Calif.
4. Educational Record Sales, 157 Chambers Street, New York, N.Y. 10007
5. Bowmar Records, Inc., 10515 Burbank Blvd., North Hollywood, Calif. 91601
6. Jam Handy Organization, 2821 E. Grand Blvd., Detroit 11, Mich.
7. Society for Visual Education, Inc., 1345 Diversey Parkway, Chicago 14, Ill.
8. RCA Victor Educational Records, Ginn and Company, Boston
9. Educational Division, Columbia and Epic Records, 51 West 52 Street, New York, N.Y. 10019
10. Folkways Records, 121 West 47 Street, New York, N.Y. 10036
11. Educational Audio Visual, Inc., 29 Marble Avenue, Pleasantville, N.Y.
12. John Gunter Audio Visual Materials Center, 1027 S. Claremont Street, San Mateo, Calif.
13. Product Information for Schools, Box 1970, Camden, N.J. 08101
14. Ampex Education Classical Music Library, Open Reel Stereo Tapes, 2201 Lunt Avenue, Elk Grove Village, Ill., 60007

The records, dances, rhythm materials, concert music, filmstrips, films, and slides cited in the catalogs of these companies should provide source material for every conceivable educational purpose.

SOURCES FOR FREE CATALOGS DESCRIBING RHYTHM, MELODY, AND ACCOMPANYING INSTRUMENTS

1. Peripole, Inc., 51–17 Rockaway Beach Blvd., Far Rockaway, N.Y. 11691 (duobass and all other classroom instruments).
2. Walberg and Auge, 31 Mercantile Street, Worcester, Mass.

3. Handy Folio Music Company, 7212 West Fond du Lac Avenue, Milwaukee 18, Wis. (melody chimes).
4. Children's Music Center, 2858 West Pico Blvd., Los Angeles 6, Calif.
5. Rhythm Band, Inc., 407 Throckmorton, Fort Worth, Tex.
6. David Wexler & Co., 828 South Wabash Avenue, Chicago 5, Ill. (build-a-tune bells and other classroom instruments).
7. Hohner Instrument Company, Andrews Road, Hicksville, N.Y. (melodica and other classroom instruments).
8. American Music Conference, 332 South Michigan Avenue, Chicago, Ill. *The Potential of Fretted Instruments in School Music.*
9. Orff-Schulwerk Instrumentarium, Music For Children, U.S. Agents, Magnamusic-Baton, Inc., 6394 Delmar Blvd., St. Louis, Missouri, 63130; also Magnamusic Distributors, Inc., Sharon, Connecticut, 06069.

Additional reference materials for playing classroom instruments will be found later in Appendix I.

FILMS FOR MUSIC EDUCATION

1. SHETLER, DONALD J., *Film Guide for Music Educators,* rev. ed., Music Educators National Conference, Washington, D.C., 1968.
2. Educators Guide to Free Films, Free Tapes, Scripts, Transcription, Filmstrips, Educators Progress Service, Randolph, Wis.
3. Audio-Visual Center of your nearest university.
4. Film catalogs, U.S. Information Service, State Department, Washington, D.C.
5. Concerts on Film Library, Mills Picture Corporation, Hollywood 28, Calif.
6. PITTS, LILLA BELLE, *Handbook on 16mm Films for Music Education,* Music Educators National Conference, Washington, D.C., 1952.
7. Ideal Pictures, 1558 Main Street, Buffalo, N.Y., 14209. Agents for distribution of many foreign government films, Pan-American Airways films, etc. Branches in other major cities. See yellow pages of your telephone directory.
8. Young People's Concert Series, Leonard Bernstein with the New York Philharmonic Orchestra, McGraw-Hill Films, 330 West 42 Street, New York, N.Y. 10036. Fourteen films from the award-winning CBS series. May be purchased or rented.
9. Walt Disney Motion Pictures, 16mm films, 477 Madison Avenue, New York, N.Y. 10017
10. I.Q. Films, Inc., 689 Fifth Avenue, New York, N.Y. 10022

SOURCES FOR CORRELATING MUSIC WITH SOCIAL STUDIES, PHYSICAL EDUCATION

1. MARVEL, LORENE, *Music Resource Guide for Primary Grades,* Schmitt, Hall & McCreary, Minneapolis, Minn., 1962.
2. McLAUGHLIN, ROBERTA, *Music in Everyday Living and Learning, Ways of Integrating Music with Other Experiences,* Music Educators National Conference, Washington, D.C., 1960.
3. TOOZE, RUTH, and BEATRICE P. KRONE, *Literature and Music as Resources for Social Studies,* Prentice-Hall, Inc., Englewood Cliffs, N.J., 1955.

4. SHEEHY, EMMA D., *Children Discover Music and Dance*, Holt, Rinehart and Winston, Inc., New York, 1959.
5. ANDREWS, GLADYS, *Creative Rhythmic Movement for Children*, Prentice-Hall, Inc., Englewood Cliffs, N.J., 1954.
6. Hi, Neighbor! Series, eight volumes and eight recordings, with games, songs, crafts, stories, dance directions, five countries in each volume; published through UNICEF, United Nations, New York, N.Y.
7. DE CESARE, RUTH, *They Came Singing*, a collection of foreign songs with English translations, Sam Fox Publ. Co., Inc., New York, 1961, with recordings from Bowmar Educational Records, 10515 Burbank Blvd., North Hollywood, Calif.
8. RAPH, THEODORE, *The Songs We Sang, A Treasury of American Popular Songs*, A. S. Barnes and Co., Inc., New York, 1964.
9. NYE, VERNICE, ROBERT NYE, and H. VIRGINIA NYE, *Toward World Understanding with Song*, Wadsworth Publ. Co., Belmont, Calif., 1967.
10. KRUGMAN, LILLIAN D., and ALICE J. LUDWIG, *Little Calypsos*, Carl Van Roy Publ. Co., Far Rockaway, N.Y., 1960.
11. GUARNIERI, ANITA, *Brazilian Songs for Children*, Carl Van Roy Publ. Co., Far Rockaway, N.Y., 1966.
12. KRUGMAN, LILLIAN D., and SYLVIA PERRY, *Song Tales of the West Indies*, Carl Van Roy Publ. Co., Far Rockaway, N.Y., 1965.
13. CHEYETTE, IRVING, and NAMIKO IKEDA, *A Child's Year in Japan*, Carl Van Roy Publ. Co., Far Rockaway, N.Y., 1969.

SUPPLEMENTARY SONGBOOKS

Probably the best source of song materials from many nations will be found in the free catalogs from the Cooperative Recreation Service, Delaware, Ohio. These songs are published in handy pocket-size folios with songs from each country at a nominal price.

The following are songbooks with special purposes:

1. CHEYETTE, IRVING, *Songs for Camp and Campus*, Pro Art Music Co., Inc., Westbury, N.Y., 1960 (with charts for recreational instruments).
2. ———, and ALBERT RENNA, *Sociability Songs with Social Instruments*, Theodore Presser Company, Bryn Mawr, Pa., 1968.
3. COHEN, MIKE, *101 Plus 5 Folk Songs for Camp*, Oak Publications, New York, 1966.
4. CROWNINSHIELD, ETHEL, *Songs and Stories About Animals*, Boston Music Co., Boston, 1947.
5. ———, *New Songs and Games*, Boston Music Co., Boston, 1951.
6. DALLIN, LEON, and LYNN DALLIN, *Heritage Songster*, W. C. Brown Company, Inc., Dubuque, Iowa, 1966.
7. ———, *Folk Songster*, W. C. Brown, Company, Inc., Dubuque, Iowa, 1967.
8. DE CESARE, RUTH, songs for foreign language study with companion LP records, includes the albums *Canciones para la clase de Espanol; Chanson pour la Classe de Français; Canzoni per la Classe d'Italiano; Lieder fur di deutsche Klasse; Songs for the Russian Class; Chants de Jeux Français*. Mills Music, Inc., New York, 1960.
9. DEUTSCH, LEONHARD, and CLAUDE SIMPSON, *A Treasury of the World's Finest Folk Songs*, Crown Publishers, Inc., New York, 1966.
10. DWYER, RICHARD A., and DAVID COHEN, *Songs of the American West*, ed. by Richard E. Lingenfelter, University of California Press, Berkeley, Calif., 1966.

11. EHRET, WALTER, *Heritage of Song*, Frank Music Corp., New York, 1966.
12. GLASS, PAUL, and LOUIS C. SINGER, *Songs of the Sea, Songs of Hill and Mountain, Songs of the West, Songs of Town and City Folk, Songs of the Forest and River Folk*, Grosset & Dunlap, Inc., New York, 1967.
13. JACOVITI, RAYMOND N., *Escuchar y Cantar*, 30 popular Spanish songs, with recordings, Holt, Rinehart and Winston, Inc., New York, 1964.
14. KLENK, GEORGE, and JEAN KLENK, *Ecouter et Chanter*, 28 French songs, with recordings, Holt, Rinehart and Winston, Inc., New York, 1964.
15. LANDECK, BEATRICE, *Songs to Grow On*, E. B. Marks Music Corp., New York, 1950, with recordings available through Folkcraft Records.
16. ——, *More Songs to Grow On*, E. B. Marks Music Corp., New York, 1954, with recordings available through Folkcraft Records.
17. LOMAX, ALAN, *American Folk Songs*, Holt, Rinehart and Winston, Inc., New York, 1948.
18. LOMAX, JOHN A., and ALAN LOMAX, *Folk Songs, U.S.A., The 111 Best American Ballads*, Appleton-Century-Crofts, Inc., New York, 1948.
19. MCLAUGHLIN, ROBERTA, and LUCILLE WOOD, *Sing a Song*, Prentice-Hall, Inc., Englewood Cliffs, N.J., 1960.
20. NYE, ROBERT E., NEVA AUBIN, and GEORGE H. KYME, *Singing With Children*, Wadsworth Publ. Co., Belmont, Calif., 1962.
21. ORFF, CARL, and GUNILD KEETMAN, *Orff-Schulwerk, Music for Children*, English adaptation Doreen Hall and Arnold Walter (B. Schott's Sohne, Mainz, Germany), American representatives, Associated Music Company, New York, 5 vols.
22. WHITE, FLORENCE, and KAZUO AKIYAMA, *Children's Songs from Japan*, E. B. Marks Music Corp., New York, 1960.
23. WOOD, LUCILLE, and LOUISE SCOTT, *Singing Fun*, Webster Publ. Co., Pasadena, Calif., 1954, with recording available from Bowmar Educational Records.

RECORDINGS FOR RHYTHMIC ACTIVITIES (PRIMARY GRADES)

1. *American Folk Songs for Children*, Pete Seeger, Folkways Records (FC 7001)
2. *Activity Songs for Kids*, Marchia Berman, Folkways Records (FC 7023)
3. *Skip Rope Games*, Folkways Records (FC 7029)
4. *Rhythms for Children, Call and Response*, Ella Jenkins, Folkways Records (FC 7308)
5. *Song and Playtime with Pete Seeger*, Folkways Records (FC 7526)
6. *Dance Along, Planned Rhythm Studies*, Folkways Records (FC 7651)
7. *Negro Folk Rhythms*, Ella Jenkins, Folkways Records (FA 2374)
8. *Adventures in Rhythm*, Ella Jenkins, Folkways Records (FI 8273)
9. *Singing Games Albums*, Bowmar Educational Records (three albums)
10. *Rhythm Time*, Bowmar Educational Records (three ten-inch records)
11. *Holiday Rhythms*, Bowmar Educational Records (three ten-inch records)
12. *Sing and Do Records*, Evelyn Atwater, Ridgewood, N.J. Four albums of delightful activity songs with action directions
13. Recordings from the basic series for each grade
14. *Dance Along Farm*, "Captain Kangaroo," Sam Fox Publ. Co., New York. Columbia (JS 287)
15. *Dance Along Zoo*, "Captain Kangaroo," Sam Fox Publ. Co., New York. Columbia (JS 288)

16. *The Rhythm Program, Primary Grades,* RCA Victor-Ginn & Co., 72 Fifth Avenue, New York. Vols. I–III (E-71, E-72, E-73), basic record library for elementary schools
17. *Primary Music,* Decca Records for the American Book Company. *Rhythm* (AS 22)

REFERENCE MATERIALS FOR ACTION SONGS, FREE RHYTHMIC PLAY, GAME SONGS

1. Teachers Manuals for the basic series:
   This Is Music, Allyn and Bacon, Inc., Boston.
   Music for Young Americans, American Book Company, New York.
   Music for Living, Silver Burdett Company, Morristown, N.J.
   Our Singing World, Ginn and Company, Boston.
   Birchard Music Series, Summy-Birchard Co.
   Together We Sing, Follett Publishing Company, Chicago.
   Growing with Music, Prentice-Hall, Inc., Englewood Cliffs, N.J.
   Making Music Your Own, Silver Burdett Company, Morristown, N.J.
   The Magic of Music, Ginn and Company, Boston.
   Discovering Music Together, Follett Publishing Company, Chicago.
   Exploring Music, Holt, Rinehart and Winston, Inc., New York.
2. *Red Book of Singing Games and Dances from the Americas,* Janet E. Tobitt, Summy-Birchard Publ. Co., Evanston, Ill., 1960.
3. *Yellow Book of Singing Games and Dances from Around the World,* Janet E. Tobitt, Summy-Birchard Publ. Co., Evanston, Ill., 1960.
4. *French Game Songs,* Ruth De Cesare, Mills Music, Inc., New York, 1962.
5. *Latin-American Game Songs,* Ruth De Cesare, Mills Music, Inc., New York, 1959.
6. *The Classroom Teacher's Piano Book,* Marjorie Hunter, Summy-Birchard Publ. Co., Evanston, Ill., 1956.
7. *Action Song Playlets,* Ruth Norman, et al., Mills Music, Inc., New York, 1956, based on various fairy tales.
8. *Action Songs for Special Occasions,* Ruth Norman, Mills Music, Inc., New York, 1952, based on various holidays.
9. *Interpreting Music through Rhythm,* Louise Humphrey and Jerrold Ross, Prentice-Hall, Inc., Englewood Cliffs, N.J., 1964.
10. *Rhythms Today,* Edna Doll and Mary J. Nelson, Silver Burdett Company, Morristown, N.J., 1965.
11. *Illustrated Games and Rhythms for Children,* Frank H. Gere, Prentice-Hall, Inc., Englewood Cliffs, N.J., 1955.
12. *First Book of Creative Rhythms,* Rosanna B. Saffran, Holt, Rinehart and Winston, Inc., New York, 1963.

MATERIALS FOR FOLK AND SQUARE DANCES

1. *Handy Square Dance Book,* Cooperative Recreation Service, Delaware, Ohio, 1955.
2. *Handy Play Party Book,* Cooperative Recreation Service, Delaware, Ohio, 1955.
3. *Handy Folk Dance Book,* Cooperative Recreation Service, Delaware, Ohio, 1955.

4. KULBITSKY, OLGA, and FRANK L. KALTMAN, *Teacher's Dance Handbook*, Bluebird Publ. Co., Newark, N.J., 1959.
5. BURCHENAL, ELIZABETH, *American Country Dances*, G. Schirmer, Inc., New York, 1918.
6. ———, *Dances of the People*, G. Schirmer, Inc., New York, 1934.
7. PITCHER, GLADYS, *Playtime in Song*, M. Witmark & Sons, New York, 1960.
8. HUNT, BEATRICE A., and HARRY R. WILSON, *Sing and Dance*, Schmitt, Hall & McCreary, Minneapolis, Minn., 1945.
9. DURAN, GUSTAVO, *Recordings of Latin American Songs and Dances*, Music Division, Pan-American Union, Washington, D.C., 1942.
10. STECHER, WILLIAM A. and GROVER W. MUELLER, *Games and Dances*, Theordore Presser Company, Bryn Mawr, Pa., 1941.
11. *Hi, Neighbor!* 8 vols., five countries represented in each, available through UNICEF, United Nations, New York, N.Y.
12. KRAUS, RICHARD G., *Folk Dancing*, The Macmillan Company, New York, 1962.
13. HALL, J. TALLMAN, *Dance, A Complete Guide to Social, Folk and Square Dancing*, Wadsworth Publ. Co., Belmont, Calif., 1963.

MATERIALS FOR RHYTHM INSTRUMENTS

1. *Little Calypsos*, Lillian Krugman and Alice J. Ludwig, Carl Van Roy Publ. Co., Far Rockaway, N.Y., 1955.
2. *Sound Sketches with Rhythm Instruments*, J. L. Vandervere, Carl Van Roy Publ. Co., Far Rockaway, N.Y., 1955.
3. *Let's Play with Classroom Instruments*, Rj Staples, Carl Van Roy Publ. Co., Far Rockaway, N.Y., 1958.
4. *Rhythm and Song*, Ruth E. Day, Willis Music Co., Cincinnati, Ohio, 1955.

MATERIALS FOR MELODY FLUTES

1. *Classroom Method for Melody Flute*, Fred Beckman, Melody Flute Co., Laurel, Md., 1952.
2. *Pipe and Sing* and *Play and Sing*, Lester Bucher, Melody Flute Co., Laurel, Md., 1941.

MATERIALS FOR RECORDER INSTRUCTION

1. *Method for Recorder*, James C. Young, Rubank, Inc., Chicago, Ill., 1949.
2. *One and All Harmonic Method for Recorders*, Allen L. Richardson, M. Witmark & Sons, New York, 1960.
3. *Recorder Playing*, Erich Katz, Clarke & Way, Inc., 35 West 21 Street, N.Y.C., 1951.
4. *Melody Method for the Recorder*, Walter D. Lanahan, Melody Flute Co., Laurel, Md., 1956.
5. *How to Play the Recorder*, Arthur Harvey, Sam Fox Publ. Co., Inc., New York, 1960.
6. *Tunes for Children*, Johanna E. Kulbach, Clarke & Way, Inc., 35 West 21 Street, New York 1954.
7. *Playing the Recorder*, Florence White and Anni Bergman, E. B. Marks Music Corp., New York, 1965.

MATERIALS FOR BELLS, FLUTOPHONES, TONETTES, MELODY FLUTES (MULTIPLE PURPOSE BOOKS)

1. *Sociability Songs with Social Instruments,* Irving Cheyette and Albert A. Renna, Theodore Presser Company, Bryn Mawr, Pa., 1968.
2. *Harmony Band Methods,* Handy Folio Music Co., Milwaukee, Wis., 1949.
3. *Fife, Jug and Bottle Band,* Adam Lesinsky, Belwin, Inc., Hempstead, N.Y., 1952.
4. *Musical Fun Books,* Rj Staples, Follett Publishing Company, Chicago, Ill., 1955.
5. *Make Music with the Bells,* Roberta McLaughlin and Muriel Dawley, Carl Van Roy Publ. Co., Far Rockaway, N.Y., 1958.
6. *Let's Play the Classroom Instruments,* Rj Staples, Carl Van Roy Publ. Co., Far Rockaway, N.Y., 1958.
7. *Jolly Come Sing and Play,* Ruth Rowen and Bill Simon, Carl Fischer, Inc., New York, 1956.
8. *You Can Play,* Paul Sterrett and Scott Wilkinson, Carl Fischer, Inc., New York, 1957.
9. *Songs for Camp and Campus,* Irving Cheyette, Pro Art Music, Westbury, N.Y., 1960.
10. *Classroom Melody Instruments,*[2] Leslie E. Woelflin, Scott, Foresman and Company, Chicago, Ill., 1967.
11. *Melodies for Music Makers,* Sally Golding, E. Lonstein, and G. Ross, Carl Van Roy Publ. Co., Far Rockaway, N.Y., 1966.

MATERIALS FOR AUTOHARP INSTRUCTION

1. *Make Music with the Autoharp,* Roberta McLaughlin and Muriel Dawley, Carl Van Roy Publ. Co., Far Rockaway, N.Y., 1958.
2. *Colors and Chords for the Autoharp,* Alice J. Ludwig and Louis L. Ludwig, Carl Van Roy Publ. Co., Far Rockaway, N.Y., 1957.
3. *Sing and Strum,* Alice M. Snyder, Mills Music Company, New York, 1957.

MATERIALS FOR MELODICA INSTRUCTION

1. *Key to the Melodica,* Marvin Kahn and Pietro Deiro, M. Hohner Co., Inc., Hicksville, N.Y., 1963.
2. *School Repertoire Series,* Marvin Kahn and John Westmoreland, M. Hohner Co., Inc., Hicksville, N.Y., 1963.

ADDITIONAL BIBLIOGRAPHY ON CREATIVE MUSIC TEACHING

KRONE, BEATRICE PERHAM, *Music in the New School,* Neil A. Kjos Music Co., Park Ridge, Ill., 1941, 1952, Chapter 5.
———, *Music Participation in the Elementary School,* Neil A. Kjos Music Co., Park Ridge, Ill., 1952.

[2] Programmed text.

MOHR, LILLIAN, and THOMAS L. HOPKINS, *Creative School Music*, Silver Burdett Company, Morristown, N.J., 1936.

MURSELL, JAMES L., *Music for the Classroom Teacher*, Silver Burdett Company, Morristown, N.J., 1951, Chapters 8 and 9.

————, *Music Education Principles and Programs*, Silver Burdett Company, Morristown, N.J., 1956, Chapters 5 and 6.

MYERS, LOUISE K., *Teaching Children Music in the Elementary School*, Prentice-Hall, Inc., Englewood Cliffs, N.J., 1954, Chapter 8.

SMITH, JAMES A., *Setting Conditions for Creative Teaching in the Arts*, Allyn and Bacon, Inc., Boston, 1967.

SNYDER, ALICE, *Creating Music with Children*, Mills Music Inc., New York, 1957.

APPENDIX II

SUGGESTED BIBLIOGRAPHY OF MUSIC MATERIALS FOR AN ELEMENTARY SCHOOL LIBRARY

BIOGRAPHY

BAKELESS, KATHERINE, *Story Lives of Great Composers*, J. B. Lippincott Company, Philadelphia, 1940.

BUNN, HARRIET F., *Johann Sebastian Bach*, Random House, Inc., New York, 1942.

BURCH, GLADYS, *A Child's Book of Famous Composers*, A. S. Barnes & Co., Inc., New York, 1939.

———, *Famous Pianists for Boys and Girls*, A. S. Barnes & Co., Inc., New York, 1943.

———, *Famous Violinists for Young People*, A. S. Barnes & Co., Inc., New York, 1941.

———, *Richard Wagner, Who Followed a Star*, Holt, Rinehart and Winston, Inc., New York, 1941.

COIT, LOTTIE E., *The Child Bach*, Theodore Presser Company, Bryn Mawr, Pa., 1943.

———, *The Child Mozart*, Theodore Presser Company, Bryn Mawr, Pa., 1942.

DEUCHER, SYBIL, *Edward Grieg, Boy of the Northland*, E. P. Dutton & Co., Inc., New York, 1946.

EWEN, DAVID, *Haydn, A Good Life*, Holt, Rinehart and Winston, Inc., New York, 1943.

———, *Complete Book of the American Musical Theater*, Holt, Rinehart and Winston, Inc., New York, 1959.

———, *A Journey to Greatness* (George Gershwin) Holt, Rinehart and Winston, Inc., New York, 1956.

———, *The World of Jerome Kern*, Holt, Rinehart and Winston, Inc., New York, 1960.

———, *Tales from the Vienna Woods* (Johann Strauss), Holt, Rinehart and Winston, Inc., New York, 1944.

———, *With A Song In His Heart* (Richard Rodgers), Holt, Rinehart and Winston, Inc., New York, 1963.

GOSS, MADELEINE, *Unfinished Symphony* (Franz Schubert), Holt, Rinehart and Winston, Inc., New York, 1941.

————, *Beethoven, Master Musician*, rev. ed., Holt, Rinehart and Winston, Inc., New York, 1956.

GRONOWICZ, ANTONI, *Chopin*, Thomas Nelson & Sons, New York, 1943.

————, *Paderewski, Pianist and Patriot*, Thomas Nelson & Sons, New York, 1943.

LEWITON, MINA, *John Philip Sousa, The March King*, Didier, Inc., New York, 1944.

LINGG, ANN M., *Mozart, Genius of Harmony*, Holt, Rinehart and Winston, Inc., New York, 1946.

MAUROIS, ANDRÉ, *Frederick Chopin*, Harper & Row, Publishers, Incorporated, New York, 1942.

MAYO, WALDO, *Mozart, His Life Told in Anecdotal Form*, Hyperion Press, New York, 1945.

NEEDHAM, IRENE B., and IRENE E. YOUNG, *Biographies of Great Composers*, Highlights for Children Publ. Co., Columbus, Ohio, 1964.

PEARE, C., *Stephen Foster, His Life*, Holt, Rinehart and Winston, Inc., New York, 1952.

PURDY, CLARE LEE, *He Heard America Sing* (Stephen Foster), Julian Messner, Publishers, Inc., New York, 1940.

————, *Stormy Victory* (Tchaikovsky), Julian Messner, Publishers, Inc., New York, 1945.

TINYANOVA, HELEN, *Stradivari, The Violin Maker*, Alfred A. Knopf, Inc., New York, 1938.

VAN LOON, HENDRICK WILLEM, *The Life and Times of Johann Sebastian Bach*, Simon and Schuster, Inc., New York, 1940.

WHEELER, OPAL, *Stephen Foster and His Little Dog Tray*, E. P. Dutton & Co., Inc., New York, 1941.

WHEELER, OPAL, and SYBIL DEUCHER, *Edward MacDowell and His Cabin in the Pines*, E. P. Dutton & Co., Inc., New York, 1940.

————, *Franz Schubert and His Merry Friends*, E. P. Dutton & Co., Inc., New York, 1939.

————, *Joseph Haydn, The Merry Little Peasant*, E. P. Dutton & Co., Inc., New York, 1941.

————, *Handel at the Court of Kings*, E. P. Dutton & Co., Inc., New York, 1943.

————, *Ludwig Beethoven and the Chiming Tower Bells*, E. P. Dutton & Co., Inc., New York, 1941.

————, *Sebastian Bach, The Boy from Thuringia*, E. P. Dutton & Co., Inc., New York, 1937.

————, *Curtain Calls for Franz Schubert*, E. P. Dutton & Co., Inc., New York, 1941.

————, *Curtain Calls for Joseph Haydn and Sebastian Bach*, E. P. Dutton & Co., Inc., New York, 1939.

————, *Curtain Calls for Wolfgang Mozart*, E. P. Dutton & Co., Inc., New York, 1941.

SYMPHONY

BARLOW, HOWARD, and SAM MORGENSTERN, *A Dictionary of Musical Themes*, Crown Publishers, Inc., New York, 1948.

DOWNES, EDWARD, *Adventures in Symphonic Music*, Holt, Rinehart and Winston, Inc., New York, 1944.

FRANKENSTEIN, ALFRED, *A Modern Guide to Symphonic Music*, Appleton-Century-Crofts, Inc., New York, 1967.

SIMPSON, ROBERT, *The Symphony, Haydn to Dvorak*, Penguin Books, Inc., Baltimore (paperback), 1966.

————, *The Symphony, Elgar to the Present Day*, Penguin Books, Inc., Baltimore (paperback), 1967.

SPAETH, SIGMUND, *Great Symphonies, How to Recognize and Remember Them*, Garden City Books, New York, 1936.

OPERA

BIANCOLI, LOUIS, *Opera Reader,* Grosset & Dunlap, Inc., New York, 1953.

DIKE, HELEN, *Stories from the Great Metropolitan Operas,* Random House, Inc., New York, 1943.

GILBERT, WILLIAM S., *The Savoy Operas,* 2 vols., Oxford University Press, Fairlawn, N.J., 1962.

LAWRENCE, ROBERT, *Boris Gudunoff,* Grosset & Dunlap, Inc., New York, 1944.

————, *The Rhinegold,* Grosset & Dunlap, Inc., New York, 1939.

————, *Siegfried,* Grosset & Dunlap, Inc., New York, 1939.

————, *The Twilight of the Gods, The Gotterdämmerung,* Grosset & Dunlap, Inc., New York, 1939.

————, *The Valkyrie,* Grosset & Dunlap, Inc., New York, 1939.

————, *Lohengrin,* Grosset & Dunlap, Inc., New York, 1939.

————, *Hansel and Gretel,* Silver Burdett Company, Morristown, N.J., 1938.

————, *The Magic Flute,* Artists and Writers Guild, N.Y.C., 1944.

————, *Carmen,* Silver Burdett Company, Morristown, N.J., 1938.

————, *Gounod's Faust,* Grosset & Dunlap, Inc., New York, 1943.

————, *Aïda,* Silver Burdett Company, Morristown, N.J., 1938.

————, *Gilbert and Sullivan's The Gondoliers,* Grosset & Dunlap, Inc., New York, 1941.

WHEELER, OPAL, *H.M.S. Pinafore,* E. P. Dutton & Co., Inc., New York, 1946.

INSTRUMENTS

BEKKER, PAUL, *The Orchestra,* W. W. Norton & Company, Inc., New York (paperback), 1963.

COLEMAN, SATIS N., *Bells,* Rand McNally & Company, Chicago, 1938.

CRAIG, JEAN, *The Heart of the Orchestra,* Lerner Publ. Co., Minneapolis, Minn., 1963.

————, *The Woodwinds,* Lerner Publ. Co., Minneapolis, Minn., 1963.

DAVIS, EDITH, and LIONEL DAVIS, *Keyboard Instruments,* Lerner Publ. Co., Minneapolis, Minn., 1963.

GILMORE, LEE, *Folk Instruments,* Lerner Publ. Co., Minneapolis, Minn., 1962.

KETTELKAMP, LARRY, *Flutes, Whistles and Reeds,* William Morrow and Company, Inc., New York, 1962.

————, *Drums, Rattles and Bells,* William Morrow and Company, Inc., New York, 1960.

————, *Singing Strings,* William Morrow and Company, New York, 1958.

KRISHEF, ROBERT K., *The Story of Recording Devices,* Lerner Publ. Co., Minneapolis, Minn., 1962.

LAPRADE, ERNEST, *Alice in Orchestralia,* Doubleday & Company, Inc., Garden City, N.Y., 1925.

SACHS, CURT, *History of Musical Instruments,* W. W. Norton & Company, Inc., New York, 1940.

SURPLUS, ROBERT W., *The Story of Musical Organizations,* Lerner Publ. Co., Minneapolis, Minn., 1963.

————, *Follow the Leader,* Lerner Publ. Co., Minneapolis, Minn., 1963.

————, *The Beat of the Drum,* Lerner Publ. Co., Minneapolis, Minn., 1963.

TETZLAFF, DANIEL B., *Shining Brass,* Lerner Publ. Co., Minneapolis, Minn., 1963.

STORIES THAT INSPIRED MUSICAL SETTINGS IN BALLET, OPERA, SUITE

CARROLL, LEWIS, *Alice's Adventures in Wonderland*, McGraw-Hill Book Company, New York, 1966.

————, *Through the Looking Glass*, St. Martin's Press Inc., New York, 1953.

COOKE, DONALD E., *The Firebird*, Holt, Rinehart & Winston, Inc., New York, 1939.

————, *The Nutcracker of Nuremberg*, Holt, Rinehart & Winston, Inc., New York, 1938.

DEUTSCH, BABETTE, *Heroes of Kalevala, Finland's Saga*, Julian Messner, Publishers, Inc., New York, 1940.

DUMAS, ALEXANDRE, *The Nutcracker of Nuremberg*, W. P. Collier Sons, New York, 1902.

EWERS, HANNS H., *The Sorcerer's Apprentice*, trans. from the German by Ludwig Lewisohn, The John Day Company, Inc., New York, 1927.

GRIMM, The Brothers, *Hansel and Gretel*, Alfred A. Knopf, Inc., New York, 1944.

HADER, BERTA, and ELMER HADER, *Mother Goose Illustrated*, Coward-McCann, Inc., New York, 1929.

HARRIS, JOEL CHANDLER, *Uncle Remus and His Songs and Sayings*, Appleton-Century-Crofts, Inc., New York, 1921.

HENDERSON, GERTRUDE, *The Ring of the Nibelung*, Alfred A. Knopf, Inc., New York, 1932.

LAMB, CHARLES, and MARY LAMB, *Tales from Shakespeare*, The Macmillan Company, New York, 1963.

LANG, ANDREW, *Blue Fairy Book* (Cinderella, Sleeping Beauty, etc.) Random House, Inc., New York, 1959.

NESBIT, EDITH, *Children's Shakespeare*, Random House, Inc., New York, 1938.

OLCOTT, FRANCES J., *Tales of the Persian Genii*, Houghton Mifflin Company, Boston, 1917.

PROKOFIEV, SERGEI, *Peter and the Wolf*, Alfred A. Knopf, Inc., New York, 1940.

PYLE, HOWARD, *The Merry Adventures of Robin Hood*, Charles Scribner's Sons, New York, 1946.

PYLE, KATHERINE, *Tales from Greek Mythology*, J. B. Lippincott Company, Philadelphia, 1928.

ROSTRON, RICHARD, *The Sorcerer's Apprentice*, Grosset & Dunlap, Inc., New York, 1941.

SANDYS, E. V., *The Story of Peer Gynt*, Thomas Y. Crowell Company, New York, 1941.

YOSELOFF, T., *Merry Adventures of Till Eulenspiegel*, T. Yoseloff, Inc., New York, 1957.

APPENDIX III

SOURCE MATERIALS
FOR LISTENING ACTIVITIES

BIBLIOGRAPHY

Children's Reading (see also Appendix II)

BALDWIN, LILLIAN, *Music for Young Listeners* (3 vols), *Green Book* (fourth grade), *Crimson Book* (fifth grade), *Blue Book* (sixth grade), Silver Burdett Company, Morristown, N.J., 1951. Contains biographies, illustrated themes, stories about the music (see recording list, p. 379).

————, *Tiny Masterpieces for Very Young Listeners*, Theodore Presser Company, Bryn Mawr, Pa., 1958. For kindergarten and primary grade children, similar in idea to *Music for Young Listeners* (accompanying recordings).

BALET, JAN B., *What Makes an Orchestra*, Oxford University Press, Fair Lawn, N.J., 1951.

BUCHANAN, FANNIE B., *How Man Made Music*, Follett Publishing Company, Chicago, 1951.

BURCH, GLADYS, and JOHN WOLCOTT, *Famous Composers for Young People*, Dodd, Mead & Company, Inc., New York, 1945.

————, *Famous Pianists for Young People*, Dodd, Mead & Company, Inc., New York, 1956.

————, *Famous Violinists for Young People*, Dodd, Mead & Company, Inc., New York, 1946.

————, *Modern Composers for Young People*, Dodd, Mead & Company, Inc., New York, 1941.

FROST, BRUNO, *A Child's Book of Music Makers*, Maxton Publ. Co., New York, 1957.

HUNTINGTON, HARRIET E., *Tune Up the Instruments of the Orchestra and Their Players*, Doubleday & Company, Inc., Garden City, N.Y., 1942.

KINSCELLA, HAZEL G., and ELIZABETH M. TIERNEY, *The Child and His Music*, University Publ. Co., Lincoln, Nebraska, 1953.

MACHLIS, JOSEPH, *American Composers of Our Time*, W. W. Norton & Company, Inc., New York, 1963.

SWIFT, FREDERIC FAY, and WILLARD MUSSER, *All about Music*, Belwin, Inc., Hempstead, N.Y., 1960.

WHEELER, OPAL, and SYBIL DEUCHER, *Biographies of Great Composers, Children's Series*, Dutton & Co., Inc., New York, 1934 through 1944, with musical examples in each book. Included are *Sebastian Bach, The Boy from Thuringia; Ludwig Beethoven and the Chiming Tower*

Bells; The Young Brahms; Frederic Chopin, Son of Poland (2 vols.); *Stephen Foster and His Little Dog Tray; Edvard Grieg, Boy of the Northland; Handel at the Court of Kings; Joseph Haydn, The Merry Little Peasant; Edward MacDowell and His Cabin in the Pines; Mozart, the Wonder Boy; Franz Schubert and His Merry Friends; Robert Schumann and Mascot Ziff; Story of Peter Tchaikovsky.*

TEACHER'S READINGS

BARLOW, HOWARD, and SAM MORGENSTERN, *A Dictionary of Musical Themes, The Music of More Than 10,000 Themes,* Crown Publishers, Inc., New York, 1948.

BERGER, MELVIN, *Choral Music in Perspective, An Enrichment Program Exploring the New and Old in Choral Music,* Sam Fox Publ. Co., Inc., New York, 1964.

————, *Instrumental Music in Perspective, An Enrichment Program Exploring the New and Old in Instrumental Music,* Sam Fox Publ. Co., Inc., New York, 1963. Teacher's Book.

CHAILLEY, JACQUES, *40,000 Years of Music,* trans. Rollo Myers, Farrar, Straus & Giroux, Inc., New York, 1964.

GROUT, DONALD JAY, *A History of Western Music,* W. W. Norton & Company, Inc., New York, 1960.

HARTSHORN, WILLIAM C., *Listening to Music in Elementary Schools,* Prentice-Hall, Inc., Englewood Cliffs, N.J., 1965.

MACHLIS, JOSEPH, *The Enjoyment of Music,* W. W. Norton & Company, Inc., New York, 1963. An introduction to perceptive listening.

————, *Introduction to Contemporary Music,* W. W. Norton & Company, Inc., New York, 1961.

MILLER, HUGH MILTON, *An Outline History of Music,* Barnes & Noble, Inc., New York, (paperback), 1947. Excellent brief descriptions of musical forms, instruments, and styles.

ULLRICH, HOMER, *Music, A Design for Listening,* Harcourt, Brace & World, Inc., New York, 1957.

COMPLETE PROGRAMS FOR ELEMENTARY SCHOOL LISTENING ACTIVITIES

Adventures in Music, ed. Gladys Tipton and Eleanor Tipton. RCA Victor. Ten albums for Grades 1 through 6, recorded by the National Symphony Orchestra, Howard Mitchell, conductor, with Teachers Guides that provide excellent procedures for developing listening skills for each composition.

Basic Record Library for the Elementary School, ed. Lilla Belle Pitts and Gladys Tipton. RCA Victor. Twenty-one albums of (78 and 45) records, including 375 classical, modern, and folk music pieces with program notes for the teacher.

Children's Library of Musical Masterpieces, Capitol Records. Twelve 10-in. (78 rpm) records of adaptations of musical classics, stories combined with music.

Complete Bowmar Listening Library, Bowmar Records, Inc. Contains 18 Bowmar Orchestral Library Albums, 256 Musical Theme Charts, 25 Meet-The-Instruments Posters, two color filmstrips with recording of Meet The Instruments, five envelopes of color study prints, with steel record storage cabinet.

Instruments of the Orchestra, Charles Walton, A Teaching Guide. RCA Victor (LE/LES 6000).
Music for Young Listeners and Tiny Masterpieces for Very Young Listeners, Lillian Baldwin, Silver Burdett Company, Morristown, N.J., and Theodore Presser Company, Bryn Mawr, Pa. Two extensive record libraries (78 rpm) based on the books of the same names.

COMPLETE PROGRAMS OF RECORDED MUSIC TO ILLUSTRATE HISTORICAL PERIODS IN MUSIC

A Basic Library of Classical Recordings, Angel Recordings, Capitol Records
The educational editor's list of recordings to cultivate a discriminating taste.
The Capitol Angel World of Classical Music Catalog includes biographical sketches of artists.
A valuable reference guide for the busy teacher

Chronicle of Music, Decca Records, Inc.
Eight Ages of History to illustrate the development of the art of music, correlated with the development of other art forms, and social structure and scientific development through the years from the Middle Ages to the twentieth century
Series A. Music of the Middle Ages
Series B. The Age of Renaissance Music
Series C. The Age of Baroque Music
Series D. The Age of Transition from Baroque to Classic
Series E. The Age of Classicism
Series F. The Age of Romanticism
Series G. The Age of Jazz
Series H. The Age of the Twentieth Century Music

The History of Music in Sound, RCA Victor
Ten volumes of LP records for the study of music history
Volume 1. Ancient and Oriental Music
Volume 2. Early Medieval Music up to 1300
Volume 3. Ars Nova and the Renaissance
Volume 4. The Age of Humanism: 1540–1630
Volume 5. Opera and Church Music: 1630–1750
Volume 6. The Growth of Instrumental Music: 1630–1750
Volume 7. The Symphonic Outlook: 1745–1790
Volume 8. The Age of Beethoven: 1790–1830
Volume 9. Romanticism 1830–1890
Volume 10. Modern Music: 1890–1950

The Story of Great Music, Time and Life, Time and Life Building, Chicago, Ill.
Contains a four-record set of performances by Angel conductors, soloists, and orchestras for each period; an illustrated book of correlated art and descriptive literature for each historical period; an introduction to the story of Western music; an essay by Jacques Barzun on "The Art and Pleasure of Listening"; and an article on "How to Get the Most Out of High Fidelity." Periods represented: the Baroque era; the Age of Elegance; the Revolutionary era; the Romantic era; the Age of Opulence; and the Twentieth Century.

FILMS AND FILMSTRIPS (See Appendix I for addresses)

Almanac Films: *Concert Hall Favorites; Violin Solos; Columbus Boys' Choir; Piano Solos by Eugene List* (15 min each)

Bowmar Records Meet the Instruments of the Symphony Orchestra: Two filmstrips to accompany recording instrumental demonstrations

Coronet Films: *Handel and His Music; Brahms and His Music; Beethoven and His Music; Mozart and His Music; Schubert and His Music; Liszt and His Music* (30 min each)

I.Q. Films, 16mm: Leonard Bernstein and the New York Philharmonic
1. *The Infinite Variety of Music*
2. *The Ageless Mozart*
3. *The New York Philharmonic in Berlin*
4. *The New York Philharmonic in Moscow*
Running time 30 min each

Jam Handy Filmstrips with accompanying recordings containing both narration and full musical reproduction:
1. Music Stories: *Peter and the Wolf; Hansel and Gretel; The Nutcracker; Peer Gynt; The Firebird; The Sorcerer's Apprentice*
2. Stories of Music Classics: *The Sleeping Beauty; William Tell; A Midsummer Night's Dream; Swan Lake; The Bartered Bride; Scheherazade*
3. Opera and Ballet Stories: *Lohengrin; The Magic Flute; Aïda; The Barber of Seville; The Mastersingers; Coppelia*
4. Great Composers and Their Music: *Johann Sebastian Bach; George Frederic Handel; Franz Josef Haydn; Wolfgang Amadeus Mozart; Ludwig van Beethoven; Franz Peter Schubert*
5. Instruments of the Symphony Orchestra: *String Instruments; Woodwind Instruments; Brass Instruments; Percussion Instruments; Melodious Percussion Instruments; The Orchestra*

McGraw-Hill Films: Leonard Bernstein and the New York Philharmonic Orchestra in the Young People's Concert Series, fourteen films from the award-winning CBS series:
1. *What Does Music Mean?* (689051)
2. *What Is a Melody?* (689060)
3. *What Makes Music Symphonic?* (689054)
4. *What Is a Concerto?* (689057)
5. *What Does Orchestration Mean?* (689163)
6. *What Does Classical Music Mean?* (689160)
7. *What Is American Music?* (689166)
8. *What Is Impressionism?* (689169)
9. *What Is Sonata Form?* (689172)
10. *Humor in Music* (689154)
11. *Folk Music in the Concert Hall* (689151)
12. *Jazz in the Concert Hall* (689157)
13. *The Sound of an Orchestra* (689175)
14. *Shostakovich's Ninth Symphony, An Analysis* (689178)
Running time 1 hr each, 16mm film, may be purchased or rented

Mills Picture Corporation Concerts on Film: Films with Rubenstein, Heifetz, and others in concert favorites

Peripole, Inc.: *The Magic of Music,* presenting the science of sound in an interesting film

Walt Disney 16mm films: may be purchased or rented
1. *Peter and the Wolf* (14 min)

2. *Toot, Whistle, Plunk and Boom* (10 min)
3. *Grand Canyon* (29 min)
4. *The Peter Tchaikovsky Story* (30 min)

SOURCES OF EDUCATIONAL RECORDS FOR CHILDREN

Bowmar Record Company, 10515 Burbank Blvd., North Hollywood, Calif. Publishers and distributors of educational recordings of folk song albums, singing games, folk dances, rhythmic activities

CBS Records, a division of Columbia Broadcasting System, Inc., 51 West 52 Street, New York, N.Y. 10019. Manufacturers of recordings in all categories, phonographs, Columbia needles

Decca Distributing Corporation, 445 Park Avenue, New York, N.Y. 10022. Educational recordings organized by age groups and grade level, called Decca Educational Plan Units

Folkways Records and Service Corporation, 117 West 46 Street, New York, N.Y. 10036, and 1460 Union Avenue, Montreal, Quebec, Canada. Manufacturers of phonograph records, tapes, filmstrips, ethnic music of the world's peoples with background texts

Greystone Corporation, Educational Activities Division, 100 Sixth Avenue, New York, N.Y. 10013, Young People's Records, Children's Record Guild, American Recording Society, educational and entertainment recordings

The Jam Handy Organization, 2821 East Grand Blvd., Detroit 11, Mich. Filmstrips in color with correlated recordings

Mercury Record Corporation, 35 East Wacker Drive, Chicago 1, Ill. Manufacturer of children's records, Childcraft-Playcraft Series. Recordings of Minneapolis and Detroit Symphonies

Music Appreciation Records. Book-of-the-Month Club, Inc., 345 Hudson Street, New York, N.Y. 10014. Producers of the Music Appreciation Educational Album and Teaching Guide of eleven LP records containing full performances of fourteen compositions. There is a spoken analysis of each work, together with a Teaching Guide (176 pp.) and a musical glossary

Radio Corporation of America, Educational Services, Camden, New Jersey. Supplies phonograph records, phonographs, tape recorders, radios, television, sound amplifiers, microphones

LIVE CONCERTS

Young Audiences, Inc., 115 East 92 Street, New York, N.Y. A nonprofit organization which arranges concerts by professional musicians for school children. There are local chapters throughout the United States. Concerts are arranged during school time, and fees are nominal, since Young Audiences engages musicians available in the area where concerts are to be provided.

APPENDIX IV

SUGGESTED BIBLIOGRAPHY OF MATERIALS FOR THE MUSICAL EDUCATION OF THE MUSIC TEACHER

AESTHETICS AND INTEGRATION OF THE ARTS

BERENSON, BERNARD, *Aesthetics and History*, Pantheon Books, a Division of Random House, Inc., New York, 1954.

COPLAND, AARON, *Music and Imagination*, Harvard University Press, Cambridge, Mass., 1952.

DEWEY, JOHN, *Art as Experience*, G. P. Putnam's Sons, New York, 1959.

EPPERSON, GORDON, *The Musical Symbol*, Iowa State University Press, Ames, Iowa, 1967.

FLEMING, WILLIAM, *Arts and Ideas*, Holt, Rinehart and Winston, Inc., New York, 1955.

FRANKENA, WILLIAM, *Three Historical Philosophies of Education*, Scott, Foresman, and Company, Chicago, 1965.

GHISELIN, BREWSTER (ed.), *The Creative Process* (paperback), New American Library of World Literature, Inc., New York, 1961.

GOWAN, JOHN C., GEORGE G. DEMOS, and E. PAUL TORRANCE (eds.), *Creativity, Its Educational Implications, A Symposium*, John Wiley & Sons, New York, 1967.

OSBORN, ALEX F., *Applied Imagination*, Charles Scribner's Sons, New York, 1953.

PARKER, DeWITT, *Principles of Aesthetics*, Silver Burdett Company, Morristown, N.J., 1927.

PARNES, SIDNEY, and HAROLD F. HARDING (eds.), *A Source Book for Creative Thinking*, Charles Scribner's Sons, New York, 1962.

PATER, WALTER, *The Renaissance*, (paperback), New American Library of World Literature, Inc., New York, 1961.

READ, HERBERT, *Education through Art*, Pantheon Books, a Division of Random House, Inc., New York, 1945.

———, and THOMAS MUNRO, *The Creative Arts in American Education*, Harvard University Press, Cambridge, Mass., 1960.

SANTAYANA, GEORGE, *The Sense of Beauty*, Crowell-Collier Publishing Company, New York, 1961.

SCHWADRON, ABRAHAM A., *Aesthetics, Dimensions for Music Education,* Music Educators National Conference, 1967.
SEASHORE, CARL, *In Search of Beauty in Music,* The Ronald Press Company, New York, 1947.
————, *Why We Love Music,* Oliver Ditson Company, Philadelphia, 1941.
SHRECKER, PAUL, *Work and History,* Princeton University Press, Princeton, N.J., 1948.
WELLEK, RENE, *A History of Modern Criticism,* Yale University Press, New Haven, Conn., 1945.
WOLD, MILO, and EDMUND CYKLER, *An Introduction to Music and Art in the Western World,* with workbook, W. C. Brown Company, Inc., Dubuque, Iowa, 3d ed., 1967.
ZUCKERKANDL, VICTOR, *The Sense of Music,* with 3 tapes, Princeton University Press, Princeton, N.J., 1959.

BASIC MUSICIANSHIP

1. Theory of Music

BASART, ANN P., *Serial Music, A Classified Bibliography on Twelve Tone and Electronic Music,* University of California Press, Berkeley, Calif., 1961.
BENWARD, BRUCE, and BARBARA G. SEAGRAVE, *Practical Beginning Theory,* with recordings, W. C. Brown Company, Inc., Dubuque, Iowa, 1963.
BIGELOW, EARL, ET AL., *Creative Analytical Theory of Music, A Correlated Course,* H. T. Fitzsimons Co., Chicago, Ill., 1948.
BOATWRIGHT, HOWARD, *Introduction to the Theory of Music,* W. W. Norton & Company, Inc., New York, 1956.
BOCKMAN, GUY A., and WILLIAM J. STARR, *Perceiving Music: Problems in Sight and Sound,* text, workbook, and recordings, Harcourt, Brace and World, Inc., New York, 1962.
BURKHART, CHARLES, *Anthology for Musical Analysis,* Holt, Rinehart and Winston, Inc., New York, 1964.
CHEYETTE, IRVING, and JOSEPH PAULSON, *Basic Theory-Harmony,* text-workbook, Pro Art Music Co., Westbury, N.Y., 1951.
CLOUGH, JOHN, *Scales, Intervals, Keys and Triads, A Programmed Text,* W. W. Norton & Company, Inc., New York, 1966.
COHEN, ALBERT, and JOHN WHITE, *Anthology of Music for Analysis,* Appleton-Century-Crofts, Inc., New York, 1965.
DALLIN, LEON, *Techniques of Twentieth Century Composition,* W. C. Brown Company, Inc., Dubuque, Iowa, 1964.
FONTAINE, PAUL H., *Basic Formal Structures in Music,* Appleton-Century-Crofts, Inc., New York, 1967.
FORTE, ALLEN, *Tonal Harmony in Concept and Practice,* Holt, Rinehart and Winston, Inc., New York, 1962.
————, and ALFRED KUHN, *Workbook in Harmonic Composition,* Holt, Rinehart and Winston, Inc., New York, 1963.
GOLDMAN, RICHARD F., *Harmony and Western Music,* W. W. Norton & Company, Inc., New York, 1965.
GREEN, DOUGLAS, *Form in Tonal Music,* Holt, Rinehart and Winston, Inc., New York, 1964.
HANSON, HOWARD, *Harmonic Materials of Modern Music,* Appleton-Century-Crofts, Inc., New York, 1961.

HARDER, PAUL, *Basic Materials in Music Theory, A Programmed Course,* Allyn and Bacon, Inc., Boston, 1965.

HINDEMITH, PAUL, *Traditional Harmony,* Associated Music Co., New York, 1944.

HOWARD, BERTRAND, *Fundamentals of Music Theory, A Programmed Text,* Harcourt, Brace & World, Inc., New York, 1966.

KRAFT, LEO, *A New Approach to Ear Training, A Programmed Text,* W. W. Norton & Company, Inc., New York, 1968.

MCGAUGHEY, JANET, *Practical Ear Training,* Allyn and Bacon, Inc., Boston, 2d ed., with workbook, 1963.

MCHOSE, ALLEN I., *Basic Principles of the Technique of 18th and 19th Century Composition,* Appleton-Century-Crofts, Inc., New York, 1951.

MURPHY, HOWARD A., *Music Fundamentals,* Chandler Publ. Co., San Francisco, Calif., 1962.

NELSON, ROBERT U., *The Technique of Variation,* University of California Press, Berkeley, Calif., 1948.

OTTMAN, ROBERT W., *Elementary Harmony,* Prentice-Hall, Inc., Englewood Cliffs, N.J., 1961.
———, *Advanced Harmony,* Prentice-Hall, 1961.

PERLE, GEORGE, *Serial Composition and Atonality,* University of California Press, Berkeley, Calif., 1962.

PERSICHETTI, VINCENT, *Twentieth Century Harmony,* W. W. Norton & Company, Inc., New York, 1964.

PISTON, WALTER, *Harmony,* W. W. Norton & Company, Inc., New York, 1961.

RATNER, LEONARD G., *Harmony, Structure and Style,* McGraw-Hill Book Company, New York, 1962.

SESSIONS, ROGER, *Harmonic Practice,* Harcourt, Brace & World, Inc., New York, 1951.

SMITH, EDWIN, and DAVID RENAUF, *Oxford Student's Harmony,* Oxford University Press, Fair Lawn, N.J., 1965.

THOSTENSON, MARWIN S., *Fundamentals, Harmony and Musicianship,* with workbook, W. C. Brown Company, Inc., Dubuque, Iowa, 1963.

VINCENT, JOHN, *The Diatonic Modes in Modern Music,* University of California Press, Berkeley, Calif., 1951.

WARDIAN, JEANNE F., *The Language of Music, A Programmed Course,* Appleton-Century-Crofts, Inc., New York, 1966.
———, *Principles of Harmony,* Appleton-Century-Crofts, Inc., New York, 1966.

2. Counterpoint

CHERUBINI, LUIGI, *A Treatise on Counterpoint and Fugue,* Novello, London, 1854.

FONTAINE, PAUL H., *Proficiency in Counterpoint,* a worktext, Appleton-Century-Crofts, Inc., New York, 1967.

GOETSCHIUS, PERCY, *Applied Counterpoint,* G. Schirmer, Inc., New York, 1902.

KANITZ, ERNEST, *A Counterpoint Manual,* Summy-Birchard, Evanston, Ill., 1947.

LIEBERMAN, MAURICE, *Creative Counterpoint,* Allyn and Bacon, Inc., Boston, 1966.

LYTLE, VICTOR V., *The Theory and Practice of Strict Counterpoint,* Oliver Ditson Co., Philadelphia, 1940.

MCHOSE, ALLEN I., *The Contrapuntal Techniques of the 18th Century,* Appleton-Century-Crofts, Inc., New York, 1947.

MIDDLETON, ROBERT, *Harmony in Modern Counterpoint*, Allyn and Bacon, Inc., Boston, 1967.

MORRIS, R. O., *Contrapuntal Technique*, Clarendon Press, Oxford, 1934.

OREM, PRESTON W., *The Art of Interweaving Melodies*, Theodore Presser Company, Bryn Mawr, Pa., 1937.

3. Keyboard Harmony

FRACKENPOHL, ARTHUR R., *Harmonization at the Piano*, W. C. Brown Company, Inc., Dubuque, Iowa, 1962.

HAMILTON, ANNA, *Keyboard Harmony and Transposition*, 3 vols., Summy-Birchard Co., Evanston, Ill., 1916.

LIEBERMAN, MAURICE, *Keyboard Harmony and Improvisation*, 2 vols., W. W. Norton & Company, Inc., New York, 1957.

LOWRY, MARGARET, *Keyboard Approach to Harmony*, Theodore Presser Company, Bryn Mawr, Pa., 1949.

McHOSE, ALLEN I., and DONALD F. WHITE, *Keyboard and Dictation Manual to Accompany Contrapuntal Harmonic Technique of the 18th Century*, Appleton-Century-Crofts, Inc., New York, 1949.

MEHEEGAN, JOHN, *Jazz Improvisation*, Sam Fox Publ. Co., Inc., New York, 1959.

PEERY, ROB ROY, *Practical Keyboard Modulation*, Theodore Presser Company, Bryn Mawr, Pa., 1944.

PELZ, WILLIAM, *Basic Keyboard Skills*, Allyn and Bacon, Inc., Boston, 1963.

SCOVILL, MODENA, *Keyboard Harmony*, Carl Fischer, Inc., New York, 1939.

4. Sight Singing

BENWARD, BRUCE, *Sightsinging Complete*, W. C. Brown Company, Inc., Dubuque, Iowa, 1965.

BERKOWITZ, SOL, GABRIEL FONTRIER, and LEO KRAFT, *A New Approach to Sight Singing*, W. W. Norton & Company, Inc., New York, 1965.

COLE, SAMUEL W., and LEO R. LEWIS, *Melodia, Course in Sight-singing*, 4 vols., Oliver Ditson, Company, Philadelphia, 1909.

CROWE, EDGAR, et al., *The Folk Song Sight Singing Series*, 13 pocket-size vols., 20 pp. each, Oxford University Press, London, 1933.

DALLIN, LEON, *Introduction to Music Reading, A Programmed Text*, Scott, Foresman, and Company, Chicago, 1967.

DARAZS, ARPAD, and STEPHEN JAY, *Sight and Sound*, Boosey and Hawkes, Oceanside, N.Y., 1965.

EHRET, WALTER, *See and Sing*, Pro Art Music Co., Westbury, N.Y., 1959.

———, *Songs for Sight Reading*, 3 vols., Pro Art Music, Westbury, N.Y., 1960.

FEARIS, J. S., and LAWRENCE HIGHFIELD, *Simplified Sight Reading*, Willis Music Co., Cincinnati, Ohio, 1946.

KANZELL, MAXWELL, *How to Read Music*, Carl Fischer, Inc., New York, 1944.

KIRK, THERON W., *Key to Sight Reading*, Pro Art Music Inc., Westbury, N.Y., 1957.

LEWIS, MAURICE A., *Solfeggio Studies*, Henry LeMoine et Cie., Paris, 1953. American agents, Elkan Vogel, Philadelphia, Pa.

WILSON, HARRY R., *Sing a Song at Sight*, Schmitt, Hall and McCreary, Minneapolis, Minn., 1954.

5. Orchestration–Band Arrangements

ANDERSON, ARTHUR O., *Practical Orchestration*, Summy-Birchard, Evanston, Ill., 1929.

FORSYTH, CECIL, *Orchestration*, The Macmillan Company, New York, 1945.

HEACOX, ARTHUR, *Project Lessons in Orchestration*, Oliver Ditson Company, Philadelphia, 1928.

JACOB, GORDON, *Orchestral Technique*, Oxford University Press, London, 1931.

JONES, JOHN PAUL, *Modern Instrumentation for Modern Arranging*, W. C. Brown Company, Inc., Dubuque, Iowa, 1947.

KENNAN, KENT, *Orchestration*, with workbook, Prentice-Hall, Inc., Englewood Cliffs, N.J., 1952.

LAKE, MAYHEW L., *The American Band Arranger*, Carl Fischer, Inc., New York, 1920.

MCKAY, GEORGE F., *Creative Orchestration*, with workbook, Allyn and Bacon, Inc., Boston, 1964.

THATCHER, HOWARD R., *Foundation Studies in Orchestration*, Carl Fischer, Inc., New York, 1959.

WAGNER, JOSEPH, *Orchestration*, with workbook, McGraw-Hill Book Company, New York, 1959.

————, *Band Scoring*, with workbook, McGraw-Hill Book Company, New York, 1960.

WHITE, WILLIAM C., *Military Band Arranging*, Carl Fischer, Inc., New York, 1926.

YODER, PAUL, *Arranging Method for School Bands*, Robbins Music Corp., New York, 1946.

6. Conducting Choral Ensembles

CAIN, NOBLE, *Choral Music and Its Practice*, Witmark, N.Y., 1932.

CHEYETTE, IRVING, *Tune Ups for Choral Groups*, Schmitt, Hall and McCreary, Minneapolis, Minn., 1951.

CHRISTY, VAN A., *Glee Club and Chorus*, G. Schirmer, Inc., New York, 1940.

COWARD, HENRY, *Choral Technique and Interpretation*, Novello, London, 1914.

DAVISON, ARCHIBALD T., *Choral Conducting*, Harvard University Press, Cambridge, Mass., 1959.

EARHART, WILL, *Choral Technics*, M. Witmark & Sons, New York, 1937.

EHRET, WALTER, *Choral Conductor's Handbook*, E. B. Marks Music Corp., New York, 1959.

FINN, W. J., *The Art of the Choral Conductor*, Summy-Birchard, Evanston, Ill., 1939.

GARRETSON, ROBERT L., *Conducting Choral Music*, Allyn and Bacon, Inc., Boston, 1961.

GRACE, HARVEY, *Training and Conducting Choral Societies*, Novello, London, 1938.

KRONE, MAX T., *The Chorus and Its Conductor*, Neil Kjos Music Co., Park Ridge, Ill., 1945.

MCELHERAN, BROCK, *Conducting Techniques for Beginners and Professionals*, Oxford University Press, Fair Lawn, N.J., 1966.

SCOTT, KENNEDY, *Madrigal Singing*, Oxford University Press, London, 1931.

SMALLMAN, JOHN, and E. H. WILCOX, *Art of A Cappella Singing*, Oliver Ditson, Philadelphia, 1933.

7. Conducting Instrumental Ensembles

EARHART, WILL, *The Eloquent Baton*, M. Witmark & Sons, New York, 1932.

FERGUSON, HOWARD, and R. O. MORRIS, *Preparatory Exercises in Score Reading*, Oxford University Press, Fair Lawn, N.J., 1930.

FISKE, ROGER, *Score Reading*, Oxford University Press, Fair Lawn, N.J., 1958.

GAL, HANS, *Directions for Score Readings*, Associated Music Publ. Co., New York, 1924.

GEHRKENS, KARL W., *Essentials in Conducting*, Oliver Ditson Company, Philadelphia, 1919.

GREEN, ELIZABETH A. H., *The Modern Conductor*, Prentice-Hall, Inc., Englewood Cliffs, N.J., 1961.

GROSBAYNE, BENJAMIN, *Techniques of Modern Orchestral Conducting*, Harvard University Press, Cambridge, Mass., 1956.

JACOB, GORDON, *How to Read a Score*, Boosey and Hawkes, Oceanside, N.Y., 1944.

KAHN, EMIL, *Conducting*, with workbooks, The Macmillan Company, New York, 1965.

KJELMERVICK, KENNETH, and RICHARD C. BERG, *Marching Bands*, A. S. Barnes and Co., Inc., New York, 1953.

NOYES, FRANK, *Fundamentals of Conducting*, W. C. Brown Company, Inc., Dubuque, Iowa, 1960.

————, *Anthology of Musical Examples for Instrumental Conducting*, W. C. Brown Company, Inc., Dubuque, Iowa, 1961.

RIGHTER, CHARLES, *Success in Teaching School Orchestras and Bands*, Schmitt, Hall and McCreary, Minneapolis, Minn., 1945.

————, *Teaching Instrumental Music*, Carl Fischer, Inc., New York, 1959.

SCHERCHEN, HERMANN, *Handbook of Conducting*, Oxford University Press, London, 1933.

STARR, WILLIAM J., and GEORGE F. DEVINE, *Music Scores Omnibus*, Part I: *Earliest Music through Beethoven;* Part II: *Romantic and Impressionistic Music*, Prentice-Hall, Englewood Cliffs, N.J., 1964.

STOESSEL, ALBERT, *The Technic of the Baton*, Carl Fischer, Inc., New York, 1920.

VAN BODEGRAVEN, PAUL, and HARRY R. WILSON, *School Music Conductor*, Schmitt, Hall and McCreary, Minneapolis, Minn., 1942.

VAN HOESEN, KARL D., *Handbook of Conducting*, Appleton-Century-Crofts, Inc., New York, 1950.

GUIDANCE TOWARD CAREERS IN MUSIC

ANDERSON, W. R., *Music as a Career*, Oxford University Press, Fair Lawn, N.J., 1939.

A Career in Music Education, Music Educators National Conference, 1962.

JOHNSON, HARRIETT, *Your Career in Music*, E. P. Dutton & Co., Inc., New York, 1945.

Occupational Outlook Handbook, U.S. Department of Labor, Washington, D.C., 1961.

SPAETH, SIGMUND, *Opportunities in Music*, Grosset & Dunlap, Inc., New York, 1966.

WILSON, A. VERNE, *Guidance in Music*, Music Educators National Conference, Washington, D.C., 1962.

HISTORY AND LITERATURE OF MUSIC

APEL, WILLI, *The Harvard Dictionary of Music*, Harvard University Press, Cambridge, Mass., 1960.

AUSTIN, WILLIAM, *Music in the 20th Century*, W. W. Norton & Company, Inc., New York, 1967.

BALDWIN, LILLIAN, *A Listener's Anthology of Music*, Kulas Foundation, Cleveland, 1948.

BARLOW, HOWARD, and SAM MORGENSTERN, *A Dictionary of Musical Themes,* Crown Publishers, Inc., New York, 1948.

BEKKER, PAUL, *The Story of the Orchestra* (paperback), W. W. Norton & Company, Inc., New York, 1963.

BERNSTEIN, LEONARD, *The Joy of Music,* Simon and Schuster, Inc., New York, 1959.

BIANCOLI, LOUIS, *The Opera Reader,* Grosset & Dunlap, Inc., New York, 1953.

BOCKMAN, GUY ALAN, and WILLIAM J. STARR, *Scored for Listening,* Harcourt, Brace and World, Inc., New York, 1964.

CHAILLEY, JACQUES, *40,000 Years of Music,* trans. Rollo Myers, Farrar, Straus & Giroux, Inc., New York, 1964.

CROCKER, RICHARD L., *A History of Musical Style,* McGraw-Hill Book Company, New York, 1966.

DALLIN, LEON, *Listener's Guide to Musical Understanding,* with workbook, W. C. Brown Company, Inc., Dubuque, Iowa, 1959.

DICKINSON, EDWARD, *Music in the History of the Western Church,* Charles Scribner's Sons, New York, 1928.

DORIAN, FREDERICK, *History of Music in Performance,* W. W. Norton & Company, Inc., New York, 1942.

DUCKLES, VINCENT, *Music Reference and Research Materials,* The Macmillan Company, New York, 1967.

FEINBERG, SAUL, *Blueprints for Musical Understanding,* with recordings, 3 series of master manuals and student study guides, Music Publishers Holding Corp., New York, 1965.

FRANKENSTEIN, ALFRED, *A Modern Guide to Symphonic Music,* Appleton-Century-Crofts, Inc., New York, 1967.

GEIRINGER, KARL, *Musical Instruments, Their History in Western Culture from the Stone Age to the Present,* trans. Bernard Mall, Oxford University Press, Fair Lawn, N.J., 1945.

————, *The Bach Family,* Oxford University Press, Fair Lawn, N.J., 1954.

GILBERT, WILLIAM S., *The Savoy Operas,* 2 vols., Oxford University Press, Fair Lawn, N.J., 1962.

GROUT, DONALD JAY, *A History of Western Music,* W. W. Norton & Company, Inc., New York, 1960.

HILL, RALPH, *The Concerto* (paperback), Penguin Books, Inc., Baltimore, 1967.

HINTOFF, NAT, and ALBERT MCCARTHY, *Jazz,* Holt, Rinehart and Winston, Inc., New York, 1959.

HITCHCOCK, H. WILEY, *Music in the U.S.,* Prentice-Hall, Inc., Englewood Cliffs, N.J., 1968.

HOSIER, JOHN, *Instruments of the Orchestra,* with Capitol recording ordered separately, Oxford University Press, Fair Lawn, N.J., 1961.

KIRBY, F. E., *A Short History of Keyboard Music,* The Macmillan Company, New York, 1966.

LANG, PAUL HENRY, *Music in Western Civilization,* W. W. Norton & Company, Inc., New York, 1941.

————, and NATHAN BRODER, *Contemporary Music in Europe,* G. Schirmer, Inc., New York, 1965.

LAWLESS, ROY M., *Folksingers and Folksongs in America,* Appleton-Century-Crofts, Inc., New York, 1965.

LONGYEAR, RAY M., *Nineteenth Century Romanticism,* Prentice-Hall, Inc., Englewood Cliffs, N.J., 1968.

LUBBOCK, MARK, *The Complete Book of Light Opera,* American section by David Ewen, Appleton-Century-Crofts, Inc., New York, 1963.

MACHLIS, JOSEPH, *The Enjoyment of Music,* W. W. Norton & Company, Inc., New York, 1955.

———, *Introduction to Contemporary Music,* W. W. Norton & Company, Inc., New York, 1961.

MALM, WILLIAM P., *Music Cultures of the Pacific, the Near East and Asia,* Prentice-Hall, Inc., Englewood Cliffs, N.J., 1966.

McKINNEY, HOWARD, *Music and Man,* American Book Company, New York, 1955.

McKINNEY, HOWARD, and W. R. ANDERSON, *Music in History,* American Book Company, New York, 1940.

NALLIN, WALTER, *The Musical Idea,* The Macmillan Company, New York, 1968.

NETTL, BRUNO, *Music in Primitive Culture,* Harvard University Press, Cambridge, Mass., 1956.

———, *Folk and Traditional Music of the Western Continents,* Prentice-Hall, Inc., Englewood Cliffs, N.J., 1965.

NEWMAN, JOEL, *Renaissance Music,* Prentice-Hall, Inc., Englewood Cliffs, N.J., 1968.

Opera Libretti in English, Oxford University Press, Fair Lawn, N.J.

PALISCA, CLAUDE V., *Baroque Music,* Prentice-Hall, Inc., Englewood Cliffs, N.J., 1968.

PAULY, REINHARD G., *Music in the Classic Period,* Prentice-Hall, Inc., 1965.

ROBERTSON, ALEC, and DENIS STEVENS (eds.), *The Pelican History of Music* (paperback), vol. 1, *Ancient Forms to Polyphony,* vol. 2, *Renaissance to Baroque,* Penguin Books, Inc., Baltimore, 1963.

ROSENTHAL, HAROLD, and JOHN WARROCK, *Concise Oxford Dictionary of Opera,* Oxford University Press, Fair Lawn, N.J., 1964.

SACHS, CURT, *Our Musical Heritage,* Prentice-Hall, Inc., Englewood Cliffs, N.J., 1955.

SALZMAN, ERIC, *Twentieth Century Music: An Introduction,* Prentice-Hall, Inc., Englewood Cliffs, N.J., 1967.

SCHOLES, PERCY A., *The Concise Oxford Dictionary of Music,* 2d ed., ed. John O. Ward, Oxford University Press, Fair Lawn, N.J., 1964.

———, *A Miniature History of Opera,* Oxford University Press, London, 1931.

SCHWARTZ, HARRY W., *The Story of Musical Instruments,* C. G. Conn, Ltd., Elkhart, Ind., 1938.

SEAY, ALBERT, *Music in the Medieval World,* Prentice-Hall, Inc., Englewood Cliffs, N.J., 1965.

SIMPSON, ROBERT, *The Symphony, Haydn to Dvorak* (paperback), Penguin Books, Inc., Baltimore, 1966.

———, *The Symphony, Elgar to the Present Day* (paperback), Penguin Books, Inc., Baltimore, 1967.

STEARNS, M. W., *The Story of Jazz,* Oxford University Press, Fair Lawn, N.J., 1956.

TANNER, PAUL, and MAURICE GEROW, *A Study of Jazz,* with recording, W. C. Brown Company, Inc., Dubuque, Iowa, 1964.

ULRICH, HOMER, *Music, A Design for Listening,* Harcourt, Brace and World, Inc., New York, 1962.

———, *A History of Music and Musical Style,* Harcourt, Brace and World, Inc., New York, 1963.

———, and BRYCE JORDAN, *Designed for Listening,* assignments in music with 4 recordings, Harcourt, Brace and World, Inc., New York, 1962.

WATANABE, RUTH, *Introduction to Music Research,* Prentice-Hall, Inc., Englewood Cliffs, N.J., 1967.

WESTERMAN, GERHART VON, *Opera Guide,* ed. Harold Rosenthal, trans. Anne Ross, E. P. Dutton, & Co., Inc., New York, 1964.

WESTRUP, J. A., and GERALD ABRAHAM, et al., *New Oxford History of Music,* with recorded *History of Music in Sound* by RCA Victor, Oxford University Press, Fair Lawn, N.J., 1960.

WHITE, ERIC W., *Stravinsky,* University of California Press, Berkeley, Calif., 1966.

WHITE, JOHN D., *Understanding and Enjoying Music*, Dodd Mead & Company, Inc., New York, 1968.

WOLD, MILO, and EDMUND CYKLER, *An Outline History of Music*, W. C. Brown Company, Inc., Dubuque, Iowa, 1964.

HISTORICAL AND PHILOSOPHICAL FOUNDATIONS OF MUSIC EDUCATION

Basic Concepts in Music Education, A Symposium, National Society for the Study of Education, Chicago, Ill. (available through the MENC, Washington, D.C.), 1958.

BIRGE, EDWARD BAILEY, *History of Public School Music in the United States*, Oliver Ditson Company, Philadelphia, 1928.

BUTTELMAN, CLIFFORD V. (ed.), *A Steadfast Philosophy* (a compendium of Dr. Will Earhart's writings), Music Educators National Conference, 1962.

DAVISON, ARCHIBALD T., *Music Education in America*, Harper & Brothers, New York, 1926.

ERNST, KARL D., and CHARLES L. GARY (eds.), *Music in General Education*, Music Educators National Conference, 1965.

FERGUSON, DONALD N., *A History of Musical Thought*, Appleton-Century-Crofts, Inc., New York, 1959.

GOSLIN, DAVID A., *The School in Contemporary Society*, Scott, Foresman and Company, Chicago, 1965.

JONES, ARCHIE N. (ed.), *Music Education in Action*, W. C. Brown Company, Inc., Dubuque, Iowa, 1960.

KAPLAN, MAX, *Foundations and Frontiers of Music Education*, Holt, Rinehart and Winston, Inc., New York, 1963.

LEONHARD, CHARLES, and ROBERT W. HOUSE, *Foundations and Principles of Music Education*, McGraw-Hill Book Company, New York, 1959.

MADISON, THURBER (ed.), *Perspectives in Music Education*, Source Book III, Music Educators National Conference, 1966.

MURSELL, JAMES L., *Human Values in Music Education*, Silver Burdett Company, Morristown, N.J., 1934.

———, *Music in American Schools*, Silver Burdett Company, Morristown, N.J., 1943.

———, *Principles and Programs in Music Education*, Silver Burdett Company, Morristown, N.J., 1956.

PITTS, LILLA BELLE, *The Music Curriculum in a Changing World*, Silver Burdett Company, Morristown, N.J., 1944.

PORTNOY, JULIUS, *Music in the Life of Man*, Holt, Rinehart and Winston, Inc., New York, 1963.

SQUIRE, RUSSEL N., *Introduction to Music Education*, The Ronald Press Company, New York, 1952.

ZANZIG, AUGUSTUS D., *Music in American Life*, Oxford University Press, Fair Lawn, N.J., 1932.

INSTRUMENTAL METHODS

1. Percussion

BARTLETT, HARRY R., *Guide to Teaching Percussion*, W. C. Brown Company, Inc., Dubuque, Iowa, 1964.

———, *Percussion Ensemble Method*, W. C. Brown Company, Inc., Dubuque, Iowa, 1961.

BUGGERT, ROBERT W., *Method for the Snare Drum*, Belwin, Inc., Hempstead, N.Y., 1942.

COLLINS, MYRON D., and JOHN GREEN, *Playing and Teaching Percussion Instruments*, Prentice-Hall, Inc., Englewood Cliffs, N.J., 1962.

GRANT, PHIL, *All American Drummer*, Mercury Music Co., New York, 1950.

HEIM, ALYN J., *Drum Class Method*, Belwin, Inc., Hempstead, N.Y., 1958.

MELNIK, HENRY, *Fundamental Method for Drums*, Universal Music Co., New York, 1940.

OSTLING, ACTON E., *Three R's for Snare Drum*, Belwin, Inc., Hempstead, N.Y., 1946.

PODEMSKI, BENJAMIN, *Standard Snare Drum Method*, Mills Music, Inc., New York, 1940.

SPOHN, CHARLES L., *The Percussion, Performance and Instructional Techniques*, Allyn and Bacon, Inc., Boston, 1967.

WALTERS, HAROLD L., *Simplified Rudiments for Latin American Instruments*, Rubank, Inc., Chicago, 1940.

YODER, PAUL, *Elementary Method for Drum*, Rubank, Inc., Chicago, 1935.

2. String Instruments

APPLEBAUM, SAMUEL, *String Builder*, Belwin, Inc., Hempstead, N.Y., 1960.

CHEYETTE, IRVING, and EDWIN SALZMAN, *Beginning and Intermediate String Musicianship*, Bourne, New York, 1952.

EDWARDS, ARTHUR, *String Ensemble Method*, W. C. Brown Company, Inc., Dubuque, Iowa, 1960.

FELDMAN, HARRY, *Unison String Class Method*, Pro Art Music, Westbury, N.Y., 1950.

KELLER, MARJORIE, and MAURICE TAYLOR, *Easy Steps to the Orchestra*, Mills Music, Inc., New York, 1951.

KUHN, WOLFGANG E., *The Strings, Performance and Instructional Techniques*, Allyn and Bacon, Inc., Boston, 1967.

MATESKY, RALPH, and RALPH RUSH, *Playing and Teaching String Instruments*, Prentice-Hall, Inc., Englewood Cliffs, N.J., 1962.

MATESKY, RALPH, and ARDELLE WOMACK, *Learning to Play a Stringed Instrument*, Prentice-Hall, Inc., Englewood Cliffs, N.J., 1966.

3. Recreational Instruments

CHEYETTE, IRVING, *Songs for Camp and Campus*, Pro Art Music, Westbury, N.Y., 1961.

———, and ALBERT A. RENNA, *Sociability Songs with Social Instruments*, Theodore Presser Company, Bryn Mawr, Pa., 1968.

DALLIN, LEON, and LYNN DALLIN, *Heritage Songster*, W. C. Brown Company, Inc., Dubuque, Iowa, 1966.

———, *Folk Songster*, W. C. Brown Company, Inc., Dubuque, Iowa, 1966.

ROWEN, RUTH, and BILL SIMON, *Jolly Come Sing and Play*, Carl Fischer, Inc., New York, 1956.

STAPLE, RJ, *Let's Play the Classroom Instruments*, Carl Van Roy Publ. Co., Far Rockaway, N.Y., 1958.

STERRETT, PAUL, and SCOTT WILKINSON, *You Can Play*, Carl Fischer, Inc., New York, 1957.

4. Wind Instruments—Brass and Woodwind

GORNSTON, DAVID, and MYRAN PALMER, *Basic Way to the Band*, B. F. Wood, Boston, 1958.

HERFURTH, PAUL, and HUGH M. STUART, *Our Band Class Book*, Carl Fischer, Inc., New York, 1957.

HUNT, NORMAN J., *Brass Ensemble Method*, W. C. Brown Company, Inc., Dubuque, Iowa, 1961.

KINYON, BERG, and MCKAY, *Band Booster*, Remick Music Co., New York, 1960.

SAWHILL, CLARENCE, and BERTRAM MCGARRITY, *Playing and Teaching Woodwind Instruments*, Prentice-Hall, Inc., Englewood Cliffs, N.J., 1962.

SKORNICKA, JOSEPH, and JOSEPH BERGEIM, *Band Method*, Boosey and Hawkes, Oceanside, N.Y., 1947.

TAYLOR, MAURICE, *Band Fundamentals*, Mills Music, Inc., New York, 1963.

TIMM, EVERETT, *The Woodwinds*, Allyn and Bacon, Inc., Boston, 1964.

WEBER, FRED (ed.), *First Division Band Course*, Belwin, Inc., Hempstead, N.Y. 1962.

WESTPHAL, FREDERICK W., *Woodwind Ensemble Method*, W. C. Brown Company, Inc., Dubuque, Iowa, 1961.

———, *Guide to Teaching Woodwinds*, W. C. Brown Company, Inc., Dubuque, Iowa, 1961.

WINSLOW, ROBERT, and JOHN GREEN, *Playing and Teaching Brass Instruments*, Prentice-Hall, Inc., Englewood Cliffs, N.J., 1961.

WINTER, JAMES H., *The Brass Instruments, Performance and Instructional Techniques*, Allyn and Bacon, Inc., Boston, 1964.

PIANO AS A MINOR INSTRUMENT

CHEYETTE, IRVING, and J. CURTIS SHAKE, *Basic Piano for the Music Educator and the Classroom Teacher*, Theodore Presser Company, Bryn Mawr, Pa., 1954.

PACE, ROBERT, *Piano for Classroom Music*, Wadsworth Publ. Co., Belmont, Calif., 1956.

RICHTER, ADA, *You Can Play the Piano*, Theodore Presser Company, Bryn Mawr, Pa., 1947.

STEINER, ERIC, *Senior Approach to the Piano Course*, Belwin, Inc., Hempstead, N.Y., 1960.

WAGNESS, BERNARD, *Adult Piano Course*, Rubank, Inc., Chicago, 1951.

VOCAL METHODS

CHRISTY, VAN A., *Foundations in Singing*, W. C. Brown Company, Inc., Dubuque, Iowa, 1965.

———, *Expressive Singing*, W. C. Brown Company, Inc., Dubuque, Iowa, 1961.

———, *Song Anthologies*, W. C. Brown Company, Inc., Dubuque, Iowa, 1961.

HAYWOOD, FREDERICK H., *Universal Song*, 3 vols., G. Schirmer, Inc., New York, 1917.

JACQUES, REGINALD, *Voice Training and Conducting in Schools*, Oxford University Press, Fair Lawn, N.J., 3d ed., 1963.

PIERCE, ANNE E., and ESTELLE LIEBLING, *Class Lessons in Singing*, Silver Burdett Company, Morristown, N.J., 1937.

PITTS, CAROL M., *Voice Class Method*, Neil Kjos Music Co., Park Ridge, Ill., 1936.

ROSEWALL, RICHARD B., *Handbook of Singing*, Summy-Birchard, Evanston, Ill., 1961.

SUNDERMAN, LLOYD F., *Basic Vocal Instructor*, Belwin, Inc., Hempstead, N.Y., 1958.

SWIFT, FREDERICK F., *Fundamentals of Singing*, Belwin, Inc., Hempstead, N.Y., 1958.

TAYLOR, BERNARD U., *Group Voice*, G. Schirmer, Inc., New York, 1936.

METHODS OF TEACHING MUSIC

1. Elementary

BERGETHON, BJORNAR, and EUNICE BOARDMAN, *Musical Growth in the Elementary School*, Holt, Rinehart and Winston, Inc., New York, 1963.

CARABO-CONE, MADELEINE, and BEATRICE ROYT, *How to Help Children Learn Music*, Harper & Row, Publishers, Incorporated, New York, 1953.

CHEYETTE, IRVING, and HERBERT B. CHEYETTE, *Teaching Music Creatively in the Elementary School,* McGraw-Hill Book Company, New York, 1969.

Children, The Music Makers, Bureau of Elementary Curriculum Development, State Education Department, Albany, N.Y.

ELLIOTT, RAYMOND, *Teaching Music,* Charles E. Merrill Books, Inc., Columbus, Ohio, 1960.

ELLISON, ALFRED, *Music with Children,* McGraw-Hill Book Company, New York, 1959.

GARRETSON, ROBERT L., *Music in Childhood Education,* Appleton-Century-Crofts, Inc., New York, 1966.

GARY, CHARLES L. (ed.), *The Study of Music in the Elementary School, A Conceptual Approach,* Music Educators National Conference, Washington, D.C., 1968.

GRAY, VERA, and RACHEL PERCIVAL, *Music, Movement and Mime for Children,* Oxford University Press, Fair Lawn, N.J., 1962.

HEFFERNAN, CHARLES W., *Teaching Children to Read Music,* Appleton-Century-Crofts, Inc., New York, 1968.

KRONE, BEATRICE P., and MAX KRONE, *Music Participation in the Elementary School,* Neil Kjos Music Co., Park Ridge, Ill., 1952.

KRONE, BEATRICE P., and KURT R. MILLER, *Help Yourselves to Music,* Chandler Publ. Co., San Francisco, Calif., 1959.

MASSIALAS, BYRON G., and JACK ZEVIN, *Creative Encounters in the Classroom,* John Wiley and Sons, Inc., New York, 1967.

McMILLAN, L. EILEEN, *Guiding Children's Growth through Music,* Ginn and Company, Boston, 1959.

MYERS, LOUISE K., *Teaching Children Music in the Elementary School,* Prentice-Hall, Inc., Englewood Cliffs, N.J., 1956.

NORDHOLM, HARRIET, and CARL G. THOMPSON, *Keys to Teaching Elementary School Music,* Schmitt, Hall and McCreary, Minneapolis, Minn., 1948.

NYE, ROBERT E., NEVA AUBIN, and GEORGE H. KYME, *Singing with Children,* Wadsworth Publ. Co., Belmont, Calif., 1962.

NYE, ROBERT E. and VERNICE NYE, *Music in the Elementary School,* Prentice-Hall, Inc., Englewood Cliffs, N.J., 1957.

PIERCE, ANNE E., *Teaching Music in the Elementary School,* Holt, Rinehart and Winston, Inc., New York, 1959.

RAEBECK, LOIS, and LAWRENCE WHEELER, *New Approaches to Music in the Elementary School,* W. C. Brown Company, Inc., Dubuque, Iowa, 1964.

RUNKLE, ALETA, and MARY L. ERIKSEN, *Music for Today's Boys and Girls,* Allyn and Bacon, Inc., Boston, 1966.

SHEEHY, EMMA D., *Children Discover Music and Dance,* Holt, Rinehart and Winston, Inc., New York, 1959.

SLIND, LLOYD H., and D. EVAN DAVIS, *Bringing Music to Children,* Harper & Row Publishers, Incorporated, New York, 1964.

SNYDER, ALICE M., *Creating Music with Children,* Mills Music, Inc., New York, 1957.

SWANSON, BESSIE R., *Music in the Education of Children,* Wadsworth Publ. Co., Belmont, Calif., rev. ed., 1967.

2. Junior High

ANDREWS, FRANCES, and JOSEPH LEEDER, *Guiding Junior High School Pupils in Music Experiences,* Prentice-Hall, Inc., Englewood Cliffs, N.J., 1953.

BEATTIE, McCONATHY, and MORGAN, *Music in the Junior High School*, Silver Burdett Company, Morristown, N.J., 1930.

COOPER, IRVIN, and KARL KUERSTEINER, *Teaching Junior High Music*, Allyn and Bacon, Inc., Boston, 1965.

GEHRKENS, KARL W., *Music in the Junior High School*, Summy-Birchard, Evanston, Ill., 1936.

HOFFER, CHARLES, *Teaching Music in Secondary Schools*, Wadsworth Publ. Co., Belmont, Calif., 1964.

HUGHES, WILLIAM H., *Planning Junior High School General Music*, Wadsworth Publ. Co., Belmont, Calif., 1966.

MONSOUR, SALLY, and MARGARET PERRY, *A Junior High School Music Handbook*, Prentice-Hall, Inc., Englewood Cliffs, N.J., 1963.

Music Curriculum in Secondary Schools, The, Music Educators National Conference, Washington, D.C., 1959.

NORDHOLM, HARRIET, and RUTH V. BAKEWELL, *Keys to Teaching Junior High School Music*, Schmitt, Hall, and McCreary, Minneapolis, 1953.

PITTS, LILLA BELLE, *Music Integration in the Junior High School*, Summy-Birchard, Evanston, Ill., 1935.

SUR, WILLIAM, and CHARLES F. SCHULLER, *Music Education for Teen-agers*, Harper & Row, Publishers, Incorporated, New York, 2d ed., 1966.

3. Senior High

DYKEMA, PETER W., and KARL W. GEHRKENS, *High School Music*, Summy-Birchard, Evanston, Ill., 1941.

Function of Music in the Secondary School Curriculum, The, Music Educators National Conference, Washington, D.C., 1952.

HOFFER, CHARLES R., *Teaching Music in Secondary Schools*, Wadsworth Publ. Co., Belmont, Calif., 1964.

LEEDER, JOSEPH, and WILLIAM S. HAYNIE, *Music Education in the High School*, Prentice-Hall, Inc., Englewood Cliffs, N.J., 1958.

Music in the Senior High School, Music Educators National Conference, 1959.

SINGLETON, IRA, *Music in Secondary Schools*, Allyn and Bacon, Inc., Boston, 1963.

WILSON, HARRY R., *Music in the High School*, Silver Burdett Company, Morristown, N.J., 1941.

MUSICAL ACOUSTICS (SCIENCE OF SOUND)

BAINES, ANTHONY, *Musical Instruments through the Ages* (paperback), Pelican Books, Baltimore, 1961.

BARTHOLOMEW, WILBER T., *Acoustics of Music*, Prentice-Hall, Inc., Englewood Cliffs, N.J., 1942.

BERANEK, LEO L., *Music Acoustics and Architecture*, John Wiley & Sons, Inc., New York, 1962.

CULVER, CHARLES A., *Musical Acoustics*, McGraw-Hill Book Company, New York, 4th ed., 1956.

HALL, JODY C., and EARLE L. KENT, *The Language of Musical Acoustics*, C. G. Conn, 1956.

HAMILTON, CLARENCE, *Sound and Its Relation to Music*, Oliver Ditson Company, Philadelphia, 1912.

KENT, EARLE L., *The Inside Story of Brass Instruments,* C. G. Conn, 1956.

LOOMIS, ALLEN, and HARRY W. SCHWARTZ, *How Music Is Made,* C. G. Conn, 1927.

MILLER, DAYTON C., *The Science of Musical Sounds,* The Macmillan Company, New York, 1916.

REDFIELD, JOHN, *Music, A Science and an Art,* Alfred A. Knopf, Inc., New York, 1928.

RICHARDSON, E. G., *Acoustics of Orchestral Instruments and the Organ,* Edward Arnold & Co., London, 1929.

WARDIAN, JEANNE F., *Physics of Sound,* Appleton-Century-Crofts, Inc., New York, 1965.

MUSIC SUPERVISION AND ADMINISTRATION

ANDREWS, FRANCES, and CLARA E. COCKERILLE, *Your School Music Program,* Prentice-Hall, Inc., Englewood Cliffs, N.J., 1958.

BOWER, ELI M., and WILLIAM G. HOLLISTER (eds.), *Behavioral Science Frontiers in Education,* John Wiley and Sons, Inc., New York, 1967.

BEST, CLARENCE, *Music Rooms and Equipment,* Music Educators National Conference, rev. ed., 1965.

COLWELL, RICHARD, *Teaching Instrumental Music,* Appleton-Century-Crofts, Inc., New York, 1968.

DWYER, TERENCE, *Opera in Your School,* Oxford University Press, Fair Lawn, N.J., 1964.

HERMANN, EDWARD J., *Supervising Music in the Elementary School,* Prentice-Hall, Inc., Englewood Cliffs, N.J., 1965.

HOUSE, ROBERT, *Instrumental Music for Today's Schools,* Prentice-Hall, Inc., Englewood Cliffs, N.J., 1965.

KUETHE, JAMES L., *The Teaching-Learning Process,* Scott Foresman and Company, Chicago, 1967.

Music Supervision and Administration in the Schools, Research Council Bulletin, no. 18, Music Educators National Conference, 1949.

SNYDER, KEITH D., *School Music Administration and Supervision,* Allyn and Bacon, Inc., Boston, 1959.

TIEDE, CLAYTON H., *Practical Band Instrument Repair Manual,* W. C. Brown Company, Inc., Dubuque, Iowa, 1962.

WAYLAND, R. H., *A Guide to Effective Music Supervision,* W. C. Brown Company, Inc., Dubuque, Iowa, 1960.

PSYCHOLOGY OF MUSIC

FARNSWORTH, PAUL R., *The Social Psychology of Music,* Holt, Rinehart and Winston, Inc., New York, 1958.

HOWES, FRANK, *The Borderland of Music and Psychology,* Oxford University Press, Fair Lawn, N.J., 1927.

KWALWASSER, JACOB, *Exploring the Musical Mind,* Coleman Publ. Co., New York, 1961.

LEHMAN, PAUL R., *Tests and Measurements in Music,* Prentice-Hall, Inc., Englewood Cliffs, N.J., 1968.

Lundin, Robert W., *An Objective Psychology of Music,* The Ronald Press Company, New York, rev. ed., 1967.

Mathay, Tobias, *An Introduction to Psychology for Music Teachers,* Oxford University Press, London, 1939.

Mursell, James L., *Psychology of Music,* W. W. Norton & Company, Inc., New York, 1940.
———, and Mabelle Glenn, *Psychology of School Music Teaching,* Silver Burdett Company, Morristown, N.J., 1938.

Schoen, Max, *The Psychology of Music,* The Ronald Press Company, New York, 1940.

Seashore, Carl, *Psychology of Musical Talent,* Silver Burdett Company, Morristown, N.J., 1919.

Swisher, Walter S., *Psychology for the Music Teacher,* Oliver Ditson Company, Philadelphia, 1926.

Whybrew, William, *Measurement and Evaluation in Music,* W. C. Brown Company, Inc., Dubuque, Iowa, 1962.

APPENDIX V

BIBLIOGRAPHY OF BASIC MUSIC SERIES OF THE LAST 100 YEARS

NINETEENTH-CENTURY MUSIC SERIES FOR PUBLIC SCHOOLS*

1. New Standard Music Reader, Benjamin Jepson, Tuttle, Morehouse & Taylor Co., 1867.
2. Loomis Progressive Music Lessons, George B. Loomis, American Book Company, New York, 1868.
3. National Music Course, Luther W. Mason, Ginn and Company, Boston, 1874.
4. Normal Music Course, Hosea Holt and John Tufts, D. Appleton & Company, Inc., New York, 1883.
5. New National Music Course, Revised Mason Course, Ginn and Company, Boston, 1885.
6. Cecilian Series of Study and Song, John W. Tufts, Silver Burdett Company, Morristown, N.J., 1892.
7. The American Music System, Friedrich Zuchtmann, King, Richardson & Co., 1892.
8. Model Music Course, John A. Broekhoven and A. J. Gantvoert, John Church Co., 1895.
9. Natural Course in Music, Frederick H. Ripley and Thomas Tapper, American Book Company, New York, 1895.
10. Novello Music Course, Francis E. Howard, H. W. Gray Co., 1899.
11. Mason Music Course, Luther Whiting Mason, Ginn and Company, Boston, 1896.
12. Modern Music Series, Robert Foresman and Eleanor Smith, Scott Foresman and Company, Chicago, 1898.

EARLY TWENTIETH-CENTURY MUSIC SERIES*

1. Congdon Music Readers, C. H. Congdon, editor and publisher, 1901.
2. The Song Series, Alys Bentley, C. C. Birchard, 1900.
3. Laurel Music Books, W. L. Tomlins, C. C. Birchard, beginning 1901.

*For descriptions of these series see Edward B. Birge, *A History of Public School Music,* Oliver Ditson Company, Philadelphia, 1928, Chapters IV to VII.

4. The New Educational Music Course, James McLaughlin, George A. Veasie and W. W. Gilchrist, Ginn and Company, Boston, 1903.
5. The Eleanor Smith Music Series, American Book Company, New York, 1908.
6. The Lyric Music Series, Arthur Edward Johnstone, Harvey W. Loomis, and William A. White, Scott, Foresman and Company, Chicago, 1912.
7. The Hollis Dann Music Course, American Book Company, New York, 1915.
8. The Progressive Music Series, Horatio W. Parker, Osbourne McConathy, W. Otto Miessner, and Edward B. Birge, Silver Burdett Company, Morristown, N.J., 1915.
9. The Universal Music Series, Walter Damrosch, Karl W. Gehrkens, and George Gartlan, Hinds, Hayden and Eldridge, 1920.
10. The Music Education Series, Thaddeus P. Giddings, Will Earhart, Ralph L. Baldwin, and Elbridge W. Newton, Ginn and Company, Boston, 1923.
11. The Foresman Books of Songs, Robert Foresman, American Book Company, New York, 1923.
12. A One Book Course in Elementary Music, Charles A. Fullerton, Fullerton and Gray, 1925.

MUSIC SERIES FROM 1925 TO 1950

1. The Music Hour Series, Osbourne McConathy, W. Otto Miessner, Edward B. Birge, and Mabel E. Bray, Silver Burdett Company, Morristown, N.J., 1927.
2. Concord Music Series, Archibald T. Davison, Thomas W. Surette, and Augustus D. Zanzig, E. C. Schirmer Music Co., 1928.
3. The World of Music, Mabelle Glenn, Helen S. Leavitt, Victor Rebmann, Earl L. Baker, and C. Valentine Kirby, Ginn and Company, Boston, 1936.
4. New Music Horizons, Osbourne McConathy, Russell Morgan, James L. Mursell, Marshall Bartholomew, Mabel Bray, W. Otto Meissner, and Edward Birge, Silver Burdett Company, Morristown, N.J., 1945.
5. A Singing School, Peter Dykema, Gladys Pitcher, David Stevens, and J. Lillian Vandevere, C. C. Birchard, 1946.
6. The American Singer, John W. Beattie, Josephine Wolverton, Grace V. Wilson, and Howard Hinga, American Book Company, New York, 1946.

MODERN MUSIC SERIES CURRENTLY IN USE

1. Our Singing World, Lilla Belle Pitts, Mabelle Glenn, and Lorrain E. Watters, Ginn and Company, Boston, 1950.
2. Together We Sing, Irving Wolfe, Beatrice Krone, and Margaret Fullerton, Follett Publishing Company, Chicago, 1955.
3. Music for Living, James L. Mursell, Gladys Tipton, Beatrice Landeck, Harriett Nordholm, Roy Freeburg, and Jack Watson, Silver Burdett Company, Morristown, N.J., 1956.
4. Birchard Music Series, Karl Ernst, Rose Marie Grentzer, and Wiley Housewright, Summy-Birchard Co., Evanston, Ill., 1962.
5. Music for Young Americans, Richard C. Berg, Daniel S. Hooley, Robert Pace, and Josephine Wolverton, American Book Company, New York, 1959.
6. Growing with Music, Harry R. Wilson, Walter Ehret, Alice M. Snyder, Edward J. Hermann, and Albert A. Renna, Prentice-Hall, Inc., Englewood Cliffs, N.J., 1963.

7. This Is Music, William R. Sur, Adeline McCall, Gladys Pitcher, Mary Tolbert, Robert E. Nye, William R. Fisher, and Charlotte DuBois, Allyn and Bacon, Inc., Boston, 1961.
8. The Magic of Music, Lorrain E. Watters, Louis G. Wersen, William C. Hartshorn, L. Eileen McMillan, Allic Gallup, and Frederick Beckman, Ginn and Company, Boston, 1966.
9. Making Music Your Own, Beatrice Landeck, Elizabeth Crook, Harold C. Youngberg, and Otto Luening, Silver Burdett Company, Morristown, N.J., 1964.
10. Exploring Music, Eunice Boardman and Beth Landis, Holt, Rinehart and Winston, Inc., New York, 1966.
11. Discovering Music Together, Charles Leonhard, Beatrice Krone, Irving Wolfe, and Margaret Fullerton, Follett Publishing Company, Chicago, 1966.

All these have accompanying albums of recordings, as well as teacher guides (see Chapter 2, p. 25, on the criteria for evaluating school music series).

APPENDIX VI

SUGGESTED BIBLIOGRAPHY OF MATERIALS FOR THE MUSICAL EDUCATION OF THE CLASSROOM TEACHER

VOCAL METHODS

CHRISTY, VAN A., *Expressive Singing,* vols. 1 and 2, W. C. Brown Company, Inc., Dubuque, Iowa, 1961.

————, *Song Anthologies,* W. C. Brown Company, Inc., Dubuque, Iowa, 1961.

————, *Foundation in Singing,* W. C. Brown Company, Inc., Dubuque, Iowa, 1965.

PIERCE, ANNE E., and ESTELLE LIEBLING, *Class Lessons in Singing,* Silver Burdett Company, Morristown, N.J., 1937.

ROSEWALL, RICHARD B., *Handbook of Singing,* Summy-Birchard Co., Evanston, Ill., 1961.

SUNDERMAN, LLOYD F., *Basic Vocal Instructor,* Belwin, Inc., Hempstead, N.Y., 1958.

SWIFT, FREDERICK F., *Fundamentals of Singing,* Belwin, Inc., Hempstead, N.Y., 1958.

TAYLOR, BERNARD U., *Group Voice,* G. Schirmer, Inc., New York, 1936.

VOCAL EAR TRAINING

BENWARD, BRUCE, *Sightsinging Complete,* W. C. Brown Company, Inc., Dubuque, Iowa, 1965.

CHEYETTE, IRVING, *Tune Ups for Choral Groups,* Schmitt, Hall & McCreary, Minneapolis, Minn., 1951.

DARAZS, ARPAD, and STEPHEN JAY, *Sight and Sound,* Boosey & Hawkes, Oceanside, N.Y., 1965.

First Year Vocalizes, Practice Aid Records, Box 209, Madison Square Station, New York, N.Y., 10010.

MYERS, LOUISE K., *Music Fundamentals through Song,* Prentice-Hall, Inc., Englewood Cliffs, N.J., 1954.

400

KEYBOARD SKILLS

CHEYETTE, IRVING, and J. CURTIS SHAKE, *Basic Piano for the Classroom Teacher*, Theodore Presser Company, Bryn Mawr, Pa., 1954.

LEACH, JOHN R., *Piano for the Classroom Teacher*, Prentice-Hall, Inc., Englewood Cliffs, N.J., 1968.

PACE, ROBERT, *Piano for Classroom Music*, Wadsworth Publ. Co., Belmont, Calif., 1959.

INSTRUMENTAL SKILLS (RHYTHM AND RECREATIONAL INSTRUMENTS)

CHEYETTE, IRVING, *Songs for Camp and Campus*, Pro Art Music, Westbury, N.Y., 1960.

CHEYETTE, IRVING, and ALBERT RENNA, *Sociability Songs with Social Instruments*, Theodore Presser Company, Bryn Mawr, Pa., 1968.

DALLIN, LEON, and LYNN DALLIN, *Heritage Songster*, W. C. Brown Company, Inc., Dubuque, Iowa, 1966.

————, *Folk Songster*, W. C. Brown Company, Inc., Dubuque, Iowa, 1967.

SNYDER, ALICE M., *Sing and Strum*, Mills Music, Inc., New York, 1957. See also bibliography in Appendix I—Materials for Melody Instruments.

SKILL IN MUSIC FUNDAMENTALS

*BARNES, ROBERT A., *Fundamentals of Music*, McGraw-Hill Book Company, New York, 1964.

*CARLSEN, JAMES C., *Melodic Perception*, McGraw-Hill Book Company, New York, 1965.

CASTELLINI, JOHN, *Rudiments of Music*, W. W. Norton & Company, Inc., New York, 1962.

DALLIN, LEON, *Foundations in Music Theory*, Wadsworth Publ. Co., Belmont, Calif., 1962.

ELLIOTT, RAYMOND, *Learning Music*, Charles E. Merrill Books, Inc., Columbus, Ohio, 1960.

*HARGISS, GENEVIEVE, *Music for Elementary Teachers*, Appleton-Century-Crofts, Inc., New York, 1968.

*HOWARD, BERTRAND, *Fundamentals of Music Theory*, Harcourt, Brace & World, Inc., New York, 1966.

NYE, ROBERT E., and BJORNAR BERGETHON, *Basic Music for Classroom Teachers*, Prentice-Hall, Inc., Englewood Cliffs, N.J., 1953.

PACE, ROBERT, *Music Essentials for Classroom Teachers*, Wadsworth Publ. Co., Belmont, Calif., 1961.

PIERCE, ANNE E., *Musicianship for the Classroom Teacher*, McGraw-Hill Book Company, New York, 1967.

TIMMERMAN, MAURINE, *Let's Make Music*, Summy-Birchard Co., Evanston, Ill., 1958.

WINSLOW, ROBERT W., and LEON DALLIN, *Music Skills for the Classroom Teacher*, W. C. Brown Company, Inc., Dubuque, Iowa, 1958.

WISLER, GENE C., *Music Fundamentals for the Classroom Teacher*, Allyn and Bacon, Inc., Boston, 1961.

*Programed instruction texts, the Carlsen text with tape recording.

TEACHING SKILLS
(METHODS AND MATERIALS)

BYER, MAUDE G., *Music Education in the Elementary School,* Fearon Publishers, San Francisco, Calif., 1957.

GRANT, PARKS, *Music for Elementary Teachers,* Appleton-Century-Crofts, Inc., N.Y.C., 1960.

KRONE, BEATRICE P., and KURT R. MILLER, *Help Yourselves to Music,* Chandler Publ. Co., San Francisco, Calif., 1959.

MURSELL, JAMES L., *Music and the Classroom Teacher,* Silver Burdett Company, Morristown, N.J., 1951.

"Music Education for Elementary School Children," *National Elementary Principal* (December, 1959), reprinted as a bulletin by the Music Educators National Conference, Washington, D.C., 1960.

RINDERER, LEO, et al., *Music Education Handbook for Music Teaching in the Elementary Grades,* English trans. Edmund A. Cykler and John R. Keith, Neil Kjos Music Co., Park Ridge, Ill., 1961.

SCHUBERT, INEZ, and LUCILLE WOOD, *The Craft of Music Teaching,* Silver Burdett Company, Morristown, N.J., 1964.

SNYDER, ALICE M., *Creating Music with Children,* Mills Music, Inc., New York, 1957.

SWANSON, BESSIE, *Music in the Education of Children,* Wadsworth Publ. Co., Belmont, Calif., 1962.

TIMMERMAN, MAURINE, *Let's Teach Music,* Summy-Birchard Co., Evanston, Ill., 1958.

MUSIC LITERATURE

See repertoire of songs and recordings from basic series for grade level taught.

BOOKS ABOUT MUSIC FOR THE LAYMAN

BERNSTEIN, LEONARD, *The Joy of Music,* Simon and Schuster, Inc., New York, 1959.

CHASE, GILBERT, *America's Music,* rev. ed., McGraw-Hill Book Company, New York, 1966.

COPLAND, AARON, *What to Listen For in Music,* McGraw-Hill Book Company, New York, 1939.

FINNEY, THEODORE, *Hearing Music,* Harcourt, Brace & World, Inc., New York, 1941.

FLEMING, WILLIAM, and VEINUS, ABRAHAM, *Understanding Music,* Holt, Rinehart and Winston, Inc., New York, 1960.

MACHLIS, JOSEPH, *The Enjoyment of Music,* W. W. Norton & Company, Inc., New York, 1955.

McKINNEY, HOWARD D., *Music and Man,* American Book Company, New York, 1956.

PORTNOY, JULIUS, *Music in the Life of Man,* Holt, Rinehart and Winston, Inc., New York, 1963.

RATNER, LEONARD G., *Music, The Listener's Art,* 2d ed., McGraw-Hill Book Company, New York, 1966.

STRINGHAM, EDWIN, *Listening to Music Creatively,* Prentice-Hall, Inc., Englewood Cliffs, N.J., 1946.

GLOSSARY OF MUSICAL TERMS

ACCIDENTAL: A symbol directing the raising (sharp ♯) or lowering (flat ♭) of a pitch a half step. The altered pitch will, therefore, be out of tonality. A natural sign (♮) cancelling the direction to alter pitch is also called an accidental

ATONALITY: Without key

BAR: A vertical line through the staff that marks measure divisions

CADENCE: The harmonic resolution at the end of a phrase, section, or piece. The traditional final cadence of a piece is usually dominant-tonic (V7–I). Cadence can also mean tempo

CANON: Exact imitation of a part by another at the same or different steps

CHORD: The simultaneous sounding of two or more different pitches

CHROMATIC: Progressing in half steps

CODA: A concluding section of a musical composition usually reiterating thematic ideas heard in the main body

COLOR: The idiomatic quality of a voice, instrument, or ensemble (orchestral quality, band quality, vocal quality, etc.)

CONSONANCE: A pleasant chord, contrary to dissonance

CONTRARY MOTION: Opposing movement of simultaneous voices

COUNTERPOINT: The art of interweaving melodies while retaining their distinct character

DIATONIC: A scale of major, minor, or modal construction having eight tones to the octave

DISSONANCE: A discordant sound; a chord sequence with intervals closer than thirds

DOMINANT: The fifth step of a scale, or the chord built on the fifth step of a major or minor scale

DRONE: Usually an interval of a fifth consisting of tonic and dominant tones sustained in the bass as accompaniment

DUET: A composition with two parts; two parts featured with accompaniment

ENHARMONIC: Tones identical in pitch but symbolized differently (E♭ or D♯)

FORM: The organization of musical materials within a composition (binary A–B or ternary A–B–A, etc.)

FUGUE: A musical form of contrapuntal composition based on developing a short single theme called the *subject* through canonic imitation at the fifth, adding *countersubjects* derived from the original theme

HARMONIC: Musical quality produced by combining tones into chords to provide a background for melody. Also the tones produced by touching nodal points of strings divided at one-half, one-third, one-fourth of their length

HOMOPHONIC: Music consisting of a melody supported by an accompaniment

IMITATION: The reiteration of a melody by another voice or instrument, creating counterpoint

INTERVAL: The distance between given tones in a scale (C–D, a second, C–E, a third)

INVERSION: The playing of a chord beginning on a tone other than its root position

KEY: The designation of the tonic tone, which establishes the point of rest or resolution in a given tonality; see *Tonic*

KEY SIGNATURE: The sharps or flats indicated on each staff determining the steps of a given major or minor scale

MEASURE: The space between bar lines organized into beats determining pulse

MELODY: A sequence of tones recognized as a significant unit

MODE: A scale organized according to the system of the ancient Greeks or the medieval church; see *Tonality*

MODULATION: Moving harmonically from a given key to a different one

MONOPHONY: A single line of melody without accompaniment

MOTIVE: The smallest unit of a musical theme

NOTE: A symbol designating a given pitch and duration; also the pitch represented by the symbol

PARALLEL MOTION: Two or more melodic lines, constantly related by the same interval

PHRASE: A musical unit made up of motives, corresponding to a phrase in a sentence

POLYPHONY: Many-voiced music in which the attention is focused on linear design rather than on melody with accompaniment

ROOT: The base note of a chord on which successive intervals are built

ROUND: A canon in which the same melody is repeated in delayed fashion, upon completion of a phrase, as the first melody continues

RUBATO: An alteration of strict tempo, usually slower, for purposes of musical effect

SUSPENSION: A nonharmonic tone held over on a strong accent from the preceding chord and then resolved to the harmonic tone on a weaker beat

SYNCOPATION: Shifting the usual accent from a strong to a weak beat

THEME: A musical idea, motive, or phrase that is the germinal seed from which the piece is developed

TIMBRE: The quality of a musical sound that is idiomatic to the voice or instrument

TIME SIGNATURE: A symbol placed following the key signature at the beginning of a piece of music, designating the number and kind of note values in each measure

TONALITY: The quality of sound of a given major or minor scale in a key. The tonality of C Major or C Minor differs from that of G Major or G Minor. Modality designates the quality of a given mode

TONE: A pitch consisting of periodic vibrations

TONIC: The first tone of a scale from which the intervals of the scale are computed, and which is the point of the scale's resolution; see *Key*

TRIAD: A three-tone chord with intervals a third apart

VIBRATO: The fluttering alteration of a pitch

VOICE: In music a melodic line as used contrapuntally

TEMPO TERMS

Very slow:	Largo (broad)
	Grave (heavy)
Slow:	Lento
	Adagio (at ease)
Moderate:	Andante (going at a walking pace)
	Andantino (somewhat faster than andante, sauntering)
	Moderato
Fairly fast:	Allegretto (a little lively, but not as fast as allegro)
Fast:	Allegro: (cheerful or lively)
Very fast:	Vivo (happy, lively)
	Vivace (in vivacious fashion)
	Allegro molto (very lively)
	Presto (quickly)
	Prestissimo (as quickly as possible)

DYNAMIC TERMS

Very soft:	Pianissimo (*pp*)
Soft:	Piano (*p*)
Moderately soft:	Mezzopiano (*mp*)
Moderately loud:	Mezzoforte (*mf*)
Loud:	Forte (*f*)
Very loud:	Fortissimo (*ff*)
Growing louder:	crescendo, also symbolized by widening arrows ($<$)
Growing softer:	decrescendo, also symbolized by diminishing arrow ($>$)
Sudden accent:	sforzando (*sf*, literally forced) accent on a single tone or chord ($\wedge$)

APPENDIX VII

MUSICAL ILLUSTRATIONS

Variants of the songs used for musical illustrations in this chart may also be found in the following basic series and supplementary songbooks. The acrostic abbreviations are coded to the titles of the series as follows:

TIM—This Is Music, Allyn and Bacon, Inc., 150 Tremont Street, Boston, Mass., 1961.

OSW—Our Singing World, Ginn and Company, Statler Bldg., Boston, Mass., 1950.

MFL—Music for Living, Silver Burdett Company, Morristown, N.J., 1956.

TWS—Together We Sing, Follett Publishing Company, Chicago, Ill., 1955.

MYA—Music for Young Americans, American Book Company, 55 Fifth Avenue, New York, N.Y., 1959.

BMS—Birchard Music Series, Summy-Birchard Co., Evanston, Ill., 1962.

GWM—Growing with Music, Prentice-Hall, Inc., Englewood Cliffs, N.J., 1963.

MMYO—Making Music Your Own, Silver Burdett Company, Morristown, N.J., 1964.

MOM—Magic of Music, Ginn and Company, Statler Bldg., Boston, Mass., 1965.

EM—Exploring Music, Holt, Rinehart and Winston, Inc., New York, N.Y., 1966.

DMT—Discovering Music Together, Follett Publishing Company, Chicago, Ill., 1966.

HS—Heritage Songster, W. C. Brown Company, Inc., Dubuque, Iowa, 1966.

Other sources include the Kiwanis Song Book, Kiwanis International, Chicago, Ill., and Children's Songs from Japan, E. B. Marks Music Corp., New York, N.Y.

Series	HS	TIM	OSW	MFL	TWS	MYA	BMS	GWM	MMYO	MOM	EM	DMT
Chapter 3 **The Barnyard Song**	69		4-155		2-21	2-42	2-69				2-4	2-8
The Steeple Bells		2-24						3-88	2-25			
Lullaby		3-100			3-136							3-116
Chiapanecas		3-103			5-92	4-118		4-6		2-162		
Chapter 4 **Baa, Baa, Black Sheep**	54	2-78	1-155						1-116			
Old Brass Wagon	262	3-13		3-121	4-95	2-97					2-19	
Tinga Layo	261	2-131 3-111			4-169		5-120		3-137		3-38	4-71
The Skaters' Waltz	74	3-148	5-154	4-67		3-32	3-79					
See-Saw Margery Daw	105				1-30							1-45
To Market, to Market		2-125	K-54									
Ten Little Indians	160		1-44			1-94	1-83					
Twinkle, Twinkle	41	2-35	2-106	1-20	1-87					2-26	2-152	1-52 2-51
Oranges and Lemons		2-63	4-164					3-76				
Chapter 5 **Greeting Song**		Kiwanis Song Book										
Clementine	176	5-129	6-67	3-5					4-22			
The Little Mohee	190		6-61		6-184		6-101					
Sweet Betsy	152	4-47 5-126	5-91			6-4	5-58					3-42 5-10
Old Hundredth		5-33		5-25	4-99		6-165	2-143			5-39	
A Song to Remember		Original										
Swing the Shining Sickle	248			3-149 4-161	3-50							
Chapter 6 **Hide-and-Seek**		2-17	also Children's Songs from Japan									
Trot, Pony, Trot		2-16			3-32							3-106
Wayfaring Stranger	5				6-183	6-38			6-109			6-83

Series	HS	TIM	OSW	MFL	TWS	MYA	BMS	GWM	MMYO	MOM	EM	DMT
The Wraggle-Taggle Gypsies				5-40			4-65				4-92	
Foom! Foom! Foom!	64				6-96	6-71			6-91			6-185
Old King Cole		Traditional										
Old Joe Clarke	229			5-61		5-70			5-40		5-74	
Sakura					6-150				2-156		3-138	
Havah Nagilah		Traditional Israeli				6-50						
Counting Song		Children's Songs from Japan										
Tumba		6-184					6-56					
Chapter 7 Lone Star Trail	82	3-20			4-47	4-142			2-197		2-30	5-107 4-64
Leavin' Ol' Texas		3-20									4-132	
Patsy		4-28										
Goodbye, My Lover, Goodbye	234	5-120										
The Campbells Are Coming		5-152				5-160						
Happy Song					3-32						3-34	5-34
On Yoshino Mountain		Japanese folk song										
This Old Man	265	1-41 4-9	1-44 2-7		2-122 2-106		1-16					2-9
Sweet Betsy	152	4-47 5-126	5-91			6-4	5-58					3-42 5-10
Erie Canal	256	5-62				6-36			5-6		5-58	5-116
Chapter 11 Oranges and Lemons		2-63	4-164									
If You're Happy		2-8									2-143	

Brahms Lullaby (RCA Victor) Listening Album 1, DMT.
Key: Under each code, the first numeral represents the book number of the series. The page number follows the dash.

INDEX

Accompaniment:
  primary grades, 11
  in songbooks, 27
Accordion, 206–209
Achievement tests, 330
  (*See also* Tests and measurements)
Activities:
  charts for, 240–241
  contemporary musical techniques, 234–241
  by grade, outline of, 290–291
  intermediate grades, 14–17, 290–291
  making instruments, 175–177, 242–259
  primary grades, 8–10, 32–52, 290–291
  song composition, 220–234
  upper elementary grades, 17–21
  (*See also* Curriculum; Games; Instruments; Rhythm; Visual aids)
Aeolian mode, 113, 120, 267
  (*See also* Mode)
Aesthetics, 341, 354, 382
Aleatory music, 237
  (*See also* Composition)
Anderson, Harold A., 217
Aptitude tests, 328
  (*See also* Tests and measurements)
Attitudes, 8, 15, 349
Audio-visual bibliography, 362
  equipment, 363
Augmented second, 123
  (*See also* Scale)
Autoharp, 187, 371
  (*See also* String instruments)

"Baa, Baa, Black Sheep," 60
Banjo, 181, 256
  (*See also* String instruments)
Barbershop harmony, 148, 150
  (*See also* Harmony)

"Barnyard Song," 41
Bartok, Bela, 273
Basic series, 397
  evaluation, 25–29
  primary grades, 11–12
  related material, 21
Bass clef, 49, 132
  (*See also* Staff notation)
Beats in music, 263
  (*See also* Rhythm)
"Beautiful Dreamer," 85
Bells, 32–52, 166–215
  "build a tune," 182
  chord, 180–181
  chromatic, 182–183
  diatonic, 42, 93, 182
  individual, 178–180
  stair, 43, 182–183
  tuned Swiss, 44, 181
  (*See also* Melody, chimes; Xylophone)
Berenson, Bernard, 341
Berg, Alban, 273
Bibliographies (Appendixes):
  action, game, rhythm songs, 369
  audio-visual methods, 362
  basic series of the last hundred years, 397
  basic series publishers, 398, 406
  correlation with social studies, 366
  curriculum building, 364
  enriched listening experiences, 377
  folk and square dances, 369
  methods for recreational instruments, 369
  music shelf for an elementary school library, 373
  musical education of the classroom teacher, 400
  musical education of the music teacher, 382

Bibliographies (Appendixes):
  supplementary songbooks, 367
Bingham, W. Van Dyke, 346
Bongo drums, 200
  (*See also* Rhythm instruments)
Boom bass, 259
  (*See also* Instruments)
Brasses, 282, 391
Broudy, Harry, 274
Bruner, Jerome, 295, 359

Cacophony, 7, 279
  (*See also* Harmony)
Cage, John, 136, 273
Canons, 141
  (*See also* Harmony)
Carlsen, James C., 323
Castanets, 200
  (*See also* Rhythm instruments)
Catalogue sources, 365
Cello, 198, 257
  (*See also* String instruments)
Chalkboard supplies, 364
Chants, 147, 156, 159
Child, nature of, 7, 8, 14, 17
Chimes, 184
Chording (*see* specific instrument)
Chords, 87–109, 136–165
  charts of, 88
  constructing, 88, 104, 138, 154
  duads, 148
  harmonic relations, 138–139
  inversion of, 88
  of nature, 137
  procedures for teaching, 88, 140
    dominant seventh, 94–96
    harmony of, 103–106, 140–165
    primary major, 87–94, 139, 156
    secondary, 99–103, 140, 161
    subdominant, 96–99
  qualities, 139
  resolution of, 138, 160
  sequences, memorization of, 160
  sign language for, 148–165
    minor scale, 161–165
  structure of, 87–90, 139–140
  triads, 105, 147, 154
  (*See also* Partials; Scale; Tendential
    resolution)

Chromatics, 106
  (*See also* Music notation; Octave; Scale)
Classroom teacher, 288–321
  lesson plan, second grade, 292–294
  methods of teaching music to, 321
  music activities, outline of, by grade,
    290–291
  preparation of, by music specialist, 288–
    289
  unit plan: second grade, 298–310
    upper grade, 310–317
  workshops for, objectives, 317–321
  (*See also* Curriculum)
Claves, 201
  (*See also* Rhythm instruments)
Clefs, 49
  (*See also* Staff notation)
"Clementine," 95
Complex pipes, 202
Composition, 220–233
  contemporary forms of, 234–241, 278–283
  development of, 136–140, 270–271, 285–
    287
  of song in class, 220–233
  structures of, 273–277
  (*See also* Harmony; Scale)
Compound meters 81
  (*See also* Meter; Rhythm)
Concepts in music education, 1–30, 353
  (*See also* Education, music)
Conducting, 57, 69, 386
  (*See also* Meter; Rhythm)
Conga drum, 200
  (*See also* Rhythm instruments)
Consonance, 136
  (*See also* Harmony)
Contemporary music, 234, 273, 351
  performing techniques, 281
  (*See also* Composition)
Correlation of music with other subjects, 11,
  17, 21, 296, 366
Count, Earl W., 346
Counterpoint, 384
  (*See also* Harmony)
"Counting Song," 130
Cowbell, 200, 247
  (*See also* Rhythm instruments)
Creativity, 216–259
  composing a song, 220–234
    procedures for, 234
  motivation, theory of, 216–219

Creativity:
  sound painting, 236–237
  (*See also* Activities)
Critical skills, 16, 19
Curriculum, elementary school music, 7–31,
    290–291
  classroom teachers: methods of teach-
      ing music to, 321
  workshops for, 317–321
  lesson plan, second grade, 292–294
  music education, changing concepts of,
    341–361
  unit plan: second grade, 292–294
    upper elementary, 310–317
  (*See also* Activities; Education, music)
Curwen, John, hand signals, 50
  (*See also* Visual aids)
Cyclical learning, 91, 149
  (*See also* Education, music)

Darazs, Arpad, 51
Decorum, 7, 10
Deduction, 56
Descants, 143, 147
Dewey, John, 260, 262, 342
Dictation, 91, 106
Diction, 106
Diminished chord, 89
  (*See also* Chords, structure of)
Discrimination, 348
Display materials, 364
Dissonance, 136
  (*See also* Harmony)
Dominant chord, 89, 94, 96, 138
  (*See also* Chords)
Dorian minor, 124
  (*See also* Mode)
Dotted notes, 61, 65
  (*See also* Music notation)
Drake, Raleigh M., 334
Dramatizing rhythms, 63, 229
  (*See also* Rhythms)
Drawings illustrating music, 47, 48
  (*See also* Visual aids)
Drones, 140, 143, 151–153
Drum talk, 63, 78
  (*See also* Rhythm instruments)
Duobass, 88, 258
  (*See also* String instruments)
Duration values, 59–62, 220–224
  (*See also* Rhythms; Visual aids)

Dykema, Peter, 334
Dynamics, 22, 264, 344
  (*See also* Music notation; Terminology)

Ear training, 3, 9, 16, 19, 62, 91, 103, 105,
    106
  (*See also* Chords; Games; Pitch; Melody;
      Scale; Voice)
Education, music: ancient theories of, 343
  classroom teachers of, 317–321
  history of, in America, 353–361
  Kodaly system, 357–358
  Orf system, 355–356
  primitive man, 347–348
  research in, 355
  Suzuki system, 358
  taste, factors influencing, 348–350
Electronic amplification, 283
  music, 278
  music board, 326
Elementary methods, 392
English *sol-fa*, 96, 161
"Erie Canal," 162
Erskine, John, 270
Evaluation:
  of creativity, 233
    of learning, 30, 327–336
    methods of, 233, 327–336
  of performance, 35, 232
  recording information, 336–337
  of series, 25
  of units, 306, 310, 317
Exotic scales, 126, 267
  (*See also* Scale)
Experimentation, 114
Expressiveness in music, 223, 264

Fahnestock, E., 335
Feedback, 320, 326
Figure illustrations, 47
  (*See also* Visual aids)
Films and film strips in music education,
    366, 380
Finger harmony, 148, 154
Fingering (*see* specific instrument)
Flash cards:
  rhythms, 59, 73, 77, 81
  tone groups, 91, 95, 103, 105
  (*See also* Visuals aids)

Flutes, 167, 371
  (*See also* Complex pipes; Simple pipes)
Focused attention, 11, 13, 341
Folk and square dance materials, 369
"Foom! Foom! Foom!" 123
Ford Foundation Contemporary Music
    Projects, 359
Foreign influences, 50, 355
  (*See also* Education, music)
Form, 32, 273
  (*See also* Composition; Harmony)
Frankfurter, Felix, 342
Free expression, 54
"Frère Jacques," 143, 240
Fundamental rhythms, 9, 15, 18
  (*See also* Rhythms)

Games:
  ear-training, 91–106
  foreign languages, 45
  melody graphs, 46–47
  musical signatures, 37–39, 237–239
  musical speech, 44–45
  questions, teaching songs by, 34–35
  rhythms: chance, 237–239
    dramatization, 63–64, 229
    drum, 63
    flash cards, 59–60, 73–74, 77
    names, 57–59
    tapped, 59
  song illustrations, 47–48
  sound imitation, 37
  (*See also* Sign language; Visual aids)
Gildersleeve, Glenn, 335
Glossary of musical terms, 403
  (*See also* Terminology)
Good music, definition, 348
"Goodbye, My Lover, Goodbye," 150
Gordon, Edwin, 334
Gorer, Geoffrey, 347
Grade outline for course of study, 290, 291
  (*See also* Activities; Curriculum)
Grand staff, 132
  (*See also* Staff notation)
"Greeting Song," 90
Guidance in music, 387
Guido of Arezzo, 50
Guiro, 200, 201
  (*See also* Rhythm instruments)
Guitar, 192, 256
  (*See also* String instruments)

Half step intervals, 44
  (*See also* Scale)
Hand harmonizing, 148, 154, 161, 164
  (*See also* Harmony; Visual aids)
Hand signals, 46, 50
Hand staff, 49, 93
"Happy Song," 152
Harmonic series (*see* Partials)
Harmonic minor, 161
  (*See also* Scale)
Harmonica, 205
Harmony, 136–165
  barbershop, 148–150
  canons, 141–143
  choir, for adding, 147–148, 158, 230
  descant, 143–147
  drone, 143, 151–154
  history of, 136–140, 270–271, 285–287
  keyboard, charts for, 209–215
  partner songs, 142
  procedures for teaching, 103–109,
      140–165
  sign language for, 148–165
    minor scales, 161–165
  skills: intermediate grades, 16
    upper grades 19, 103–109, 136–165
  (*See also* Chords; Partials; Scale; Tenden-
      tial resolution)
Hartshorn, William C., 274
"Havah Nagilah," 128
"Hickory, Dickory, Dock," 85
"Hide-and-Seek," 113
Historical development of music, 285, 287
  (*See also* Composition; Harmony)
Homemade instruments, 175, 285, 387
Humming choir, 156
"Humpty Dumpty," 141

"If You're Happy," 295
Imagery, 3, 5
Improvisation, 278
Induction, 56
Inflection, 264–265
Information, recording of student, 336
    inventory, 337–339
Instrumental skills, 10, 18, 20, 27, 55, 159,
    165, 166–215
Instruments, 166–215
  adding to vocal performance, 231–232
  making, 175–177, 242–259

Instruments:
  methods for, 390
  sound painting, 234–235
  (*See also* specific instrument)
Intermediate grades, 14, 27, 290–291
  (*See also* Activities)
Interpretation of music symbols, 56
Intonation, 262
Inventory records, 337
Ives, Charles, 273

Janáček, L., 273
Japanese scales, 111, 153
  (*See also* Scale)
Junior high school methods, 393

Key, 116–125
  charts of: major scale, 119
    minor scale, 126
  signatures, 23
  (*See also* Music notation; Scale)
Key signatures, 110, 115, 119, 126
Keyboard charts (*see* Visual aids)
Keyboard harmony, 133, 209, 385
  (*See also* Harmony)
Keyboard scale and chord finder
  (*See* Visual aids)
Kindergarten, 7
  (*See also* Primary grades)
Kingsley, Howard J., 354
Knuth, William, 335
Kodaly, Zoltan, 51, 357
Kwalwasser, Jacob, 334, 335

Ladder graphs, 25, 41, 43, 104, 107, 109,
  121, 122, 124, 126, 128, 130, 267–269
  (*See also* Scale)
Lansbury, John, 336
Latin American percussion, 199, 259
  (*See also* Rhythm instruments)
Leading tone, 42, 88
"Leavin' Old Texas," 144
Leger lines, 49
  (*See also* Staff notation)
Lesson planning, 29, 276, 290
  (*See* Curriculum)
Listening, 260–287
  bibliography, 377

Listening:
  contemporary music, 273–283
  films and film strips, 380
  planning lessons for, 274–278
  skills: intermediate, 14, 16–17
    primary grades, 9, 13
    upper, 14, 19–20
  traditional music, 275–283
  (*See also* Recorded music)
Literacy in music, 30, 348
  (*See also* Music notation)
"Little Mohee, The," 97
Locrian mode, 129
  (*See also* Mode)
"Lone Star Trail," 144
"Lullaby," 297

McMurray, Foster, 217–219, 232, 342,
  351
Madison, Thurber, 226
Major chords, 89, 94, 96
  (*See also* Chords)
Major scales, 115
  (*See also* Scale)
Mandolin, 195
  (*See also* String instruments)
Maracas, 200, 201
  (*See also* Rhythm instruments)
"Mary Had A Little Lamb," 236
Measurement in music education, 327
  achievement, 330
  aptitude, 328
  imagery, 329
  objective tests, 332
  standardized test, 333
Mediant, 88
  (*See also* Harmony)
Melodic minor, 122
  (*See also* Scale)
Melodica, 205, 371
Melody, 9, 15, 18, 19, 26, 32, 37, 88, 262
  bells, 178
  chimes, 184
  constructs, 141, 278
  contemporary, 278
  flutes, 174, 370
  graphs, 46
  names, 46
  songs, 80
  (*See also* Pitch consciousness; Scale; Sign
    language; Voice)

Memorizing chords, 160
  (*See also* Chords)
Meringue, 68
"Merrily We Roll Along," 168
Meter:
  compound, 82–83
  signature, 25
  $\frac{2}{4}$, 56–68
    conducting of, 221–222
    dramatizing, 63, 229
    drum talk, 63
    duration patterns, 59–62, 220–224
    faster rhythms in, 64
    flash card games, 59–60
    rhythm score developing, 64–66, 229
    syllabic rhythm, 57–59
    syncopation, 66
    tempo and mood, 68
  $\frac{3}{4}$, 68–78
    flash card games, 73–74
    tempo changes, 73
  $\frac{3}{8}$, 74–78
    flash card games, 77
    movement to, 74–77
    tempo changes, 77
  $\frac{4}{4}$, 81–82
  $\frac{6}{8}$, 71–81
  (*See also* Rhythms)
Microtones, 137
Minor chords, 88, 89, 101, 104, 157, 159, 161
  (*See also* Chords)
Minor scales, 120
  (*See also* Scales)
Minor third, 123
  (*See also* Chords)
Mode:
  generally, 112, 265–269
  major: Aeolian, 113
    modified, 130, 267
    Dorian, 112, 267
    Ionian, 112, 267
    Locrian, 129–130, 168, 269
    Lydian, 129, 269
    Mixo-Lydian, 269
    Phrygian, 126–128, 267, 269
  minor: Aeolian, 120–125, 268

Mode:
  minor: Dorian, 124–125, 268
    Ionian, 268
  mixed, 125
  (*See also* Scale)
Monroe, Will S., 353
Mood, 68, 81, 138, 227
Motor-rhythmic skills (*see* Rhythms)
Mozart, W. A., 217
Mueller, Kate Hevner, 336, 344
Mursell, James L., 217, 219, 232, 260, 261, 345, 359
Music, reactions to, conceptual, 351–352
    physiological, 345–346
Music corner, 2, 12–13
Music education (*see* Education, music)
Music lesson, planning, 10–11, 29–30
  (*See also* Curriculum; Song)
Music notation, 1–6, 16, 19, 32–52, 216–234
  glossary, 21–25, 282, 403–405
  (*See also* Games; *Sol-fa* syllables; Staff notation; Visual aids)
Music specialist, 288–340
  classroom teachers, preparation of, 288-289
  unit consultant, 294–317
    unit plan: second grade, 298–310
      upper grades, 310–317
  workshops for, 317–321
Musical acoustics, 394
Musical activities (*see* Activities)
Musical concepts, 3, 4, 12, 21, 30, 341–361
  (*See also* Education, music)
Musical forms, 285
  (*See also* Style)
Musical illustration sources (*see* Appendix VII)
Musical speech, 44
  (*See also* Games; Rhythms)
Musicality, 360
Musikits, 176, 242
Musique Concrète, 278

Natural minor, 120
  (*See also* Scale)
Nettl, Bruno, 348
New performing techniques, 281
  (*See also* Contemporary music)
New sound sources, 278
  (*See also* Contemporary music; Sound painting)

Notation (*see* Music notation)
Notebooks, 16, 19, 22, 42, 49, 52, 238
Nuance, 6, 265
Numbers, 37

Objectives, 1–31, 341–361
  instrumental, 167
  current, 358
  Yale seminar, 360
Ocarina (*see* Simple pipes)
Occidental scales, 119, 268
Octave, 110
  (*See also* Scale)
"Old Brass Wagon," 64
"Old Hundreth," 100
"Old Joe Clarke," 125
"Old King Cole," 124
"On Yoshino Mountain," 153
"Oranges And Lemons," 84, 296
Orchestra:
  classroom, 116–215
  objectives for, 167
Orchestration, 386
Orff, Carl, 25, 273, 355
"Organ Point Chant," 146
Oriental scales, 120, 269
  (*See also* Scale)
"Our Halloween Song," 227, 228
Overtones (*see* Partials)

Palisca, Claude, 360
Pandean pipes, 172
  (*See also* Simple pipes)
Parker, DeWitt, 261, 341, 344, 352, 354
Partials, 137
  (*See also* Chords; Harmony)
Partner songs, 142, 145
"Patsy," 146
Pentatonic scales (*see* Scale)
Pentatonic songs, 40, 42, 111
Percussion instruments, 176, 242, 283
  methods, 390
  techniques, 397
  (*See also* Rhythm instruments)
Pestalozzian influence, 353
Phenix, Philip, 362
Philosophy of music education (*see* Education, music)
Phrase line, 34, 55, 230
  (*See also* Rhythms)

Physiological reactions to music, 345
Piano:
  charts for scale and chord fingering, 133–135, 209–215
  melody, transferring to, 225–227
  scale on, teaching of, 110–120
Pianolin, 189
Pitch consciousness, 35
  definition, 344
  difficulties, 36
  ear training for, 9, 35–37
    chord intervals, 91–109
    nature of, 262, 344
    octaves scale intervals, 115–118
Plan unit, lesson (*see* Curriculum)
Polyrhythms, 238
Pop bottle band, 169
Pratt, Carroll C., 270
Prepared piano, 283
Primary grades, 7, 292, 293
  attitudes to be developed in, 8
  characteristics of children, 7–8
  melody, developing concepts of, 32–52
  musical activities for, 9–14
  rhythm, developing concepts of, 53–86
Procedures of teaching:
  chords, 87–109, 136–165
  classroom teachers, 288–340
  composing, 216–259
  harmony, 87–109, 136–165
  instruments, 166–215
  listening, 260–287
  rhythm, 53–86
  songs, 32–52
  (*See also* Activities; Curriculum)
Programmed instruction, 322-327
Psaltery, 187
  (*See also* String instruments)
Psychology of music, 341–361
  bibliography, 395
  (*See also* Education, music)
Pulse (*see* Rhythm)

Question approach to teaching songs, 34
  (*See also* Songs)

Recorded music, 9, 13, 14, 35, 232, 278
  elementary listening, 378
  historical periods, 379
  rhythmic activities, 368

Recorded music:
 sources, 381
 (*See also* Appendix III)
Recorders, 202, 370
Recording by tape, 16, 19, 233
Recreational instruments, 166–215
 methods, 391
 (*See also* specific instrument)
Redfield, John, 137, 140, 266, 270, 346
Resource consultant, 288–340
Rests, 62
Rhythm, 53–86, 262–264, 344
 activities, 53–86, 292
 aleatory, 237
 beat, varieties of, 83–86
 clock, 53
 conducting, 221
 concepts, 53
 creative 54, 230
 development of, 262
 dramatizing, 63, 74, 227
 drum talk, 63
 duration patterns, 59–62, 220–224
 flash cards, 59, 73, 77
 fundamental, 32, 54
 interpretation of, 54, 63
 listening to, 59
 phrase, 53, 230
 polyrhythm, 238
 primary grades, 9, 15, 18, 54
 reactions to, 56
 recordings for, 378
 sound effects, 230
 symbolizing, 56
 unusual, 278
 of words, 53, 57
 (*See also* Games; Meter; Rhythm instruments; Visual aids)
Rhythm instruments:
 description of, 178, 242–248
 Latin American percussion, 199–202
  castenets, 201
  claves, 201
  cowbell, 202
  drums, bongo and conga, 200
  guiro, 201
  maracas, 201
Rote teaching, 34
 (*See also* Song)
Rounds, 49, 140, 143
Rugg, Harold, 217

"Sakura," 127
Scale:
 forms of, 24–25, 265–269
  chromatic, 110, 265
  gypsy, 127
  major, 24, 43, 116–120
   relation to partials, 138–139
  minor, 24, 120–125, 268
  oriental, 110, 112, 113, 126, 129
  pentatonic, 24, 41, 93, 110–116, 216
 harmonizing of, 139, 148–165
 introducing, 42–46
 ladder graphs, 25, 267–269
 octave, 110, 265
 theory of, 265
 (*See also* Chords; Harmony; Key; Mode)
Schrammel, H. E., 335
Schoen, Max, 352
Schoenberg, Arnold, 273
Seashore, Carl, 334
Secondary chords, 99, 154
 (*See also* Chords)
Senior high school methods, 394
 (*See also* Curriculum)
"See-Saw Margery Daw," 75
Sensing meters, 53–86
 (*See also* Meter)
Sensory perception, 1–6
Serial tone row, 278
 (*See also* Composition)
Shepherd's pipe, 171
 (*See also* Simple pipes)
Sight singing, 385
Sign language, 37–42, 148–165
 John Curwen, hand signals, 50–51
 Kodaly, 358
"Silent Night," 85
Simple pipes, 167–174
 procedures for teaching, 167–168
 types of: flutophone, 172–173
  melody flute, 174
  ocarina, 172–173
  pandeau pipes, 172
  pop bottles, 169–170
  shepherd's pipe, 171–172
  song flute, 172–173
  tonette, 172–173
  transverse flute, 170–171
"Skaters Waltz", 69
Sociological aspects of music, 350
 (*See also* Education, music)

Sol-fa syllables, 39–46
  English system, 96
Song:
  composition in class, 220–234
  procedures for teaching, 10–11, 34–52
    phrase method or rote approach, 34
    question approach, 34–35
  sound effects, 230, 234–237
Song flute, 173
  (*See* Simple pipes)
"Song to Remember, A," 102
Song sources, 406
Songbooks, 25–29
Sound effects, 231, 242
Sound kits, 242
Sound sources, 230, 278
Sound studio, 242
Staff notation:
  clef: bass, 132
    treble, 48–50
  explanation of, 225–227
  hand staff, 48–50
  (*See also* Music notation; Visual aids)
Standards, 341, 349
"Steeple Bells, The," 43, 92
Stetson, Raymond, H., 346
Stockhausen, Carl Heinz, 273
Stravinsky, Igor, 137, 273
String bass, 199, 257
String instruments:
  procedures for teaching, 185
    fretted strings, 187–188
  types of: autoharp, 185–186
    banjo, tenor, 191–192, 256
    bowed (violin, viola, cello, string bass), 196–199, 255, 257
    duobass, 188, 258
    guitar, six-string, 192–194, 256
    mandolin, 194–196
    psaltery, 187
    ukulele, 189
  vibrations and resonance, 185
Student records, 336
Style in music, 272, 285, 350
Subdominant chord, 88, 96, 148, 156
  (*See also* Chords)
Submediant, 88, 103, 158
  (*See also* Harmony)
Supertonic, 88, 104, 158
  (*See also* Harmony)
Supervision, 288

Supervision:
  bibliography, 395
  (*See also* Music specialist)
Supplementary songbooks, 367
Suzuki, Shinichi, 358
"Sweet Betsy from Pike," 100, 157
"Swing The Shining Sickle, " 107
Syllabic rhythm, 57
  (*See also* Rhythms)
Syllables, 44
Symbol (*see* Music notation)
Syncopation, 66
  (*See also* Rhythms)

Tanglewood symposium, 360
Teaching (*see* Procedures of teaching)
Teaching equipment and supplies:
  audio-visual, 362
  chalkboard, 364
  educational recordings, 365
  films for listening, 366
  films for music education, 366
  recorded music libraries, 365
  (*See also* Appendix I)
Tempo, 22, 54, 68, 73, 77, 81, 227, 263, 283
"Ten Little Indians," 82
Tendential resolution, 45, 87, 94, 138
  (*See also* Harmony)
Terminology, 22, 227, 282, 403
Tests and measurements, 327–333
  (*See also* Evaluation)
Theme and variations, 275
Theory of music bibliography, 383
"This Old Man," 156
Thorpe, Louis P., 334, 349
"Three Blind Mice," 143
Tilson, Lowell M., 334
Timbre, 32, 271, 328
Time for music, 10
"Tinga Layo," 67
"To Market, To Market," 79
Tolbert, Mary R., 1
Tonal beauty, 34, 261
  (*See also* Melody; Pitch; Sign language; Song; Voice)
Tonal memory, 49, 328
Tonal relations, 37
Tonal spectrum, 278
Tonality, 224, 266, 278
Tone bells, 178
Tone quality, 35, 106

Tonette, 167
Tonic chord, 90
   (*See also* Chords)
Torgerson, T. L., 335
Transposing, 93, 112, 114, 160
   (*See also* Harmony; Key)
Transverse flute, 170
   (*See also* Simple pipes)
Triads (*see* Chords)
"Trot, Pony Trot," 114
"Tumba," 131
"Twinkle, Twinkle, Little Star," 84

Ukulele, 189, 190, 254
   (*See also* String instruments)
Unit construction, 288–340
   Afro-American music, 310
   "Music of Mexico," 307
   outline for, 294
   The Zoocus, 298
   (*See also* Activities; Curriculum)
Unit consultant, 294
Upper grades, music, 17, 290–291

Varese, Edgar, 273
Viola, 198, 255
   (*See also* String instruments)
Violin, 197, 255
   (*See also* String instruments)
Visual aids:
   duration patterns, 59–62, 220–224, 237–239
   flash cards: for ear training, 91–106
     for rhythms, 59–60, 73–74, 77
   hand staff, 48–50, 225–227
   illustrating songs, 47–48
   keyboard charts, 93, 147, 209–215
   keyboard scale and chord finder, 103, 108, 110–120, 147, 225
   melody graph, 46–47
   phrase line, 230
   scale ladders, 24–25
     major, 42–43

Visual aids:
   scale ladders: pentatonic, 39–42
   sign language, 37–42, 148–165
   (*See also* Games; Rhythm; Scale; specific instruments)
Vocal methods, 392
Vocal skills, 9, 15, 18, 105, 115
Voice:
   harmony, 140–165
   pitch placement, 115–118
   play, 37
   quality 8, 14, 36, 106
   skills 9, 15, 18
   tone, improving, 106
   vocalizes, 105, 116
   (*See also* Chords; Harmony, Melody; Pitch; Song)

Wagner, Richard, 263
Water glasses, 176–177
"Wayfaring Stranger," 115
Webern, Anton, 273
Whistler, Harvey S., 334
Whitley, Mary T., 354
Whitner, Mary Elizabeth, 342
Wind instruments, 169, 249
Wing, Herbert, 334
Woodwinds:
   methods, 391
   new techniques, 282
Wordsworth, William, 349
Workshops for classroom teachers, 317
"Wraggle-Taggle Gypsies, The", 121
Writing music, 16, 25, 292
   (*See also* Music notation)

Xylophones, 184

Yale University, seminar, 360

Zanzig, Augustus D., 33